THE BEST OF GOLF DIGEST

1950-1975

THE BEST OF GOLF DIGEST

THE FIRST 25 YEARS

A Golf Digest Book
Trade book distribution by Simon and Schuster

CONTENTS

Published by
Golf Digest, Inc.
A New York Times Company
297 Westport Avenue
Norwalk, Connecticut 06856

Book Trade distribution by
Simon & Schuster
Rockefeller Center
630 Fifth Avenue
New York, New York 10020

First Printing
ISBN: 0-914178-07-5
LC: 75-18529
Printed in the
United States of America

FOREWORD

The first issue of *Golf Digest* was published out of my bedroom in 1950. At 16 pages digest-size, it was something less than a collector's item.

During the next 25 years, the game of golf grew from a minor diversion in the United States, with a few major championships, to a major sport with a year-round season. It not only awakened assuredly from a war-time slumber, but became a lifestyle for millions of Americans. We have named this period, 1950-1975, the Silver Era of Golf. Certainly no 25 years in the history of any sport has sparkled with more growth and personality.

Golf Digest magazine was part of this growth, and the men and women who wrote for it and contributed their talents to it are a story in themselves.

Out of the Navy and back in my home town of Wilmette, Ill., after World War II, I became an avid weekend golfer on the daily-fee courses that abound in the Chicago area. In those days there was not much coverage of tournament golf in newspapers, and existing golfing magazines were unavailable at newsstands or most golf courses. Published instruction consisted largely of essay material only a graduate engineer could comprehend, supplemented by small sequence photos.

One of my golfing buddies, Bill Vanderpool, and I decided to look into the possibility of publishing a golf magazine. From the beginning, we believed golf was a fun game, that becomes more enjoyable the better you play it. Our aim was to come up with a magazine that provided readers with a balance of easy-to-understand instruction and service articles along with entertaining and informative human interest features.

When we began, Ben Hogan was dominating golf. He was surrounded by colorful stars like Lloyd Mangrum, who looked like a casino croupier; Jimmy Demaret, golf's first notoriously fancy dresser; the irrepressible Sam Snead, and a fastidious Dr. Cary Middlecoff. Babe Zaharias and Patty Berg were the big names in women's golf. But despite the impact of such famous figures, golf was not really big business. Wilson, Spalding and MacGregor were the only big names in manufacturing. The Walgreen Po Do was a leading golf ball. Nobody could pronounce Titleist.

Against this background, we started *Golf Digest* as a part-time venture. Bill Vanderpool was offered a new job a few months before we were ready to put out the first issue of *Golf Digest,* and didn't think he would have the time to proceed with the magazine. So, together with an associate (Gordon Smith) from the television station where I worked, we put out two local issues in 1950. Our loss was $150. That fall Gordon accepted a job in television in another part of the country and happily abandoned the project. Jack Barnett and Howard Gill joined me in 1951. We went on to publish four issues and sent Gordon Smith a check for $75— his half of the first year's loss. The three of us had gone to New Trier High School together in Winnetka, where Jack had been sports editor of the school paper and Howard had written a column on jazz. Then we all went on to Northwestern University.

In those early days we would stay up half the night (we all had full-time jobs elsewhere) arguing with each other and planning issues. Our first office, other than my bedroom, was acquired late in 1951 in preparation for going big time with six national issues in 1952. It was one small room in Evanston's original post office building. The floor tilted 20 degrees, which portended the uphill battle ahead. The building was condemned and razed six months later, and we moved into a loft that had been a paint shop on, believe it or not, Davis Street in Evanston.

One of our most encouraging boosts came in 1952. At that time, George S. May conducted by far the richest tournament in golf, his $100,000 World Championship at Tam O'Shanter. The man George assigned to run the press tent was Chet Possum. Possum made the mistake of questioning the credentials of one of the most popular (and cantankerous) sports-casters in Chicago, Tom Duggan. Just before Tom was rebuffed, he had been attracted to our *Golf Digest* display, which consisted largely of a couple of cute young models selling copies of the magazine. On his show that night, Tom told Chicago that the most exciting thing about George S. May's tournament was *Golf Digest.* To prove it, he paraded all of us in front of the camera, including the models.

Another big boost was the Ike button incident. After Gen. Eisenhower moved into the White House in 1953 he tried to minimize discussion about how often he played golf, where he played and what he shot. I got a friend of mine, a White House correspondent for NBC, to pin a big button on Ike as he came off the course one day at Augusta National. It read: "Don't Ask What I Shot." Photographers were there, and it made all the front pages and TV news shows. By now we had gone national, and we saw it as a promotion for us. We offered to send a button to anyone in the country who requested one, figuring we'd get the names of a bunch of golfers and convert them into subscribers. We paid for and sent out about 100,000 buttons, received a lot of publicity but unfortunately our ink and our faces from the project were a little red. So was the face of my friend from NBC, Ray Scherer, who was then emerging as a nationally known news correspondent.

Now we really were facing a cost squeeze. Howard Gill's family was growing, and he needed more money than we could afford to pay him. He even raised chickens on the side. I was still working in the television business and coming down to the magazine office at night. Jack Barnett decided to retire as editor, continuing to contribute articles while working at another job, later to come back on a full-time basis.

We brought in a young newspaperman from Danville, Ill. An editorial purist, John May has always been somewhat defiant of the business world that has contributed greatly to our success. Whenever he was introduced to one of our advertising salesmen, he'd comment, "Oh, another one of those commercial types. Don't sell too many ads. We need all the room we can get for editorial."

John May is still with us, as our senior editor. Around the office they call him Big Daddy. He serves as a steadying hand and preserves our editorial continuity.

Big things were happening in golf in the mid-1950s. In the 1953 Tam O'Shanter, Lew Worsham holed out a wedge shot on the 72nd hole to win the tournament. It caught the attention of the nation and thrust golf to the forefront on the sports pages. Then an anonymous club pro from Davenport, Iowa, Jack Fleck, made a birdie putt on the 72nd hole of the 1955 U.S. Open at San Francisco to tie Hogan, and then beat him by three strokes in the 18-hole playoff the next day. Jack Barnett was there following Fleck during the fourth round. There weren't more than a half dozen people with Fleck early in the round, since everyone figured Hogan had it won. Today thousands claim to have followed Fleck around.

Those exciting developments were harbingers of the golfing explosion soon to come. We at *Golf Digest* now were looking confidently ahead.

Howard Gill held the titles of editor and publisher, and filled that dual role with a flair. He kept the company of a select circle of golf journalists that included Charlie Bartlett of the Chicago Tribune, Bob Drum of the Pittsburgh Press and Dan Jenkins of the Fort Worth Press, who wrote in a lively no-holds-barred style—and kibitzed late at night in a no-bars-held style. Dan went on to Sports Illustrated and fame as a best-selling author. In our early days he contributed several memorable articles to *Golf Digest,* including one about the redoubtable George Low that is reprinted in this volume.

In 1959 we took on a young writer, Dick Aultman, who had played golf at Northwestern. Possessor of a technically analytical mind, he brought a sharp logic to the product. He moved to Connecticut with us in 1962, the year we enlarged the format of the magazine, and in 1966 he became editor. He went on to achieve wide note as a writer of instruction books, among them the classic, *The Square-to-Square Swing.* Altogether, Dick has written or helped write eight instruction books. A free-lance writer today, he still serves as a contributing editor to *Golf Digest* and is a member of our golf schools instruction staff.

Our next editor was a bombastic Britisher, Ken Bowden. I met Ken, then editor of the British publication *Golf World,* at the 1965 Ryder Cup matches at Royal Birkdale, England. *Golf World,* incidentally, today is owned by Golf Digest, Inc. Ken came to work for us in 1969, giving us an international tone and perspective. In 1972 he left to form his own company, handling corporate promotions in golf. Ken collaborated in 1973 with Jack Nicklaus to write *Golf My Way.*

In 1967 we hired a bright young newspaperman from Kansas who was working as a sports editor in Oklahoma City. Nick Seitz wrote one brilliant feature article after another for us. He had been a philosophy major in college, and brought to his work a depth, flavored with a nice touch of humor, which has earned him many national writing awards. He became editor in late 1972, and continues to handle that assignment with great distinction. Several of his articles are reprinted in this volume.

Our different editors have approached the job in ways accented somewhat differently, but the over-all effect has been a well-rounded progression. It has given us improved art direction as well as improved text. John Newcomb is our present highly capable art director who designed the book you are holding.

Newcomb and Seitz are backed by strong staffs. The writing of current editors May, Cal Brown, Larry Dennis, Dwayne Netland and Kathy Jonah will be found frequently in the ensuing pages, as will the writing of our "alumni" who still work closely with us: Aultman, Bowden, Hubert Mizell and Larry Sheehan. Also essential to this project was the help of books coordinator Charlene Cruson, managing editor Jay Simon and librarian Fran Delphia.

The selection of material which appears in this volume was a collective effort of the editorial staff. The introductory comments which begin each section further explain the selection process. Readers should bear in mind that the articles are arranged, for the most part, in the same chronology they appeared in *Golf Digest.* The stories reflect the perspective of the years in which they were written; in some cases, although time has obsolesced the facts, we have not changed them in order to preserve the story's unique flavor.

In 1969 we sold *Golf Digest* to The New York Times. Jack Barnett retired to pursue other publishing interests in Connecticut. Howard Gill continues as publisher and I'm still around as president and editor-in-chief. We not only expect *Golf Digest* to continue to pioneer in golf journalism, we think the best of *Golf Digest* is yet to come.

—*William H. Davis*

THE CHANGING GAME

The suspicion is strong that golf, which is among the most venerable of sports, has undergone more dramatic change in the past 25 years than in the previous 250, on virtually every level. Producing this 25th anniversary book has given the editors of *Golf Digest* a welcome opportunity to review and put in perspective the highlights of this rambunctiously exciting quarter century.

The first section of the book is devoted to the most significant of dozens of developments. The opening essay, by the noted golf journalist and historian Herbert Warren Wind, takes a broad, personalized overview of the changes of the past 25 years, not all of them necessarily signifying healthy progress.

The essay grew out of a 1972 series Wind did for the magazine, "Can Golf's Great Traditions Survive the '70's?" Wind updated the series for the book.

The rest of the section points up *Golf Digest's* basic role as a service publication. Much of our magazine content is instruction for playing the game better and much of it features the glamour of the tour, but there is another vital category. On our editorial planning sheets we refer to it cryptically, if not too cleverly, as "non-instruction how-to" (every issue contains at least one such article and usually more).

"Non-instruction how-to" includes the large area of equipment coverage, a sampler of which you will find in this section. It is the abiding aim of our staff, led by associate editors Larry Dennis and Cal Brown, to keep our readers abreast of new technological developments in materials and design, particularly ones that can affect their play. We try not to get sidetracked by the deluge of cosmetic and marketing differences in the equipment business, knowing that most top lines are quality products with the same essential traits in common.

To report technological developments before they are made public, the editors regularly keep in contact with key research and development men in the industry. The editors visit equipment plants and testing facilities to tune in on the latest experimental thinking. The equipment articles excerpted here are staff-written with only a couple of exceptions.

J. Victor East and John Baymiller, still on the magazine's masthead as technical consultants, did early reporting on how balls and clubs influence the golf swing, on swing-weight, and on other compelling equipment subjects. Our coverage since has grown to include an annual equipment section each January issue, previewing the new lines, and frequent treatments in the intervening issues.

Our service coverage often has taken the form of vigorous crusading, as in the cases of course architecture, handicapping and slow play. We have hit these subjects hard and repeatedly, not always with as much effect as we would like, but often with rewarding results for the game. Dr. Francis Scheid's computerized handicapping studies, for example, have inspired the U.S. Golf Ass'n to give the higher handicapper more of the help he needs to get an even game.

It's been an amazing and fascinating 25 years, as the following pages show.

THE STATE OF THE GAME

BY HERBERT WARREN WIND
March, 1972
updated 1975

Is there any greater pleasure in this astonishing age of tele-mechanics and microcircuitry than to lean back on a wintry weekend and watch the latest installment of the professional golf tour? Flick— the dull, gray, all-too-familiar world is dispatched and in its stead life sparkles as it should, a plexus of soft blue skies, olive fairways, palm fronds rustling in the breeze, pretty girls in big hats and small dresses and, in the foreground, a clutch of able young golfers knocking the pins down. Some weekends this is only the beginning of the show. For example, I think we all remember those amazing editions of the

Desert Classic which brought us Arnold Palmer chatting just off the edge of the 18th green with his good friends General Eisenhower and Bob Hope. Golf, we knew then if we hadn't realized it before, was the "official game" of our era—the common ground, the shared enthusiasm, the Cloth of Gold that drew together the heroes from such separate worlds as sports, government and entertainment.

The coming of warm weather— golf weather—hardly lessens the lure and the impact of televised golf: an average of 11 million viewers tune in to each tournament telecast. For many of us during the

late 1960s, no morning of the year could compare with that Saturday morning in July when the final round of the British Open was telecast "live via satellite," and we saw the likes of Nicklaus, De Vicenzo and Jacklin making their moves on the hallowed hard-pan of Muirfield, Hoylake and Lytham St. Annes. True enough, we didn't have Howard Cosell on the scene explaining what was wrong with linksland golf, the Lake Poets and the British way of life in general, but then you can't have everything.

These are unpredictable times, however, and no one knows what lies ahead for golf. It may continue to grow and become an even more lustrous part of the national and global scene. Or, for no apparent reason, it may suddenly lose its privileged place in the scheme of things, like baseball, piano lessons, the polo coat, the well-made Broadway play, the Packard, penmanship, railroad travel, dance music, the bakery wagon and countless other faded glories that in earlier eras loomed as unshakable as the English pound and the American Legion. Accordingly, I think it would be an excellent idea if we paused for a moment and reflected on the golden age of golf we have lived through in the last quarter of a century.

Here are just a few of the things that happened in the 25 years between 1950 and 1975:

1. Not that figures tell everything, but the number of golfers increased as never before—in the United States from three million to 16 million. Similarly, the number of courses in the U.S. rose from under five thousand to over 12 thousand. (A hundred years ago, by the way, there were fewer than 50 golf clubs in the whole world. A mere handful lay beyond the borders of Scotland, and there was only one, Royal Montreal, on this side of the Atlantic.)

2. The total prize money on the American tournament circuit in

1950 came to $460,000. Today it has climbed to over $8,000,000. In 1950 Sam Snead was the leading money winner on the tour with a haul of $35,758. Last year 20 golfers earned over $100,000 on the American tour—*and no fewer than 74 earned over $35,758.*

3. Since the war, such significant new international competitions as the World Cup (for two-man professional teams), the Eisenhower Trophy (for four-man amateur teams) and the Espirito Santo Trophy (for three-woman amateur teams) have solidly established themselves. They have not been completely dominated by the traditional golf powers either.

4. Where the modern champions are concerned, one can go on and on dealing in warranted superlatives. In this period Ben Hogan reached the climax of his career. While Harry Vardon, Bob Jones and Jack Nicklaus should be rated Hogan's equals—after all, they accomplished as much in their times as he did in his—Hogan, with the assistance of modern equipment, stands by himself as the finest striker of the ball and the most accurate shotmaker the game has ever known.

This period also produced Arnold Palmer, perhaps the most exciting figure to appear on the American sports scene since Babe Ruth. Under a new USGA rule, anyone using the word *charisma* in writing about Palmer is henceforth subject to a two-stroke penalty and loss of down, so we will content ourselves with saying that Palmer's appeal has been so extraordinary that he has made contact with everyone—young and old, male and female, golfer and non-golfer, American and foreigner, poet and laborer. In doing so, he widened the game's appeal and brought to it its largest audience ever.

In addition, there is Jack Nicklaus, an unprecedented combination of sophisticated power and spectacular technique. Jack has had more crests and valleys in his career than most tournament golfers, but when he has been at the top of his game he has several times unleashed a sustained brilliance that no other player in the long history of golf has approached. This, of course, is

what Bob Jones had in mind when he remarked in 1965, after Nicklaus had broken practically all the records for the Masters Tournament, "Jack Nicklaus is playing an entirely different game—a game I'm not even familiar with."

There is no question that Peter Thomson, who won five British Opens between 1954 and 1965, is the greatest Australian golfer of all time. There is little question that Gary Player is the greatest South African golfer of all time—a notch superior to the remarkable Bobby Locke. There is a very good chance that Mickey Wright may be the greatest woman golfer of all time—she is a much finer shotmaker than Babe Didrikson Zaharias, and her competitive record far surpasses that of Joyce Wethered, her only other conceivable peer. There is a good chance, too, that Gene Sarazen, who at the age of 68 played a 74 on his second round in the Masters, may be the best player for his age who ever lived . . . unless it is Sam Snead.

One could go on and on, but let us leave it at this, for the point must be amply clear: in the last quarter of a century, golf has prospered mightily in just about every way. For some observers, it reached an untoppable peak when Alan Shepard assembled his trusty 6-iron on the surface of the moon, though others were even more impressed when King Hassan II of Morocco summoned his favorite playing pro, Billy Casper, for a practice session less than two weeks after he had survived a palace uprising in the summer of 1971.

I mention all this because a main purpose of this article is to point out that, despite its voluminous prosperity and over-all health, there are quite a few directions in which golf is moving these days that are cause for concern. To say it another way, a good many of the finest things about golf are in the process of being forgotten. Change, of course, is inevitable. Frequently it is beneficial, though this is not always the case. In any event, the people who are involved in golf should at least be more aware than most of them are of new trends and forces that have come into the game.

Widely considered the most knowledgeable and articulate American golf writer of all time, Herbert Warren Wind is a frequent contributor to *Golf Digest*. His books include *Thirty Years of Championship Golf* with Gene Sarazen, *The Greatest Game of All* with Jack Nicklaus and *The Story of American Golf*. He is a member of the staff of The New Yorker Magazine.

What we hope to do here is discuss the changing scene in some detail and try to put the good things and the bad things about it in a reasonable perspective.

For me, the atmosphere in and around tournament golf has lost a good deal of its old sporting flavor. As I see it, this has come about to a large extent because there is too much money in professional golf nowadays. Curiously, it is not the *amount* of the prize money that bothers me—that is not out of line with purses and salaries in other sports or, for that matter, with what the leaders in business and other professions are currently making. (Indeed, each week when I pick up *Golf World* magazine, one of the features I turn to first is "The PGA Tour Statistics" which lists the leading money-winners. Without really being aware of its fiscal import, I study the list with the same intensity I expend each Sunday morning during the baseball season on the major league batting averages, for I love the sense of continuity that these regular tabulations give you.) At the same time, it is probably the huge increases in prize money over the past decade—in 1960, remember, a $50,000 tournament was a whopper—that account for the almost institutionalized decorum with which most circuit pros now go about their appointed rounds. To mix a metaphor, they seem to be walking on egg shells, only too well aware of what a good thing professional golf is and eternally vigilant lest they do anything that might kill the goose that lays the golden eggs. "Tournament golf has become so cut and dried that I don't enjoy watching it on television any more," a friend of mine, a non-golfer, was explaining recently. "Practically every guy has the same set of gestures. They all walk onto the green the same way. They all line up their putts the same way. If they hole the putt, they all turn on the same kind of a smile and tip their hat the same way. When they're interviewed they all say the same thing: They were 'fortunate to play so well this week against this fine group of gentlemen.' It's all so calculated and unspontaneous that it's positively eerie." I think my friend goes too far, but there is

more than a germ of truth in what he says.

For myself, one aspect of the financial picture that worries me is that tournament prize money is comparatively small pickin's compared to the sums a champion can make from television commercials and other product endorsements. (Mark McCormack, who manages Palmer and Player and quite a few of the other leading golfers, deserves the credit for creating the new levels of payment. He was able to sell Palmer to top manufacturers at movie-star prices as a man who connotes excitement and glamor to the average consumer, and after that the other players of the first rank were able to command higher fees.) In order to break through the barrier that separates the merely successful touring pro from a Sports Hero like Palmer and thus qualify for the really big money, a golfer must not only demonstrate that he has the ability to win a major championship (the U.S. Open, the British Open, the Masters or the PGA) but also show that he has the stuff to get across to the public as a Personality with a capital P—someone whom you and I want to identify with, consciously or subconsciously; someone who has such a strong appeal for us that if, say, he drives a white Essex, we'll want to drive a white Essex.

As a result, what we have today in the tournament world is a situation where a number of the players just below the first five appear to be much more interested in improving their images than in improving their golf. To exaggerate a bit for effect, here, moving up the fairway, comes Phil Familyman followed by as many of his nine children as the tournament officials will allow inside the ropes. Phil is obviously devoted to them. In the next twosome, bestowing that non-stop smile on the spectators, we have Glenn Golden who is trying desperately to get himself across as the personification of youth, blondness and a sunny disposition. Compared to Glenn, the Man from Glad is grubby and negative. Coming into view now with that choppy, rugged stride is Hardy Competitor, a fellow who wants the fans to know that he never stops fighting and who has worked up a large repertoire of gestures and cries that transmit this admirable quality. For instance, when Hardy saw how warmly the spectators responded when Gary Player punched the air with his fist after holing a good-sized putt, he devised that marvelous variation whereby he punches the air with a left jab, a right uppercut and a left hook, in that order. And so on and on. (Who said there weren't individuals on the tour!) Among the new acts, the most successful by far is Lee Trevino's, and while granting Trevino's natural charm and ebullience, I am inclined to think that it owes its success to the fact that he is such an astonishing golfer. It brings one back to Walter Hagen. If he had not been such a great shotmaker, he would not have been such a great showman.

The more that golf becomes a branch of the entertainment world and a means to an end rather than an end in itself, the more it is bound to surrender that rare and special flavor that the world of sports possesses when it is at its best. Some people love it, of course, when a Dave Hill is in an eloquently rude mood, or a Cliff Richey tears up the taped line of a tennis court to dramatize his wrath over a linesman's call, or a Muhammad Ali throws a tantrum at a weigh-in. For them, this is Color. The true sports fan, I suggest, finds these moments uncomfortable and irrelevant. They are not what drew him to the event. Color for him is function. It is there inevitably when skillful athletes perform their dazzling deeds. For him, consequently, golfers are most glamorous when they are totally absorbed in playing golf.

Quite often these days when I am watching a fine young golfer who is wooing his gallery all too deliberately, I find myself thinking of Ben Hogan, for if ever a man epitomized the Old School, it is Hogan. There were stretches in his career, in fact, when his demeanor on the course was undoubtedly too severe. With his enormous pride and his passion for perfection, Ben couldn't stand to play poor golf, and whenever he struck a really bad patch, he would pack up and leave the tour, head for the practice

tee and slave away monastically until he had corrected the cause of his trouble and was back on his stick again. The idea of continuing to play tournaments at these times because he might pick up a little prize money or gain some other commercial benefit—this was anathema to him. No different from anyone else, Hogan wanted to make money through his golf, but his standards were exceedingly high and, if my memory is correct, the only product he ever endorsed (other than golf equipment, golf slacks and golf shoes) was Ben-Gay, an ointment he used and found effective. With Hogan, golf came first, and he gave it everything he had. You felt this whenever you saw him in action, and this is what made watching him such an incisive and indelible experience.

Since Hogan's philosophy of life is so utterly different from that of the young men on the other side of the generation gap, some of his encounters with them have been very interesting. I am thinking particularly of the television interview he consented to tape with Chris Schenkel in the spring of 1970 when, as the tour was trouping through Texas, Hogan joined it for the tournaments in Houston and Fort Worth. The way it was told to me, Schenkel took aside the young producer who would be handling the interview and impressed on him how important it was to cut out all the Sixth Avenue gingerbread when the sequence with Hogan was shot. The young producer said he understood perfectly. The next day, when Hogan, after finishing a satisfactory round, arrived at the corner of the clubhouse set aside for the interview, the young producer studied how he looked and then asked him if he'd mind raising the visor of his cap half an inch. "Yes, I would," Ben replied politely but firmly. "This is how I wear my cap."

This is not the last mention we will be making of television. It is impossible to overstate its power or overemphasize its influence on our lives. There are times when television seems more real than life itself—as if it were the substance and life were the shadow. Each year the feeling grows among all of us that if something isn't shown on

television, then it just didn't happen.

Television has affected all sports to a considerable degree, but none quite as much as golf. To begin on a light note, it has, we noted earlier, dictated a whole new style of deportment for tournament players. Over the first 14 holes of his round, a player who is either in the throes of a bad slump or simply having a bad day may make no effort to hide his irritation with himself and the world in general. After a poor shot, he may toss his club petulantly toward his caddie. After a good shot, he may take elaborate pains to ignore the applause of his gallery. However, once he reaches the tee on the 15th hole (or whatever is the first hole on which the TV cameras are positioned), bingo, off goes the Mr. Hyde grimace and on comes that winning Dr. Jekyll smile. His manners are impeccable. You sense that, deep down, this man has integrity. If he ran a prep school, you would send your son there, no questions asked.

Television's greatest disservice to golf, perhaps, is that it has helped to virtually eliminate match play as a form of competition for the game's best players. At the present time the pros engage in match play in this country only every four years when it is our turn to host the Ryder Cup. As a general rule, match play is more fascinating to watch than stroke play, but because the shape it can take is so unpredictable, it just doesn't suit television. How can a network make plans to televise live the finishing holes of a 36-hole final when there is a fair chance that one of the players may wrap it up, say, 9 and 8 or 8 and 6 when the show has barely gone on the air. You're locked out then; there is no other action on the course to turn to.

There are a hundred other chances for snafu. For example, due to some unforeseen delay or to just plain slow play, the lead match in a Walker Cup or Ryder Cup competition may be only on the 12th green at air time, and this is going to present some nice complications if the network has arranged to cover just the last four holes. In the 1971 Ryder Cup, it worked out the other way. Ten minutes after the start of the telecast, the

14

American team got the point it needed to clinch the match, so the rest of the golf was of no consequence. No head of a network sports division (and no sponsor) is going to invite the implicit headaches of match play when stroke play is so much easier and safer. *There,* since the whole field will be completing the 18 holes, you know pretty well when each contender will be coming into camera range and how long he'll be staying there.

Stroke play calls for fundamentally conservative and unimaginative tactics. The key is to avoid serious error. The essence of match play, on the other hand, is immediate, all-out response. For instance, if you and I are playing a par-4 and you put your approach shot five feet from the flag, I must reply with an equally excellent approach or face the probable loss of that hole. Or let's say that we are playing a short par-5 (like the 475-yard 13th at the Augusta National) and you have hit such a prodigious drive that you can easily get home with an iron. Well, after my ordinary drive I must make up my mind then and there whether I should try to whack a career shot all the way to the green, knowing that I may well make an irredeemable error and present you the hole on a silver platter. Match play, you see, is much more of a joust. It calls for a doughty, resourceful competitor, the sort of fellow who is not ruffled by his opponent's fireworks and is able to set off a few of his own when it counts. It calls for a Walter Hagen. Back in the days when the PGA Championship was a match-play affair, Hagen won it five times. From 1924 through 1927, he carried it off four years in a row, and over that span won 40 consecutive matches.

The most fervid match that Hagen ever lost was the final of the 1923 PGA, and it offers a superb illustration of the thrills that match play can produce. Up against Gene Sarazen, the one contemporary of his who was intrinsically as tough as he was, Hagen, all square after the morning 18 at the Pelham Country Club in Westchester, struck a bad stretch and trailed by three holes after the 27th. He won the 28th when he put his niblick approach next to the pin, but could

make no further headway against young Sarazen—Gene was only 21—until the 34th, which he won. Only one down now. However, on the 35th, a par-5, it looked all over for Walter when he hooked his second shot out-of-bounds. Holding his cool, he dropped another ball and laced a long brassie all the way to the green. There he dropped a 20-foot putt for his par and, when Sarazen three-putted nervously from 30 feet for a six, Hagen won a hole that had seemed irretrievably lost. Match all square. On the 36th, two pars.

On into extra holes, the two opposing camps of rooters charged up and voluble. On the 37th, a halve in pars. Now the 38th, a short par-4 that doglegged acutely to the left, with a high stand of trees commanding the angle of the dogleg. Hagen, with the honor, hit a good drive down the center of the fairway. Sarazen impulsively decided to bite off a bit of the corner. He hooked the shot badly and it went crashing into the trees. Here he was very lucky. The ball, which easily could have ricocheted out of bounds, was found lying in deep rough but in a position which afforded Sarazen an opening to the green. He made the most of that break. Digging down with his niblick, he tore the ball out of the matty grass and sent it bounding onto the green. It rolled to within two feet of the hole.

"I looked over to see what dent that recovery had made in Walter's armor," Sarazen recalled many years later. "He was visibly shaken. I had never seen Hagen lose his poise before, and I doubt if any man in the gallery had. When he finally played his wee pitch, he floofed it, like a duffer, into the trap between him and the green. His fighting instinct surged back then. He made a brave effort to hole his third shot from the trap. When he failed by inches, he had lost the PGA Championship." Yes, there is nothing like match play to bring out the dynamic qualities of golf.

If we are generally denied such treats as Hagen vs. Sarazen these days, it is wrong to imply that it is all television's fault. Long before the medium was sufficiently advanced technically to consider doing golf, the pros, as individuals, were looking for a good excuse to do away with match play as the format of the PGA Championship. Over 18 holes even the best player in the world can lose to a man with a hot putter, and it is rough enough for a star's self-esteem to be beaten in a head-to-head encounter by his peers, let alone by some upstart bumpkin. When a friend calls over to a name pro and asks him how he came out, how galling it is for him to have to answer, "I lost 3 and 2." It is all so definite, so pejorative. How much nicer and unbruising it is, after he shoots a similarly mediocre round in a stroke-play tournament, to be able to answer the same question, with an attractive shake of the head, "Three over, can you believe it? Hit the ball perfectly but couldn't buy a putt. Must have missed half a dozen under four feet." (I am convinced, by the way, that the reason tennis players are so taut and temperamental during a tournament—off the court as well as on—is that there is no such face-saving luxury as stroke-play competition in tennis. The threat of losing a match hangs continually over the head of the tennis player, and that makes for enormous pressure.)

The PGA must shoulder a fair share of the blame for the passing of its match-play championship. Of course, the PGA does need money to operate, and in this day when the television networks aren't particularly interested in contracting for the rights to a match-play event, you can understand why the association veered toward stroke play. The PGA actually began veering that way many long years ago, for all too often its match-play championship proved a financial bust. If Sam Snead and the one or two other gate attractions were eliminated in the early rounds, the public stayed away in droves the rest of the week.

One final point which, while it has nothing to do with match play, is extremely relevant. In the middle 1960s, the USGA made a revolutionary alteration in the Open, dispensing with the traditional double round of 36 holes on the third and final day and adopting the format of a single round on four days. I would suppose that gaining another day's television audience

and, with that, a more bountiful television contract had something to do with this move. For many of us, however, this was a mistake, because we feel that the Open was a better championship when it required 36 holes on the last day. There are any number of golfers who can get through 18 holes even on an Open course without their swings coming apart, but 36 is an entirely different proposition: if your swing has a basic flaw, it will disintegrate under the attrition of that ever-increasing pressure. Only a truly sound golfer can stand up to it, which is the way it should be in the national championship. As a result, the old Opens developed a drama all their own. (Just the other day, I had a letter from a veteran golf enthusiast, a Mr. Joseph Hyland of Staten Island, in which he spoke of this. "Some of the most exciting moments of my life," he wrote, "were spent at Merion and Winged Foot and Baltusrol and a half dozen other places around three or four o'clock on those Saturday afternoons).'' As someone or other said once—it was either Andra Kirkaldy or Chairman Mao— when the USGA revamped the Open, it lost a championship and gained just another tournament.

It comes down to this, more or less. During the past decade, it has often looked as if the whole world was turning itself inside out just to accommodate the CBS, NBC and ABC camera crews. The golf world certainly has, at moments. It is about time that it realized that its first responsibility is to further the best expression of golf.

There's no need to worry about television; it will adjust. For example, if the USGA decided to return to the climactic double round in the Open, the network telecasting the event would undoubtedly accord the championship at least as much air time, and possibly more than it is presently getting. This isn't meant to imply that it would be an equally simple matter to get the networks to cover match-play golf as stroke-play golf, but should the PGA re-introduce pure match play at a significant level, it would be surprising if the networks didn't quickly learn how to cope with the new and special problems involved. After all, light

portable equipment is where television is heading, and even with the present largely stationary equipment, the BBC does a pretty fair job covering the annual eight-man-field World Match Play Championship.

Are we right to take the game of golf this seriously? I think we are. What comes to mind, as I write this, is William Hazlitt's famous essay on Cavanagh the Fives-Player, written in February, 1819, upon the death of John Cavanagh, the greatest handball player of his time. Here is the heart of it:

". . . It may be said that there are things of more importance than striking a ball against a wall— there are things indeed that make more noise and do as little good, such as making war and peace, making speeches and answering them, making money and throwing it way. But the game of fives is what no one despises who has ever played at it. It is the finest exercise for the body, and the best relaxation for the mind. The Roman poet said that 'Care mounted behind the horseman and stuck to his skirts.' But this remark would not have applied to the fives-player. He who takes to playing at fives is twice young. He feels neither the past or the future 'in the instant.' Debts, taxes, 'domestic treason, foreign levy, nothing can touch him further.' He has no other wish, no other thought, from the moment the game begins but that of striking the ball, of placing it, of making it . . .''

Hazlitt's words, I would think, apply to every good game. They certainly do to golf. ∎

ADVANCES IN EQUIPMENT

MOLDED BALLS—HOW GOOD ARE THEY?

June, 1967

Solid, man, solid! That is the word in the golf ball industry these days. And while "solid" does not quite accurately describe the makeup of the new molded balls, it does reflect the impact their backers hope they will make this year.

After what amounted to a practice round in 1966, the non-wound ball is challenging aggressively for a share of the golf ball market in 1967.

In fact, according to its proponents, the new sphere will eventually replace the conventional wound rubber ball that has been with us for over 65 years.

A. G. Spalding & Bros., Chicopee, Mass., one of the largest golf ball companies in the country, created the most significant stir when it came out with a non-wound ball this March [1967]. Spalding, of course, is also continuing conventional ball production.

As well as being the first of the new balls to sell for the "quality price" of $1.25, the Spalding Executive is the only one to take the "two-piece" approach by putting a cover on a molded center.

What are they saying about this new ball? Its backers claim: that only the golfer will smile, the ball won't; that it will not chip, break or go out of round; that it will fly truer and putt straighter than conventional balls; that it will hit the fairways more often because its slower spin means less hooking and slicing, and that it will last indefinitely and can't be affected by temperature.

Also, the claimants say, molded balls can be made rounder than wound balls. And, since the manufacturing operations are reduced at least by half, the non-wound ball can be made and sold cheaper. They claim that the average golfer will be able to hit the molded ball farther, yet won't be able to recognize any difference in click or feel.

What are the criticisms leveled against the new ball? Critics claim that it breaks up sometimes and that the paint chips off. They say it lacks consistency, feel, backspin,

hang, click, is still unproven and falls short of the distances achieved by conventional balls.

While the methods of making a conventional ball vary (and manufacturers guard their secrets closely) generally they begin with a thin-walled rubber sphere that has been filled with some substance and frozen. Sometimes a solid center of steel, nylon or rubber is used. Around this center pellet is wound a vulcanized rubber thread of about 30 yards that is under enough tension to stretch it to more than 245 yards.

Two molded hemispheric shells of compounded balata rubber are knit to the wound center by heat treatment in a mold which also forms the dimples on the surface. The ball is cured or vulcanized to toughen the cover and make it resilient.

The final acceptance or rejection of molded or "non-wound" balls lies strictly with the golfers themselves. And, quite likely, their decision will be based primarily on a ball's ability to provide that one all-important characteristic—maximum distance.

—*John E. Teehan*

SURLYN: MORE DURABILITY, EQUAL DISTANCE

April, 1971

The recent development of a new plastic ball covering called Surlyn may significantly alter golf ball manufacturing, and provide golfers with hard-to-cut "distance" balls.

Most ballmakers agree that the golf ball has just about reached the peak of its development so far as distance is concerned. For the past decade research has been primarily aimed at making the ball more durable and resistant to cutting,

without reducing its quality of resilience, which is the major distance factor.

Surlyn is the latest material to emerge in the search for cut-and-scuff-resistant golf ball covers. It is a thermoplastic invented by Du Pont and, like its cousins parafin and polyethylene, is derived from petroleum. But it is a lot tougher than its chemical relatives —a .38 caliber bullet fired from seven feet will not penetrate a ¾-inch slab—and it can be molded to either a solid or wound-rubber core.

Toughness is not the only quality that makes Surlyn attractive to

many manufacturers. It is cheaper than balata and easier to produce. The fact that Surlyn covers can be injection-molded by pouring the molten material around the center is an advantage over the compression-molding process required with balata, according to Roy H. Kinsey, Du Pont product manager. "It's much faster. There are fewer steps, and the result is greater consistency in the covers," Kinsey claims. There is also some evidence that Surlyn-covered balls go as far as, and in the case of irons shots, farther than, some top-grade balata-covered balls.

—*The Editors*

17

THE FULL STORY ABOUT THOSE ALUMINUM SHAFTS

March, 1968

This closeup photo of their tip ends shows the difference in wall thickness and diameter between the two leading aluminum shafts (LeFiell's, left, True Temper's, center) and a typical steel shaft (right). Both LeFiell's smooth shaft and True Temper's tapered one are less shiny and weigh less than the present steel shaft.

The aluminum golf shaft is the biggest change in club manufacture in 40 years and its full-scale introduction in 1968 will have a major impact on golf, from manufacturer to club professional to weekend player.

The aluminum shaft is fatter, costlier and duller in appearance than the steel shaft, but few experts believe these characteristics will impede its acceptance. It already has captured the public's imagination to an extraordinary degree, and seems certain to produce the most dramatic turnaround in the industry since the changeover from hickory to steel shafts in the 1920s.

At the outset, let it be clear that the merits of the new shaft have yet to be proven conclusively. No one really knows how good—or how bad—it may turn out to be. Scientific tests, though encouraging, are far from complete. All indicators point to a period of experimentation and improvement over the next two or three years before the jury—millions of golfers—returns with a verdict.

Yet the golfing public, traditionally eager to try something new, is clamoring for the new shaft, linking it with the romance of space-age metallurgy and the charisma of Arnold Palmer, the first man to win with aluminum shafts on the professional tour.

The demand right now, in the words of one club manufacturer, has zoomed "out of sight." If this demand for aluminum shafts continues through the spring and summer at its present rate, it well may outstrip the supply.

Opinion on the new shaft is divided but predominantly favorable, especially from club professionals who see it as a can't miss business-builder and clubmakers who look on aluminum as the first real breakthrough in improving clubs since steel replaced hickory.

For years, clubmakers have searched for a lighter golf shaft that would still be as strong and durable as steel. The theory is that you can swing the lighter club faster and hit the ball farther.

Aluminum had long been one of many materials investigated, but available alloys—mixtures of two or more metals—had been considered too soft. Only in recent years did a new alloy appear—developed for aerospace tubing—that seemed to have the necessary strength characteristics. Since aluminum is not as strong as steel, to get the same resistance to bend it was decided that the shaft wall should be thicker than the wall of steel shafts. Because aluminum has more flex than steel, clubmakers found that they had to increase the outer diameter as well as the wall thickness to produce a shaft as strong and torsion-free as steel.

This wider, thicker-walled shaft required more metal, but it was still lighter than a steel shaft. The over-all savings per shaft is between ½ and ⅝ of an ounce, roughly 15 per cent of the average driver shaft's total weight of 4½ ounces.

The claimed points of advantage of the new aluminum shafts, all of which will be promoted by the industry are: lighter clubs at the same swingweight, more distance, less torsion and shock and, thus, better control.

Why the sudden, overwhelming demand? Dan Sheehan, vice president of LeFiell (pronounced Le Fell) Co., Santa Fe Springs, Calif., a major supplier of aluminum shafts to the club manufacturers, observes: "The golfer is a guy looking for innovations, just waiting for something new, that little extra edge."

One problem that haunts most of the manufacturers is uncertainty about the true extent of the public's interest. This lack of knowledge about the market, combined with the expense of retooling and reorganizing production facilities and procedures, has many industry leaders jumpy. Yet, most are optimistic about the future and have shifted production schedules on aluminum into high gear.

True Temper and LeFiell, the dominant suppliers of the shafts to manufacturers, are both gearing for increased production, but the extent to which they can supply the demand this first year remains uncertain. And True Temper's chief of the golf shaft division, Gurdon Leslie, looks at the current furor with a long-range view. "Our goal is a very slender, lightweight shaft made of a very stiff material. The ultimate shaft hasn't been made. We're still looking for it."

There is some difference of opinion over who will benefit more from the new shaft, the weekend player or the professional. Cary Middlecoff suspects that it may benefit the "swinger" more than the "hitter." Not only will he develop more clubhead speed, it is reasoned, but the added "feel" of the heavier head will allow him to time his swing more easily.

Arnold Palmer thinks it will be a real boon to the senior golfer because it will tend to tire him less and allow him to swing faster with the same effort. Arnold says his father, Deacon Palmer, pro at Latrobe (Pa.) C.C., lowered his scores when he switched to aluminum clubs and now won't go back to steel. With no scientific measurements to prove this one way or the other, answers will have to await the test of actual play.

Touring professionals will no doubt be slow to switch to the new shafts. They are usually reluctant to change tools, particularly when their games are going well. Wilson's Joe Wolfe believes that it will take a while before aluminum, or any equivalent shaft, catches on among the tour stars but "in the long run, when they accept it, aluminum will have it made."

Even though his company is moving into aluminum slowly, MacGregor's Bob Lysaght admits it is a change in concept comparable to steel's replacing hickory in the 1920s. "I keep remembering the old Scotchman I worked with in those days. He bet steel shafts wouldn't last a year."

—Cal Brown

CLUBS THAT HIT STRAIGHTER, BALLS THAT GO FARTHER

December, 1971

Over recent years there has been a growing feeling among knowledgeable golfers that many modifications in equipment were more cosmetic than functional, more sales-oriented than scientific.

But there *have* been scientific approaches to various aspects of the designing of golf clubs and balls by many American manufacturers. And they have never occurred with quite such depth and intensity as now.

Out of this new plunge into science emerges a long-range promise for every golfer. By joining scientific findings to the experience and subjective knowledge of golf professionals and veteran clubmakers, manufacturers ultimately hope to sell each golfer implements more perfectly suited to his size, shape and level of skill.

Dr. Alistair Cochran's and John Stobbs' ambitious book, *The Search for the Perfect Swing,* perhaps triggered the new plunge into research and development. Dunlop of Great Britain, expanding on Dr. Cochran's ideas, came up with Maxpower clubs, incorporating new shafts, which the company said made it possible to match the feel of clubs within a set "dynamically" (while in motion) rather than statically.

In his studies, Dr. Cochran also had suggested that iron heads would be more efficient if weight were moved from behind the center of the blade and redistributed toward the toe and heel. He showed that with such a club, less twisting would result from off-center shots. Prior to the publishing of Cochran's book, a Redwood City (Calif.) engineer named Karsten Solheim was independently experimenting with the same principle. At first Solheim incorporated the idea into his now famous Ping putters. Later he designed iron clubs with heads hollowed out in back, and with the weight relocated toward the toe, heel and sole.

Now more than a half-dozen clubmakers feature adaptations of the same principle in 1972 lines.

Scientists at other companies have been working harder than ever to improve the golf ball. Uniroyal, after a three-year investigation into flight, spin and aerodynamic characteristics, is now ready with a ball radically different from any other on the market.

The rattling of test tubes and whining of computers have also been noticeable at Faultless and at Princeton Chemical Research, as they strive to develop a solid ball that will be as resilient as it is cut-proof.

Shakespeare, the highly successful fishing rod company which tried with limited success to market a glass golf shaft several years ago, is now developing a shaft made of graphite filament that, it claims, is 12 times as strong, but almost half as light, as steel. Such a development could radically alter both the tools of the game and the techniques for playing it.

Here is a rundown on the major science-based equipment developments for 1972:

Iron Heads

Shortly after Acushnet entered the club market two years ago, it asked research and development director Dr. John W. Jepson to develop a much-expanded research program. The first objective was to discover where on the clubface golfers of different ability hit the ball.

Field tests showed that expert golfers hit the ball flush on the "sweet spot," or center of gravity, only 41 per cent of the time. The less-skilled player, the tests proved, hits the ball on the sweet spot of his club only about 21 per cent of the time. Armed with this and other data, Acushnet devised a clubhead so weighted at the toe and heel that it minimized the differences in carry and direction between shots hit on the sweet spot and shots hit off-center. The effect of the new design, very simply, is to increase any golfer's margin for error by widening the hitting area from which he can produce a good shot.

Shafts

Probably more attention has been paid to the shaft than any other piece of golf equipment in recent years. The object of most research has been to lighten the shaft, so that more weight can be put into the clubhead without increasing the over-all weight of the club. Theoretically, this produces longer hits and better club "feel."

Such research produced the aluminum shaft of several years ago, and then the lightweight steel shaft which has now virtually replaced it as the standard material.

The appearance of the lightweight steel shaft was due primarily to Ben Hogan, who did not like the way aluminum performed and who, through his own equipment company, and in cooperation with True Temper Corp., developed the Apex shaft. This lightweight steel shaft is lighter than regular steel shafts because it has a thinner wall, but just as strong because its diameter is thicker.

It was in this atmosphere of change that Dunlop began a program to develop a set of clubs in which every club from wedge to driver would swing with the same "dynamic feel."

To produce such a set, a new type of shaft was needed, one graded by its flex and recovery characteristics, while in motion, rather than simply by stiffness. Thus Dunlop evolved a new shaft pattern which, it is claimed, flexes and recovers identically from driver through the wedges, given the same force of swing.

In America, Shakespeare has

developed two shafts, one of graphite, the other a composite of glass and tough resins, that are both lighter than steel or aluminum.

The new shafts weigh between 2.6 and 2.8 ounces in a driver, as compared with 3.75 to 4.5 ounces for driver shafts made of aluminum or steel. Shakespeare claims the graphite and composite shafts are also superior to steel in terms of the feel.

Swingweight

Several U.S. manufacturers are experimenting with systems to improve on the swingweight system of matching clubs. Spalding is marketing a new line, called MV-2, and PGA Victor will introduce a line called Par Excellence in 1972. In both lines club are related within a set by dead weight.

The Par Excellence line is also interesting in that it features two design changes that are specifically aimed at helping the average golfer add distance. These features are increased loft and longer shafts.

Balls

Uniroyal has made a dramatic departure from convention by devolping a golf ball with fewer dimples, each of which is six-sided.

The new ball was developed in consultation over three years with Dr. John D. Nicolaides, professor in the department of aerospace and mechanical engineering at Notre Dame. Uniroyal and Nicolaides developed a ball with 252 hexagonal dimples positioned at random. Conventional balls have 336 round dimples lined up in rows. Uniroyal discovered that randomly oriented dimples produce more lift. Its scientists claim that dimples arranged in straight rows create tiny flat surfaces between the rows, which generate no lifting force from the air.

Called the Royal Plus Six, the new ball uses a new polymeric solid core, a new type of rubber winding, and a Surlyn cover.

Both Faultless and Princeton Chemical Research have changed the chemical formula of their solid golf balls, following lengthy research programs. Solid golf balls are made from polybutadiene, a type of synthetic rubber, mixed with other ingredients like resin and a hardening agent.

The initial velocity of the new ball is five feet per second faster than previous solid balls, according to Gene Lukinac, technical manager of the Faultless golf ball division. This produces an increased carry of seven yards over the previous Faultless solid ball.

—The Editors

STORE-LINE OR PRO-LINE CLUBS?

January, 1973

You're thinking about buying new golf clubs for the season to come. You can walk into a retail store and pick up a set for less than $100. You also can pay more than $400 for a set in a golf professional's shop.

Why do club prices range so widely? What are you getting for the money? Is there a difference that will help you become a better and happier golfer?

A *Golf Digest* inquiry indicates that pro-line clubs have the edge over their store-line cousins in four areas:

• New designs and materials are introduced first in pro-line clubs.

• Better and/or more expensive materials are selected for pro-line models.

• More care and precision go into the manufacture of pro-line clubs. Tighter and more frequent inspection makes for finer tolerances, fewer rough spots and greater uniformity. Pro-line clubs also are generally better finished —more paint, polish and decoration —than store-line models.

• There is greater variety in specifications in pro-line clubs, facilitating better fitting to individual requirements by the golf professional.

The differences look like this:

In pro-line models, much effort is made to achieve uniformity of "geometry"—loft, lie, degree of offset and so forth—in each set of clubs. In addition, two or more of various techniques are used to produce uniformity of "feel" in each set. These include swing-weighting (arrived at by correlating the weight of the clubhead and the weight of the grip end with the length of the grip end with the length of the shaft) and matching by shaft flex, or sometimes by balancing static or "dead" weight.

Each manufacturer's best store line usually is registered (the specifications are recorded by the manufacturer for possible later duplication) and swing-weighted but is ordinarily available only with a medium-flex shaft. (The retailer usually sells it for just a few dollars less per set than pro-line models.) After that, there is less concern— often none at the bottom end of the line—about achieving uniformity of either geometry or feel.

In the golf professional's shop, the player often wants clubs personally tailored to his particular size, strength, experience and playing ability. The professional, whose livelihood depends on offering expert advice and highly personal service, wants to have them for him. So both the retailer and the consumer are, in effect, putting pressure on the manufacturer to custom-build clubs.

Persimmon, the traditional wood-head material, has been largely replaced by wood-laminates. Thin sheets of wood—usually maple— are glued together to form a strong, workable block. Most manufacturers claim it is just as effective in striking the ball as persimmon and has the advantages of greater strength and imperviousness to climatic changes, thus keeping the static weight and swing-weight more constant. The overly hard feel of the early laminates has been virtually eliminated by the development of new adhesives that require less glue between the wood sheets.

The wood used in laminates for pro-line clubs is top-grade. Coarser grades usually are used for store-line clubs.

In the making and finishing of woods, pro-line heads are more precisely machined and sanded than the store-line variety.

There is a strong swing to the use of stainless steel in top pro lines because of its durability and lasting finish. Stainless steel heads, which will not corrode, almost always are made with a technique known as investment or "lost-wax" casting. More expensive than the traditional forging and machining, this process casts each head separately in its finished form, including decoration.

The cast heads are becoming increasingly available in the store lines. Because they are produced from cheaper materials and sell for less, they obviously lack some of the esthetic appeal as well as some of the qualities of weight distribution and consistency that cast pro-line clubs have.

Pro-line forged heads are usually more precisely machined and finished to achieve finer tolerances in loft, lie, degree of offset, size of hosel and over-all weight and balance.

Shaft manufacturers do not grade their shafts "pro-line" or "store-line." They make four basic quality grades, each in a variety of weights, strengths and flex characteristics. Materials used in each grade of shaft differ negligibly. A shaft's quality is governed primarily by the thickness of the wall, which largely controls weight, and by the "stepping pattern," which lessens the diameter of the shaft in stages and establishes flex characteristics. The closer to the clubhead the final "step" is, where the shaft wall is thinnest, the stiffer the flex characteristics.

Because each "step" requires an individual operation, a shaft with more stepping patterns obviously is costlier to produce.

—Ken Bowden

WOULD YOU PAY $100 A CLUB?

January, 1973

For just about $1,120 (that's $100 per wood and $80 an iron), you can buy a set of golf clubs with a new shaft made of graphite yarn, a major breakthrough in club manufacturing.

The black graphite shafts are being offered by two companies—Shakespeare, Columbia S.C., and Aldila Precision Golf, Inc., San Diego, Calif. Much of the work on the new shaft has been done by Shakespeare's chief product design engineer, Frank Thomas.

"Graphite yarn has about a fourth the specific gravity of steel and twice its tensile strength," Thomas explains. "In making steel or aluminum shafts, you can vary some of the shaft qualities (flex, stiffness, etc.) but you are limited by the fact that the material cannot be altered.

"Graphite yarn, on the other hand, can be varied at will because the thin, hairlike threads are spun, or wound, onto a mold to form the hollow shaft. This allows us to make a shaft with any torsion stiffness, flex strength or weight we desire. Graphite shafts have a more evenly distributed flex throughout the shaft because we can make them stiffer than ordinary shafts near the tip. Graphite shafts do not have a flex point, as such, and this allows the entire shaft to store and release more energy."

Graphite shafts weigh about half as much as comparable steel shafts (2.1 to 2.9 ounces for graphite vs. 4.2 to 4.5 for steel).

A number of tour players, among them Gay Brewer, Phil Rodgers and Tom Shaw, are playing with the new shaft. Brewer, who has had a lifelong problem keeping his tee shots straight, began hitting the fairway consistently when he switched to a graphite-shafted driver, and had a big year in 1972.

"I have so much confidence in this new driver," Brewer says, "it's changed my whole attitude."

Aldila Co. is backed by Glen Campbell, Andy Williams and Rodgers and is run by James Flood, a two-time club champion at La Costa. Although both Aldila and Shakespeare agree that graphite shafts can produce 10 per cent more distance than steel, they prefer to emphasize that, because of its lighter over-all weight, more golfers notice greater club control with the new shafts.

The ideal golf shaft, theoretically, would be a very thin, perfectly rigid connection between the clubhead and the golfer's hands, because it would eliminate deviation. Graphite shafts represent a giant step toward this ideal, because they can be made lighter and stiffer than steel shafts.

—Cal Brown

DIMPLES ARE BIG

January, 1973

The big news in golf balls for 1973 is dimples. Acushnet, the giant of the ball-manufacturing industry, has announced that its Titleist ball will have fewer dimples (324 instead of 336) that would be 15 per cent larger and 10 per cent shallower than before. The new ball, which goes on the market in January, will remain otherwise unchanged, having the same construction, cover material, initial velocity and lift force.

Acushnet has been facing growing competition from solid and Surlyn-covered balls, such as the Spalding Topflite. In its continuing pursuit of product improvement, two years ago it introduced a new dimple shape, the K-2, as an intermediate step in its cover redesign.

Dimples on golf balls are a good deal more useful than they may appear. They're there to give the ball lift so it will stay airborne longer.

Way back in the 1850s, when the gutta percha ball replaced the original feather ball, golfers found that this rubber ball performed better after it had been roughed up in play. In 1908, Englishman William Taylor "invented" the dimple, reasoning that a more or less regular pattern of slight depressions in the ball's surface produced the most desired effects of lift and control.

Most ball-making companies eventually settled on molds which had 336 dimples distributed in rows around the 1.68-inch sphere, mostly because there was only one man in America, Ralph Atti of Union, N.J., who could make a decent golf ball mold, and he made them all with 336 dimples.

There has been a certain amount of experimentation, mostly between 1908 and 1925, with changing the number, shape and depth of golf ball dimples. Scientists had suggested that better aerodynamics would improve golf ball performance. But no one in the golf business had any reason to pursue the idea very hard until a year ago, when Uniroyal came out with its Royal Plus-6 that had 252 hexagonal dimples (*Golf Digest,* December, 1971). The ball went farther, Uniroyal claimed, and seemed to fly higher, particularly downwind. And it did not go unnoticed that Royal's new ball began doing well in the market place. The dimple race was on.

The man who did the work for Acushnet is Dr. John Jepson, the company's tall, pipe-smoking research director, who explained the reasons.

"We were not just looking for added distance, although the new Titleist will carry an average of five to 10 yards farther with a driver. We also wanted to see if we could design dimples that would produce less left and right deviation in flight," Jepson said. "You do this by reducing the drag force—the resistance to forward motion exerted on the ball by the air it is passing through."

This happens with the new Titleist because the larger dimples are closer together and the spaces between them are thinner, more sharply edged and less variable in thickness, presenting a more uniform, rougher surface.

—*The Editors*

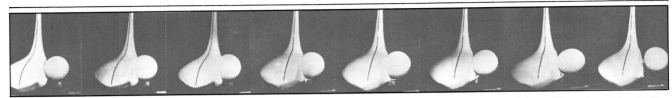

Here's the way a golf ball can look when being compressed by a strong swing with a driver. Note how the ball flattens against the clubhead and then appears to spring away. This rare sequence was taken with an open shutter with exposures being triggered by a light flash lasting only three-millionths of a second. This entire action took place in .0004 of a second, using a driving machine set to whack the ball over 230 yards.

WHAT DOES BALL COMPRESSION MEAN TO YOU?

January, 1974

If you play golf three or four times a month, you probably spend upward of $75 a year on golf balls. You're always in the market. And when you think about making a golf ball purchase, the term "compression" likely comes to mind.

Some balls are marked 100 compression. Some are marked 90, a few 80. But what does it all mean? *Golf Digest* made an in-depth study of golf ball compression. Here are the answers to some questions you perhaps should ask before you buy golf balls the next time.

Q: Simply speaking, what is golf ball compression?

A: It's the measure of a ball's hardness. A golf ball is placed between two parallel plates of a vise-like machine. One plate is fixed, the other moves under a spring with 200-pound force. The more a ball can be squeezed by the machine, the lower the reading on the compression gauge. The harder a ball, the more it resists pressure and the higher the reading.

Q: How do scientists measure golf ball compression?

A: The standard American golf ball, which is 1.68 inches in diameter, is placed in a compression machine and "squeezed" under a constant pressure. Balls that can be squeezed from the normal 1.68 size down to 1.58 inches are said to have a compression reading of 100. For every one-thousandth of an inch more a ball is mashed, the compression reading drops one point. For every one-thousandth of an inch less a ball is deformed on this compression machine, the reading goes up a point.

Q: What does compression mean in distance off the tee?

A: When you talk pure distance with no other factors concerned, all golfers should get more yardage from the highest compression ball.

Q: Why then shouldn't everyone play 100-compression balls?

A: While you may get five or 10 additional yards playing a 100-compression ball instead of a 90, you may decide against using the 100 due to a rock-like feeling when you strike the ball.

Q: When you purchase a box of a dozen balls, are they all the exact same compression?

A: The odds are a million-to-one that you will ever buy a dozen perfectly matched balls. It is common to find a difference of eight compression points between the hardest and softest ball among your dozen. What you really are buying is a compression range and not an exact compression. If you purchase balls marked as 100s, you usually get anything from 91 to 99. Balls marked as 90s are mostly between 82 and 90 compression.

Q: Do higher compression balls cut more easily?

A: Yes. High compression balls of conventional construction are wound extremely tight and are more likely to have a "smile" cut in their hides by mis-struck shots.

Q: How does weather affect compression?

A: Cold weather makes a ball harder. Your 90-compression golf balls suddenly feel like 100s. It comes back to what you "feel" at impact. Most touring pros will switch to a lower compression ball when the temperature drops below 50. If they normally play the 100, they'll go down to 90. —*Hubert Mizell*

THE CASE FOR LIGHTER CLUBS

December, 1974

"The average man could probably play better with his wife's clubs."

Frank Beard, *Golf Digest* playing editor who made the above observation, is convinced that almost every golfer should be using lighter clubs.

Albert Einstein was no golfer or he would have told the golfing public the same thing Beard advocates. Einstein and his fellow physicists have long known that force equals mass times velocity squared. In other words, the faster you swing a driver the farther you will hit the golf ball. You can swing a lighter club faster.

Jim Dent, the current long-driving king of the tour, agrees with Einstein and the physicists. After winning the *Golf Digest*-Tournament Players Division distance contest this year, he told our readers to swing as light a club as possible.

Star teaching professional Bob Toski, who stresses the value of a light grip pressure in this issue, says that lighter clubs make it easier to grip the club lightly. "The average player doesn't have to work as hard to swing a lighter club," he says.

The most practical avenue to a lighter club is the shaft. It's the controlling element.

We've come a long way since the days of the hickory shaft, which weighed as much as 8½ ounces.

The first improvement on hickory, in the 1930s, was steel, which now weighs about 4½ ounces. By the mid-1960s the weight of shafts was lowered to four ounces with the appearance of lightweight steel and aluminum. Many still feel aluminum is a useful club for the average player, but it didn't catch on. The dull appeance, the insistence of some touring pros that it felt too "soft," and its fat look worked against aluminum.

Lightweight steel gained better acceptance and accounts for about 20 per cent of the shaft market today. Although the shaft is slightly larger in diameter than regular steel, the walls aren't as thick, saving weight.

Stainless steel, which made an abortive appearance several years ago, is back on the market in limited supply. The problem with stainless has always been finding the proper alloy. It is about the same weight as lightweight steel.

Today, the golf club industry also is working with a lighter-than-lightweight steel, with titanium and with graphite. A titanium driver shaft weighs 3½ ounces, the lighter-than-lightweight steel only 3 ounces and graphite ranges between 2.3 and 3.6 ounces.

Titanium is a metal widely used in the aerospace industry and even in pots and pans. It is plentiful and has exceptional strength, but it is expensive to extract from the earth

and is difficult to shape into shafts. One of the reported assets of titanium is its resistance to torque. Just this fall a new titanium shaft came on the market in limited quantities. Drivers are priced in the $100 range.

The 3-ounce steel is only in the first experimental stages. The shafts have very thin walls—which is why they're lighter—and are very flexible.

Graphite, which burst onto the scene in 1973, has since captured the imagination of the golfing public —but only 2½ per cent of the club market. Graphite has been called the most dramatic single innovation in golf since hickory shafts were supplanted by steel. Stories of greater distance have been numerous.

Many knowledgeable golf people claim graphite is a boon to women players and seniors.

Why then has graphite cornered such a small portion of the market? Several reasons, but cost remains the most conspicuous. Graphite woods run from $85 to $150 each, the irons from $70 to $125. A full set of graphite clubs can cost more than $1,500.

In addition to cost, another reason for the slow acceptance of graphite is confusion over fitting the clubs to individual players and their games. In the beginning, finding the correct shaft to match a golfer's needs was mainly a guessing game. The trial and error method is still used today, but there does seem to be a majority opinion about a starting point—going to higher swingweights and stiffer shafts.

In the beginning there were opposite viewpoints about flexes. One major company offered 15 flexes and another big firm offered only one. Today, the consensus is to offer a range of flexes comparable to those in steel.

Most club golfers playing graphite have bought only drivers. Is that good or bad?

Paul Runyan, a member of the Golf Digest Professional Teaching Panel, warns of potential dangers. "It throws off your timing. You should use all graphite or none," he says.

On the other hand, Jimmy Wright, teaching professional from the Inwood (N.Y.) C.C., believes you

can play with just a graphite driver. "I think it can help a golfer produce a smoother tempo that will carry over to his steel clubs," he says.

The USGA's Frank Thomas takes a position in between Runyan and Wright. Thomas says, "Graphite is good if you have it in all your woods, not just your driver."

The pros and cons of graphite irons have been all but overlooked amid the hoopla about the drivers and longer belts off the tee.

Peter Kostis, professional at The Hamlet, Delray Beach, Fla., puts it this way: "With graphite I feel I'm hitting an 8-iron when I'm using a 4-iron. Who doesn't feel more comfortable hitting shorter irons?"

Touring pro Jim Wiechers says, "You can swing graphite irons with less physical effort and the ball gets in the air quicker."

Touring pro Phil Rodgers says, "I have hit more classic-looking iron shots since starting to use graphite. I'm able to stop the ball on the greens quicker since I get more spin. I feel graphite irons can be a definite advantage for the medium to high handicapper, especially older players who have lost some strength."

Ladies PGA tournament professional Sandra Haynie says, "The ball jumps off the clubface. For irons you have to adjust your club selection or you'll be hitting the ball too far."

On the other side, some advanced players claim they cannot maneuver the ball as well with graphite shafted irons—cannot deliberately fade or draw it.

The earlier graphite shafts had less resistance to torque (or twisting) than steel. The more the shaft twists, the less chance there is of the clubface returning squarely to the ball. Although improvements have been made through the use of additives and different methods of applying the graphite fibers, many industry experts seem to feel the shafts still do not equal their steel cousins in torque-resistance.

If you're not in the market for graphite and you want to try lighter clubs, what can you do?

The obvious first answer is lightweight steel.

Second, you can go to a lower swingweight. A club swingweighted C6 does not *have* to be lighter in static weight than a D2, but it normally will be. The trend on the men's tour is toward lower swingweights.

You can custom-order a steel-shafted club, of course, to make it lighter and still retain acceptable swing characteristics.

But this can be a time-consuming and more costly process.
—*James McAfee*

WHAT IRONS ARE BEST FOR YOU—FORGED OR CAST?
January, 1975

No new feature since the steel shaft has "changed the face" of the golf equipment industry as radically as the investment cast ironhead.

Among top lines sold in pro shops only, the percentage of cast clubs has risen from zero four years ago to about 75 per cent now. Over-all, counting store-line clubs too, cast clubs have cornered amost 50 per cent of the market.

All the approximately 40 manufacturers (except custom designer Kenneth Smith) make investment cast clubs, while only 15 also make forged clubs. MacGregor and the Ben Hogan Company joined the trend to cast clubs for the 1975 model year. Wilson, the giant of the industry, makes two top-grade forged lines in men's clubs which combined apparently outsell its cast model, but indications are the cast club is its most popular single seller.

Forgings will not disappear in the immediate future—if ever—for a couple of reasons. In the first places, the established companies have substantial capital investments in equipment to produce forged heads. Secondly, forged clubs are much less expensive to make per club, which has to be a factor during the current economic slowdown. Finally, there still are many traditionalists who favor the look and feel of forgings.

What are the differences in the manufacturing techniques? Basically, in the castings process an exact replica of the club is turned out each time by pouring melted steel into a mold, whereas in the forging process a piece of steel in the general shape of a club is produced and must be finished with several milling, grinding and engraving operations.

A plus for the cast process is that it requires much less capital outlay for machinery, the reason so many new companies have been able to get into the business. No

company that has gone into golf in the last three years makes anything but cast clubs.

Another advantage is that investment casting allows the use of stainless steel. The stainless variety—harder than mild steel— can be forged, but not easily. Because it is corrosion-resistant, containing a greater percentage of chromium, there is no need for the chrome plating that must go on heads forged from mild steel.

Cast clubs don't tarnish or nick as easily, but chrome-plated forged clubs, properly cared for, will look good for years.

The other differences for the consumer probably lie not so much in the inherent capabilities of the two processes as in what the manufacturers are doing with them. The cast clubs on the market today tend to have a larger head. This can be an advantage to most players, although it sometimes turns off the better golfer. Larger forged heads could be made.

Great strides have come in recent years in better distributing the weight in clubheads to help off-center shots and enable the average player to get the ball in the air more readily. Weight redistribution is a direct offshoot of the casting process, although it is done in forged clubs, too.

A big difference between cast and forged clubs for the average player is the price. The manufacturer must make a major investment in master models for cast clubs, and cast heads cost approximately $3 as opposed to 50 cents apiece for forged. The consumer pays anywhere from 11 to 35 per cent more for cast than forged irons.

Investment cast clubs are made by the "lost wax process," basically the same method used to make fine bone china. A set of bronze master models is built incorporating all the features of the eventual heads, down to the last detail of scoring lines and engraving. From these master models, permanent female molds are made. Into these molds is injected hot liquid wax which when

cooled forms a replica of the master model.

The wax replicas are attached to a "tree" and dipped alternately into a liquid ceramic material, a dry silicone sand mixture and back into the ceramic to obtain a coating of the proper thickness—the investment process. Then the tree is heated until the wax inside is melted and runs out—hence the "lost wax." The ceramic molds that remain are heated, molten metal is poured in and allowed to cool, and the ceramic shells are broken away. A series of polishing, weighing and painting operations completes the process.

The forged process also begins with a set of master models, but they are oversize in places to allow for machining operations, and they contain no scoring lines or other engraving.

A two-piece plaster casting is made from each master model. From these castings a special machine mills the two halves of a steel forging die. The two halves of the die are matched and fastened in a forge hammer. Red-hot round bars of metal are placed in the two halves of the die and pounded into the shape of the die by the hammer.

After trimming, grinding and other touch-up operations to remove the rough edges, the heads are sent to the manufacturer. There a series of milling operations is necessary to give the head its approximate weight, back design and desired shape. Next, the hosel hole must be bored and reamed. Scoring and polishing, buffing, chrome plating and painting complete the forging.

There seem to be several advantages to the manufacturer in the casting process. Weight, size, loft and lie specifications can be closely controlled, while in forgings the variables of die wear and individual operator techniques have to be considered. Casting gives the option of more complex shapes and designs, which can add cosmetic appeal to clubs.
—*Larry Dennis*

LET'S BUILD COURSES THAT ALL GOLFERS CAN ENJOY

BY RICHARD S. TUFTS
May, 1968

The average golfer is inclined to become emotional when talking about golf course architecture. Just listen to a discussion on the subject in the average locker room and much too often it will go somewhat as follows:

"Boy you should see that new Backbreaker Country Club. I played it last week and it is terrific. When the XYZ Open was played there only two pros were able to break par!"

"Yah, but you never played Polo-field Club. Biggest greens I ever saw. I hit all but two of them in regulation figures and ended up with an 87. Some course!"

And so it goes . . . but you never hear of these fellows giving up their membership at Pleasant Oaks and joining these "monster" courses.

Perhaps the time has come for a better understanding of golf course architecture and a realization of the fine skills which can create a course that is a pleasure, rather than an ordeal, to play, one that presents an ever-changing challenge to golfers of every degree of ability, and one that can be maintained in good condition at a reasonable cost. It seems in recent years golf course architecture has moved away from the sound principles which are so apparent in the great British links courses and in the work of the fine American architects who built courses in what might be termed the Donald Ross Era (1900-1940).

Whether we realize it or not, one of the great attractions of golf is

that it takes us away from the artificiality which surrounds our daily living and brings us out into nature's great outdoors where the scenes which meet the eye are restful and beautiful. In order that we may derive maximum pleasure and benefit from our golf, it is the first obligation of the golf course architect to develop, in every way possible, the natural beauty of the terrain with which he is working.

To be sure, the task of carefully fitting a course to its surroundings requires more of the architect in both time and ability, but those who buy his services should be willing to pay generously for this extra effort. It is unfortunately true that modern equipment makes it too easy to change the face of nature, for man can only imitate at best, and the great holes in golf are those that nature built for us.

No golf hole can be considered great unless it offers a challenge—but not a burden—to every golfer

who plays it. There is no fun in playing a hole which lacks challenge, nor is there any fun if the challenge creates misery. This is a simple proposition, but one which severely tests the ability of the architect. By far the easiest thing to do is to build a spectacular hole, one which presents the scratch golfer with a real problem. A far more difficult task is to create the same sort of hole for the 25-handicap player. The really supreme test is to design a hole which challenges, yet entertains, both scratch golfers and 25-handicappers.

Perhaps the best way to discuss how to make golf courses challenging yet enjoyable is to consider the play of a hole, stroke by stroke, by three golfers of three degrees of proficiency: Mr. Big, Mr. Average and Mr. Poor.

From the tee, length presents no great challenge to Mr. Big. He enjoys knocking the cover off the

Richard Tufts is one of the most distinguished figures in American golf history. He was the owner of Pinehurst for many years, a recognized authority on turf and a pioneer in the science of setting up a course for tournament play. He is also a past president of the United States Golf Ass'n.

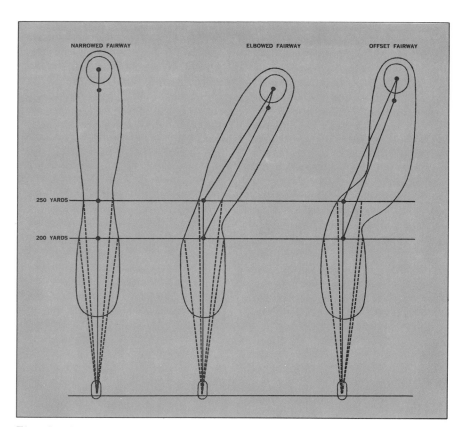

The simplest way to reduce the premium on long hitting is to restrict the area into which the longer player strikes the ball. This requires greater accuracy off the tee from the long hitters if they are to enjoy the advantages of a shorter second shot. The most direct methods of accomplishing this are shown in the diagrams of a 420-yard, par-4 hole. They are (left) narrowing the fairway; (center) the elbow hole; and (right) the offset fairway.

The area around the putting green makes the most severe demands upon the skill and ingenuity of the architect and at the same time distinguishes the really great hole from the merely good one.

Above we have a green in which normal cup locations have been indicated. This green is properly located on a small knoll, with a gradual slope away from the left front area, balanced by a bunker on the right. This is a well-designed green and would make an interesting hole except for the fact that the player who fails to reach the putting surface has a rather easy time of it, unless he happens to be in the bunker.

In the center diagram we see an effort to penalize mis-hit shots by the use of bunkers. To the left of the green, nicely fitted into the depression, is a large bunker of white sand, which makes a very striking picture. Smaller supplementary bunkers have been added. The objection to this is that it gives the hole an artificial appearance. If this treatment is used on every hole it certainly adds a great deal of monotony to both appearance and play.

The treatment accorded the third hole (below) may be best described as the Donald Ross method. The entire circumference of the green is protected by a series of cleverly designed hollows, mounds and ridges. From every position around the green a skillfully played and delicate little shot is required to reach any cup location. Every type of shot is called for, from a running ball played with a putter or 3-iron up to drop shots and cut shots played with wedge or niblick. Best of all, these are not the kind of shots which can be performed only by a strong-handed golfer. It is skillful golf at its best.

ball and getting home with an 8-iron second shot on a hole designed for a 4-iron, but this does not test his skill. He should be required to meet the challenge of accuracy. This can be accomplished by using various devices to narrow the area into which his longer tee shot will land and roll. Elbow holes, offset fairways, or the simple narrowing of the fairway will do the trick. If possible, these landing areas should be developed by the use of such natural features as trees, hills, hollows, etc.

It is a mistake for Mr. Big's shorter hitting brethren to think that they can fully enjoy the design of a golf hole when played from the back tees constructed for the use of Mr. Big. Mr. Average should move forward on the tees to a point where he can enjoy the same challenge with his tee shot that Mr. Big does with his. Mr. Poor, who probably will create his own problems from the tee, will derive challenges on his second shot from the problems that confronted Mr. Big's initial shot.

Failure to require accuracy from the tee for the big hitter is probably one of the most serious failures in American golf architecture. Demanding accuracy is important to retain the element of skill in golf. It is also the most practical method of preventing our courses from becoming outdated. Better equipment has made it possible to strike the ball farther and farther, but it is impossible for physical reasons to add more length to many of our great courses. To retain the skill and pleasure of the game we must increase the requirements for accuracy of our big hitters by penalizing inaccuracy, or perhaps by providing greater rewards for accurate placement.

The crucial shot on each hole is the shot to the green, whether it be from the tee on a par-3 hole, the second shot on a par-4, or the third on a par-5. Any play which precedes this shot serves only as preparation for this important shot. It may, therefore, be said that the situation of the green makes or breaks the hole. Donald Ross felt so keenly about the importance of properly situating greens that it was his practice to select the best available sites for his greens before even considering the location of his holes.

What should be the problems of our three golfers on this all-important shot to the green? On a par-4 hole, Mr. Average, playing from a shorter tee, will be in approximately the same position reached by Mr. Big from the back tee. Mr. Poor, after his second, should be somewhat ahead of them. On the par-3 holes perhaps the use of proper tees will place them in relatively similar positions. Except for the very long par-4s and par-3s, Mr. Big will be using an iron with a rather high trajectory and hazards (bunkers and water hazards) short of the green present him with no particular problems. However, since Mr. Average will be using a wood or a long iron, his shots will be coming in low with run, and hazards short of the green may make the shot unfairly difficult for him. The same may be said for Mr. Poor, unless due to lack of length he is unable to reach the trouble at all. Thus the problem of providing a fair and interesting test for our three golfers is best solved by placing the troubles to the right and left of the green and behind it, while leaving the front relatively open.

If there is a serious weakness in golf today it is the premium put on putting. The larger the green the greater this premium, and the less interest there is in the shot to such a large target. A delicate pitch shot adds variety to the play of a hole, and an added requirement for skill as compared to a long putt from the same distance. The extra large green, therefore, adds nothing to the skill or pleasure of golf. It adds only to the cost of the game, because these beautifully manicured surfaces are very expensive to maintain. A green should be no larger than is necessary to distribute the wear from the traffic on it and to provide an adequate number of interesting locations for the hole.

Large sand bunkers near the green also add little to the pleasure or skill of golf. Like large greens, bunkers must be classified as expensive luxuries. They present no problem to Mr. Big, who usually finishes about as near to the hole from a bunker as he does on a chip shot of the same length. But for Mr. Poor, handicapped by lack of strength and experience, bunkers are usually pure torture. Another objection to bunkers is the element of luck introduced both by the position of the ball in the bunker and the nature of its lie. On most holes a bunker or two around the green is essential in adding character to the hole and as an aid in estimating distance to the green; however, the really great holes in golf have been designed with at most only one or two well-placed bunkers.

Thus our three golfers have now played their shots to a green of modest size which is not severely bunkered. Those nearer the hole should be rewarded, while those who have failed to hit the target should be presented with a variety of fair and interesting problems. As has been suggested, the excessive use of hazards is not recommended. Nor is the use of rough and long grass close to the putting surface a proper way to increase the playing difficulty of these delicate little shots. By far the most satisfactory treatment is the development of gentle undulations, little ridges and slopes which flow gracefully about and slightly into the putting surface. Such conditions call for a great variety of interesting shots which may require the use of irons with every degree of loft, from the wedge to the putter. These are skillful little shots, never unfairly difficult but challenging to the skills of all.

Because of the large number of courses being built today, the supply of experienced golf architects is hardly adequate to meet the demand. A golf course is a work of art and requires careful and loving attention to every detail. The site must be carefully studied, the plans developed with individuality, and the little refinements meticulously perfected during the course of construction. Donald Ross, in a retrospective frame of mind in his later years, once commented that his single regret was in not having given more attention to fewer courses. ∎

25 YEARS OF GOLF FASHION: FROM PLEATS TO POLYESTER KNITS

BY KATHY JONAH

The knit shirt was introduced following World War II and heralded the modern era of practical golf clothing. Men's slacks in the 1950s, however, were still baggy and cuffed and women wore Louise Suggs golf dresses that fell below the knee.

Since then we've shaped the slacks, hiked the hemlines and made double-knits the popular choice for golf apparel. And the future? The challenge of the 1970s is making polyester double-knits look and feel like natural fabrics. The kind, naturally, we wore in the '50s.

The 1950s
Jimmy Demaret (upper left) modeled pleated slacks and a shirt of Thalspun, billed as a "new fabric that looks like wool and wears like iron." The longer-length golf dress (upper right) was priced at $14.95. A classic from the '50s (bottom): the bell-sleeved alpaca sweater.

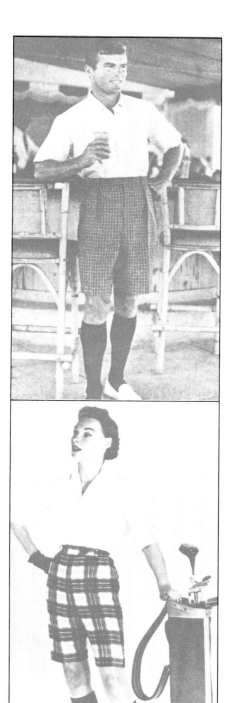

Through the '60s
*The heyday of Bermuda shorts.
This pair of men's Bermuda's
(top) was dubbed Tee-Top Tartans.
The women's Viyella flannel shorts
retailed for $12.95.*

Into the '70s
*Polyester double-knits were
introduced for golf in the late 1960s
and were the golfwear look in the
early 1970s. Typical are these
Dacron double-knit slacks ($32.50)
and Dacron double-knit dress ($42).*

CRISIS IN CLUB GOLF

BY MAX BROWN
AND THE EDITORS
March and April, 1971

Many of America's 4,600 private golf and country clubs today are beset with economic and social problems that threaten their very future. Operating costs are going up at an alarming rate. Added or increased taxes are imposing further financial burdens. Young people—potential club members—are questioning the relevance of the country club life style in an era of tumultuous social change and reform.

In the present inflation-recession cycle, club dues are going up astronomically. Assessments are added upon assessments. Now, the average man is threatened with being priced out of the country club.

Here are the major economic problems facing American country clubs in this new decade:

PROPERTY TAX RATES SOAR
Property taxes are skyrocketing in many areas, and clubs in other parts of the country are afraid the trend may be contagious. Instead of being taxed on the basis of "recreational use," many clubs are being assessed on the basis of "best land use." For a club located in or near a city, this practice can prove disastrous. The land may be assessed at the same rate as nearby highrise apartments, for example. In one Midwestern area, some clubs recently have been assessed at five times what they once were.

NEW INCOME TAX BURDEN
The 1969 Federal tax law imposes an income tax on clubs previously exempt. The new law, which remains to be clearly defined via specific IRS regulations, provides that all non-member income and investment income of clubs, less certain expenses, will be taxed at regular corporate rates.

For small, traditional, member-only golf clubs, this tax law may not pose much of a problem. But for the large, general-purpose club which offers dining and banquet rooms, and possibly living facilities and the like for non-member use, there may be trouble.

How tightly the IRS defines such terms as "non-member usage" or "unreleated business income" will determine exactly what problems clubs face, and their magnitude.

EMINENT DOMAIN THREAT
As land becomes increasingly scarce, there is a greater threat to clubs all over the country from eminent domain—the constitutional right of government to purchase private land for the public good, such as for the building of schools, highways and parks. All levels of government—local, county, state and federal—may exercise this right.

In such a case, the club would receive compensation from the government, but it is highly doubtful if the sum would be enough to cover the cost of buying other land, rebuilding and starting over. A *Golf Digest* survey did indeed reveal that 10 per cent of clubs were worried about possible government takeover of their land.

SERVICES COST MORE
In the past 15 years there have been uninterrupted increases in both country club operating costs and in revenue and dues income. Costs are now beginning to outstretch income. According to a condensed financial profile of 75 country clubs throughout the country prepared by Harris, Kerr, Forster & Co., the average income clubs received from each member during 1970 was $1,245, an increase of $45 over the previous year. Average expenses of clubs per member were $1,217, an increase of $61 over the previous year. This left the typical club with only $28 per member to spend on debt service or capital improvements, as compared with $44 in 1969.

A specific blow to some clubs was the 1969 Wage and Hour Act, which brought social clubs of a certain size under the provisions of Federal minimum wage laws for the first time.

MEMBERSHIP APPLICATIONS DOWN
No country club likes to admit its waiting list is bare, but at the moment the desire to join many clubs in the U.S. is "practically non-existent," in the words of an industry spokesman.

The phenomenon may be temporary—as young executives, professional people and other potential members ride out the period of high costs and tight money—but in the meantime clubs face an obvious financial handicap.

THE PEOPLE PROBLEM
The social problems confronting many of the nation's 4,600 private golf clubs are not so easily defined, but they surely exist, in varying degrees of seriousness.

There is the continuing challenge of racial and, to a lesser extent, religious discrimination in private clubs. For example, the courts of several states are presently hearing the question of whether a state liquor authority has the right or duty to withhold a license from a private club which practices discrimination. If it is decided that state authorities do have that right, some golf and country clubs may find themselves in the legal spotlight.

The legal aspect of the problem is not to be taken lightly. A private golf club may be open to legal attack today on two flanks. First, the Civil Rights Act of 1964 prohibits discrimination in places of public accommodation. It is possible that a club loosely under-stood to be private may, in fact, be a place of public accommodation for several reasons, such as that it operates its facilities for a profit, or advertises for new members, or lacks machinery for recruiting members on a truly selective basis. Proprietary (non-member-owned) golf clubs especially may be vulnerable to such interpretation. Second, states regulate clubs in various ways, including via liquor licenses. It is possible that a state, by licensing a facility where discrimination is practiced, may be seen to be in violation of the equal protection clause of the Fourteenth Amendment.

On the other hand, courts are not likely to tolerate government interference in genuinely private sectors. In a 1964 opinion, Supreme Court Justice Goldberg probably made the point as well as anyone: "Prejudice and bigotry in any form are regrettable, but it is the constitutional right of every person to close his home or club to any person, or to choose his social intimates and business partners solely on the basis of his personal prejudices, including race. These and other rights pertaining to privacy and private association are themselves constitutionally protected liberties."

STRATEGY CHECKLIST FOR MEETING THE CRISIS

LEGAL

1. Examine the new regulation governing social clubs issued by the Internal Revenue Service. This regulation interprets the Tax Reform Act of 1969 specifically in terms of social clubs.
2. Obtain expert advice from qualified tax attorneys or accountants in interpreting the new regulation and in deciding how to act. Certain clubs already committed to a certain amount and kind of non-member activity could possibly be better off abandoning their non-profit tax-exempt status, but such a decision should await careful study of the IRS regulation.
3. Hire an attorney qualified in the field to advise you on what, if any, problems the club could face in the civil rights area. Is the club within the meaning of the public accommodations section of the 1964 Civil Rights Act? Is the club's liquor license, or any other government-regulated activity of the club, vulnerable to interpretation under "equal protection" provisions of national or state constitutions? Should the club decide to abandon tax-exempt, non-profit status (above), would that decision make it vulnerable to civil rights litigation?
4. Examine your conditions of membership, stated or implied. Are they morally defensible in the light of current national public attitudes?
5. Every club would do well to create and appoint a "watchdog" committee to stay abreast of contemporary developments in law affecting the status of private clubs.

POLITICAL

1. Seek to combat unfair land or other taxes by collective, preferably statewide, action in concert with clubs having similar interests.
2. Seek support of conservationist groups on issues such as open-space legislation by which clubs in urban areas could continue to survive through favorable tax assessments.
3. Seek maximum cooperation from state, regional and national organizations and associations in golf. A state golf association can represent member clubs in state legislation on such issues as property taxation. Club managers, professionals, golf course superintendents may be members of these national organizations, and they should be encouraged to work toward greater unity and more effective collective action.
4. Communicate to your state and national legislators (who may be dependent on the support of your club's members) your position on important issues.

IMAGE-BUILDING

1. Work to put the media serving your area (sports and news editors, radio and TV commentators, etc.) on your side, by getting to know them personally. Watch the local media outlets for attacks on clubs and answer these sanely, cogently and with well-reasoned arguments.
2. Humanize your relationship with the surrounding community. An ideal way to do this might be to occasionally open your course for civic or charitable usage, or by junior or high school golf programs. Open your course to the community for winter sports activities such as skating or tobogganing if possible. Keep your caddie program vital and interesting; support caddie scholarship programs.
3. Explore and exploit means for communicating to your community the value of the golf club in terms of open space, and as land providing ecological, recreational and residential green-belt benefits.
4. Do not neglect internal public relations. Make sure all members are aware of the problems of the club, at the earliest moment and in the greatest and clearest detail. Explain honestly and in detail any and all economies in facilities and services, and any and all increases

in dues and assessments.
5. Encourage youthful participation. How many clubs, for example, have booked a rock band for a dance or party lately?

OPERATIONAL

1. Check your operating efficiency. Conceivably your club could benefit from stricter and more highly centralized organization. It is almost impossible for a large part-time committee, composed of people earning a living in areas widely divorced from club management, to collectively run an efficient club. Hire good club management personnel and let them get on with the job.
2. Remember, too, that turnover among key club officers contributes to inefficiency. A greens committee chairman who serves only one year is likely to contribute less to the economy of that department than one who serves for five years.
3. Compare the cost of increased mechanization with the cost of labor in such areas as course maintenance.
4. Examine all possibilities for increasing the use of your plant. Most clubs use their plant fully only on weekends and holidays. Consider five-day memberships, two-day memberships, non-family memberships, and so on. Try to develop off-season member functions (for clubs in northern areas) such as bowling, snow-mobiling, or even cultural or professional theatrical events to get people out to the club.■

YOU'RE NOT GETTING ENOUGH STROKES

BY FRANCIS SCHEID, Ph.D.
June, 1971
updated October, 1973

A computer analysis of some 500,000 golf matches was programmed in this study to test the validity of the current USGA handicap system. It was found that higher-handicapped players always suffered under today's system.

The underlying question is, of course, how to arrange matches that are fair.

USGA handicaps
Clearly, the search for a fair golf match must begin with the handicapping system. The current system of the USGA uses the 10 lowest "differentials" of a player's last 20 rounds. A "differential" is the rating of the course subtracted from the score shot. Say, for example, that a player's last 20 scores are:

86 83 84 87 87 **81 80 82 79** 86
81 81 87 84 85 **79 83 79** 83 **82**

All the above rounds were shot on a course rated at 69. His 10 lowest differentials are found by subtracting 69 from the 10 bold-type scores. The total 10-round differential is 117, the average 11.7.

His official USGA handicap is 85 per cent of this average, rounded off to the nearest whole number. Since 85 per cent of 11.7 is close to 9.9, he has a handicap of 10.

Here's how the effectiveness of such handicaps was tested.

500,000 two-ball matches
From an abundant supply of scorecards actually turned in by members of Plymouth (Mass.) Country Club, the 20 most recent

Professor Scheid received his doctorate in mathematics from MIT in 1948. Since then he has been teaching math at Boston University. A golfer since 1961, he now carries a 9-handicap. Since this article was first published Dr. Scheid's words have been heeded. Beginning in 1976, handicaps will be figured by multiplying the average differential by 96 per cent, a rise from the current 85 per cent. The author had recommended that this factor be raised to 108 per cent.

rounds of 50 golfers were retrieved for this study. Hole-by-hole scores for these 1,000 rounds were memorized by the IBM-360 computer at Boston University. Each round was associated with a number identifying the golfer who shot it. The official USGA handicap of each man was then computed from best 10 of the 20 rounds available.

With all these rounds in the computer, and with each handicap figured, it became possible to "play" a high number of theoretical matches. By choosing a pair of players and requiring the better player to give the weaker a certain number of strokes, the computer could rapidly match every round of one player against every round of the other.

How many strokes to equalize
Here are two examples from the study:

For matches between opponents with a difference in handicaps of seven—say a 17 and a 10—to be equal, nine strokes are needed by the weaker player to give him equal opportunity to win. For a handicap difference of 20, more than 25 strokes by the weaker player are needed.

What it shows is that for a two-ball match to be fairly handicapped, the better player should give his weaker opponent 127 per cent of the difference between their handicaps. Stated another way, each player's USGA handicap should be increased 27 per cent.

In stroke play, this study produced almost exactly the same figures.

Better-ball competition
Member-guest, member-member, and four-ball play all involves matching the better ball of a two-man team against that of one or more competing teams. The average better-ball scratch score of 10-15 combinations is about nine strokes above the course rating, the average better-ball score of a 12-13 combination is 10 shots over and a 1-24 combination is only three over. Though the combined handicaps total 25 in each case, a 1-24 combination will average seven shots lower than a 12-13 on better-ball score at scratch play.

The odds if you don't get more shots

Difference between USGA handicaps of two golfers	Odds against weaker golfer breaking even if he receives only USGA allotment of strokes (column 1).	Actual number of strokes needed by weaker player to equalize match
20	83-17	25.4
19	82-18	24.1
18	80-20	22.9
17	79-21	21.6
16	78-22	20.3
15	76-24	19.0
14	75-25	17.8
13	73-27	16.5
12	71-29	15.2
11	70-30	14.0
10	68-32	12.7
9	66-34	11.4
8	65-35	10.2
7	63-37	8.9
6	61-39	7.6
5	59-41	6.4
4	57-43	5.1
3	56-44	3.8
2	54-46	2.5
1	52-48	1.3

What it takes to equalize

Since better-ball events are usually played at 85 or 100 per cent of handicaps, corresponding competitions were included in the study. At two-ball play, we found that the odds became equal if the competitors played at about 127 per cent of their USGA handicap.

In better-ball play this allowance should be 107 per cent.

Extensive experiment thus supports and sharpens a conviction that golfers have had for many years. Players should not receive the same percentage of their USGA handicap in two-man team play that they do in individual matches. Better-ball competition requires the players receive only 107/127, or about 84 per cent, as many strokes as they get in man-to-man, two-ball matches. Obviously, it benefits the low-handicap players engaged in a four-ball match to make two-ball matches on the side with higher handicap players in the group.

Choosing a partner

The optimum strategy appears to be: take the strongest partner you can find, but if no one better than you is interested, then take a partner about five strokes worse than you, this being the ideal spread.

Four-ball

It seemed wise to study four-ball matches, however, since they usually are held at match instead of stroke play, with strokes being awarded off the lowest handicap present rather than off scratch.

The results of more than 250,000 computer matches shows that events played at less than 100 per cent are not a good investment for high-handicappers.

Suggestion

What the experiment suggests is that current handicaps be increased by 27 per cent. The simplest way to do this would be to follow the current USGA method of finding the player's average differential—using the 10 lowest differentials of his last 20—but then produce his handicap by multiplying this average by 108 per cent, instead of the current 85. Fair two-ball matches could then be played at 100 per cent of the new handicaps and fair better-ball matches at about 85 per cent. ■

HOW'S YOUR HANDICAP ON TOUGH TRACKS?

You're tough at home, but can you win on the road? You're a 15-handicapper at Executive Golf Club, the little 5,900-yard course behind the Gateway Shopping Center. On most Saturdays you usually make your freebie strokes count and manage to survive in dollar Nassaus.

Then you receive the big invitation. Your general manager asks you to his club, Marvelito Country Club. You've always dreamed of playing Marvelito, but you cringe at the thought of its toughness . . . those fairways famed for tightness, the crater-like bunkers and greens faster than Interstate 95. You wonder, shouldn't I be getting more than 15 shots at Marvelito? You're absolutely right.

If Marvelito, as a great test of skill, has a course rating of 73, it is my mathematical deduction that your 15 handicap at Executive Golf Club should be increased to 17 for your round as a guest at Marvelito. By the same token, if you reciprocate and invite your general manager for a game at Executive, he should have his handicap sliced due to the comparative easiness of your course which is rated at 66. For instance, if he's a 17 at Marvelito he should be reduced to a 15 at Executive.

My figures are based on 6,000 scorecard results being fed into a computer. These were rounds shot by all types of golfers with greatly varying skills. My survey included five courses of greatly varying toughness, including four in Massachusetts and the Firestone Country Club in Akron, Ohio.

The table below covers almost every golfer with an established handicap. It encompasses courses with easy ratings of 66 to the extremely tough course rated at 74.

Scratch players or near-scratch players get no handicap adjustment in the Scheid System. Course ratings are supposed to be the score which scratch players should shoot, no matter how tough the layout. If a scratch player shoots 66 on a course rated 66, then he should be expected to shoot 73 on a course with a 73 rating.

HOW TO USE TABLE
Find the rounded-off rating of your home course among the figures across the top line.

Run your finger down the column until you find your established handicap. If your handicap is listed twice, use the one with the asterisk.

Once you have located that figure, the adjustment—if any—can be found by going to the left or right from your handicap on the same horizontal line until you are under the rating of the course you plan to visit.

EXAMPLE: If your home course has a 72 rating and your handicap is 15 and you are planning to visit an easier course with a 68 rating, your handicap for that round will be 14.

COURSE RATINGS →

← HANDICAPS

66	67	68	69	70	71	72	73	74
1	1	1	1	1	1	1	1	1
2	2	2	2	2	2	2	2	2
3	3	3	3	3	3	3	3	3
3*	3*	3*	3*	3*	3*	3	4*	4
4*	4	4	4	4	4	4*	4	5
4	5	5	5	5	5	5	5	5*
5	5*	6	6*	6	6	6	6	6
6	6	6	6*	6	7*	7	7	7
7	7	7	7	7	7	8	8	8
7*	8	8	8	8	8	8*	8	9*
8	8*	9	9	9	9	9	9*	9*
9	9	9*	9*	9*	9*	9*	9	10
9*	9*	9	9	10*	10	10	10	11
10	10	10	10	10	11	11	11	11*
10*	11	11	11	11	12	12	12	12
11	11*	12	12	12	12*	13	13	13
12	12	12*	13	13	13	14	14	14
13	13	13	14	14	14	14*	14*	14*
13*	14	14	14*	14*	14*	14	14	15
14	14*	14*	14	14	15	15	15	16
14*	14	15	15	15	16	16	16	17
15	15	16	16	16	17	17	17	18
16	16	16*	17	17	18	18	18	19
17	17	17	18*	18	18*	19	19	20
17*	18*	18	18	19	19	20	20	20*
18	18	19	19	20	20	20*	20*	20
19	19	20	20*	20*	20*	20	21	21
20	20	20*	21	21	21	21	22	22
20*	20*	21	21	21*	22	22	23	23
21	21	21*	22	22	23	23	24	24
21*	22	22	23	23	24	24	25	25
22	23*	23	24*	24	25	25	26	26
23	23	24	24	25	25*	26	26*	26*
24	24	25	25	26	26	26*	27	27
25	25	26	26	26*	26*	27	27	28
26	26	26*	26*	27	27	28	28	29
26*	26*	27	27	28	28	29	29	30
27	27	28	28	29	29	30	30	31
27*	28	29	29	30	30	31	31	31*
28	29	29*	30	31	31	31*	31*	32
29	30	30	31	31*	31*	32	32	33

WHO ARE ALL THOSE WOMEN AND WHAT ARE THEY DOING ON MY GOLF COURSE?

BY LARRY DENNIS
July, 1972

Tuesday was not the favorite day for caddies at Elmwood Country Club, except maybe for Porky Henchal and a few others. Tuesday was Ladies Day and Porky, because he was the oldest and strongest, would be chosen by the good players, like Kathryn McMurray or Lorraine Booth or Alice Kewley or Beulah Williams.

Jake Hemphill and Dale Hayes always wound up with a couple of the better players apiece. So did Tom Braak, who was the pro's son and could help the ladies with their games.

The rest of us, back in those summers of the 1940s in Marshalltown, Iowa, faced a long morning's work, because that about exhausted the supply of women who could make it around in under 100—or maybe 150—and in less than five and a half hours. Which meant we always wound up missing jobs with the men who played after all the women were off.

If you were particularly unlucky on Tuesdays, you drew Emma Purcell. She's gone now, rest her soul. She seemed 100 then, which was a lot better than she scored. Once a local champion, she was reduced to playing doggedly and interminably. In retrospect, that's admirable, but she drove many an Elmwood caddie into early retirement.

Tuesday pretty much took care of it for most of the women. A lot of the time they weren't even allowed on the course, to the smug satisfaction of most men.

Today things are different at Elmwood—which now has 125 women players with registered handicaps—and at most other courses across the nation. The women are driving and chipping and putting all over the place, with surprising skill, and those of us who might have traces of prejudice remaining from our caddie days had best swallow them in a hurry. In the last decade, the female of the golfing species has become the flora of the fairways, and she is not about to wither. To wit:

• Women golfers now make up almost one quarter of the United States golfing population and play 40 per cent of the rounds recorded. In 20 years those figures may well double!

• Women have become vital to the economy of the golf shop, particularly in the apparel lines.

• The Ladies Professional Golf Ass'n tour is rapidly increasing in stature and prize money, to the point where the girls finally are getting the recognition they deserve as fine athletes.

• Women have broken the barriers and are landing jobs as teaching professionals and even head pros at golf clubs.

• The attitude of the male chauvinist golfer is changing, however slowly, and women are moving close to divot-digging equality of opportunity.

It has been a long struggle. If Mary Queen of Scots indeed popularized the game back there in the 1500s, it took her sisters a while to attain parity.

The boom began about 1960. According to the National Golf Foundation, which keeps track of such things, there were 478,142 adult female golfers (who played at least 15 rounds each) in this country in 1947. In 1950 there were 610,700 and in the ensuing 10 years the growth piddled along to only 875,000.

Then suddenly everything on the golf course seemed to be coming up female. By 1965 there were 1,685,000 women swinging along, and by 1971 the legions had grown to 2,143,000. Of these, 408,000 were private club members, 842,000 played at daily fee courses and 893,000 at municipal courses, representing an increase of 150 per cent in just 11 years. During that span, the male golfing population increased only 110 per cent, from 3,202,000 in 1960 to 6,731,000 in '71.

The end is nowhere in sight. In 1971 there were 1,126,000 junior golfers tabulated by the NGF. Probably half of them are girls. One good barometer is the USGA girls' junior tournament, whose entry list grows each year and forces the repeated lowering of the handicap requirement (now down to 15 from 20 in 1965).

Last year, 116 high schools in

the country sponsored girls' golf, until recently unknown at that level. Says Dick Schafer of the National Ass'n of State High School Athletic Ass'ns, "Starting an individual sport like golf is the result of demand by the girls."

Reasons for the growth are many and obvious. Women have more free time and money than ever before. They are outdoors-conscious, recreation-conscious, exercise-conscious. Golf fits. The sport is "in." Television glamorizes it. So does your friendly local golf professional.

"One reason for the growth, I think, is that the golf professionals in recent years have promoted women's golf," says P. J. Boatwright, executive director of the USGA.

They have. Gleefully. The economic impact of women's golf is staggering. In apparel, sales have more than doubled in a decade, and in the last couple of years the percentage of increase is even larger. Greater wearability and higher fashion styling in women's golf clothes has brought the girls rushing to the counter. (It also has influenced men's fashions to brighten up.) In 1971, women's apparel was the third largest contributor to gross sales in pro shops with a dollar volume of $26 million.

Equipment manufacturers have taken heed. The PGA/Victor Co., an innovator in women's golf lines, came out five years ago with ladies' multi-colored wood sets, pastel balls and bags, clubs in aluminum shafts (and later lightweight steel) and other refinements the company felt would prove that the girls would buy top-line quality. They do. Most other companies are now making similar efforts. Educated guesses in the industry place the sales of women's equipment at double that of five years ago. The woman golfer is no longer satisfied to take her husband's and son's hand-me-downs.

She is no longer satisfied with much that has been her lot as a second-class golfing citizen. She is aware that she is keeping clubs in business. For years the venerable Winged Foot Golf Club in New York was known as a men's club. Ladies were *persona non grata*. When women finally began to play, they

found only a small upstairs room set aside for changing their shoes. Seldom were they permitted on the club's two courses. Today they get preferred daily starting times on one course or the other, and last month they celebrated the grand opening of their own cocktail lounge. Tommy Armour, who used to tipple at Winged Foot, no doubt turned over in his grave.

There is no doubt that women can play. Watching the women on the pro tour provides proof enough. And much as he might hate to admit it, the average male golfer probably should be watching them.

"We've tried hard to convince people that the average golfer can learn more about how to hit the golf ball by watching our girls than by watching the men," says Bud Erickson, executive director of the LPGA. "Some of the men pros have said the same thing. The average guy's strength and the woman pro's strength are comparable."

Oddly enough, from its beginning the gals' tour attracted more men fans than women.

"We went through a phase when there were very few women watching," says LPGA President Cynthia Sullivan. "Now we gear our promotion more toward women. It's due to the changeover of players. We have an attractive show, and maybe we can get the women to feel we're not just big athletes out there."

The LPGA influence extends into the merchandising game, Cynthia believes. "I feel we're going to be able to help sales," she declares. "Male pros are putting more women pros in their shops, realizing that they're good retailers."

The LPGA itself is growing in many ways. From a single tournament just 22 years ago, the women's tour has blossomed into a parade of almost 30 events worth nearly a million dollars in 1972. At least three tournaments are on television this year.

The $110,000 Dinah Shore-Colgate Winners Circle Championship, richest event in women's history, drew the fifth largest New York area viewing audience of all 1972 telecasts through April. It was outranked by the Crosby, Williams, Hope and Masters tournaments and beat out

eight other men's events on the tube.

David Foster, president of Colgate-Palmolive and the driving force behind the tournament, created a concept which utilized the woman pros in TV commercials and gave great impetus to the over-all tour.

The LPGA now has more than 200 members, up from 128 in 1964. Only 75 or 80 are tour players, which means that more are infiltrating the clubs in teaching jobs and head professional positions. The LPGA, in fact, recently established a teaching division.

Gloria Armstrong has had no problems teaching either men or women at Atlanta, although she admits her playing reputation undoubtedly helped her both in getting the job and gaining acceptance with the members. She would like to be a head pro some day, but is realistic.

"I think it's a long way off," Gloria says. "Because more men play and pay the dues, they have more respect for a man than a woman. They feel more secure having a man pro. They feel men are better business-type people, although I don't agree with that. I certainly see more women as pros in the future. A lot of us have paved the way. There are a lot of women teachers with good reputations around the country."

Some barriers are still there. One club, on a recent Thursday, barred tour pro Cynthia Sullivan from playing with three men, the best of whose handicap was 12, because the rules prohibited women on the course before 2 p.m.

But the barriers are crumbling. The male holdouts usually don't have wives playing the game. Those who do are finding it increasingly nice to have a mate who can play golf with them on vacations or zip out for a quick nine in the evening after work, maybe with the kids, too.

As long as hubby can choke back any pointers he might be inclined to offer, everything is lovely. A basic rule of this new male-female relationship on the links is that love means never trying to tell your wife why she's hitting it dead sideways. ■

IT'S TIME TO GET TOUGH WITH SLOW PLAY

BY LARRY DENNIS
May, 1974

In 1965, *Golf Digest* became the first magazine to appear with a cover story advocating that play on the nation's golf courses be speeded up. A couple of other magazines followed with similar efforts. In 1968 the National Golf Foundation launched its "Speedy" campaign to combat slow play.

Unfortunately, there has been no marked effect on the game. The 3-hour round of 25 years ago is gone. Now, 4½ hours is considered speedy, five or longer probably is the average and we are headed toward six.

It's time to get tough in the fight against slow play.

It is difficult to measure the effect of slow play in terms of the game's relative popularity and on the rate of attrition of players. The shocking fact that there is attrition is frequently summed up in the expression, "I'm switching to tennis."

The National Golf Foundation claims the number of golfers in the country is 13,550,000, up five per cent from 1972 and up 13.4 per cent from 1970. There is no concrete statistical evidence to back this up, however.

On the other hand, a 1973 survey by the A. C. Nielsen Co. shows that the number of tennis players has grown to 20,377,000, double the 10,650,000 that Nielsen says were playing in 1970.

The most serious effect of slow play on the course is the anguish suffered by those who still play and love the game. And their plight will not get better unless conditions change.

Joe Jemsek, who owns public-fee courses in the Chicago area, cites figures to show he is moving an average of 100 fewer players a day than he was 40 years ago. This is a common problem, and it means lost revenue.

Given this discouraging outlook, it is easy for potential golf course investors to opt for businesses other than golf. That means even more overcrowding until the growth in numbers of players ceases altogether. When that happens, the sport begins to die.

The disease can—and must—be checked. Play can be speeded.

Last July, 60-year-old Matthew Alcorn of Verona, Pa., walked three golf courses—including fabled Oakmont—following an average golfer's route of play from tee through green and on to the next tee. The average walking time was one hour and 27 minutes. Since the act of addressing and striking a ball can be done quite deliberately in 15 or 20 seconds, that leaves a lot of dallying time in a five-hour round.

Joe Dey, long-time executive director for the U.S. Golf Ass'n and for five years commissioner of the PGA Tournament Players Division until his recent retirement, feels that two persons should play a round of golf in 2½ hours or less. Three people should play in three hours or less and four people in 3½ hours or less, he believes.

Dey says, "There's only one thing effective against slow play—a two-shot penalty." He points out that 12 such penalties were meted out on the professional tour in 1973, with the result that the traditionally dilatory pros have cut their average playing time below 4½ hours and are heading toward four.

The two-stroke penalty obviously applies only to the tour. What can be done to make the amateur play faster?

After an 18-month nationwide study in which every known method for speeding play has been evaluated, *Golf Digest* is presenting three major proposals which could eliminate the problem, systems or procedures which can be instituted at clubs and other courses.

These remedies can work. The responsibility lies with you and your fellow players. Demand that your golf course follow these rules. We also are presenting lists of other specific speed-up actions you can incorporate into your club rules and into your personal habits of play.

THREE HARD-NOSED SUGGESTIONS

1. ENFORCE THIS NEW
ACCOUNTABILITY SYSTEM
The low-handicap player in a group
keeps his players moving. If the
group ahead allows a hole to open
up in front of it, the low handicapper
warns the low handicapper in that
group to close the gap by speeding
up or allowing the trailing group to
go through. Failure to cooperate is
reported to the golf committee by
filling out a brief form on the reverse
side of the card.

There must be a predetermined
enforcement system with appropriate penalties to be meted out by the
golf committee or other governing
body. Provisions also must be made
to insure that the first group on the
course plays quickly. Urge your
club or golf association to give it a
try. The accountability cards will be
printed and made available at cost
by *Golf Digest*.

2. INSTALL SLOW-PLAY
CHECKPOINT SIGNS
Sign No. 1, setting a 2-hour limit
per nine, should be placed on the
first tee as a reminder to players to
look at their watches and play
briskly. Sign No. 2, establishing an
80-minute "par" for the first six
holes, goes on the seventh tee.
Sign No. 3 should be placed just
off the ninth green, clearly visible.
Sign No. 4, allowing 80 minutes for
the first six holes of the back nine,
goes on the 16th tee.

These signs are available at a
cost of about $4 each from Standard
Manufacturing Co., 220 E. Fourth
St., Cedar Falls, Iowa 50613, or from
any of Standard's many dealers.
Make an effort to see that they are
put up on your course.

3. PLANT 150-YARD MARKERS
By knowing how far he is from the
green, a player should not have to
walk ahead of his ball. He will be
able to make his club selection
much more quickly. These indicators
—widely but by no means universally
used already—would be particularly
helpful on resort courses, where
most of the traffic is unfamiliar with
the layout.

There is nothing in the rules that
prohibits these markers, even for
tournament play. The USGA
normally does not use them in its
tournament competition, but it
does not force a club to uproot
trees or bushes that may be
serving as yardage markers. If
you use shrubbery be sure it is
clearly defined.

Encourage your club or course to
provide 150-yard markers.

OTHER WAYS TO SPEED UP PLAY

WHAT AN INDIVIDUAL CAN DO
• Concentrate and plan ahead . . .
be thinking about your next shot,
about where to place your bag or
handcart or where to park your
golf car; save your funny stories
for the bar.
• Be prepared to play when it's
your turn . . . select your club, line
up your shot or study your putt,
make your practice swings while
others are playing. When it's your
turn, address your ball and hit it.
• Walk briskly.
• Carry a spare ball.
• Take no mulligans or practice
shots.
• Don't stop with playing partners
while they hit . . . go to your own
ball.
• Don't walk beyond your ball
more than a few paces.
• Watch ball into rough and mark
it; hit a provisional.
• Be realistic when waiting to
hit to a green or off the tee . . .
usually the waiters can't get there
with a cannon.
• Learn how far you can hit the
ball.
• When out of the hole and

heading for triple-bogey, pick up.
• Mark your scores as you walk
to the next tee.
• Learn the rules.

WHAT GROUPS CAN DO
• Forget honors . . . first man off
green and on the tee, hit it; play
when ready in fairway, even
simultaneously, so long as you don't
interfere with other players.
• Putt when ready . . . don't wait
for outside player if he's not ready.
• Shorter hitters play first as soon
as group ahead is out of range.
• If a group behind is pressing
you, wave it through . . . then
speed up.
• Only one man look for his ball
in rough and only for two minutes.
• Wave up following group on
par-3s, particularly longer ones.
• Make your match and lay your
bets before you get to first tee.

WHAT CLUBS AND
COURSES CAN DO
• Insist that new players/
members have a certain level of
proficiency and knowledge of
rules and etiquette.

• Ban winter rules.
• Train caddies properly.
• Allow golf cars on the fairway.
• Be realistic about starting
times to avoid over-crowding.
• Start from both No. 1 and
No. 10 tees.
• Be sure starter admonishes
each group to play briskly.
• Use rangers to push slow
players.
• Run a fun tournament to expose
golfers to fast play.
• Create a "slow player of the
week" award and post the winners.

FOR FASTER PLAY
IN GOLF CARS
• If two are riding, player first to
hit should make his logical club
selection, then take two more clubs
—one longer and one shorter. While
he's preparing to play the other
rides to his ball. Don't wait for
each other.
• Park car in direct line from
green to next tee.
• At green, driver should bring
other player's putter if he doesn't
already have it (which he should).

2: INSTRUCTION

GREAT METHODS AND GREAT TEACHERS

Continuity and correlation in presenting instruction material are imperative for a magazine that reaches two million readers each month. As the selections in this section demonstrate, we strive to fulfill an instructional philosophy that emphasizes fundamentals that will enable more of our readers to make more lasting improvement.

Golf Digest believes that most golfers can best learn to play within an over-all method. By understanding cause and effect within a method, golfers will be able to recognize problems in their swings and will have answers to rely on under pressure on the course.

We have always endorsed teaching that leads to a sound game over the long haul. We don't believe in temporarily remedying a fault by invoking a second fault.

The methods that follow share several crucial traits: each is designed to develop a repeating swing; each has a strong inner consistency; each is geared to all levels of golfers and represents the outcome of hundreds—thousands—of hours of teaching.

Golf Digest was an early proponent of the "modern golf swing." It probably was first brought to the public's attention by J. Victor East, our long-time technical consultant, in his 1959 article "Why the Americans Beat the British." In it East alluded to the "square" concept favored by American professionals as opposed to the rotating or twisting of the clubface with the hands by British pros. The idea of squareness—the forearm, back of the left hand and the clubface starting and remaining aligned throughout the swing—has

persisted in our instruction material from that time, evolving into and beyond the famous Square-to-Square Method.

Obviously the methods vary somewhat. There's more than one workable way to swing a golf club, just as there's more than one road to Philadelphia (assuming you want to go to Philadelphia).

Also, different "word pictures" get across to different people. Different types of visual styles get different responses.

On the face of it, a method like Bob Toski's "Touch System" is very different from "Square-to-Square," for example. Toski approaches his subject more from the standpoint of how the swing should feel to a player, while Square-to-Square is more of a positional approach.

But the two methods have in common such bedrock modern precepts as controlling the swing with a strong left side, starting with your grip pressure in the left hand at address and continuing through the ball.

In our endeavor to relate one method to another, explaining the important similarities and differences, we increasingly have come to rely on our Professional Teaching Panel. The leading group of golf experts in the world, it consists of Jim Flick, John Jacobs, Eddie Merrins, Henry Ransom, Paul Runyan and Toski. Twice a year we meet with them in lengthy, tape-recorded round-table sessions. They review all our instruction content before it passes into print.

A burgeoning schedule of Golf Digest Instruction Schools helps acquaint some of our readers with these star teachers on a face-to-face basis. More important to the mass of our readership, the schools serve as testing laboratories that help us learn what players at all handicap levels need and want, and how we

can help them more.

Golf Digest's stable of instruction artists includes the best in the business with Tony Ravielli, Jim McQueen, Stan Drake and Red Wexler. Illustrating the golf swing is an exceedingly difficult thing to do, but we feel these men accomplish it with both striking clarity and appealing aesthetics.

The work of all these top artists and teachers, along with others, is included in this section. They are examples of a 25-year effort we like to think has contributed to the improvement of the breed.

Preceding page: Bob Toski, a leading player who has achieved even greater fame as an instructor, shows a pupil how it's done.

40

USE THE BASEBALL GRIP

BY JOHNNY REVOLTA
April, 1959

I believe that within 10 years the baseball grip will be taught and used almost exclusively.

I know it would be if I were the only golf instructor in the world, for I have had phenomenal success teaching it.

Golfers need only look to the touring professional ranks to find a pair of outstanding golfers who use this grip.

Art Wall won Bing Crosby's National Pro-Am this winter over those tough courses at Pebble Beach, Calif., and in 1958 he was the fifth-ranking pro in both Performance Averages and money won. Bob Rosburg's steady play won him the 1958 Vardon Trophy for having the lowest scoring average.

Both of these prominent professionals use the baseball grip, and always have. They wouldn't use any other, and recommend it for all players.

Henry Cotton, the famed English pro, has used the grip for this reason. He says:

"I do not say it is the grip for every one, but I tried it out for nearly a year when I was playing spasmodically—no more than twice a week—and it worked."

In 1953 Johnny Bulla started using the baseball grip. He has commented that he would have been better all along if he had always used it. And both Jack Burke and Jimmy Demaret have said that if they had it to do over again they'd start and stick with the baseball grip.

One of the most common admonitions given in regard to the golf swing is "relax—don't tighten up." The word relax really doesn't fit. Webster says it means "to make less firm, rigid, or tense; to slacken."

But the words "don't tighten up"

Johnny Revolta is a former tour star and one of the nation's leading instructors.

In the 10-finger grip (left), the right arm is in proper position with the forearm muscle on the right side, the right arm under the shot. The weight of the upper body is in position. The common tendency to overdo the right-hand position in the overlap grip is shown at right. This throws the body out of balance.

With the baseball grip (left), it is easier to swing the club away from the ball in good tempo. Using the overlapping grip (right), Revolta shows the tendency to twist the club away from the ball.

Bob Rosburg says:

The baseball grip gives me more hand control and a free swing.

When I got out of college I spent about six months trying to use the Vardon overlapping grip. I found that it was useless—I lost all wrist action at the top of my swing.

Because all of the fingers are on the club, this grip also gives a better feel. This makes those delicate shots that much easier.

I believe that all women and most men, particularly those with smaller hands, should use the baseball grip. Those with larger hands wouldn't benefit. After all, the man who invented the grip, Harry Vardon, had very large hands.

I don't think there are any real disadvantages, except that you have to put up with people talking about the funny way you grip.

Art Wall says:

I think that anyone who would like more power would be wise to try the baseball grip. I personally feel that my hands are stronger and that my swing is freer with this grip.

Power comes from a firm grip and a free swing. The baseball grip does both for me. My wrists feel loose and certainly devoid of tension.

The only danger I find in this grip is that my right hand has a tendency to overpower the left. I must frequently check this point for when I get careless I am likely to hook.

The way I avoid this is to feel that I am leading my swing with my left hand as I start the downswing. Also, I see that when I take the grip both of my hands are well on top of the club.

The baseball grip is the perfectly natural way to hold a club. That's why I started using it, and I'll never change.

---

mean just what they say, and tightness is probably the cause of more poor golf shots than any other single factor.

You have seen this type of approach to the ball—possibly done it yourself:

The player walks up to his ball, takes his stance, grasps the club with his left hand and then carefully puts his right hand in place. Then comes a slight finger adjustment and—CRUNCH—the grip tightens. You can almost see, and surely feel, the tension telegraphing from the fingers, up the arms, into the shoulders and throughout the body. In a fraction of a second the golfer is one rigid mass of frozen muscles.

These frozen muscles can't possibly go through the flowing motions of a smooth, well-oiled swing.

I contend that most of the tension built up in the average golfer stems directly from use of the Vardon, or overlapping grip. Although this grip certainly has its place, I believe that most golfers would hit the ball straighter and farther if they used the baseball grip.

Here is how to take that grip:

The left hand is placed on the club with the thumb slightly down the right side of the shaft. It is a "finger palm" grip—not completely in the palm. The "V" formed by the thumb and forefinger should point directly over the right shoulder.

This left hand position is no different than in the Vardon or any other grip. Getting it correct should be a simple matter. The problems arise in placing the right hand on the grip.

A common way to start placement of the right hand in the Vardon grip is to lock the right little finger around the left forefinger. Right away this develops tension, mainly on the underside of the right forearm.

The next step is usually to grasp with the thumb and forefinger, turning the right hand to the left. This tightens and strains the muscle on the upper side of the forearm. Result: tension in the whole right arm.

With the 10-finger grip, all fingers of the right hand are on the club, with the V of the right hand also pointing over the right shoulder. That makes it easier for the average golfer to take the grip without distorting any muscles. That's the most important point.

In starting the backswing, the baseball grip makes it simpler to swing the club away freely. The Vardon grip will often cause the golfer to twist the club away.

The club must be SWUNG away WITHOUT distortion in order to get the swing off to a good start. It may be swung slow or fast, depending on your own particular rhythm, but it has to be swung.

This swinging is made easier by the fact that the wrists are looser for both cocking and uncocking with the baseball grip. This gives the golfer a feeling of freedom that no other grip can produce.

An additional advantage of the baseball grip is that it helps keep the right arm closer to the body, and under the shot at impact. A "flying" right elbow, especially at the top of the backswing, will produce all sorts of errors—including hitting too soon.

The Vardon grip, on the other hand, tends to move the right elbow away from the body at address and therefore during the swing.

Judging from the speed my students have developed sound swings using the baseball grip. I'm convinced that anyone else can do the same. The baseball, or 10-finger grip will be the grip of the future for almost all golfers. ■

DIARY OF A TEACHING PRO

BY HARVEY PENICK
EDITED BY BETTY HICKS
May through September, 1960

I don't know any shortcut to playing golf well. Let's make that clear from the start. If I had a sure-fire secret to golfing success, I'd probably be a millionaire—and I'm not.

Yet, the notes I've collected during 37 years of teaching may help some players improve their games. I hope so, because I firmly believe that the most important duty of a club professional is to give sound instruction.

For 30 years I have coached the University of Texas golf team in addition to my duties as professional at the club. I have discussed with students from all parts of the country the help they have received from their local golf instructors and as a result I feel I know well many pros who have never met me.

Thus, The Country Club of Austin has been sort of a private classroom for me where indirectly the greatest teaching professionals in the United States have educated me in the intricate and elusive art of golf instruction.

Entry, February 20, 1925

No two golf pupils are alike. But there are pitfalls which seem to face three types of players. There do not seem to be too many exceptions:

1. Women listen too well and too often, especially to people who do not understand the golf swing. Everyone wants to give them advice.

2. The average man tries to play like a tournament player.

3. Tournament players—especially young ones—try to play like someone else instead of being themselves.

When his diary appeared, Harvey Penick was head professional at the Austin (Tex.) C.C. and University of Texas golf coach. Since retired, Penick still is sought for lessons by amateur and touring pro alike. He has developed many outstanding players, the latest on tour being Tom Kite and Ben Crenshaw.

Entry, October 5, 1929

The follow-through is important because it tells so much about what has gone on in the swing before it.

Correct use of the hands in the hitting area is very often the answer to balance.

Taking the club back inside on the backswing will cause the body to turn. There is no need to try to produce turn. Be leisurely on the backswing—not slow. So many players who try to be slow just put the club up there to the top.

Women need a hook for distance.

The body moves on pitches. We should neither try to make it move nor try to hold it still. Just let it move. The follow-through should be the same length as the backswing on short shots.

Entry, February 28, 1930

There are not too many things that all fine golfers do in common. But players I'd like to play like observe three fundamentals:

1. They have good position to the ball.

2. They all pause momentarily at the top. I'd rather call it "gathering the swing together" than pausing.

3. They all have a little waggle or a forward press.

I get a kick out of discussing golf with J. K. Wadley, an oilman from Texarkana. He knows as much about the golf swing as anyone I've met, pro or amateur. He mentioned a boy from Fort Worth he'd like to see go somewhere in golf. If J. K. says the boy has the ability, I don't even have to see him swing to believe it.

I hope I recall his name right as being Nelson—Byron, I think.

Entry, June 5, 1931

I'm finding that too many pupils get ahead of themselves. That is, they try to perform a lot of the finer points that they hear the good players use. Too often the pupil tries this too soon—before he learns the fundamentals of a good swing.

I think we swing by feel. The swing is not made up of a lot of parts. When it has separate parts it isn't natural and ceases to become a swing.

I'll jot down the fundamentals of grip, stance and swing which I think the average man golfer should heed before he goes on to something else.

Most players develop a swing to fit their grips. Poor grips must be offset by compensations in the swing.

Many players know where to point the V's between their thumbs and forefingers, but they fool themselves by twisting the skin of their hands to that position. Or sometimes they move their grips over or under with their shoulders.

I like to see a pupil move his hands into position with his hands and wrists only, not with his arms and shoulders, too.

Having the "V's" of both thumbs and forefingers point between the right shoulder and right cheek seems to fit most regular players. As players progress they usually make the V of the right hand—and sometimes both V's—point about at the chin. Pointing both V's at the chin may cause the average player to lose power and slice. It is up to the individual to find which is best for him.

I advise the pupil not to cure his slice by moving the V's to the right of the right shoulder, nor to cure a hook by pointing the V's too far left. Too much cure just produces other troubles.

A closed stance (right foot pulled back a bit from the line of flight) is generally better for distance. With this stance it is easier to get a full turn going back and to get inside the ball on the downswing. Use the closed stance to best advantage on drives and from good lies on long fairway shots.

An open stance (left foot pulled

Teacher Penick (right) with Betsy Rawls, one of many women stars he has instructed.

Jimmy Demaret looked like this in 1937 when he went around Penick's Country Club of Austin in 28-32—60.

back from line of flight) is better for shorter shots where direction is the main object. Also, it is a bit easier to follow-through with this stance. On very short shots it is all right to open the stance as much as you want because there is not much backswing turn. (I didn't say there was no turn or pivot on these shots.)

One golf swing should work for both iron and wood shots. Generally speaking, an iron is hit on the downswing. However, I don't think there should be too much effort applied to hit down on the ball. A conscious effort to hit down often results in a shank. I'd rather apply a few tips that will cause a player to hit down on the ball, rather than actually tell him to do it. Here are a few tips that might help:

Keeping the weight either equally on both feet or a little more on the left at address will help in hitting the ball on the downswing.

It is all right to play the ball anywhere from the left heel back toward the center of the stance, but the ball should be more toward center if the student is having trouble hitting down.

Keeping the hands a little forward at address also helps in hitting down.

A good wood shot is either hit at the lowest point of the swing arc or a little on the upswing. Here are a few aids to do this:

Distribute weight equally on both feet at address or a tiny bit more on the right to help hit on the upswing. I like to see that the initial move of the club on the backswing is started with the left arm and side.

The club, hands and the left arm form about a line to the ball on irons. However, it is all right to have the hands slightly back if you are trying to hit wood shots on the upswing.

Entry, March 19, 1933
You hear a lot about keeping the head still, but now that we have good ways to photograph the swing we can see that the head does move. At least this is true in all the good players.

I've looked at pictures of Jimmy Demaret—a fine swinger. His head doesn't just turn to the right and left, but it also moves up and down.

Bobby Jones also let his head move.

Only a physically powerful person, I would think, could consciously try to keep his head steady and not give up something else as a result.

We hear a lot about timing, too, but I haven't shaken hands with many people who understand it.

It seems to me you have to get a good swing and then learn the timing to fit it. A player could have good rhythm and still not hit the ball well if he'd been in bad address position in the first place.

Entry, August 10, 1934
Practice is awfully important, especially to tournament players. But there's a lot of wasted practice.

I suggest practicing as long as you are fresh. You'll do yourself more harm than good if you hit balls after fatigue has set in.

Practice at first to correct mistakes. When the mistakes are pretty well cured, practice should then be similar to playing. Hit a driver and then an iron, or a drive, a fairway wood and an iron, just as though you were playing a hole.

Lessons are a big help in making practice worthwhile. The pro can tell you what to achieve through practice and how to achieve it.

Every good player is a practicer, though some spend more time than others. They try to hit each first shot well, not the second or third. You don't get mulligans in a tournament.

Entry, May 4, 1935
A woman asked me today, "What about a forward press?"

I told her to imagine how she would swing a heavy bucket of water. She no doubt would find it easier to swing back if first she gave a slight forward movement to get the bucket in motion.

It's the same with the golf swing. If you precede the backswing with a slight forward movement, you'll start everything going back together.

Entry, August 2, 1937
Jimmy Demaret came up from Houston today and sure shot up our golf course. He had 28-32-60.

I talked to him afterward and he's working on a theory that the elbows should stay together in the swing. He doesn't mean tight together, or in to the body. He just tries to keep them the same distance apart throughout his swing.

Entry, December 20, 1940
The worst trouble pupils have is that they try to think of the thousand-and-one things they hear. We all have to check our mistakes, but it's impossible to go through the list before each stroke.

It's so important not to give up a golf swing in an effort to do some minor or inconsequential thing. I've seen a lot of players with a good straight left arm. Trouble is, they gave up their golf swings to do it.

It is helpful to remember that corrections may throw you off for a while. If I knelt on my knees and played for a long time, it would throw me off to swing while standing on my feet.

One should not look for gradual improvement in making corrections. Improvement usually comes in jumps. A player will be a 100 shooter; then he shoots a 90. He then usually stays from 90-100 for six months or a year. Then he shoots an 85 and stays between 85 and 90 for a while. The better he gets, the smaller the jumps.

Confidence is a result of a good swing and of good shots.

Entry, April 19, 1945
Good players have the power to think while they are competing. Most golfers are not thinking, even though they believe they are. They are only worrying.

Entry, October 15, 1946
There was a young girl from the University who came to me for a lesson today. She wore blue jeans and a bad grip. I've never seen a better, though unpolished, prospect.

Betsy Rawls is quite shy. I'm not too wordy either, so little was said during the lesson. But I don't think she'll need much talking to. If she can get some breaks, and some time from her studies there's no telling how far she might go.

Entry, September 12, 1953
Too many women hit behind the ball. The two very good women golfers who come to mind that have this problem are Betty MacKinnon and Mary Lena Faulk. I've worked with both of them when they've been through Austin in the past, and both have trouble with close lies. I think the problem stems from swinging *too much* from the inside. So many women think they have to do this to get distance.

Entry, September 30, 1955
Women golfers too often listen too well to too many people. Everyone has advice for them on how to hit a golf ball and most females are too sensitive to refuse it and too conscientious about making corrections.

Most women learn golf from their husbands—or try to learn from them. Husbands invariably tell their better half to "look at the ball" or "keep your head down."

I showed the lady from San Antonio that I can look at the ball and still miss it.

Husbands also say, "Relax!" The Lord didn't start women with any excess power when it comes to hitting a golf ball. They must be *taught* to hit it. They have to be careful neither to relax nor to tense up.

Women must have sound swings to get distance. They may have to give up accuracy to get yardage. Men usually have the ability to hit the ball hard.

Because a woman must hit it just as far as she possibly can I believe in starting a woman with a full and forceful swing. The study of muscles has proven that if you start hitting easy you will more likely continue to swing easy. Hitting too easy is a common error among women.

Weaker women are better off with a long swing if they can maintain their timing. How can we learn to time the swing? I'd say work a lot on short shots, imagining you are swinging a water bucket. And don't spill the water!

Entry, March 4, 1958
Many have said that Sam Snead has a "picture swing." I guess Sam does look pretty effortless when he swings a golf club, but I'll bet he's using every available muscle, either consciously or unconsciously, to move that club just as fast as possible in the hitting zone.

Frequently it's a scratch player who spoils a good golfer in the making. Players just starting to come along use their natural ability. Then they hear some remark, casual or otherwise, and the boy ruins his style trying to be like somebody else.

Mickey Wright said to me not so long ago, "I sure wish I could get my hands high, like Betsy [Rawls]."

I had to tell her, "You don't want your hands high. You just like what Betsy has done with her hands high."

A player just can't develop someone else's golf swing. This is the kind of imitation which leads players into developing shots which are just the opposite from their natural styles.

Nelson has a short swing. Bobby Jones had a long swing. But they both worked out their swings in the way best suited for them, with the help of competent and interested coaches.

Entry, January 1, 1960
If you asked me to name my most challenging job as pro here I'd have to tell you this:

I have to try and keep older players as good as they were when they were younger. These are pupils I have had for 25 or 30 years. Or perhaps I am only trying to keep them good enough at golf to want to go on playing.

At any rate, golf is a wonderfully challenging game, both for the par-shooter and the high handicap player. If publishing these excerpts from the notes I've accumulated over many years has stimulated any player to work on his game with renewed interest or given a newcomer incentive to take up the sport, I'll say the whole thing has been more than worthwhile.∎

HOW SENIORS CAN LOWER THEIR SCORES

BY JIMMY DEMARET
AND THE PROFESSIONAL PANEL
August, 1964

Amateur golfers often improve with age because increased leisure time in their "senior years" allows them to play more frequently.

Take two people with the same ability, let one play once a week and the other four times a week, and the latter will beat the once-a-weeker 90 per cent of the time.

Two other things can contribute to lower scores for seniors:

1. Stick to a pattern of play.

2. Use equipment that compensates for the slowing up of muscles and reflexes.

Forget about fancy shots that depart from your pattern. Play the same way all the time.

I have seen many great golfers who hooked the ball to the left all of their lives. Bill Mehlhorn and Craig Wood, as well as myself, were among the first who faded every shot to the right. If you "miss it the same way" all the time you have the percentages going for you, and an advantage over the fellow who hooks it one time and fades it the next. If you are a natural hooker or fader, go with the game you have and allow for the shot to curve. Of course, this doesn't necessarily apply to the young fellow coming up or the aspiring pro who has a lot of time to practice and develop a better game.

When choosing equipment you must realize that your swing changes slightly as you get older. Your turn and the length of your swing are apt to become restricted. You may lose clubhead speed and, as a result, distance.

I have found that by using slightly lighter woods and irons I get almost

as much clubhead speed now, at 54, as I did 10 or 15 years ago. Now I'm using a D-0 swingweight with the driver while formerly I was swinging D-2, D-3 or even as high as D-4. Ben Hogan, who will be 52 on Aug. 13, is now swinging about a C-9, and he tied for ninth in the Masters and fifth in the Colonial National Invitation this year.

The length of your clubs should depend on your build. I'm 5'-10" and use woods and irons that are a half-inch longer than the normal of 43 inches for the driver and 39 inches for the 2-iron. I think many shorter people, my height or less, could use a slightly longer shaft to give themselves a little wider swing arc. This, along with a "flatter lie," probably will add a few yards to shots, though longer clubs may be more difficult to control. A taller person may not need the longer shaft. He usually has good leverage because of his long arms and greater height.

Jimmy Demaret, the first player to win the Masters three times, is now co-owner with Jack Burke of Champions Golf Club in Houston.

PANEL COMMENTS

SAM SNEAD: We need help from equipment

I agree wholeheartedly with Jimmy's comments on using lighter clubs as you get older. Now that I'm a senior golfer, I know you need all the help you can get from your equipment. As a golfer ages he gradually loses his ability to generate clubhead speed. His turn isn't quite as full and his swing loses some snap. A lighter club will help him swing the club faster and retain much of the distance he would otherwise lose.

Since greater clubhead speed at impact is also one of the things that makes a shot fly high, the senior golfer who has lost speed might have trouble getting the ball up in the air enough when using a driver off the tee. I have switched to a 1½-wood and this might help other seniors.

I feel that shorter-than-average players often need longer clubs. The so-called standard length club is made for the person of average height. The shorter person, by using a longer club, can increase the size of his swing arc and get more distance.

(The average golfer who swings a 43-inch driver at a clubhead speed of 120 feet per second in the hitting area can attain a clubhead speed of 123½ feet per second with a 44-inch driver, providing he can swing it at the same hand speed.)

JACK BURKE JR.: Allow for a consistent curve

I would like to enlarge on Jimmy's advice that a senior golfer simplify his method of play. Some people don't understand that no one can hit a golf ball straight consistently. You have to allow for a curve. The player who knows which way his shot will curve has the advantage over someone who hits one shot to the left and the next to the right. The latter player must always aim for the center of the fairway. If his shot slices or hooks more than half the width of the fairway, he's in trouble. The player who can count on hooking or slicing can aim down the right or left side of the fairway as a safe landing area.

All professionals, when hitting to a green from long range, aim to one side of the green and try to make the ball curve in slightly toward the hole. They don't aim at the flag except with high-lofted clubs like a 9-iron or a wedge, which seldom produce badly hooked or sliced shots.

BYRON NELSON: Play the safer shot
Because the average senior's nerves aren't as steady and his eyesight isn't quite as sharp, one of the hardest shots for him to play is the little, delicate pitch shot with a wedge or high-numbered iron. I have seen older players achieve more success by using a 4- or 5-iron hitting a running chip shot. It's a little safer when you don't have that delicate touch.

On long shots, I have observed that older players who score consistently well don't worry whether they hook or slice the ball a little—just so they get the same action on it every time. If they slice or hook, they just allow for it. Just so the curve isn't so extreme that it gets the golfer in trouble or cuts his distance too much. At their stage of the game, it sometimes isn't practical for seniors to take their swings apart and try to rebuild them. Minor improvements might be in order, but not a major overhaul.

One reason senior golfers appear to be straighter than young players, and more consistently avoid trouble, is simply that they don't hit the ball as far. A short drive to the right or left may stay in the fairway while a longer drive, hit off-line at the same angle, will reach the rough.

I haven't found that seniors putt as well as some people would lead you to believe. There are exceptions, but I think most seniors are consistent putters rather than exceptionally good or bad putters. Playing regularly makes them more consistent. They retain their timing and coordination even though their nerves and reflexes aren't as good as they once were.

GARY PLAYER: Slight hook increases distance
As a golfer gets older he might do well if he develops a slight hook on his shots. Senior golfers usually need more distance, and a hooked shot eventually rolls farther than a sliced shot because it flies through the air with less backspin. It's often a good idea for seniors, and

short-hitting younger players, too, to get a driver with a hooked face, turned to an angle that looks slightly to the left of the target. This type of clubface helps apply right-to-left hook spin to the ball.

Thinner-than-normal grips can also help a golfer develop a little hook because they allow him to get more wrist action into his shots. Thick grips rob the wrists of their flexibility and strength and therefore make it difficult to hook a ball unless you have abnormally large or strong hands.

I think a senior can retain or even improve his strength and suppleness if he swings a weighted practice club. It tones the muscles and that's very important.

One advantage senior golfers have, and it often saves them strokes, is that they don't get upset as easily as many younger players.

PAUL RUNYAN: Play often, but practice, too
There isn't a thing Jimmy Demaret said that I would disagree with, but I would like to enlarge on a few points.

Jimmy's contention that the four-times-a-week golfer has an advantage over the once-a-weeker ties in with my theory that, as we get older, we should take our exercise in smaller but more frequent doses. I feel the 50-and-over golfer should play from three to five times a week, even if he finds it expedient to cut his game to nine holes on some days. What a boon it would be to all golfers, and particularly the seniors, if my friend Rod Munday's dream came true. Rod feels golf should consist of two sides of six holes each. I think most doctors will contend that some of the good derived from the exercise of the first 12 holes often is undone by the fatigue acquired in the last six holes of an 18-hole round.

I think all frequent golfers would help themselves if they cut out that fourth or fifth round each week in favor of a leisurely two-hour practice session, with half the time spent on or around the putting green or the sand bunker. I would rather have a well-practiced mediocre swing than a better swing that has had little practice.

The inroads of time can be

arrested effectively by the daily, gentle swinging, golf fashion, of some long, heavy object such as a hoe, rake or shovel. This must be done daily but only for a few moments.

The soundest advice in Jimmy's article concerns the length and weight of clubs. There is a tendency for the tall player to use extra-long clubs. This may be necessary to assure proper posture but often the taller golfer with long arms doesn't need the extra club length to produce a large swing arc. It is the shorter golfer who more often needs longer clubs to maintain good distance.

Certainly, the older player should use clubs that are lighter, but not necessarily whippier. The whippier clubs, in my opinion, decrease one's ability to control the direction without giving an appreciable distance advantage.

PANEL TIPS
1. Most good golfers play all of their longer shots with the same curve. It is impossible to hit the ball consistently straight, so a senior with a consistent hook or slice should live with it and allow for it —if it isn't so severe that it kills his distance.

2. Lighter clubs can help seniors increase clubhead speed and distance. Shorter-hitting players can also increase clubhead speed by using slightly longer clubs, which expand the swing arc, if the golfer is able to manipulate them with no loss of angular speed.

3. A slight hook increases distance by adding roll. Thinner grips and a "hooked" clubface —that looks slightly to the left— help a golfer hook the ball.

4. Seniors who have trouble getting sufficient height on their drives might do well to switch to a 1½ wood, which has slightly more loft.

5. A senior should try to play frequently, even if only nine holes at a time, but should also devote two hours a week to practice if at all possible.

6. Muscle tone can be maintained by daily swinging a weighted practice club or a long, heavy object such as a hoe, rake or shovel. ∎

THE SQUARE-TO-SQUARE GOLF SWING: MODEL METHOD FOR THE MODERN PLAYER

BY DICK AULTMAN
February, 1970

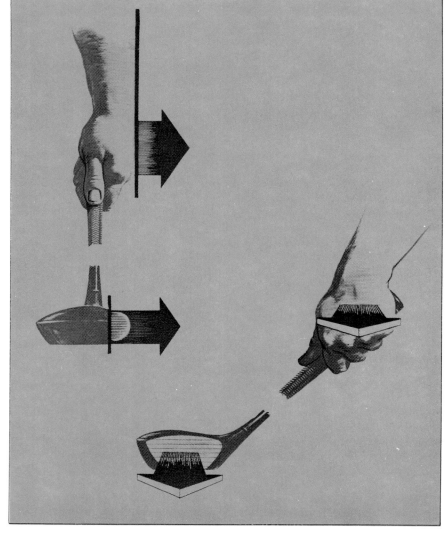

The early golfers, those who set set the swing patterns for future generations, played the game with wooden-shafted clubs. These shafts were very flexible, or "soft," by modern standards and had a tendency to twist during the swing. This twisting, or torque, action made it difficult to square the clubface with the target line during impact. Only by relying on their hands and wrists to flip the clubface back to a square position could the golfing pioneers hit straight shots with much consistency.

The Square-to-Square method detailed here is taken from *The Square-to-Square Golf Swing: Model Method for the Modern Player,* by Dick Aultman and the editors of *Golf Digest,* and from the follow-up book, *Square-to-Square Golf in Pictures,* by Jim Flick with Aultman. Flick is the head professional at Losantiville C.C. in Cincinnati and director of golf at The Hamlet, Delray Beach, Fla. A member of Golf Digest's Professional Teaching Panel, he has earned a reputation as a top instructor and student of the game. Aultman is a former editor of *Golf Digest* and is now a contributing editor.

Thus, our ancestors became largely "hands" players. During their backswings many right-handed golfers would rotate the clubhead with a clockwise turning of the hands and forearms. The left hand would more or less roll over the right, and the toe of the clubhead would turn away from the ball in advance of the heel. On the downswing these golfers could square up the clubface and thus hit straight-flying shots, only if they reversed the procedure by rolling their hands and forearms in a counterclockwise manner. They found that by gripping the club with the right hand turned well to the right, more under the clubshaft, it was easier to maneuver the clubface back to a square position at impact.

During the 1930s and after World War II, however, certain developments occurred in golf, largely in America, that caused players to seek a simpler, more reliable method of striking a golf ball.

The advent of steel shafts, which had less tendency to twist, greatly lessened the need for manipulation of the clubhead with the hands. Players, led by the American professionals, found that the less they rotated the club clockwise with their hands during the backswing, the less they needed to compensate with counterclockwise movement on the downswing to square the clubface at impact. By minimizing the moving parts they found that they minimized the chances for error.

Because of automatic sprinkling systems, American courses became wetter and lusher, which led to an increase in ball diameter (to the present 1.68 inches). The tendency of this larger ball to rise more easily than the 1.62-inch ball that most other countries continued to favor, diminished the need for hand action —the Scottish "flick-the-clubhead" technique—during the downswing. American players discovered that they achieved greater control over the height and accuracy of shots with a body-oriented swing that "pulled" the clubhead solidly and smoothly through the hitting area.

And then, perhaps catalyzing all the other factors, was the matter of distance, the urge and the necessity to hit a golf ball ever farther. The larger ball needed more forceful, accurate striking if it were to travel as far as its predecessors. Courses were getting longer and more "holding." Incentives grew greater and competition tougher on the professional tour. Success began to depend more and more on sheer yardage and less and less on finesse. And the steel shafts would take all the stresses that the most Herculean players could apply.

Golfers like Byron Nelson, Ben Hogan and Sam Snead pioneered the new method. They took the accent off hands and put it on the bigger muscles of the body, especially those of the back and legs, the major sources of athletic power. Arnold Palmer, Jack Nicklaus and many others—even more power conscious—carried the new techniques into the '60s, improving on them as they went.

So was born the Square-to-Square Method.

Today, in America particularly, the Square-to-Square Method is filtering down and influencing the swings of average club golfers. Increasingly, leaders of the golf teaching profession are studying and refining the Method and are teaching it to fellow professionals through schools, seminars, and clinics sponsored by the PGA.

Yet, though the Method has evolved to a high degree in the swings of many of the world's best golfers, though it has been discussed and partially promulgated in books and articles, and though it is being taught by professional instructors, it has never been presented in totality in the printed form.

Sometimes partial understanding can be more damaging than no understanding, especially when trying to build a golf swing. In researching the Square-to-Square Method, the editors encountered reservations from some players and

professional teachers about certain aspects of the concept. Invariably, however, the editors later found that such reservations resulted from misunderstanding, or from failure to understand the Method as a whole.

The purpose of this series is to explain the Square-to-Square Method as a total concept. The editors of Golf Digest feel that this explanation must necessarily involve detailed instruction about, for instance, correct gripping and setting up to the ball, as well as actual swinging.

Some professionals think of their pupils as being either Stage I, Stage II, or Stage III players. Generally a male Stage I player cannot break 100 for 18 holes on a course of over 6,000 yards. Stage II players will normally shoot in the 90s and middle-to-high 80s. Stage III players shoot in the low 80s and better.

The Square-to-Square Method is least applicable to the Stage I golfer. Such a player—especially if he is a beginner—usually faces the basic problem of putting the club into motion; of making a fluid, fast swing of the clubhead. Such players need first to develop freedom of movement, the sense of swinging the club forcefully, then learning how to channel that energy. The Square-to-Square swing, however, emphasizes the elimination of superfluous movement. It is designed, for example, to minimize hip turn and "wrist action." It is based on the principle that the simplest swing—with a minimum of moving parts—is the best swing.

This is not to say that Stage I golfers cannot benefit from studying Square-to-Square principles. They can in a variety of areas, including, for example, the stress the method places on left-side control.

But most of those who teach Square-to-Square would agree that the Method is best suited to the more experienced golfers in Stages II and III.

The editors of Golf Digest would like to make it clear to those readers who choose to follow and to apply the Method that any major overhaul of one's golf swing necessarily involves both a fair amount of practice as well as some —hopefully infrequent—periods of discouragement. Learning the

Square-to-Square Method calls for retraining muscles so that the normally weaker left hand, arm and side can dominate the normally stronger right hand, arm and side.

The professionals who teach the Square-to-Square swing have found that it is best if pupils start with short shots, then gradually move toward full-shot swings with the longer shafted clubs.

By starting with chip shots, you will be able to concentrate on the fundamentals of grip and setup and backswing without concern about distance gained. Also, you will be able physically to handle the shorter clubs more easily during the early stages when you are developing left-side muscles and "teaching" them to control your swing.

After learning to apply Square-to-Square techniques to these short shots, and after any changes in grip and address position begin to feel normal, you can then beneficially proceed to full shots with a 9-iron. Move on to full shots with longer irons only after you can swing the 9-iron through impact and beyond with the square position of the left hand and forearm remaining intact.

Finally, those who teach the Square-to-Square swing would warn that learning the Method will necessarily cause most players to alter old familiar habits. Because alterations in grip, address posture and the swing require conscious mental direction, your swing may lose, temporarily, much of its normal smoothness. This must be expected. Don't be discouraged when it happens.

Such changes also will cause you to feel new unfamiliar sensations and these will make you feel insecure. At times as you address the ball, it will seem impossible that you can make a successful shot. You will be tempted to allow the image of a bad shot to creep into your mind's eye. Square-to-Square instructors advise that you consciously replace these negative images by visualizing the flight pattern of a successful shot. Visualizing successful shots is a technique by which leading golfers allow their subconscious to direct their muscles and nerves toward making a successful swing. Such visualization is even more important to the learning golfer.

49

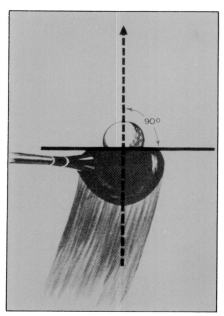

"Square" impact: If clubface looks down the target line during impact, it is considered "square," because the clubface itself forms a 90-degree, or "square," angle with the target line. To make a "perfect" golf shot, the clubface must be "square" during impact. It also must be moving along the target line at ball level and at maximum speed.

SQUARE-TO-SQUARE: WHAT IT IS, WHAT IT CAN DO

To make a "perfect" golf shot certain mechanical requirements must be met during impact—that split second when the ball is being squashed against the clubface.

First, the clubface must be "looking" down the line along which the golfer intends that the ball should fly. When the clubface does look down the target line during impact, it is considered "square." It forms a 90-degree, or "square," angle to that line. If, during impact, the clubface is looking either to the right or the left of the intended line of flight, the ball can *never* fly in the direction that the golfer has chosen (although admittedly it may end up at his target via a hooking or slicing route).

Second, in order to execute a "perfect" golf shot the clubhead must be moving *along* the intended line—and at ball level. If it is not moving along this line, if it is traveling from outside or inside this

line during impact, the clubhead, depending on how it is facing, will push the shot to the right or pull it to the left, or strike the ball a glancing blow and apply some degree of sidespin. The glancing blow not only reduces force—and thus the distance of the shot—but it also causes the ball to spin off to the left or right of the target line.

Third, the "perfect" golf shot, to travel its fullest distance, must be struck with the maximum amount of clubhead speed that the golfer can generate.

There are several ways in which the Square-to-Square Method promotes "square" clubface, on-line clubhead path and maximum clubhead speed during impact. These advantages of the Method will be explained shortly. The explanation will be more meaningful, however, if we first look briefly at just what Square-to-Square means.

For years the position of the golfer's clubface at the top of his or her backswing has been described as either "closed," "open" or "square."

If the clubface looks more or less straight up to the sky it is considered "closed." Many golfers, and some teachers, feel that from such a position the golfer must make some sort of compensation during the downswing in order for the clubface to be "square"— looking down the target line— during impact. Theoretically, if such compensation is not made, the clubface will remain in a closed position so that it looks to the left of target when it contacts the ball. The golfer who swings from a "closed" clubface position at the top of his swing to a "square" clubface position at impact is said to have a "closed-to-square" swing.

The so-called "open" position at the top of the backswing finds the clubface looking more or less straight out, in the same direction the golfer is facing. Many golfers and teachers believe that from this position the golfer must make a different sort of compensatory movement on the downswing to avoid an "open" face at impact. Such a swing would be designated "open-to-square."

If at the top of the swing the clubface is positioned about

midway between "closed" and "open," it is considered "square." From a square clubface position at the top of the swing, the golfer can, theoretically, return to a square impact position without any compensatory movements. Many golfers consider this to be a "square-to-square" swing.

However, those who teach the Square-to-Square Method do not follow the old system of assigning designations of "closed," "square" and "open" to *clubface* positions. These teachers feel that judging the swing on the basis of clubface positions has been misleading to both pupils and instructors.

Because a golfer's grip and swing plane can distort the true meaning of clubface position (other factors such as length of backswing also affect clubface positioning), progressive instructors prefer to describe the proper "square" position in a different manner. Generally, they refer to the "square" position as pertaining to *the relationship between the back of the left hand, wrist and lower forearm while swinging in proper plane.* When the back of the left hand, wrist and lower forearm form a *straight line,* the golfer is considered to be in a "square" position, if he is swinging on a sufficiently upright plane. This position is called "square" because it is the ideal position that the left hand, wrist and lower forearm should be in during a "square" impact.

In the true Square-to-Square swing now being used by the leading players and taught by progressive professionals, this straight-line relationship of the back of the left hand, wrist and forearm is established either when gripping the club, or during the early stages of the backswing. Thereafter, it is firmly maintained through impact with absolutely no independent hand manipulation at any point during the swing.

Thus, in the true Square-to-Square swing, the golfer actually establishes his proper "square impact" position of left hand, wrist and lower forearm at the *start* of his swing, and then he merely retains this position thereafter as he brings his bigger leg and back muscles into the shot.

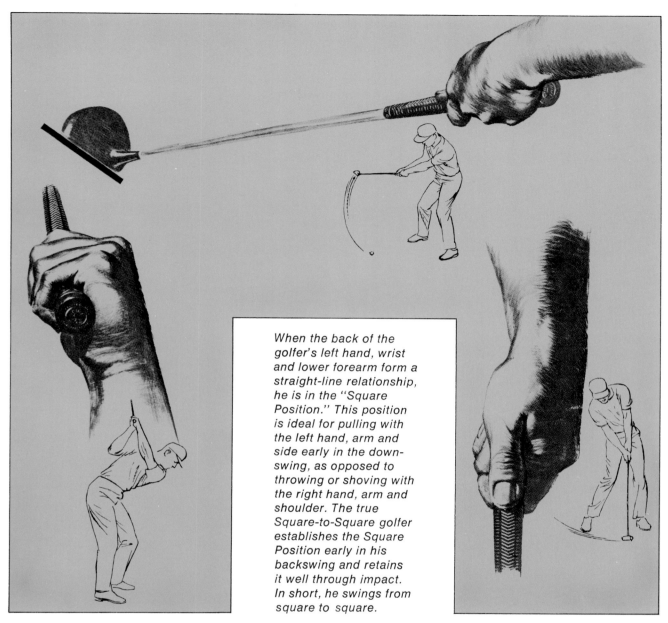

When the back of the golfer's left hand, wrist and lower forearm form a straight-line relationship, he is in the "Square Position." This position is ideal for pulling with the left hand, arm and side early in the down-swing, as opposed to throwing or shoving with the right hand, arm and shoulder. The true Square-to-Square golfer establishes the Square Position early in his backswing and retains it well through impact. In short, he swings from square to square.

The Square-to-Square swing evolved because leading players sought an "edge" over their fellow competitors. Players who learn this method today will enjoy the same edge over those who employ less efficacious methods. The advantages derived from enjoying the Square-to-Square Method include:

1. A better chance for square contact with the ball, because the clubface "looks" down the target line for a greater duration of time and space as it moves through the hitting area.

2. More distance as a result of "squarer" contact of the clubface on the ball.

3. More distance through greater use of the large muscles of the back and legs, rather than the smaller muscles of the hands, wrists and arms.

4. More distance through greater retention of clubhead speed through impact, because the Method stresses and generates a stronger left side. The right side has less chance to take over and dissipate clubhead speed before impact.

5. More consistency because of less manipulation of the club with the hands and wrists. The swing is simpler because it uses fewer moving parts. This means that the golfer's timing and rhythm need not be absolutely perfect in order to produce acceptable shots.

6. Greater control because the golfer works the club and left side toward proper impact position during the slower moving backswing, rather than during the faster moving downswing.

7. Elimination of slicing caused by failure to rotate clubhead back to square position during down-swing.

8. Elimination of hooking caused by collapse of the left wrist during impact.

And, finally, learning the Square-to-Square Method provides the golfer with a definite, clearcut avenue towards improvement. It enables him to know always *exactly what he is trying to do.* This, as all golfers whose games are now based on constant experimentation will appreciate, is a major psychological plus-factor, and a great stimulus to working for improvement.

SQUARE-TO-SQUARE GOLF IN PICTURES

BY JIM FLICK
WITH DICK AULTMAN
May and June, 1974

The premise of Square-to-Square is that you are more likely to produce perfect impact if you *pull* your club into position during the early stages of your forward swing than if you *throw, push* or *shove* it.

The easiest position from which to pull the club is the so-called "Square Position." This position is one in which the back of your left hand, wrist and forearm form a straight-line relationship. It is called the Square Position simply because the pulling action that can be applied from it gives you your best chance of contacting the ball squarely. If you establish this straight-line relationship either at address or early in your backswing, and maintain it to near the finish of

your forward swing, you are, in fact, swinging from square to square.

Most golf swings—I'd say about 99.9 per cent— involve too much pushing, shoving or throwing of the club early in the forward swing. Invariably, the right hand dominates the left and the shoulders dominate the legs. Put a muscularly dominant hand, arm and shoulder *behind* a clubshaft which you are trying to swing forward. Instinctively, they will try to assume control.

The results are all too familiar—slicing, pulling, hooking, fat shots, topped shots, even shanks. All result from over-controlling the club with the right hand and/or the right arm and shoulder muscles early in the forward swing. Also, throwing the club with the right hand often wastes centrifugal force so that the clubhead actually decelerates into the ball.

The main goal of the Square-to-Square Method is to help you minimize the role played by your right hand and right-side muscles, and to increase the influence of your left hand, your left arm and side and your legs. Though golf is a bilateral game, the Square-to-

Square Method is designed to give your weaker, less developed parts an equal billing so that you can strike the ball squarely more often and with increased clubhead speed.

Again, the main reference point in the Square-to-Square swing is the so-called "Square Position," in which the back of your left hand, wrist and forearm form a straight-line relationship, with no inward cupping or outward bowing at the back of the wrist.

Though the Square-to-Square Method does increase your chances of facing the clubhead down the target line during impact, in no way do I mean to imply that the clubface looks at the target throughout the entire swing. Actually, the clubhead rotates about 90 degrees as you make your backswing turn, and then about 180 degrees in the opposite direction during your entire forward swing.

I would also like to clarify that while the Square-to-Square Method does increase the span in which the clubhead is moving along the target line through impact, this is not to say that it never leaves this line. As in all golf swings, the clubhead

moves to the golfer's side of his target line fairly early in the backswing, remains on this side until near impact, and then returns to the golfer's side shortly thereafter.

The Square-to-Square grip

A proper Square-to-Square grip puts control of the club largely in the last three fingers of your left hand. It is this control that, if maintained during your swing, helps you pull, rather than throw, the club into proper position for square impact.

The Square-to-Square grip is one in which your palms more or less face each other and align with the clubface. Thus, both palms are relatively "square" to the target line. If there is to be any departure from this palms-facing, clubface-aligned relationship, it should be that your right hand faces a smidge more skyward. Most players run into trouble if their right hand tends to crawl over the thumb of their left. This gives over too much control of the club to the thumb and forefinger of the right hand, which in turn activates the top-side muscles— the "throwing" muscles—of the forearm.

In the Square-to-Square grip, the thumb of your left hand extends down the top of the clubshaft, or slightly right of top, so that the back of this hand also aligns more or less parallel with the clubface and thus is also square to the target line.

Should you employ this Square-to-Square grip immediately or should you move to it gradually over a period of time and practice? I've found that this depends on three things: (1) how long and how much the pupil has played with his or her present positioning of the hands; (2) how great the variation of this present positioning is from the aligned grip and, most importantly, (3) how much time the student can spend practicing to develop familiarity with the new grip. Unless you have played relatively little golf, or unless your hands' position is already close to being aligned with the clubface, I suggest you make the transfer gradually. A major change all at once probably will feel foreign and uncomfortable. It may produce mental tension and perhaps affect your alignment and your swing adversely.

How firmly should you grip the

club? I feel that light is better than tight. Too much grip pressure in either hand creates arm and shoulder tension that stifles freedom of arm movement.

One goal of the Square-to-Square swing is to minimize the control exercised on the clubshaft by the right hand. There are two primary danger points to be aware of at address: (1) strong pressure in your right hand, and (2) stiffening pressure with the right arm, especially in the area around the elbow. Both of these pressures create tension that cannot easily be broken down.

You will also need just enough pressure joining your hands so that they will not move apart as you swing. I suggest you accomplish this by gently nudging the base pad of your right hand forward—toward the target—against the thumb pad of your left hand.

The Square-to-Square setup

Most golfers give too little thought to how they aim the clubface and set up to the ball. This is unfortunate. Without question, the way you *prepare* to swing directly

The overriding purpose of the Square-to-Square Method is to produce a swing in which the club is pulled during the downswing, not thrown or shoved. Professional Johnny Miller (top photos) uses his legs, left arm and the last three fingers of his left hand to produce this pulling action. The amateur (below) throws the clubhead with his right hand and shoves it with his right arm and shoulder. Photos 1, 2 and 3 show Miller positioning the club and himself to pull the club down and forward. He does so by SWINGING his arms and the club freely, as opposed to the amateur's LIFTING. By pulling during his downswing (photos 4, 5 and 6), Miller retains his wrist cock much longer than the amateur, who throws and shoves with his right hand, arm and shoulder. Miller also keeps his left wrist and hand in firm control through impact and beyond (photos 7 and 8). The amateur's throwing-shoving action with his right hand and shoulder forces his left wrist and arm to collapse during impact. His clubhead is up and off-line, reducing his chances for square contact and straight shots.

determines *how* you swing.

One way to improve your ability to aim the clubface properly is by using an "intermediate target," a technique employed by many professionals, including Jack Nicklaus. First, stand behind the ball so that it is between you and the target as you face down the line. Visualize your line of flight. Then select a spot on that line a few feet in front of the ball. Concentrate solely on the line from the ball to the spot. Since the intermediate target is relatively close at hand, this line is short. You'll find it relatively simple to square the clubace to it accurately. Thereafter:

1. Play the ball forward. If you play the ball about opposite your front heel on all normal shots, you will develop your legs and learn to use them as leaders in your forward swing.

2. Set most of your weight on the inside of your back foot. This positioning allows you to make a full, free backswing with little or no additional shifting of weight away from the target. Almost any and all weight-shifting you must make during your swing will be forward, toward the target, during your forward swing.

3. Your legs should feel alive and springy. As you address the ball they should already feel ready to slide forward at the start of your forward swing, ready to *pull* your arms and club through impact.

4. Your arms and shoulders should feel soft.

5. Bend forward from your hips with your back fairly straight. For your legs to lead your shoulders in your forward swing you need some "separation" between your legs and upper body. This separation is best established at address by bending forward from your hips and letting your arms hang freely.

6. Align your shoulders, hips and knees parallel to your target line.

Setting the angle

Now I'm going to discuss how and when to cock your wrists. I refer to cocking the wrists as "setting the angle." Setting the angle is a simple concept, but vital to the success of any golf swing, especially Square-to-Square.

The sides of the "angle" are your left arm and the clubshaft itself. The

Shown here are professionals Gary Player and Tom Weiskopf, who address their shots in a way that helps them apply a pulling force during their forward swings. Player sets up with his back straight and his knees flexed, his legs alert and ready to go. His hands fall well inside a vertical line down from his eyes. Weiskopf sets his upper body well behind the ball with most weight on the inside of the right foot. The knees are cocked toward the target to encourage driving the legs forward.

angle forms at the top of the wrist of your left hand, at the base of the thumb.

Why set an angle? The answer to this question should be fairly obvious. Imagine trying to swing a golf club stiff-wristed. You wouldn't hit it very far.

Your ability to produce a maximum force during impact, and to transfer that force squarely to the ball, is directly related to how you set and retain and release the angle as you swing. Setting the angle improperly makes the job of retaining it until the right time all but impossible.

Maintaining maximum clubhead speed and producing square contact during impact is best achieved with a swing that *pulls* the club into position during the early stages of the forward swing.

To set the stage for pulling the club on the forward swing, you must learn to set the angle in a way that (1) breaks down the influence of normally dominant muscles and (2) builds up the role of normally subordinate muscles.

Specifically, you should seek to set the angle—to cock your wrists

—with the last three fingers of your left hand. When these fingers assume control, they activate the muscles on the underside of your left forearm. It is these three fingers and these underforearm muscles, along with your legs, that should lead and pull the clubshaft into position during your forward swing. So long as these muscles control the clubshaft, you can pull the club forward, delay your release of centrifugal force and also maintain on-line movement of the clubhead longer through the impact area.

The actual setting of the angle during the backswing must be done smoothly and with these last three fingers. As you cock your wrists with these last three fingers, you should move into what we call the "square position." Once in this position, the back of your left hand, wrist and forearm form a straight-line relationship. You should see no inward cupping or outward bowing at the back of this wrist. The only bending of your left wrist is at the base of your thumb, not at the back of the wrist.

Setting the angle is a gradual process. It should be done

smoothly, without jerking the clubhead upward quickly. Still, some golfers do most of their angle-setting earlier than others. I'll categorize golfers into three types —(1) swing and set, (2) swinging set and (3) set and swing.

Swing and Set describes a relatively late setting of the angle. The wrists are cocked, near or at the top of the backswing and in some cases further cocked early in the forward swing. Late-setting is best for players whose swings are relatively inhibited, who need more body turn. This technique calls for excellent rhythm and timing, a relatively slow swing pace, strong left-hand control and outstanding lower-body and leg leadership on the forward swing.

The Swinging Set: This technique finds the wrists hinging gradually during the backswing— from start to finish—with little or no additional cocking early in the forward swing. The swinging set does not encourage quite so much freedom of movement as the swing-and-set style, but it does provide a somewhat earlier establishment of left-hand dominance. There is less likelihood of losing control of the club at the top of the swing and then grabbing hold with the right hand.

Set and Swing: Here the angle is set largely before the hands reach shoulder height during the back-swing. Control of the club is given

over to the last three fingers of the left hand throughout the entire swing. The golfer moves into the straight-line, square position during his takeaway.

The set-and-swing technique not only establishes left-hand, target-side control early, but in so doing places the club in excellent position to be pulled—not thrown or shoved—during the forward swing. This technique often produces a relatively upright arm swing. It all but eliminates flippiness at the top of the backswing.

An early setting of the angle is best suited to golfers who already have long, free-flowing swings with plenty of body turn.

Early setting does encourage picking up the club with the hands and arms in a jerky, rhythm-inhibiting movement during the takeaway. So the set-and-swing golfer must take care that he sets the angle while his arms swing freely and thus turn his shoulders and hips fully.

Retaining the angle
To achieve a full release you must hold the club lightly and swing your arms freely throughout your forward swing.

This free-swinging release not only produces a full explosion of centrifugal force, but also helps to (1) square the clubface to the target line; (2) swing it along that line and (3) extend the left arm and

clubshaft to put it at ball level all during impact.

Our method for retaining the angle is, again, to apply largely a pulling force, rather than a throwing, shoving or pushing force.

For your pulling hand to control your downswing, it is best to retain a light, passive grip with your throwing hand. For most golfers this requires conscious effort.

The best way I know to retain control with your pulling hand is to maintain your Square Position through impact and on to the finish of your swing.

In all good golfers we see that while the back of the left wrist remains firm and uncupped throughout most of the forward swing, it does rotate counterclock-wise a full 180 degrees. This rotation occurs as the arms swing past the body through the striking area. The back of the left hand, wrist and lower forearm turn a half circle, just as if they were a page turning in a book. Without this free rotation, you cannot square your clubface back to the target during impact, except by flipping it with your right hand or shoving it with your right shoulder.

Another way to retain left-hand control is to start your downswing at a leisurely pace. The faster your hands move the club from the top of your swing, the sooner your throwing hand will take over and dissipate your angle. ■

Correct setting of the angle requires control of the clubshaft largely with the last three fingers of the left hand. This left-hand control breaks down tension in the right side, as demonstrated by Dave Hill.

Bruce Crampton's strong driving results largely from his ability to retain the angle formed by his left arm and clubshaft until late in his downswing, yet still release this wrist cock fully by impact.

THE TOUCH SYSTEM FOR BETTER GOLF

BY BOB TOSKI
July through October, 1971

The first thing I'm going to do to make you a better golfer is ask that before you read any farther you find yourself a pen or pencil and a piece of paper. Seriously! Go ahead. I'll wait.

Now, if you've done that, I'd like you to write your name three or four times *as fast and as legibly as you can.* I will do the same.

Let's compare signatures. I've reproduced mine here in the actual size that I wrote it. Are your handwriting strokes as light and as consistent as mine? Are your letters as tall and as deep and as wide? Or

The look of 'feel'
The uninhibited, smooth-flowing motion of the expert's golf stroke usually reflects itself in his handwriting. Is your signature similarly free of heavy-handed jerkiness?

are your lines heavier, or your letters smaller? Does your handwriting seem as "free" as mine, or does it appear more controlled?"

And who do you think wrote the fastest, you or me? I'd better warn you that I've raced against dozens of "signature signers," and only a handful have written faster than I did. And none of them wrote as legibly.

What does all of this mean? Why did I ask you to write your name? I did so because I believe—I *know*—that there is a definite link between the way a person writes his name and the way he, or she, plays golf. I can watch a person sign his name, and then, almost invariably, describe correctly how he swings a golf club. The person who writes fast and smooth with big loops like I do usually makes a full, free, rhythmical swing, with his hands moving quite high on the backswing. The person who writes with a heavy-handed, jerky stroke and makes small letters usually has a relatively short, fast, jerky backswing.

Hold your pen or pencil as tight as you can and try to write your name. I'll bet that your writing suddenly becomes slower, and less legible, than normal. Why? Because you over-control the pen. The same thing happens when you over-control a golf club. Hold the club too tight and you'll lose clubhead speed and rhythm. You won't hit the ball as far, or as straight.

Why can I drive a golf ball 250 or 260 yards and keep it in play almost every time? Certainly not because of my size or strength; I weigh barely 125 pounds when my wallet is full. That's why Sam Snead calls me "Mouse." I hit the ball far and straight simply because I have developed a high degree of *feel* for the rhythm and motion and timing of a proper swing. It's the same sensitivity for rhythm and motion that lets me write so fast and so legibly.

I know that with your cooperation I can teach you a similar feel for the proper golf swing. Once you develop this feel, you will make golf shots you never dreamed you could achieve.

Renowned as one of the country's finest teachers, Bob Toski is a member of Golf Digest's Professional Teaching Panel. He authored this book with Dick Aultman.

I believe there are a FEW "mechanics" of golf—note the stress on "few"—that anyone who hopes to play well must first master. If you haven't already done so, you must learn, for instance, how to hold and aim the club, and how to align yourself to the ball and the target.

Mechanics will take you only so far, however. I strongly suspect that most people who read this series will have failed to reach their true potential as golfers because they have not gone beyond learning the mechanics of the swing. Most players get so wrapped up in mechanics—the so-called fundamental moves and key positions —that they never apply them with the freedom of movement and sensitivity of clubhead motion that allows a Chi Chi Rodriguez—or a Bob Toski—to hit drives 50 or 100 yards past men twice his size.

What we'll really be getting down to is making you aware of your God-given ability to *feel*. I'll tell you in many, many different ways how a super golf swing should *feel;* how your grip should *feel;* how your backswing should *feel;* how impact should *feel;* how your knees should *feel.*

Given a clear track, the human mind and nervous system can perform amazing feats of coordination. You don't need to "tell" your body what to do, where to move, into what position. In fact, this sort of mental direction merely clutters up the computer of your mind and keeps it from functioning smoothly. The golfer who stands over the ball for half a minute is merely feeding his mind a lot of extraneous information—"keep your head down," "hold on tight at the top," "hit with your left knee"—that it doesn't need. Ask almost any star golfer what he thinks about when he's over the ball and he'll tell you he's imagining how the shot will look, or feel. Or possibly he's thinking about one "key move" that will help create the feel he wants. He trusts his subconscious to take over from there.

We program ourselves to produce proper golf swings by experiencing, again and again, reactions to successful shots. The more successful golf shots you experience, the easier it becomes to reproduce them. The more you

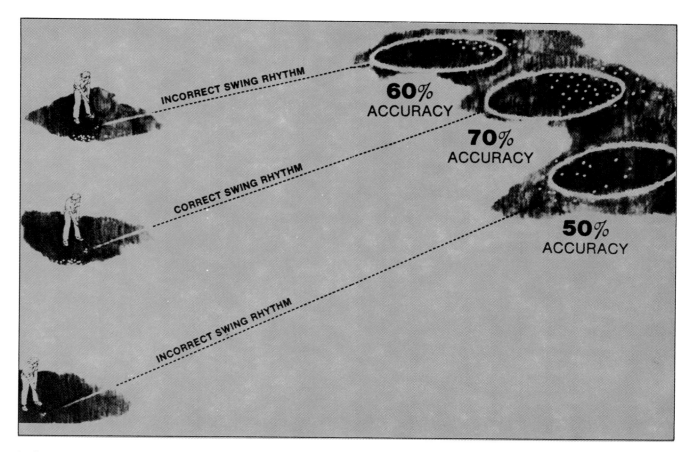

INCORRECT SWING RHYTHM

60% ACCURACY

CORRECT SWING RHYTHM

70% ACCURACY

INCORRECT SWING RHYTHM

50% ACCURACY

feel, say, proper hand action during impact, the more readily you'll be able to duplicate such movement subconsciously. The more times you watch the flight of successful shots, and relate that sight to the feel of your swing and the club striking the ball squarely, the better you will be able to duplicate such a shot in the future by merely summoning forth the corresponding feel. Never turn your back on successful shots. Watch the ball until it stops rolling.

Can a novice golfer learn the sensation—the feeling and sight—of successful shots? How does a 25-handicap player build a "success pattern" of solid driving when he only hits one or two solid drives in a whole month of play? The answer is that he can build "success patterns" in his computer-like mind only if he learns golf the way I teach it—*from the green to the tee.*

Anyone can experience the feel of solid contact and see successful results on two-foot putts. And that's exactly where I think golf should first be learned—from two feet away. That's where I will start to teach you to play by feel.

You may find it necessary to putt from this distance for only five or 10 minutes before progressing to longer putts, short approach shots and, eventually, the full swing. But if you follow my prescription, you won't move on to a longer shot until you have experienced, with reasonable frequency, the *feel* of success with shorter shots. Should you falter along the way and lose the feel of, say, a full 5-iron shot, I will ask you to step backward in your training and re-establish a success pattern with a shorter iron.

Now I'm going to present you with a wide variety of mental pictures to tell you how your swing should feel.

After you understand *mentally* how the swing should feel, you must work toward developing a given *physical* sensation. I'll tell you, for instance, how it feels to make a certain sequence of movements. It will be up to you to practice until it feels right in your swing. *BUT NEVER TRY TO ACHIEVE MORE THAN ONE SENSATION IN EACH SWING.*

OVER-ALL SWING SENSATIONS
Nobody ever hit the ball on the backswing. Yet, many golfers take the club back so fast that it seems they're trying to do just that. It's no wonder they lose control of the club.

Find your basic rhythm
Select a target area of about 15 paces in diameter. First, hit 50-100 shots to this target with your most-lofted club, using a very relaxed, easy swing. Note what percentage of your shots finish in the target area. Repeat the process from 10, 20, maybe 30, yards farther out, but with the same club. Again, figure the percentages of successful shots. Note at which distance you are most accurate. The swing rhythm used at that distance is the rhythm you should feel you are using on all full shots with any club.

Hands feel unified

Imagine that your hands blend together throughout your swing like a good dance team. The left hand controls the right gently and smoothly, just as the male dancer leads the female. The two partners never separate.

Others swing back too methodically, then slash at the ball with their hands because they feel they must do something to create clubhead speed. Whatever speed they do generate is largely wasted before impact because they use their hands too soon.

A good mental image for these golfers is that of an automobile stuck in mud or snow. Recall how you'd try to rock the car out. You would put it in reverse and slowly roll the wheels up the back edge of the rut. Then you'd put it in forward gear and slowly—to avoid spinning the wheels—accelerate. You'd keep doing this until you were able to accelerate gradually forward. Back slowly, then gradually faster forward. Picture this in your mind. Sense how it would feel inside the car. Imagine the same movement back and forth when you swing the golf clubs.

The place where you can really feel the motion of your golf swing is in the movement of your arms. Try swinging a golf club with your eyes closed. Without the ball in view to distract you, and with your sense of sight eliminated temporarily, you become acutely aware of the motion of your arms as they move back and forward. You'll feel the rhythm of your swing.

Try this. Take a deep breath and then swing the club before you let out any air. I asked a friend of mine, Bill Michaels, to try this and he thought I was some kind of nut. But he soon found that it was all but impossible to tense up during his swing so long as he held his breath. It's a beautiful reaction. There is practically no way you can push or shove or force your swing. It's a great way to get the feeling of swinging your arms freely, without over-controlling the club.

Your hold on the club should feel consistently *light*—not loose nor tight—throughout your swing. Also, the pressure of *one hand against the other* should remain constant all the time.

As you swing, imagine that your hands are like a good dance team. They're close against each other, moving together. There's never any separation between the two. The man—your left hand—is the leader. Your right hand responds to your left, but they never move apart or squeeze together tightly.

You really don't need very much grip pressure, even during impact. I prove this time and again to my pupils by making shots in which I actually *let go* of the club *before* impact. The club zings through the air down the fairway 40 or 50 yards, and the ball flies almost as far as on a normal shot. If it's possible to hit a shot almost normal distance without any hold on the club at impact, how much grip pressure do you really need on a regular shot?

Watch different pros playing in a tournament, live or on TV, and you'll soon find one whose swing gives off to you a sense of rhythm that you

feel you can adapt to your own game. Visualize the pace of that player's swing over and over in your mind's eye. Then try to duplicate it in your practice sessions.

I don't think there is a simpler or better way to get the feel of smooth rhythm and proper timing than through practicing your putting. Merely concentrate on making solid contact with the ball. This will force you to eventually start making well-timed strokes. And this new-found sense of timing and smooth rhythm will carry over into your longer shots.

ADDRESS POSITION SENSATIONS

The club will actually feel thinner some days than others. It's best when it does. And it will feel thin more often if you hold it lightly with just enough pressure to control its movement—no more, no less.

As you address the ball, don't squeeze any part of either hand, but *feel* or *sense* that you are going to control the club with the last three fingers of your left hand. These

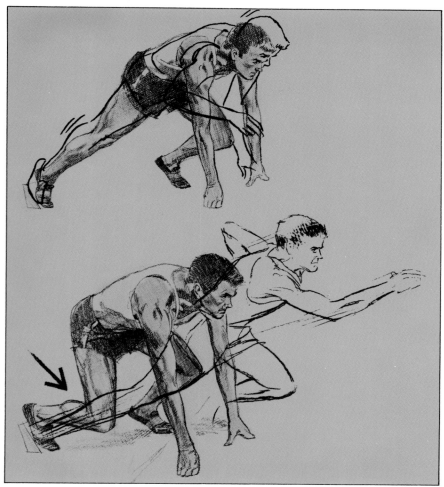

you prepare to return the shot, you're not even aware of making a backstroke. The ball, because it is moving, occupies your full attention. You don't have time to think about *how* you are moving the racquet back. Consequently, a good tennis player will unconsciously swing his racquet back and turn his shoulders without any rush or hurry. It's a smooth turning away.

Try to feel that your golfing backswing has the same pace that you'd give your tennis backstroke. Remember that in golf, as in tennis, all you are really doing on your backswing is placing yourself and your club in position to drive the ball forward.

TOP-OF-SWING SENSATIONS
You should feel a slight tension, just a little discomfort, across your back and down your left side at the top of your backswing. This indicates that you've built up some kinetic energy to be released later, during impact.

If you don't feel this slight discomfort, something has relaxed. You may have let your left arm bend too much, or collapsed the back of your left wrist into a "cuppy," concave position. You may have swung your hands too far *around,* rather than *over,* your back. Or you may simply have failed to complete your turn.

Near the top of your backswing, your moving clubhead will want to keep moving over your shoulders. You should feel resistance to this movement in the last three fingers of your left hand, since these fingers are farthest from the moving clubhead. With these fingers in control you'll be in good shape to *pull* the club back to the ball with your left side and arm and hand leading the way.

Unfortunately, most right-handed people follow the natural pattern of letting their right hand resist the

---

three fingers should feel ready to "rule" both hands throughout your swing. Your right hand should feel as if it's doing little more than caressing the club.

Around Old Baldy Lodge in Wyoming, where I taught in the summer, you can see a lot of deer. The graceful springing action they make—the agility, the speed, the distance they can jump—is really fantastic. Yet, these supple animals do not have big muscles and tendons and bones in their legs. What they do have is great flexibility and smoothness of movement—springlike action.

You don't see the deer stand rigid and stiff before they jump. They'd lose their agility. They'd get tense, and tension and stiffness inhibit movement in everything, including the golf swing. Perhaps you stand over the ball too long before you start your swing.

Your knees should feel positioned so that if you bounced on them they'd bend toward the ball. To get this feeling, you must point your right knee slightly inward to the left.

Your left side should feel slightly stretched as a result, even though your left knee is also flexed slightly. What you're doing is more or less previewing your impact position at address.

Try addressing the ball with the clubhead off the ground. Swing it back from this mid-air position. You may not hit the shot squarely, but you'll get the feel for proper control —rather than over-control—of the club.

BACKSWING SENSATIONS
Your right arm and right side should feel as if they are asleep during your backswing. Your left hand, arm and shoulder should be able to move them aside at will.

During your backswing imagine that you're standing on a slick floor, or even a sheet of ice, without any spikes on your shoes. This will force you to "hold on" with your feet. It will give you the proper leg resistance you should feel during your backswing.

If you've played a racquet sport such as tennis, you know that as

Timing your downswing

The feel of the proper downswing is similar to sitting in a canoe being gradually drawn toward a waterfall. You should feel that your legs and left arm are pulling the clubhead toward the ball, slowly at first, then faster and faster until it "swooshes" through. This feeling of gradual acceleration will occur only if your shoulders follow, rather than lead, your legs.

moving clubhead and thus take over control of the club at the top of the backswing. This opens the door for a right-hand-dominant throwing action on the downswing, resulting in premature releasing of energy and flipping of the clubhead across, rather than along, the target line.

Should you pause at the top of your swing? I'm told the club never really stops moving, but I do think that it's a good feeling to strive for if you often swing too fast—if you tend to move into your downswing before you've completed your backswing. The feeling of pausing will give you a greater sensation that you are in control of the club as it changes direction.

Your hands should feel "quiet," but firm, at the top of your swing. You should feel as if you've "placed" the club in position, and that your left hand is ready to pull it back to the ball.

Swing your club to the top of your backswing and then stop. Where on your feet do you feel your weight? Ideally it should seem more or less equally distributed between the inner half of your right foot and the inner half of your left foot. Your weight on your right foot should feel more toward the heel, on your left foot more toward the sole.

DOWNSWING SENSATIONS

I'd like you to imagine that you are sitting in a canoe in the middle of a small lake. Since one end of the lake is lower than the other, gravity pulls you in that direction, toward a small waterfall.

You sit in the canoe and you can feel it being pulled slowly toward the waterfall. It's a smooth pull—no jerks. But as you get closer, the pull gradually becomes stronger and stronger. The boat moves faster and faster. You can't stop it. Suddenly, you're over the waterfall, swoosh . . . splash . . . and you're hurtling down the stream.

Your clubhead is just like that canoe. It starts from an almost static position. Then it begins to move slowly, then gradually faster, but always smoothly. It's being pulled down and forward toward the ball, faster and faster, then, "pow," and it's gone, lashing through the ball and beyond.

The downswing of a good golfer may also look unified to some people, but we've learned from high-speed movies and photos that it really isn't. The downswing is really a sequence of movements. If everything moves in proper sequence, we have proper "timing."

The over-all feeling you should

have on your downswing is that, first, your left heel is returning to the ground and pulling your knees and hips laterally to the left. These, in turn, are pulling your left arm down and forward and your right elbow into your side. Your arms are leading your hands and your clubhead is lagging behind everything. Then, suddenly, you experience the *reaction* of the wrists unhinging and the clubhead squaring up to, and lashing through, the ball. If your timing is correct, this uncocking of the wrists will feel automatic with no conscious effort on your part.

The problem is that most of us relate power to our backs and shoulders instead of our legs. Naturally, whenever we try to hit the ball far, we rely too heavily— and too early—on our shoulders. This destroys the proper sequence of movement—timing.

If your shoulders come into play too soon in your downswing—you are probably slicing or pulling your shots—I suggest you practice part-swing shots of 40-60 yards. Try to feel that on your downswing you are swinging with your arms and legs, but holding back the return movement of your shoulders.

Imagine that you are holding a golf ball very lightly in your fingers and tossing it toward a wall with an easy underhand-sidearm motion. This is the relaxed flowing motion you should feel with your right arm and hand as you swing down and through the ball.

Imagine that you are holding a rug-beater in your left hand. You've got a rug hanging on the line. You're standing toward one edge of the rug and you're going to *backhand* the swatter against the rug. Make this motion, never letting the back of your left wrist collapse. You hit and hold. This is the firmness your left hand should feel as it moves into and through the hitting area.

To put these two feelings together,

take a 7-iron and hit some shots in this fashion. Swing the club down and into the ball as you normally do, but then "hold" firm with your left wrist and arm immediately after impact. Try to finish your swing as soon as possible after you've struck the ball. Hit and hold.

This drill will give you the proper feeling of hand movement through impact. You'll feel as if the hands are moving under control, but with authority. You'll feel a bit of a snap that you won't experience when you try to overpower the ball with your right shoulder.

Terry Bradshaw, the pro football quarterback, once told a friend of mine that when he throws a football he feels as if he's doing it with his forearm instead of his hand. It seems to him that his hand just happens to catch up and finally releases the ball.

The downswing in golf is much the same. Obviously, we don't hit the ball with our forearms—we hit it with the clubhead—but the feeling should be that your forearms—not your hands—are swinging the club into position to hit the ball. Only at the last split second should you feel your hands finally square the clubface and swing it through the ball.

When you swing *through* the ball and strike it squarely, it will feel "light" during impact. It will seem that it has jumped off the clubface quickly, as if it hadn't resisted the moving clubhead at all. The mis-hit shot will feel heavy and dull and slow in moving off the clubface. You will sense the ball's resistance.

As I mentioned earlier, the sensations I've described are those that most golfers experience when they execute the swing properly. But not all golfers will be able to relate to all these sensations. Just pick those that make sense to you. And, above all, as you practice your full shots, never try to achieve more than one of these sensations during any given swing. ∎

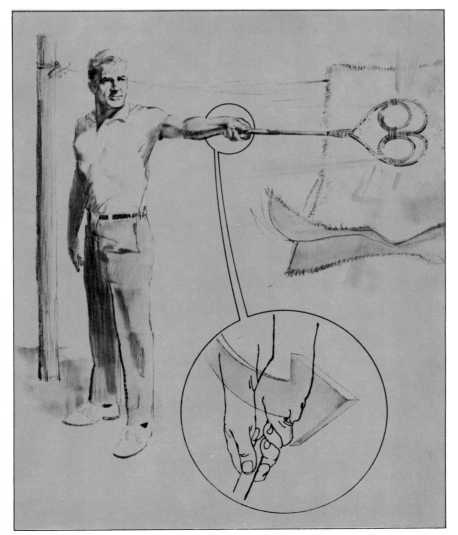

Left wrist feels firm
Your left wrist should feel as firm through impact as it would if you were backhanding with a rugbeater. You should feel no inward bending at either the top or back of the wrist.

I CAN GET YOU OUT OF THE SAND WITH ONE HAND

BY CLAUDE HARMON
September, 1972

I don't know why any golfer would want to play sand shots with one hand—except perhaps occasionally to shake up an opponent—but the fact that you could do so once you mastered my system indicates, I think, its simplicity and effectiveness.

Obviously a system that allows you to move the clubhead through the sand with only one hand is a system that requires relatively little physical effort.

Because my system results in a thin cut of sand, it allows you to take a LONGER cut with minimal effort. Textbooks tell us to contact the sand only two inches behind the ball. I insist that my pupils strike the sand AT LEAST four inches behind the ball. This requires both hands on the club, of course, but using my system I can actually enter the sand 10-11 inches behind the ball and still make a successful shot. Thus, my system, once mastered, all but guarantees that you'll no longer dig deeply into the sand and fail to get the ball out, nor catch it thin and skull it over the green.

Your shots from normal lies will fly high, settle gently and stop quickly. You'll find that those deep greenside bunkers are no problem.

Also, you'll find it possible to swing aggressively on those very short sand shots that otherwise would require an extremely delicate half-swing.

Claude Harmon is head professional at Winged Foot G.C., Mamaroneck, N.Y., and Thunderbird Ranch and C.C., Palm Springs, Calif.

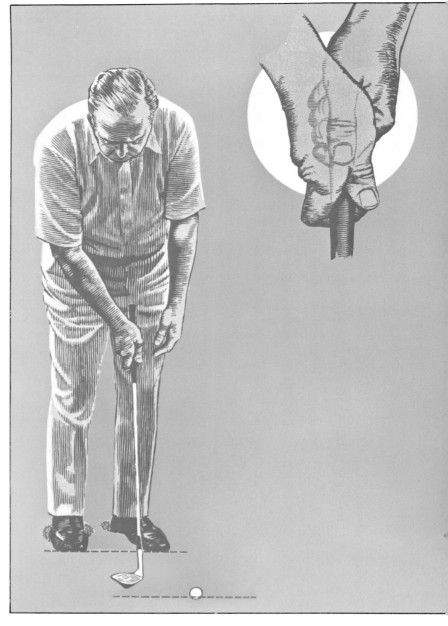

The setup

Step up to the ball in the sand as you would for a normal wedge shot from the fairway, but with only your right hand on the club. Choke down the shaft about an inch farther than normal with this hand and open the clubface so that it looks well to the right of target.

Then place your left hand on the shaft so that the thumb is on top of the cylinder and the back of the hand looks down the target line.

Open your stance by turning your entire body to the left until the clubface looks only slightly—a few degrees—to the right of target, and the back of the left hand now faces to the left of the target. Also, step back from the target so that the ball is well ahead of your left toe and your hands "trail" the clubhead.

Initially choking down on the club compensates for the general lowering of your body that will occur when you dig in your feet. Placing your left thumb on top of the club with the back of the hand facing down the target line prohibits any extensive closing of

the face when you swing into the sand. Such closing would cause a deep cut into the sand.

Maintaining a slightly open clubface at address allows you to strike firmly with your right hand without fear of closing the face and taking too much sand. The face will merely return to a square position.

Playing the ball well forward lays back the clubface, increasing its loft and lowering the rudder. The result is a high shot with a shallow cut of sand.

The swing

With your weight largely on the left side, pick up the clubhead quickly by immediately cocking your wrists. Your entire backswing is sharply upward.

Lead your downswing with a full weight shift to your left side. Throw the clubhead sharply downward, largely with your right hand, into the sand four or more inches behind the ball and straight forward toward the target. Try to clear a 10-12-inch rectangle of sand fore and aft of ball.

Weight to left at address and early wrist cock encourages a sharply ascending-descending swing pattern needed to get the clubhead under the ball.

Leading the downswing with a weight shift to the left side is vital to provide maximum length of cut through sand, thus avoiding skulled shots. This shifting also pulls the clubhead down and then under the ball while it is moving along rather than across the target line. On-line clubhead path allows ball to fly out readily on a forward-flying cushion of sand.

Throwing club downward at least four inches behind the ball provides safe margin against catching ball first, assuring a sufficiently deep cut to clear under bottom of ball.

PRACTICE DRILLS AND CHECKPOINTS FOR SAND PLAY

Draw two parallel lines about one foot apart in the sand. Start at one end of the lines and practice-swing your way to the other. Try to make your sand divot extend all the way from one line to the other.

Place the head of a sand rake about 15 inches behind your ball. Practice taking the club back and up with a severe, early wrist-cocking until your clubhead easily clears the top of the rake.

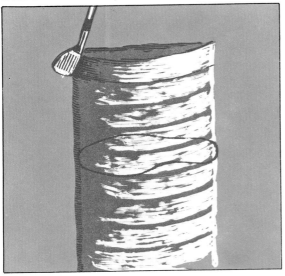

Practice hitting shots with only your right hand on the club. Strive for a long, thin cut of sand.

Check the position of your clubface about midway into your follow-through, when the clubhead is about hip high. The face should be looking more or less skyward and with the club itself extended toward the target. If it faces to your left, you've probably closed the face prior to its cutting under the ball.

SWING AROUND YOUR SUSPENSION POINT

BY PAUL RUNYAN
August, 1971

What is the biggest challenge for the learning golfer? Developing a sound grip? Correct posture and alignment at address? Proper initiation of the backswing and downswing?

All are important, certainly, but they are only parts of the bigger challenge, which is simply to make square contact with the ball.

Let's be honest: there are literally dozens of things that each of us could work on which, if mastered, would probably improve our swings and our chances of making solid contact. But who can possibly perfect all of the parts? There are too many variables. Consider this:

Imagine that the top of your left shoulder is the center of a circle. An imaginary line from this shoulder tip to the base of the ball forms the radius of the circle. Let's say that at address this radius measures approximately 60 inches.

Now, let's assume that all of the many variables that go into hitting a golf ball are functioning correctly. You stand the proper distance from the ball, which is positioned correctly in relation to your stance. Your grip is good. Your bend from the waist is just right. Your knees are flexed precisely the right amount. Your shoulders turn on the perfect plane. During your downswing your left arm straightens the correct amount. Your knees bend and move just as they should . . . and so on.

If all these things—and a dozen or two others—function properly, you will hit the ball squarely. But what if one of them goes out of kilter? What if this 60-inch radius has become 61 inches by impact? All things being equal, such lengthening would cause the club-

Paul Runyan is a former PGA champion, noted teacher and member of the Golf Digest Professional Teaching Panel.

head to reach the earth in back of the ball. How far back? Simple geometry tells us a foot or more!

The point I'm trying to make is that we must admit that we cannot hope to perfect all of the variables, no matter how hard we practice. Instead, we must find one variable which, if perfected, will automatically cause solid contact reasonably often.

During 43 years of teaching golf, I have found one variable which, if perfected, produces such a result. This variable concerns what I call the "suspension point" of the swing; the point at the nape of the neck, a spot midway between the shoulders where the top of the spine protrudes and becomes part of the neck.

I believe that most golfers, by keeping this suspension point as nearly immobile as possible while still swinging rhythmically, will greatly increase their ability to contact the ball solidly reasonably

often. It's the best—and simplest—way that I know to develop consistent shotmaking.

I suggest you think of your suspension point as being the axis or hub of your swing. Think of it as being the point around which you turn your shoulders. Even your head may turn, with your shoulders, around this point, so long as the point itself does not shift radically.

It is most important that your suspension point not raise or lower during your swing. We have seen that any increase or decrease in the distance from the left shoulder to the ball can, theoretically, greatly disrupt your chance for solid impact.

A simple way to detect any movement of your suspension point is to have a friend stand behind you, with a club in hand, resting the grip end on your suspension point as you swing.

Once you learn to swing around

HOLD SUSPENSION POINT LEVEL

POINT LIFTED

POINT IN NORMAL POSITION

POINT LOWERED

Your head may rotate with your shoulders around your suspension point to add rhythm to your swing, but the point itself should never raise or lower. Altering its position upwards or downwards tends to raise or lower the clubhead so that it fails to swing solidly into the back of the ball.

TOPPED SHOT

BALL NOSEDIVES, DRIBBLES ALONG GROUND

SOLID SHOT

BALL FLIES MAXIMUM DISTANCE

FAT SHOT

GROUND SLOWS CLUBHEAD, REDUCES DISTANCE

your suspension point, moving it as little as possible, I suggest you check one point in your address position. See that your left arm is extended, with your hands sufficiently high, so that there is very little, if any, bending or wrinkling at the top of your wrist.

Any bending, or "break," formed between your arm and clubshaft at address will tend to have straightened out by impact, as a result of centrifugal force pulling the clubhead outward, away from your body, during the downswing. By extending your left arm at address, you minimize the amount you further extend during the swing. You will greatly increase your chance for solid contact.

The concept of the suspension point as your swing axis also helps explain the varying types of shots you hit. For example, if your clubhead contacts the ground behind the ball, you will hit a "fat" shot, a "sclaff." If your clubhead reaches the ground at the same time the clubface reaches the ball, you have what I call a "lob" shot. All things being equal, and given a good lie, this is the ideal shot. The club does not cut into the turf, but rather sweeps the ball away at the correct trajectory relative to the clubface loft.

Not all of us are so skilled, however. Therefore, to be sure to avoid sclaffing (hitting "fat" shots) we may have to plan to hit what I call "pinch" shots. On such shots the clubface reaches impact just before it contacts the ground, just before it reaches the bottom of its arc. Thus, the pinch shot, since it involves taking turf in front of the ball, allows us to avoid hitting behind the ball. The lob shot is more preferable to the fat shot, especially with irons, which tend to cut into the turf more frequently than do the woods.

I suggest you try varying your shots, between lob and pinch, by the positioning of your suspension point at address. Given a constant ball position, the farther to the left —toward the target—a right-hand golfer positions his suspension point, the more he tends to pinch the shot. The more he positions his suspension point to his right, the closer he comes to being able to hit the lob shot. But if he positions his suspension point too far right, he risks hitting the ball "fat."

In determining the degree you should try to pinch your shots, several factors must be considered.

First, the more you pinch a shot, the lower it will fly.

Second, you can afford to apply more pinch with the more-lofted short irons than with the less-lofted long irons and fairway woods.

Third, every golfer must find his own proper positioning of his suspension point. It will vary with one's ability.

I suggest that you conduct an experiment to establish your ideal suspension point positioning for various shots. First, go to the practice range and take out your most-lofted club. Hit several shots with varying degrees of pinch. Find the greatest amount of pinch you can produce with this club and still achieve sufficient elevation on the shot.

Note where your suspension point is positioned in relation to the ball on these shots. Is it even with the center of the ball or is it a half-inch or one inch in front of or behind the ball? Once you've established this relationship, "memorize" it. Then repeat the process with the next less-lofted club, and the next, and so on through the bag.

You will soon see a pattern emerge. As you progress to less-lofted clubs, your suspension point will necessarily move to your right in relation to the ball. You'll find yourself needing more lob and less pinch in order to hit shots sufficiently high into the air.

In the end, you will have established a reliable position for your suspension point on any normal shot with any club in the bag. Thereafter, merely extend your left arm at address and swing around your suspension point.■

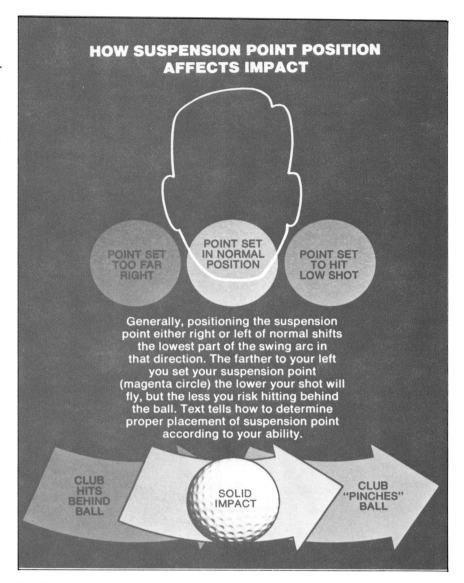

HOW SUSPENSION POINT POSITION AFFECTS IMPACT

POINT SET TOO FAR RIGHT

POINT SET IN NORMAL POSITION

POINT SET TO HIT LOW SHOT

Generally, positioning the suspension point either right or left of normal shifts the lowest part of the swing arc in that direction. The farther to your left you set your suspension point (magenta circle) the lower your shot will fly, but the less you risk hitting behind the ball. Text tells how to determine proper placement of suspension point according to your ability.

CLUB HITS BEHIND BALL

SOLID IMPACT

CLUB "PINCHES" BALL

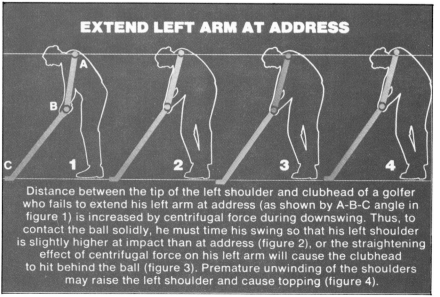

EXTEND LEFT ARM AT ADDRESS

Distance between the tip of the left shoulder and clubhead of a golfer who fails to extend his left arm at address (as shown by A-B-C angle in figure 1) is increased by centrifugal force during downswing. Thus, to contact the ball solidly, he must time his swing so that his left shoulder is slightly higher at impact than at address (figure 2), or the straightening effect of centrifugal force on his left arm will cause the clubhead to hit behind the ball (figure 3). Premature unwinding of the shoulders may raise the left shoulder and cause topping (figure 4).

PRACTICAL GOLF

BY JOHN JACOBS
February, 1972

FIRST, UNDERSTAND WHAT YOU ARE TRYING TO DO

The only purpose of the golf swing is to move the club through the ball square to the target at maximum speed. How this is done is of no significance at all, so long as the method employed enables it to be done repetitively.

That is my number one credo. It is the basis on which I teach golf. It may sound elementary, but I am certain that the point it makes has been missed by most golfers. Ninety-five per cent of the people who come to me for lessons don't really know what they are trying to do when they swing a golf club.

Slicing

Usually, golfers who are slicing shots to the right instinctively begin aiming their clubface to the left. This forces them to play the ball farther forward than normal and to turn their shoulders into an open position, parallel to the direction the club is looking. With the ball forward and the shoulders open, their hands are forced into a "slice" grip. With the misaligned shoulders forcing the clubhead to cut across the ball from outside to inside the target line, and with the clubface still open during impact, the increased slice spin accentuates the ball's left-to-right flight pattern.

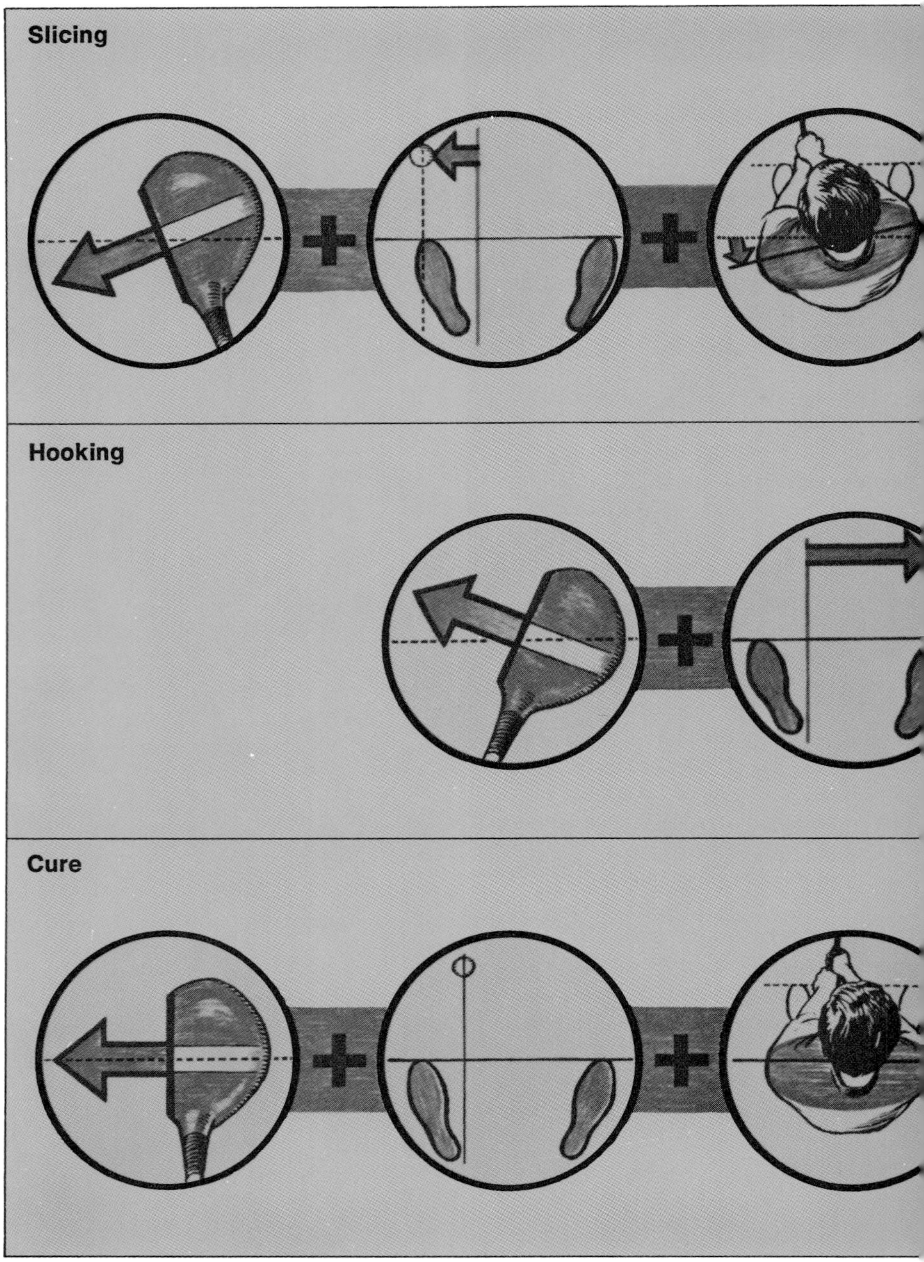

Slicing

Hooking

Cure

This article was excerpted from the book *Practical Golf* by John Jacobs with Ken Bowden. Jacobs is Europe's leading golf instructor and now a member of Golf Digest's Professional Teaching Panel. Bowden then was editorial director of the magazine.

Cure *To end hooking, slicing, pulling or pushing, the golfer must first swing in a manner that moves the clubhead along the target line during impact. Such a clubhead path is best achieved by first aiming the clubface down that line. This encourages proper ball positioning, which produces proper shoulder alignment— parallel to the target line. With the ball properly positioned and the shoulders square, the golfer tends*

Their prime concern is to get into certain "positions" during the swing. Therein, they believe, lies the elusive "secret" of golf. They have either never known or have long forgotten that the only reason such positions are necessary is *to get the club to swing correctly through the ball.*

Do one thing right in the golf swing and it will lead to another right. Do one thing wrong and it will produce another wrong. In this sense, golf is a *reaction* game. Never forget that fact.

The thing we all react to most is the face of the club. You must realize—and never forget—that incorrect alignment of the clubface at impact on one shot affects the entire golf swing on the next shot. Any cure is not to be found in swing "positions." It lies in *developing a grip and swing that brings the clubface square to your swing line at impact.* Do this and all your reactions will be correct.

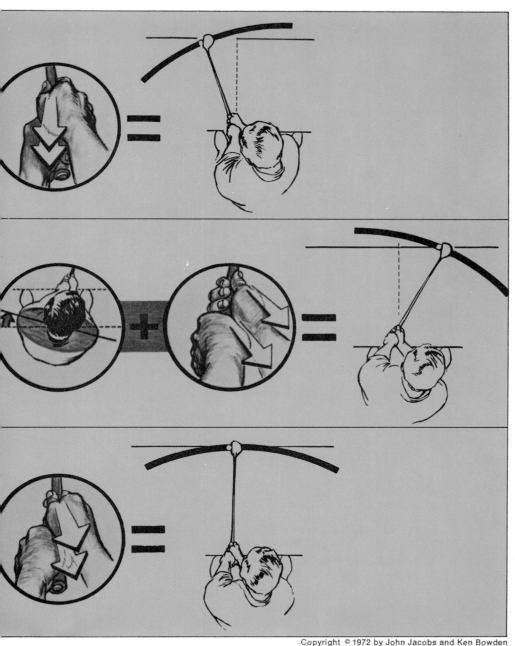

Hooking
Golfers who are hooking shots from right to left instinctively begin aiming their clubface to the right. Aiming to the right forces the ball farther back in the stance which, in turn, closes the shoulder alignment. Playing the ball back with the shoulders closed forces the hands into a "hook" grip that will roll the clubface closed to the swing line before or during impact. With the clubface looking left of swing line, and the clubhead moving parallel to the shoulder line—from inside to outside the target line— the ball takes on even more hook spin than previously. The shot's right-to-left pattern is accentuated.

position his hands properly on the club so that he can return the clubface square to his swing line— and thus his target line—during impact. All ingredients are thus present for a straight shot.

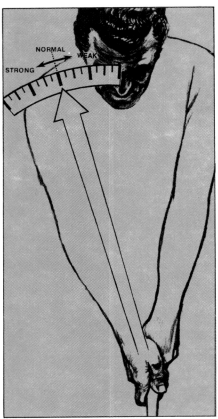

The correct grip for you is the one that delivers your clubface square to your direction of swing during impact. Start with your "Vs" pointing to "Normal"—midway between your nose and your right shoulder. If the flight of your shots tells you that you are delivering the clubface to the ball looking to the right of your swing line, move both your hands gradually towards your shoulder. If your shots tell you that the clubface is arriving at the ball looking left of your swing path, move both hand's "Vs" gradually toward your nose. Your grip is right for you when your shots fly on a straight line, even though you may be to the left or right of target.

YOUR GRIP DETERMINES HOW YOU PLAY

If clubface alignment at impact is golf's critical "geometrical" factor, then how the golfer holds his club — and thus controls this alignment — is the supreme factor in determining the success or failure of his shots.

Much as many golfers would like to be able to ignore this fact, it is inescapable. The old saw, that you never see a good golfer with a bad grip or a bad golfer with a good grip, is pretty true. Whether you are a beginner or a seasoned player seeking improvement, finding a grip that *naturally returns the clubface square to your swing line* is your absolute first priority, your inescapable starting point. If you are an established golfer, but feel you have never reached your full potential at the game, it is a 5-to-1 chance that your grip is at the root of your problems.

First, I want you to forget anything you have read or heard that suggests that there is one, and only one, way to hold a golf club. Find the grip that enables *you* — not Arnold Palmer or Jack Nicklaus or Tony Jacklin — *to face your club in the direction you are swinging it during impact, while swinging at speed.*

SET UP SO YOU CAN SWING THE CLUB ON TARGET

Let's assume that you're now holding the club in such a way that at impact it faces, more often than not, the same direction it is traveling. The ball flies fairly straight, but its straight-line flight is still to the left or right of target. What are you going to do to get the ball to finish on target? You are going to shift yourself around at address, because *instinctively* you know that this will help you to swing the club along the target line at impact.

"Setup" is a phrase for a golfer's alignment, including his stance and posture at address. Your grip determines where your clubface looks during impact, but your set-up position determines in which direction you'll swing the club through the ball.

Setting up correctly involves a careful ritual.

1. You grip the club correctly for *you,* as we have already spelled out.

2. Maintaining that correct grip, you aim the club correctly by placing it behind the ball so *that its bottom edge is exactly at right angles to your target.*

3. Having gripped and aimed the club correctly, you arrange your body and limbs in the position that most easily and naturally allows you to *swing along the line established by the aim of the clubface.* This means simply that you stand with your shoulders, chest, hips, knees and feet at right angles — or "square" — to the clubface.

It is vital to set the clubhead behind the ball first, with its face precisely at right angles to your desired line of flight. Most people start out wrongly here. Looking along the line of the shot, they stick their feet in what they believe to be the right position, and *then* they dump the clubhead down behind the ball. It could be pointing anywhere, and generally is.

It is essential to get the clubhead behind the ball first, not only so you can aim yourself relative to it, but to ensure that the ball is in the correct position relative to your feet. Positioning the feet first causes bad ball positioning because the club, when finally grounded, can be either too far to your left (forward) or right (rearward). If the ball is too far forward in your stance, your shoulders are dragged round to aim left of target, causing that old outside-to-inside clubhead path through impact. If the ball and club are too far right, the shoulders will tend to align to the right of target, promoting an exaggerated in-to-out swing.

The way to constantly check your setup is to remember that the first part of the ball's flight — its direction before sidespin takes effect—indicates the direction in which you were swinging the club at impact.

The first priority of proper alignment is that your *shoulders* be parallel to the target line when the clubhead is placed squarely behind the ball. Many good golfers play from open or closed positions of the feet, but almost all good players address the ball for normal shots with their shoulders and upper torso pretty much parallel to the target line.

Because the right hand is lower than the left on the club, the right shoulder should set up lower than the left. This produces a slight tilt of the upper body to the right, which in turn places your head *behind* (right of) the ball. (And here it must *remain* until after impact, even though it may turn on its own axis a little during the swing.) Unless you are so tilted, it will be difficult to swing the club straight through on target. Indeed, setting the right side too high at address is one of the game's most common faults.

"TIMING"

Timing is a common word in the lexicon of golf. It relates to coordinating all the movements that comprise the swing. But let's be more specific.

We have seen that the swing is, in fact, a combination of two distinct motive forces and patterns of physical movement. One force is body action, and by "body" I mean the whole of the upper torso, plus the hips, legs and feet. This unit generates power by coiling and uncoiling.

The other unit of motive force is what most people simply call "hand action," but which I prefer to call arm, wrist and hand action. Working as a swinging unit, the arms, wrists and hands supply some power to the shot, although their main function is to transmit to the clubhead the much greater power generated by the winding and unwinding of the body.

If you can grasp this simple concept of the golf swing, you should have no difficulty in understanding what timing is all about. In fact, probably without my spelling it out, you will have suspected that a perfectly coordinated or timed golf swing is one in which the coiling and uncoiling action of the body coordinates with the swinging action of the arm-wrist-hand unit— *to deliver the clubhead squarely to the ball with maximum speed at the moment of impact.*

Once you understand how the body pivot and the arm-and-hand swing interrelate, it is easy to diagnose and correct poor swing coordination for yourself. The way your shots fly tells you whether the two are in balance or not.

Let's assume that your playing methods are basically sound. You use a grip that normally returns the clubface correctly. You aim the clubface and yourself properly. There is nothing seriously wrong with the shape of your swing. You should, therefore, hit straight and solid shots. But you are not. You are slicing a lot of shots, and topping or thinning others.

When this happens the fault is almost always poor coordination. If you are slicing or topping shots, simply slow down your lower-body unwind and increase the use of the clubhead by speeding up your arm swing. Hit *earlier* with the clubhead and *later* with the body, until the flight of the ball tells you that you have struck a balance. Think predominantly of swinging the clubhead down and through the ball with your arms *before your shoulders unwind.*

If you have other problems, if you are hooking the ball or hitting

Picturing a golfer standing on one track of a railroad to hit a ball down the other track is one of the most popular teaching analogies. It is used so often because it so perfectly conveys the ideal of aligning one's body parallel to the target line. Such a setup encourages swinging the clubhead through the ball along—rather than across—the target line. Because the right hand rests lower than the left on the clubshaft, the right shoulder must similarly set "under" the left.

"Timing"

1. Body too far ahead leaves clubface behind hands and thus open to swing-path; swing-path out-to-in across target line; club approaches ball too steeply. Results: whiffing, slicing, topping.

2. Body "blocking" hands and arms, causing wrists to roll, closing clubface; swing-path in-to-out across target line; club approaches ball too shallowly. Results: hooking, sclaffing, smothering.

3. With body clearing path for arms to swing clubhead along target line, hands deliver clubface square to swing-path and target line; club approaches ball at correct level to make solid contact. Result: straight, powerful shots.

shots fat, you need the opposite treatment. Your coordinative problem is simply that your arm and hand swing is *ahead* of your body unwind.

Again the cure is simple. Just speed up your leg and hip action relative to the movement of your arm-wrist-hand unit.

WHATEVER YOUR METHOD, YOUR ARMS MUST SWING

The fundamental action in the golf swing is without a shadow of doubt the swinging of the arms. If you are to play well, you must swing them freely. "I do," you say.

I would suggest, sir and madam, if your handicap is between 36 and 12, that you do *not*. You may *think* you make a free arm swing, but my experience tells me that somewhere in your swing, if you have not yet progressed to the limit of your natural golfing ability (which is far higher than most players will believe), something is interfering with the free, fast flailing which should and could be your arm action.

The arm action in golf has had surprisingly little attention. Millions of words have been written about hands, shoulders, hips, feet, but hardly a thought seems to have been given to the arms as such.

I think this is chiefly because the arms in golf are confused with the hands. Indeed, in much teaching, "hands" is used as a synonym for "arms." "Swing the club (or the clubhead) with the hands" is an adage almost as old as the game itself, and still sums up probably the most widely accredited "method" today. Yet, if you think about it, you soon realize that the hands themselves *cannot* swing the club. All they can do is to hold on while the arms swing it.

It seems to me that how the hands work is determined not by any involuntary or independent action of these extremities themselves, but by arm movement.

The reason why the arms must swing freely is quite simple. When they do we are able to apply the clubhead to the ball at our maximum speed. When they do not, we are generally forced to apply *ourselves* to the ball; the flail of the arms is replaced by a heave of the shoulders.

How does one acquire a good arm swing? The simple exercise that I have found helps more than any other to promote the feel of a good arm swing is to hit balls with your *feet absolutely together*. In this position it is virtually impossible to make a shot other than with a free swinging of the arms, hands and clubhead, because any excessive use of the body leads to complete loss of balance.

Two of the most common faults in golf prevent the arms from really swinging. One is prematurely turning, or spinning the shoulders into the shot on too horizontal (flat) a plane. The other fault is prematurely uncocking the wrists—the release of power long before the clubhead is in position to strike the ball squarely. This jerky attempt to force clubhead to ball with the hands from the top of the swing often results from the misdirected effort to increase clubhead speed with "hand action" instead of a full, free swinging of the arms.

In fact, both premature application of the shoulders and upper body and too early release of the wrists result, nine times out of 10, from insufficient or late arm swing. Any player suffering from lack of power or poor balance should have one simple thought at the top of his backswing: to start down with his arms, to make *his arms swing the clubhead down and through the ball.*

It is, of course, a fact that the good player's downswing is started and led by the legs and hips (and this has become a fundamental of teaching). But, believe me, it is no good for the player who lacks a free arm swing to think of starting his downswing with his hips. Doing so will simply lead to an early unwinding — a heaving — of his shoulders.

To my way of thinking, almost every movement in the golf swing is subject to a full, free arm-swing, but the fact has rarely been emphasized for the simple reason that the good players who write books on golf usually make the erroneous assumption that, like themselves, their readers have both strong hands and free-swinging arms.■

This happens in *every* good swing
Stand facing any good golfer and watch the space between his hands and right shoulder during the downswing. You will see that it quickly widens. Then watch any golfing friend who slices the ball repeatedly. The space between his hands and right shoulder will not widen as fast because he swings his shoulders instead of his arms. The speed at which all good golfers widen this angle is proof positive that, although the lower body initiates the downswing, leg and hip action must always be married to a fast, free arm-swing.

SWING THE HANDLE— NOT THE CLUBHEAD

BY EDDIE MERRINS
February and April, 1973

I am going to give you what may be the single, most important piece of golf instruction you will ever receive in your life. This is the key to my method, the one positive thought that will allow you to make a mechanically perfect golf swing. That thought is simply to:

SWING THE HANDLE OF THE CLUB WITH YOUR FOREARMS

Please ponder that sentence awhile. It represents the one overriding thought you should have on every normal golf shot you make.

I do not believe it is possible to make a perfect golf swing every time. We are all human, and the human factor is bound to prevent us on occasion from producing machine-like perfection. However, I do believe that swinging your end of the club with your forearms represents the *mechanical means* for producing a perfect swing. The closer you can come to executing this one, simple thought, the closer you will come to enjoying perfection in your golf game.

You see, your hands and your wrists directly influence the head end of your club for good or for bad—usually the latter. Your arms, and only your arms, directly affect the top portion of your club. Let's face it, you can turn your body back and forth all day, but you will not move the golf club until your arms also begin to swing. Or you can flip the club back and forth with your hands and wrists until the end of time, but primarily this manipulation will move only the clubhead.

The point is simply that you can swing the handle of your club only by swinging your forearms. And only by swinging the handle end

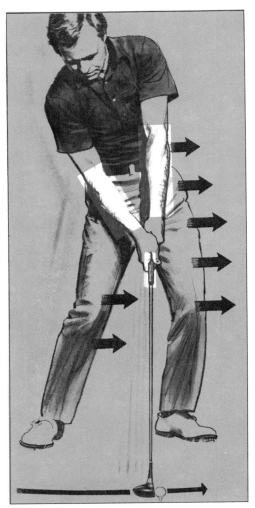

Swing this way . . .

. . . Not this way
In the ideal golf swing, the player's legs, body, arms and entire club all accelerate forward through impact. This forward movement takes place only if the golfer accelerates the grip end—the handle—of the club. And only the arms, swinging freely, can accelerate the handle. Whenever the player throws the clubhead forward with his hands and wrists, the top end of the clubshaft reverses direction, thus slowing down the forward movement of the body, legs and arms. This slowing down can reduce shot length but, more important, it causes mis-alignment of the clubface and distortion of the clubhead arc. Mis-hit shots normally result. The arms should swing the handle, not the hands and wrists the clubhead.

Excerpted from the book *Swing the Handle— Not the Clubhead* by Eddie Merrins with Dick Aultman, this article is a reflection of the method Merrins has used to gain his place as one of golf's outstanding teachers. He is a member of the Golf Digest Professional Teaching Panel.

with your forearms can you eliminate the bad shots that result from misdirecting the head end with your hands and wrists.

In this article I will tell you *HOW* to swing your end—the handle—of the club. Then I will explain a dozen reasons *WHY* applying this technique will make you a much better golfer.

First, I would like you to extend your arms and the clubshaft horizontally in front of you and begin swinging the club back and forth around your body. You should make more or less the same circular arc, first around to the right and then to the left, that a baseball batter would make in swinging his bat back and through.

Be sure that at all times you are swinging the grip end of the club with your forearms. There should be no flipping of the clubhead with your wrists.

You will note that as you swing the club around to the right on your backstroke, your left forearm tends to roll above your right. As you swing the grip end of the club back to the left, your right forearm gradually rolls above your left. You are swinging the club around your body in a semicircular arc with your forearms rolling over each other as they swing the grip end of the club. This is the same basic arm motion that you will be using in your golf swing.

As you simulate the baseball swing, you should note that your body wants to turn as a *result* of your arms swinging the handle of the club. This may seem like a fine point, but it does simplify the swing considerably to know that your body and shoulders turn as merely a *reaction* to your arm swing. Once you learn to swing the handle of your club with your forearms, you need no longer concern yourself with how to turn your body. It will happen *automatically.*

Once you have mastered the feeling of swinging the grip end of the club around your body in a semicircular arc with your forearms, you should make similar swings with the clubhead brushing the ground. Now you will be swinging on a plane that is somewhere between horizontal and vertical. This will put your semicircular swinging motion into

YES

NO

Proper wrist action
The only type of wrist action needed—or desired—while swinging the handle is that which lifts and lowers the club. If the grip is proper, this hinging will occur at the base of the thumbs, producing wrinkles there rather than at the back of the wrists. This wrist action gives the swing height and leverage and lowers the clubhead to the ball during the downswing. Improper wrist action—hinging the back of the wrists—misaligns the clubface, throws the clubhead off track and tends to decelerate the forward swinging of the arms.

a somewhat upward-downward-upward pattern.

As you make this swing, you should find that your wrists are starting to hinge, but only at the *base of your thumbs,* at the *top,* not at the *back,* of the wrists. This is the type of hinging and unhinging that allows you to connect the clubhead to the ball. It is the type of wrist action that gives additional length and leverage to your swing. It is not the type of wrist action that you would use to flip your clubhead backward and forward.

The best way to keep your hands from independently influencing the clubhead is to see that your arms accelerate as they swing down and through the impact area. So long as your arms accelerate—even on short chip shots and putts—you can swing the top end of your club. If your arms lag, your hands and wrists will take over and begin to flip the head end—the wrong end—of the club. You will begin to mis-hit your shots.

Following are some of the benefits you will enjoy as a result of swinging the handle:

1. You will avoid "hitting from the top." This common fault occurs as a direct result of accelerating the clubhead with your hands and wrists either consciously or subconsciously—early in your downswing. Among other things, you waste power prematurely, before impact. You lose distance. Accelerating the handle end of the club with your forearms makes it impossible to accelerate the clubhead prematurely with your hands and wrists.

2. You will avoid hooking. Hooking occurs when your arms quit swinging the handle end of the club. Then your hands and wrists take over and they flip the clubface into a closed position, so that it looks to the left of the target during impact. This cannot occur as long as your grip is correct and your arms swing the top part of the club.

3. You will avoid slicing and shanking. Both of these problems result from the clubface being open—turned to the right—during impact. For some reason, the golfer has failed to square his clubface to the target line by the time it reaches the ball. This failure may be due to a subconscious fear of hitting from

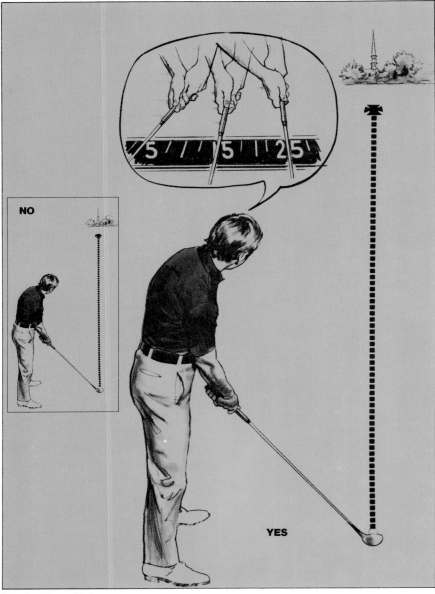

Controlling distance

On all shots—especially drives—it is vital to select a target based not only on direction, but also distance. Failure to consider distance in target selection leads directly to an uncontrolled swing and mis-hit shots. Once you have selected your target you should relate the length of the forthcoming shot to the speed at which you will swing your arms through impact. Imagine a speedometer with a top speed of, say, 25 miles per hour. On full-out shots you would try to accelerate your arms up to that speed. On mini-shots, such as chips, you might only accelerate up to, say, three miles per hour.

the top and hooking. Whatever the motivation, swinging the handle with the forearms in a semicircular arc automatically begins to turn your clubface toward a square position early in your downswing, just as swinging the handle of a tennis racquet on the forward stroke squares the string portion to the ball.

4. You will reduce fat and topped shots. Overactive hands and wrists tend to flip your clubhead downward so that it reaches the lowest point of its arc *behind* the ball. It either contacts the ground (fat or scuffed shot) or continues on—now moving upward from its low point—to catch the ball on the upswing (topped shot). Swinging the handle with your forearms eliminates this overactive use of your hands and wrists.

5. You will add distance through better coordination. By accelerating the top of the club with your forearms, you automatically accelerate the forward movement of your hands and the clubhead. Everything moves in the same direction— forward. As we have seen, trying to accelerate the clubhead forward with your hands and wrists encourages the top of the club to lag. No longer is everything moving forward in a coordinated effort.

6. You will add distance through employing your stronger side. Most right-handed golfers have a dominant right side. Using this strength incorrectly can cause problems, such as hitting from the top. For this reason, much golf instruction stresses building up left-side control. Swinging the top of the clubshaft with your forearms eliminates such problems because your hands and wrists remain relatively passive—your right hand isn't allowed to break down your left wrist, as occurs when hitting from the top. Instead, you are free to use the strength of your right side to generate maximum arm speed through the impact area.

7. You will add distance by swinging THROUGH, rather than TO, the ball. Most golfers subconsciously overestimate the weight of the ball and its resistance to the clubhead. They swing *TO* the ball instead of *THROUGH* it. This subconscious reaction causes some lessening of clubhead speed and

Controlling direction

The initial direction of a golf shot as it leaves the clubface (left) is determined solely by the path of the clubhead at impact. Determine this path by the direction in which you extend the handle of the club with your right arm as it moves through the hitting area. Think of the handle as a pointer. If you wish to start a shot to the right of target, you would extend the pointer in that direction with your right arm through impact. The principle is similar to that used in tossing a ball in an underhand-sidearm fashion. The ball begins its flight in the direction you extend your throwing arm.

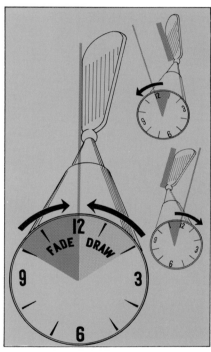

Controlling shape

The direction a shot curves depends on where the clubface is looking during impact. Control the facing of the clubface by timing the turning of the club's handle with your forearms during the downswing. Imagine the end of the handle as a clock dial. When the 12 is on top of the dial, the clubface looks down the path on which it moves. For straight shots, turn the handle so the 12 returns to the top of the dial during impact. To curve shots to the left, turn the handle so number 1 or 2 is on top during impact. Dial 10 or 11 to curve shots to the right.

loss of distance. Thinking of accelerating the arms *forward* eliminates the tendency to direct the clubhead AT the ball.

8. You will add distance by utilizing the full strength of your body, rather than just your hands and wrists.

9. You will find it easier to control the length of your approach shots. The speed at which you swing the handle of the club with your forearms directly determines the distance you will hit the shot with a given club. This means that you need to consider only one variable —the speed at which you swing your arms—when hitting less-than-full approach shots.

10. You will mis-hit fewer shots. The ideal golf swing is a simple swing, free from unnecessary frills. The simpler the swing, the easier it is to repeat. Repetition breeds consistency. Swinging the handle of the club with the forearms is a relatively simple maneuver. When you add wristiness, you add moving parts. You unnecessarily complicate your action. You run the risk of flipping the clubface out of position.

11. You will learn to use the same swing with all of your clubs. Clubs are designed so that all within a given set will feel the same when swung. But golfers usually do not swing all clubs the same way. They will use a different swing with a 2-iron than with a 9-iron. I think one reason for this is that the clubheads within a set vary in appearance. Because they look different, the golfer subconsciously directs himself to swing them differently. When you direct your attention to the *handle* of the club, instead of the *clubhead,* you eliminate this troublesome impression. Since all the grip ends look the same, you will tend to swing them all the same. Why make a dozen different swings when your set of clubs is designed to require only one?

12. You will eliminate bad shots caused by mental confusion. All golfers know how a multiplicity of thoughts while swinging can ruin shots. Such thinking confuses your subconscious so that you cannot make a "natural" swing. The Merrins Method eliminates trivia by requiring only one overriding thought while swinging. I trust by now you know what that thought is.■

GAIN MORE LEVERAGE— START DOWN SLOW

BY DICK AULTMAN
September, 1973

How do the pros hit the ball so far with so little effort? After watching a Snead, a Crampton, a Littler, a Boros or a Nicklaus fire tee shots 250-300 yards with an almost lazy swinging motion it is frustrating for a golfer with comparable physical assets to wind up, slash with every available muscle and watch in disgust as the ball bananas 180 yards into the right-hand rough .

Something is wrong here, obviously. The harder we swing, the faster our tee shots fall.

Most golfers are cursed with what Chicago professional Paul Bertholy calls the "hit impulse." This impulse is strongest on shots where the premium is on length— on drives, shots into a strong wind, shots from deep rough, on approach shots where we sense we might not be using quite enough club.

Professional players have learned to sublimate this instinctive behavior pattern. Most of us have not. The hit impulse is fiercest at the start of the downswing.

The answer? Simply start your downswing slowly. Try to start down slower than you went back, with your hands and arms passive.

Long drivers are those who best restrain their hit impulse at the start of the downswing. As early as 1903, Harold Hilton, later a U.S. Amateur champion, wrote of S. Mure Ferguson, one of the long hitters of the day:

"On the upward swing Mr. Ferguson always appears to take the club up in a most leisurely and deliberate fashion, and maintains this leisurely method at the beginning of the downward swing . . . he always appears to be swinging slowly."

Later, in 1932, the immortal Bobby Jones elaborated on Hilton's observation. Jones stressed that Ferguson "maintains this leisurely method at the beginning of the downward swing. We hear 'slow back' on every side but 'slow back' is not enough. There are numbers of players who are able to restrain their impulses to this extent, but who, once back, literally pounce upon the ball with uncontrolled fury. It is the leisurely start downward which provides for a gradual increase of speed without disturbing the balance and timing of the swing."

The best modern evidence is the swing of Nicklaus. It shows up in the accompanying sequence photos carefully calibrated and measured by Vance Elkins, a New Jersey systems analyst with a background in engineering.

Jack's hands and arms actually move *slower* during the start of his downswing than during the latter portion of his backswing. Since Nicklaus has one of the slowest backswings in the game this observation is all the more significant.

Dr. David Williams, a British scientist, reached the conclusion a few years ago that, all things being equal, the more leisurely the hands and arms start down, the greater the clubhead speed at impact. In his book, *Science of the Golf Swing,* Dr. Williams mathematically analyzed sequence photographs of Bobby Jones swinging a driver.

To appreciate the significance of Dr. Williams' findings, you must understand the principle of leverage. Grasp a golf club about six inches from the clubhead with your thumb and forefinger and hold it in front of you horizontally. The clubhead's weight seems almost insignificant. Now, slide your thumb and forefinger to the grip end of the shaft and try to hold the club. Your thumb and forefinger no longer can hold the shaft horizontal.

You have increased the length of the lever, the distance between your fingers and the clubhead. Though the clubhead's actual weight remains the same, its effective weight has increased tremendously.

In your golf swing the length of the lever is the distance between your clubhead and the axis of your swing, a point midway between your shoulders. At the top of your backswing this lever is short and easy to control. Williams found that Jones, at that point, applied only two pounds of force, hardly more than the weight of the club.

Thereafter, Williams broke Jones' downswing into two stages. The first, which took about two-thirds of the elapsed time of his entire downswing, brought Jones' left arm into a near-horizontal position. During that stage Jones' wrists remained fully cocked as his hands, arms, shoulders and club moved as a unit. The length of his lever— the distance between the clubhead and the point midway between his shoulders—was constant.

From that point through impact— Stage Two—his wrists began to unhinge, but only as a natural reaction to the centrifugal force of the moving clubhead. The length of the lever increased and rapidly built up the effective weight of the clubhead to 107 pounds just before impact. The outward-pulling centrifugal force became so great near impact that Jones was merely hanging on to the club to control the force of its movement.

At no point did Jones apply more than one pound of right-angle pressure to the clubshaft, the type of pressure he'd need to accelerate the clubhead solely with his hands and wrists. At no point did he throw the club with his right hand or "hit from the top." During the first three-fourths of Stage One, the pressure Jones applied in *pulling along*—not throwing—the clubshaft increased from two pounds to only six pounds. In other words, he started down leisurely.

"The general problem in starting down too quickly," says touring professional Frank Beard, "is that you tend to start with the hands. They are the only part of your body connected to the club—they're free agents. It's easy to move them first and much easier to move them fast than slow. We're violent people anyway and when we see that little ball sitting there we just want to get at it."

Beard draws a parallel between the golf swing and the way a topnotch athlete runs the mile.

"A good miler always paces himself," Beard points out, "so that

78

59°
Wrist
Cock

103°
Wrist
Cock

Bandleader Lawrence Welk, an avid middle-handicapper, over-controls the club with too much hand-arm force early in the downswing, uncocking his wrists too quickly. From this point to impact he pulls with an average of 50 pounds force and drives the ball about 200 yards. Had he reached Jack Nicklaus' late-hit position (below) and then applied the same 50-pound force, he would have driven 239 yards.

Jack Nicklaus' minimal hand-arm force starting down (see additional photos next page) allows him to reach this ideal late-hit position. From here to impact he pulls with an average of 70 pounds of force and drives the ball 270 yards. Were he in the Welk position, to drive 270 yards he would have to apply 135 pounds of force, an impossibility.

he has a finishing kick left. He saves his biggest burst of speed for the last 200 or 300 yards.

"That's what a golfer should strive to do. Instead of starting the downswing swiftly from the top, you want to accelerate smoothly, not reaching real speed until you're coming into the hitting zone."

HOLD THE CLUB LIGHTLY

Bob Toski, a member of *Golf Digest's* Professional Teaching Panel, reasons that tightening of the hands on the club results in overcontrol. Therefore he wants his pupils to apply only light grip pressure, especially with the right hand, throughout the swing. Toski realizes that the grip pressure will increase automatically as clubhead speed builds up during the downswing, but he wants to avoid suddenly grabbing the club at any point.

SLOW YOUR BACKSWING

As Jones notes, a slower backswing does not guarantee a leisurely start to the downswing. But it can help. Many players swing the club back so fast that they must grab it at the top or early in the downswing merely to maintain or regain control.

LEAD WITH THE LEGS

The technique most used by better players to avoid applying early downswing pressure with the hands is to lead the downswing action with a lateral thrusting and turning of the legs and lower body. If the shoulders do not spin concurrently, this move gradually pulls the hands and arms downward into proper striking position with the wrists remaining "frozen." Thereafter, centrifugal force demands that the wrists unhinge automatically at the proper time, so long as the golfer does not tighten them with an abrupt increase of grip pressure.

Nicklaus states, "A major fault of the average golfer is starting the downswing with his hands and arms *before* his legs and hips have begun to work. Inevitably this brings his shoulders into action too early and his clubhead is thrown forward outside the target line, producing that weak pull-slice."

SWING YOUR ARMS FREELY

A major reason golfers suffer from the hit impulse is the mistaken belief that hand and wrist action, consciously applied through the hitting area, will increase distance.

Byron Nelson, another member of *Golf Digest's* Professional Teaching Panel, put his finger on the problem when he said, "You tell a person to hit with his hands and sure enough he'll hit too soon."

Good advice is to swing the arms freely through the hitting area and merely let the wrists unhinge automatically as a result of centrifugal force. This is the main point of Eddie Merrins' recent book, *Swing The Handle—Not The Clubhead.* Merrins feels that over-attention to the clubhead causes golfers to overcontrol it with their hands and wrists. By merely swinging the grip end of the club freely with the forearms, he explains, the hands and wrists will take care of themselves.

USE MORE CLUB

One simple way to overcome the hit impulse and thus start down slower is just to use more club than normal on all shots to the green. On drives try to fly the ball 15 or 20 yards *shorter* than normal.

Chances are excellent that golfers who use these tactics will experience the same result that touring professional George Archer once did while still an amateur. He was practicing 9-iron shots and

The difference of some 70 yards between the drives of Jack Nicklaus and Lawrence Welk is determined largely by the way they start their downswings. Nicklaus exerts less pressure on the club than does Welk in the early stages and thus preserves his wrist cock until much later. This results in greater club-head speed—175 feet per second vs. 133.5 feet per second—at impact. While Nicklaus moves his left arm only five degrees between the first and fourth photos, Welk starts down faster and moves his arm 10 degrees. This difference in speed of arm movement directly affects one's ability to retain wrist cock. The faster the arms move, the more difficult it is to retain the hinging. This is dramatically demonstrated by the fact that throughout the first nine photos Nicklaus actually increases his

Dutch Harrison walked by.

"I was making a nice pattern of balls out there—all pretty close together," Archer recalled. "Dutch watched me for a while and then said, 'Hit one short of the pile.' I swung easier, but the ball landed in the middle of the pattern. 'Go on,' said Dutch, 'hit one short.' I swung still easier, and again the ball landed among the others."

Perhaps Archer's experience best illustrates the paradox mentioned in the first paragraph of this article—"How the pros hit the ball so far with so little effort."

The truth is that the portions of most pros' swings most apparent to the eye—the backswing and the start of the downswing—are being executed with little effort. The pros have learned how to avoid over-controlling the club. It is the hit impulse that requires all that effort you may feel in your swing, power-sapping effort that is robbing you of distance. Start down slower and hit it swifter! ∎

NICKLAUS-WELK SWING COMPARISON

Photo No.	Left Arm Angle		Wrist Cock Angle		Lever Arm Length		Pulling Force On Shaft		Clubhead Velocity	
	JN	LW	JN	LW	JN	LW	JN	LW	JN	LW
1	177°	121°	85°	143°	4.58	2.26	−2	1	−15.4	−4.3
2	176°	120°	89°	142°	4.45	2.31	0	2	− 6.8	3.4
3	174°	117°	91°	141°	4.38	2.35	1	3	1.1	6.0
4	172°	111°	91°	139°	4.38	2.43	2	4	5.9	12.1
5	164°	104°	97°	137°	4.15	2.52	3	5	8.8	13.8
6	150°	95°	107°	130°	3.93	2.81	5	10	14.3	27.4
7	133°	84°	114°	119°	3.48	3.28	7	20	27.5	40.4
8	118°	75°	115°	97°	3.44	4.15	10	35	32.6	62.7
9	91°	58°	118°	77°	3.32	4.85	36	30	54.9	81.8
10	64°	43°	103°	59°	3.92	5.36	50	25	97.1	77.8

LEGEND

Left Arm Angle—*The number of degrees this arm must move before reaching a position perpendicular to a line across the toes at or near impact.*
Wrist Cock Angle—*The number of degrees the left wrist must unhinge in order for left arm and clubshaft to form a continuous line.*
Lever Arm—*The distance in feet between the base of the golfer's neck and his clubhead.*
Pulling Force On Shaft—*The amount of effort in pounds being exerted by the golfer on the club in the direction its grip end is pointing. (Expressed in a minus term when effort is applied in opposite direction.)*
Clubhead Velocity—*The average clubhead speed generated in feet per second between the photo in question and the previous photo in the sequence. (Expressed in minus terms when clubhead is still moving away from the ball.)*

About the numbers

The figures presented in the analyses of the Nicklaus-Welk swings were computed for Golf Digest by Vance Elkins Jr., of Freehold, N.J., president of Sight-Line Industries, as part of his investigative efforts to apply mathematics and physics to golf equipment. The figures were derived from careful measurement of the photos and the application of appropriate formulas. While unobtainable variables such as exact ball compression and the effect of wind on the drives prohibited complete accuracy, the reader may assume that Elkins' figures are sufficiently precise to substantiate the points of this article.

wrist cock by 33 degrees while Welk decreases his by 66 degrees. Because Nicklaus gradually increases his wrist cock, the length of his effective lever arm —the distance from the back of his neck to the clubhead—gradually shortens until his wrists finally begin to uncock between photos nine and 10. Since Welk's wrists are already uncocking throughout this period, his effective lever arm is gradually increasing in length. By starting down with less pressuring of the club with his hands and arms—and driving with his legs instead—Nicklaus actually increases his leverage until near impact. Welk begins to lose leverage at the start of his downswing because like most golfers, he exerts too much pressure too early.

ONE MOVE TO BETTER GOLF

BY CARL LOHREN
WITH LARRY DENNIS
April, 1975

The purpose of a golf swing is to deliver a blow with an implement that will send a small ball flying far ahead and in the desired direction.

Sounds simple enough, doesn't it? It isn't. To strike the ball far and straight, that implement—your golf club—must be swung with enough speed, at the proper angle of descent and on the proper path. Right away you've got yourself all kinds of complications.

There is nothing natural about a golf swing. If somebody says you are a natural golfer, he means you have excellent coordination. That helps, but it still doesn't get you halfway home. Ben Hogan once said that the first time you pick up a golf club, every instinct that comes to your mind is wrong. Watch a child the first time he or she is given a golf club and told to swing at a ball. The club is picked straight up and delivered with a strong right-sided blow as if the ball were a log waiting to be split with an ax.

Overcoming this instinct to hit *at* the ball with the dominant right side has been the curse of the golfer since the game was invented. Proposed solutions have filled countless pages of golf instruction through the years. Countless dollars have been poured into the pockets of countless teaching professionals by pupils searching desperately for the way. By the time the average player has been inundated with all the theories of arm movement, leg movement, weight shift to and fro, wrist cocking and uncocking, hand action and other components of the complex golf swing, his mind is spinning so rapidly he has very

little chance of understanding what a good swing is, let alone making one.

Right now I'm going to give you one thought that will clear away the fog, one move that correctly done will give you an effective, repeating golf swing and will send you on your way to a lifetime of better golf.

Start your swing with your left shoulder. At the moment of takeaway, the very beginning of the backswing, start your left shouder *turning around your spine.* One small area of the body . . . one move. I'm not asking you to change your swing. I just want you to give it a *new start.*

Most golf instructors stress that a turn must occur, but they attach no significance to *when* it takes place.

I believe it must be the first thing that happens in your swing. The first and only action you need think about is to start turning the left shoulder around. Since this one move is going to make you a better striker of the golf ball, I'm going to dwell on it at some length.

The important thing to remember about this move and the action that follows is that the shoulders turn rather than tilt in relation to the spine. On the backswing, they revolve around your spine much as a searchlight sweeps around a lighthouse, at right angles to your spine.

That proper revolution will be accomplished if you simply think of starting to turn your left shoulder in the direction you're facing. I emphasize that I'm only talking about a *start.* The rest of the turn will follow naturally. I don't want you to think about anything except starting this move, for reasons I'll explain later.

When I discuss the left shoulder I'm not talking about a spot. I'm talking about the entire left shoulder area, the upper left side of your trunk. I've never seen a player make a good, honest shoulder movement without having the shoulder, upper arm, back and chest area move simultaneously.

When the left shoulder swings out, the right shoulder of course swings back. This movement, this swinging of the two shoulders around the spine, is what maintains

the axis for your swing. It also is a big factor in creating the windup of the back muscles which results in that all-important windup.

Here are two key thoughts that may help you to make this move correctly:

1. Think of starting to make a small U-turn with that left shoulder. Imagine starting the left shoulder turning to where the right shoulder is. It won't get there, but this has been a helpful concept to many of my pupils. Again, concern yourself only with the start and not with trying to turn the shoulder all the way.

2. Visualize your upper body being in a tube; turn your left shoulder—and with it your right—in a perfect arc within that tube, without moving your body even one degree laterally. It may help you feel as if you are turning in a *small* area rather than a larger one to start winding the muscles as soon as possible.

Make this move in a relaxed manner, with a complete absence of tension in the upper body. Any tenseness when you get ready to start the swing will result in an inability to make this move properly. But if you are properly relaxed, this initial move is your transport to success.

One of the major problems in the golf swing is that battle to keep the left side in control while the right tries to overpower it at the wrong time. Please understand that the right side certainly is vital in the golf swing. It helps provide the power that gives you distance in your shots. So the right side must come into play, but only at the proper time, with the left side still in control as it guides the swing through the area of impact with the ball and gives you the accuracy which golf demands.

Unfortunately, this proper application of right side power goes against our basic instincts. When our arms and hands get as far back as they can go and we subconsciously are faced with the prospect of hitting that ball sitting motionless down there, our stronger right side is commanded to spring into action.

That's our ruination. Almost every missed shot is the result of the right side overpowering the

This article was excerpted from the book *One Move to Better Golf* by Carl Lohren with Larry Dennis. Lohren is head professional at North Shore C.C., Glen Cove, L.I., N.Y.

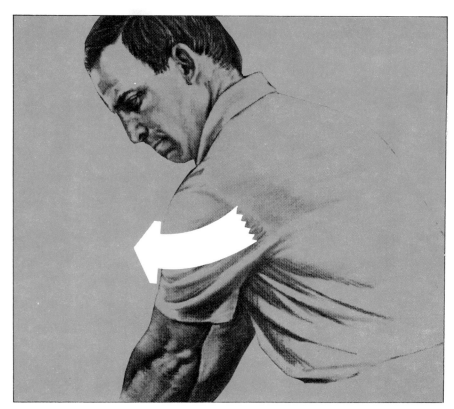

Carl Lohren demonstrates the one move, the turning of the left shoulder around the spinal axis at the start of the backswing. This he feels is the key to a consistent, powerful swing.

left at the beginning of the downswing or any time prior to impact. The topped shot, the "fat" shot in which you strike the ground before the ball, the pull or hook to the left, the slice from left to right —the overly active right side is the culprit in almost every case.

But when the left side does not yield control, when you are able to return clubface to ball with the left in command until it is time for the right to act, when you have found a way to subdue those right-side instincts at that critical moment when the backswing changes into the forward swing, you can produce a swing that delivers more powerful, accurate shots than you ever thought possible.

The one move I've given you accomplishes this, because it establishes four fundamentals which have been incorporated into all the great golf swings in history. These four fundamentals are interrelated; one does not function as effectively without the others. Together they give you the correct golf swing we're after. One of the features of this swing is that the forward swing

will react to the backswing, almost like a reflex.

The first of these fundamentals is to maintain your vertical axis on your backswing. The axis, is in effect, your spine. It must remain fixed as your shoulders turn around it on the backswing.

Maintaining this backswing axis does two things:
● It helps build up and retain power by keeping you from swaying during the backswing.
● By keeping your swing in one place, it helps you return the clubface at impact square to or facing the target.

The second fundamental is to keep the radius of your left arm swing the same from the beginning of the swing through impact. This radius is the span from the left shoulder to the left hand. Maintaining it does three things:
● It returns the clubhead to the spot behind the ball from which it started, neither higher nor lower.
● It insures maximum width of the arc of your swing.
● It contributes to the buildup of clubhead speed and power.

The third fundamental in a good

swing is to stay within the boundaries of your swing plane. The swing plane is the line your club follows as you swing up and down. You establish this plane at address. It can be pictured as an imaginary line drawn from the toe of the club up over your shoulders. Envision this plane as a flat surface—a pane of glass, for example—leaning against that imaginary line and placed along the line of your shoulders. Your swing can fall below that line but should never rise above it and break the imaginary pane of glass anytime in the backswing after the club has begun to swing inside the intended line of flight.

Even though the plane in and of itself does not do anything, it is the easiest way to visualize this direction of path on which the club is swung.

Moving the left shoulder first starts the swing in the correct plane. It prevents the body or arms from throwing your swing outside that plane. Maintaining this correct backswing plane keeps your swing in the right direction.

The fourth fundamental is to begin winding your upper body early so that it can wind up fully. This induces as a reflex the correct forward swing and contributes most of the power in your swing. An early windup does three things:
● It insures that you will stretch the muscles in the upper left side of your body.
● It removes the slack from your swing, creating a force against the lower body so intense that your instinct is to relieve that force by moving into the forward swing with your left side leading, not the right.
● It keeps the right side from taking over when it might otherwise want to at the beginning of that forward swing.

The creation of windup and the subsequent reaction to it is vital in producing a sound swing. But this windup can be effective only if it is accompanied by the other three fundamentals—maintaining your axis on the backswing, keeping your swing radius the same from start to impact and swinging your club on the proper plane. Without these fundamentals, the benefits of a good windup would be dissipated.■

GREAT PLAYERS AND THEIR SECRETS

In addition to methodologies like the foregoing, *Golf Digest* always has presented other, complementing types of instruction like shorter specialty treatments that can contain the thought that "clicks" for the reader (our one-page Instant Lessons, featuring a single tip and drawing that work together as a bright image, rank high in every reader survey).

We often have gone to the great players of the era to get their key thoughts. They might not be teachers or mass communicators, and their concepts might need translating and visualizing, but their sensitivity and dedication result in important insights. Often they go on to illustrious teaching careers — witness Bob Toski. In a sense, they are the proving ground for the golf swing.

At a meeting of our Professional Teaching Panel and Advisory Staff, Jim Flick, a member of the former, asked Samuel Jackson Snead, a member of the latter, what he thought about under tournament pressure. Since Sam has withstood tournament pressure better than any mortal ever, everyone in attendance sat up a little straighter and turned toward the man who has won a record 84 events.

"I try to keep my grip pressure constant, from the first hole to the last," Snead said. Flick loved the line, and has been using it to help teach his pupils ever since.

The leading player of his time comes to enjoy a special status in theorizing about the game, particularly if he is articulate and studious. Bobby Jones played such a statesmanlike role in his day and Jack Nicklaus is playing it today. Nicklaus regularly writes exclusive instruction for *Golf Digest,* in collaboration with contributing editor Ken Bowden and contributing artist Jim McQueen, and it is a much-quoted feature on the tour and among weekend golfers.

Nicklaus does not pretend to tell everyone how to play. He explicitly states that he is saying how *he* plays, and he invites you to try his way and see if it works for *you.* Obviously, he feels he has something to offer the average golfer, but he also knows he is far from average himself and not in daily teaching contact with 15-handicappers.

The star tour players, whose thinking and swings are brought out in this section, can serve as instructive models for the attentive weekender. By closely observing the swing of a tour player whose physique and temperament are similar to yours, you can improve your own game.

That's why *Golf Digest* runs swing photo sequences of the top players, often asking leading teachers to analyze them and relate them to club golfers.

In this section we sample the secrets of great players from Hogan, Snead and Nelson to Nicklaus, Player and Miller. We have made the selections trying to include as many leading players as possible and also to cover a balance of content. There are helpful tips on driving, long-iron play, rhythm and tempo, sound practice, putting and scrambling, to name some of the subjects.

The ultimate test of golf instruction always is whether it works on the course, under fire. The players on the following pages have made more low numbers than anyone else in history.

PUT IMAGI-NATION IN YOUR GOLF GAME

BY HORTON SMITH
August, 1961

Today's professional tour features more players with solid golf swings than ever before. Yet, as in the past, only a small nucleus wins most of the top prizes. With so many good players competing, why don't more of them win the big money?

I think the answer to this puzzling question lies partly in that most of the leading pros possess an inner ability to imagine or visualize the possibilities of a shot situation to a greater degree than do most of the also-rans.

The touring pro's ability to imagine or visualize a shot beforehand cannot be observed by the gallery, but it most certainly is an important part of his golf skill. And it is a phase of golf that anyone—pro or amateur—can develop.

The shot from the first tee in the Masters tournament at the Augusta National Golf Club offers a good example of how imagination plays a part in my golf game.

On this hole a large sand trap guards the right side of the fairway about 225 yards out. Years ago this hazard was no problem because I could carry it with a normal drive under normal wind conditions. But today my shorter driving forces me to play to the left of the bunker.

To help myself avoid the sand, in my mind I block out the right third of the fairway, including the trap. Thus I imagine the entire target area as being only two-thirds of the actual fairway.

My imaginary "fairway" is more narrow than the real one, but it is still wide enough to hold a fairly straight tee shot. And I know that if I keep the ball in this area, I'll have no problems on my second shot.

Imagination in golf originates with your eyes. You see the ball and the place where you want the shot to

Horton Smith, who died in 1963, won the Masters in 1934 and 1936 and later was recognized as one of the game's leading teachers.

finish. Next you make a mental note of the many variables that go into shot planning, such as the lie of the ball in the grass and character of terrain on which the ball sits; distance to the green; wind direction and strength; character of the turf, both near the ball and the target, etc.

Then you imagine the best route your ball should take to finish on target, and the flight pattern it should assume. Finally, you imagine or sense how your swing should feel to produce this type of shot.

Imagination enters into every golf shot, from the drive to the putt. It helps provide a basic plan of action.

On tee shots I not only block out hazards by "narrowing" the fairway, as on the first hole at Augusta, but also I like to imagine that I'm sweeping the ball off the tee.

On approach shots I visualize not only the flight the ball should take, but also how it will act after hitting the green. If the greens are soft, I imagine the ball sitting down after two or three short hops. If they are hard, I visualize the ball bouncing high and rolling. Thus, I make a predetermined shot plan—whether to hit the ball well into the green, or to play it short and allow it to roll to the flag. I always visualize a landing.

Sometimes when I'm hitting into a strong headwind, I will picture in my mind that the flag is on the back fringe, or even over the green. This helps assure that I will hit enough club to buck the wind and still reach the actual flag position.

When my pupils have trouble with sand shots, often I find it helps them if I make a good blast shot from the sand and then place a ball in its correct position in the sand divot. Thus the pupils can imagine beforehand how the eventual divot in the sand should look after the shot has been made. They are able to establish a shot pattern which is based on a mental picture.

In putting I try to visualize a path or trough or string connecting my ball with the hole and stretching along the line I expect the ball to roll. I also try to imagine a nice smooth stroke with the putter, a firm clicking sound as the putter-face meets the ball, and a true, free-rolling of the ball along the imaginary path.

Imagining the click of a putt is one way of anticipating beforehand how the actual shot should sound. It might also be helpful to imagine the thud of a sand shot, the brushing of the grass on a short approach shot, or the whistle of the club shaft on the downswing of a full wood or iron shot.

Imagination or visualization is a form of concentration. Visualizing an aspect of the shot at hand gives you something concrete on which to focus your thinking. However, a danger lies in negative visualization —imagining bad shots.

One of my pupils once had a phobia that he would hit behind the ball on his short pitch shots. I asked him to imagine that he was swinging a giant safety razor instead of a golf club, and that he was trying to clip the grass with it. I pointed out that with too upright a swing he might cut into the ground, just as he would dig into his face with an actual razor. I also pointed out that a too level stroke would fail to shave either his whiskers or the grass. I had him brush the grass back and forth with the sole of the club to get the feel, sight and sound of this double brushing, which is the key to a properly hit pitch shot. No digs, no tops—just a proper arc with a slightly flattened spot at the bottom.

Soon he got the idea and began hitting his pitch shots successfully with a proper stroke. I don't know that my advice altered his swing very much, but it did take his mind off the possibility of missing the shot.

The more you develop your ability to visualize, more new aids for shot planning will pop into your mind.

Your over-all concentration will improve and you will realize the double satisfaction of not only hitting good shots, but also of hitting them according to your advance planning. Your good shots will become more a matter of skill than of luck.■

MAKE YOUR LONG IRONS PAY OFF

BY BYRON NELSON
October, 1962

The long irons bring out the real "class"—or lack of it—in a golfer. There are thousands of players who shoot in the middle 70s, but relatively few move down into the scratch or plus handicap range. Lack of consistent skill with the 1-, 2-, 3- and 4-irons is often the Achilles Heel for these otherwise competent golfers.

Often the beginner finds it difficult to hit his shots into the air with a wood club. Thus he or she relies on the long irons for fairway shots that really should be struck with a wood. Merely through usage the beginner becomes fairly proficient with the less-lofted irons.

However, after the golfer finally solves the problems of hitting wood shots into flight, he often neglects his long irons. His practice sessions begin to stress the drives, short irons and putts—the so-called "payoff" shots.

The vicious circle now has started. Because he haś not practiced his long irons, the golfer shuns their use during play. He falls into the habit of "easing up" on 4-wood shots when he should be swinging all-out with a 2- or 3-iron. Confidence in—and skill with—the long irons further diminishes. Finally, a golfer often avoids frustration by not even practicing the long irons at all.

This is a tragedy, for long-iron practice not only develops skill with these important golf weapons, but it also helps develop sound swing habits that will improve one's technique with other clubs.

Practice with a long iron will help you learn to stay down to the ball and to develop a proper left-side lead and increased hand action on all kinds of shots.

Byron Nelson is one of golf's legendary figures and a member of the Golf Digest Advisory Staff.

THE GRIP

There is one thing that is an absolute necessity on long iron shots: You must have a firm grip.

I don't mean that you should squeeze the club; just feel that you have a firm tension in both hands. I can take my hands off the club immediately after hitting a shot and see indentations in them where I have gripped.

Gripping firmly is particularly important for long irons because if you don't, you'll not turn your shoulders completely on the backswing and your hands won't go high enough. It takes a long full arc to be a good long-iron player. Nobody with a short, choppy swing ever played long irons well.

I like to feel the pressure of the two hands against each other. This assures me that my hands are snugly together on the club, working as a unit during the swing.

I also like to grip far enough down the shaft so that there is a little club sticking out behind the left hand. This gives better club balance and control and minimizes chances of the club slipping during the swing.

A long, smooth swing is a must for the best long-iron shots. A firm grip will encourage a full pivot and consequently a long turn on the backswing.

BALL POSITION

A properly struck long-iron shot will find the club meeting the ball and the turf almost instantaneously, though it should contact the ball first. The clubhead should slightly skin the turf in front of the ball.

I feel the correct position for the ball on long irons is slightly— normally not more than an inch— inside the left heel. I've noticed that good long-iron players usually position the ball a bit farther forward than those less skilled.

The most important thing about ball positioning on the long irons is to make certain that your hands are ahead of the clubhead—more toward the target—at the address position.

TEMPO

You hear a lot about fast swings and slow swings. I feel that such discussion is immaterial for this reason: The speed of one's swing is of little importance so long as it is *smooth* and *unified*.

The average player seems to have trouble making this smooth swing. Even some better players get too anxious to hit the ball. And this anxiety is often predominant in the long-iron swing since many players lack confidence in these clubs.

I like to think, "1, 2, 3, hit"—sort of a waltz tempo—during my swing.

Once the player has adopted a smooth rhythm to his swing, he need only make certain that everything—hands, arms, shoulders, hips, legs and feet— move together as a unit on the backswing in rhythm with the clubhead. Even your head may *turn* slightly with this unit, but don't let it move sideways or up-down.

DOWN, INTO AND THROUGH

We have seen how the backswing is a "package deal." By the same token, I think of the downswing as a "chain reaction."

First step in the chain is the left side. It moves *into* and *through* the ball, pulling the hands *down, into* and *through*. The hands, in turn, pull the clubhead *down, into* and *through*. "Down, into and through." Those are the key words on long-iron shots.

The left side must go through

the shot. It shouldn't stop at the ball and wait for hands to catch up. The hands will do that automatically. With the left side leading through the hitting area, the wrists will uncock late in the downswing, exploding the hands and, in turn, the clubhead into the ball at maximum speed.

This late release of the wrists—produced by the left-side lead—is the only way to get the utmost power and distance from your swing.

If the player becomes too anxious and rushes the downswing with his hands and arms, he will lose his left-side lead. The wrists will uncork prematurely, dissipating clubhead speed before the ball is struck.

Chances are good that the golfer who has hit through the shot with the left side leading will have no trouble fulfilling another very important phase of long-iron play —staying down with the shot.

Too often when using a less-lofted club, such as a 2-iron, a golfer feels he must lift the ball into the air with his body. He straightens up on the downswing and tries to scoop the ball.

This merely arrests the smooth turning of the left side through the ball, encourages a premature release of the wrists, and discourages square contact.

Trust in the loft of the club to put the ball into flight without any lifting on your part. Remember the key words *down, into* and *through*.

THE FINISH

The finish cannot be forced. It is the automatic result of what occurred before—good or bad—in the swing.

I will guarantee a fine high finish to any golfer who applies the other major points on long-iron shots that I have made in this article:

1. A firm grip.
2. A smooth, even-tempoed swing.
3. A package-deal backswing with everything moving as a unit.
4. A chain-reaction downswing with the left side leading the hands and clubhead down, into and through the ball.
5. Practice. ■

At the very start of the downswing, weight should be quickly transferred from the right side to the left. The hips turn first, leading the hands and club into the ball.

These correct impact action drawings show how the right shoulder lowers, the left side leads hands and clubhead down, into and through the long-iron shot.

BUILD YOURSELF A COMPLETE SWING PATTERN

BY JULIUS BOROS
December, 1963

When I first became a touring professional in 1950 the most popular and successful golf swings were those of Sam Snead and Ben Hogan. Both were "swingers." They moved the club back from and through the ball with little or no apparent effort, yet drove the shots farther than did most professional golfers before or since.

There are still some "swingers" on the tour—Gene Littler, Dow Finsterwald, Bobby Nichols are examples. But most of today's better players—Arnold Palmer, Jack Nicklaus and Gary Player, for example—use a power swing to

Winner of three major championships and almost a million dollars on tour, Julius Boros has been noted for his rhythmic, consistent swing.

varying degrees. These are "hitters." They take the club back and return it to the ball using every iota of their God-given power. Their swings imply, "The heck with how we look —hit the ball hard!"

The success of the hitters no doubt influences the swing styles of amateur golfers around the world. It could well be that the Palmers and Players are breeding a generation of amateur golfers who at least appear to be trying to knock the cover off.

However, this year a "swinger" won the U.S. Open. Possibly my success with the more easy-flowing, rhythmical "swinging" swing will encourage some golfers to adopt this style. I hope so because I strongly feel that a swinging swing is much easier for the ordinary golfer to control than is the power swing. I also feel that the difference in distance generated by each style is negligible. To control a fast swing, which requires split-second hand action, a golfer must play often. The weekend golfer will have less trouble keeping a swinging swing operable than he would an all-out power stroke.

Developing a "swinging" swing is principally a task of the mind. Deliberate thinking will prepare you for a coordinated unhurried swing.

To this end every golfer should follow a pattern before every swing. I never vary my pre-shot motions, whether driving or putting. I have confidence in this pattern. I know what I am doing before every shot.

As I approach the ball from behind I decide on the shot's direction and trajectory. I decide which club will give me best results.

I prefer not to take practice swings before a shot. This might interrupt my pre-swing pattern. From the moment I take the club from my bag or my caddie until my swing is completed, I want a steady, deliberate pattern of motion.

Once I have the club in my hands I stand aside from the ball, re-check the line to the target, assume my grip, and finally, with my feet close together, I place the clubhead squarely behind the ball.

I feel that these actions can and should be adopted by every golfer. They form a logical and reliable pattern.

The rest of the pre-swing pattern, which involves widening of the stance and waggling of the clubhead, may vary with the individual. I will describe what I do. You may accept my method or reject it, providing you do employ some sort of pattern that repeats itself on every shot.

After I have placed the clubhead behind the ball with my feet still close together, I move my left foot to the left. At the same time I again reaffirm my line and raise the clubhead over the ball in a semi-waggle.

Next, I move my right foot to the right and return the clubhead to behind the ball.

Finally, with my feet spread the proper width for the shot at hand, I take a final waggle and begin my backswing with no conscious pause beforehand.

All of this is done in a rhythmical flow of motion. It's almost like a dance step. People tell me you could time my pre-swing pattern with a stop watch and it would always be the same. You should strive for a consistent pattern.

When I'm executing my "swinging" swing I never feel that I am going to "crush" the ball. I never try to apply maximum power to any shot. I want to remain in control of my swing and the clubhead at all times. ∎

To help execute a smoothly timed,"swinging" swing, count "one and . . ." on the backswing and "two" on the downswing. The backswing is slower than the downswing and it requires twice as many counts.

MICKEY WRIGHT: EASY DOES IT

BY PAUL RUNYAN
February, 1965

What you can learn from Mickey Wright's swing	See	Benefits to your game	How to incorporate these tips into your swing
Grip club so that palms more or less align with clubface at address.	1	Helps keep clubface in proper position throughout swing so it faces target line during impact.	Imagine palms as being extension of clubface when placing hands on club. See that back of left hand and palm of right faces target.
Assume powerful address position that more or less duplicates position at impact.	1 & 7	Pre-sets body, arms and legs for square return of club to ball.	Address ball with left arm extended and knees slightly bent. Position right hip and shoulder slightly lower than left hip and shoulder.
Take club away from ball without rolling wrists to right or left.	2-4	Helps provide proper swing plane. Swing will flatten if wrists roll to right. It becomes too upright if wrists roll to left.	Take club back in conjunction with tilting and turning of shoulders and hips.
Keep right knee joint bent throughout backswing.	2-4	Allows freedom of movement in feet and legs so that weight shifts smoothly.	Maintain same amount of bend at right knee joint throughout backswing as was present at address. Be careful that knee does not buckle to right.
Increase wrist cock during downswing.	5	Further stretches tendons of back, legs and arms, helping you uncoil powerfully on downswing.	Uncoil your hips and shift weight to the left on downswing while clubshaft is still moving up toward horizontal position on the backswing.
Employ hips-shoulders-arms sequence on downswing.	5-7	Tilting and turning of hips, then shoulders, ahead of arms on downswing builds up and maintains speed of clubhead.	Think "hips-shoulders-arms" and practice this downswing sequence in slow motion. Then gradually increase speed.
Retain constant position of swing's suspension point at base of your neck throughout the swing.	1-10	Provides consistent swing plane which results in square club-ball contact.	Maintain consistent flex in your knees and bend at waist so head stays in its original position. Retain weight "inside" feet so head does not sway laterally to right or left.

THE DOCTOR PRESCRIBES

BY CARY MIDDLECOFF
1965 through 1969

On planning putts:
make a mental picture of a
perfect putt

I like to check the contour of the green by looking at the area between my ball and the cup from the side. Usually I'll study it from both sides. I take note of the cup itself. If the right side of the cup looks higher than the left, the putt will break left, and vice versa.

Then, I make a mental picture of a perfect putt—the ball following a certain line and traveling at the proper diminishing speed to drop in the center of the cup just as its force is spent.

I don't advise trying to putt over a predetermined spot between the ball and the hole. When I try this method my sense of how hard to hit the putt deserts me.

In determining the speed of the green, I look for "shine." If the surface gleams, I know the green is fast and if it's dull, slow. If you're playing in mountainous country you can be reasonably sure that the green slopes away from the highest peak, even though it may appear level. In flatlands, the grain nearly always runs in the direction of the setting sun. The grain will also run toward any nearby large body of water. One word of caution: don't put so much emphasis on lining up the putt that you forget to stroke it properly.

On sand shots:
get the ball up quickly

Back in the days when I was a good sand player, I liked to imagine that there was a small mound directly in front of the ball. This helped me concentrate on getting the ball up quickly, so it would clear this imaginary obstacle.

One of golf's all-time great players and a member of Golf Digest's Advisory Staff, Dr. Middlecoff made these comments in a series of Professional Teaching Panel critiques.

A quick rising shot is encouraged by laying back the clubface at address. The open stance, the ball well forward, and the hands behind the ball combine to give the clubface more loft, and the ball to rise faster.

Dave Marr's description of the shot—"skim"—may be just the word golf instruction needs to explain sand techniques. His idea to skim off a thin layer of sand from under the ball is invaluable. The words "blast" and "explosion" are misnomers.

I have always let the distance I hit behind the ball determine the length of the shot, rather than to regulate distance by the force of the swing.

On clubhead path:
visualize swing as hub
and wheel

Too many golfers think of the swing as a pendulum-type thing—straight back and straight through the ball. A more illuminating way to visualize it, I believe, is to think of the clubhead following the rim of a tilted wheel with yourself as the hub of the wheel.

For the average golfer, I advocate first taking the clubhead back a little outside the line of flight. That way he will be making a well defined and easily recognizable movement. As he shifts from backswing to downswing, the hips rotate back to the left and the right shoulder comes under so as to get full power of the body behind the shot.

On head position:
strive to keep head still

A golfer can allow his head to turn during the swing, provided that he keeps it in one position relative to the ball. However, in order to avoid any lateral or up and down movement of the head, my advice to the average golfer is that he try to keep his head perfectly still.

I have seen some good players who move their heads laterally to the right on the backswing. Because they are good athletes and have great muscular coordination, they are able to return the head to its original position on the downswing.

On the delayed hit:
just let it happen

The delayed hit is a result of correctly transferring the weight to the left side, pushing off with the right foot, and turning the hips back to the left.

The delayed hit, which is the opposite of "hitting from the top," is indispensable to a good swing. It cannot be forced. I think the way to achieve success with a delayed hit is to develop a clear concept of it, and then let it happen. Arching the body to the left on the downswing while the head and feet remain as anchor points develops a maximum power build-up. A lot of golfers mis-hit iron shots through trying to swing as hard as they do with the driver. Since so many golfers swing even the driver too hard, the fault becomes even more pronounced on iron shots.

On long-iron play:
hit down and through

Many average golfers have trouble with the long irons because they think they must put something extra into their shots with these clubs. They do not trust these clubs to do the work for which they are designed. Golfers seem to think the ball will not get airborne unless they scoop it off the turf, instead of hitting down and through. This scooping motion is the most prevalent of all long-iron faults.

On occasion I have suggested to golfers who fear the long irons that they replace the 2-iron with a 5-wood. However, this is really a give-up measure, because the 2-iron, when mastered, is definitely the more effective club, especially in a strong headwind when you need a low-trajectory shot.

Any player who can hit good short and medium iron shots can learn to hit the long irons by maintaining the same basic tempo. Mastering the long irons is largely a matter of overcoming fear and gaining confidence.

On right elbow position:
"flying" elbow can
lengthen arc

It is not necessary to keep the right elbow close to the body on the backswing. Some lifting of the elbow makes it easier to keep the left arm properly extended for a full swing arc. However, it is impossible to swing the clubhead into the ball from inside the intended line of flight if the right elbow does not point more or less downward at the top of the swing, and then move back into the side on the downswing.

On the backswing turn: shorter turn OK for average player

A 90-degree shoulder turn and a 45-degree hip turn on the backswing is ideal, but it takes a supple man to make that much of a turn, especially in the shoulders. Something less would be fine for many average players, as little as 70 degrees for the shoulders and 35 for the hips. The 2-1 ratio would still be correct.

Keeping the left heel on the ground for as long as possible on the backswing does improve control. I'd say it ought to stay there until the golfer feels he must lift it to complete his backswing. Even then the lift should be minimal. This low left heel helps keep the weight inside the balls of the feet during the backswing, where it should be.

On left-side control: muscles must stretch on backswing

There should be a distinct feeling of the muscles of the left side being stretched as the backswing progresses. There should be a sense of live tension in the muscles that control the movement of the left hip and left shoulder.

The downswing should be initiated by the left hip and arm. When the muscles of the left side are stretched on the backswing, it is easy and natural—virtually automatic, in fact—to start the downswing with the left hip and left arm leading. Starting the downswing with the hands is the great swing-killer.

As to the action of the left side on the downswing, I think some lateral movement of the hips—while the head stays "back"—is essential to a good swing.

On how to compete: "the swing's the thing"

As a matter of personal opinion, I have always felt that while physical conditioning and mental attitude are important, the swing is the thing. I'm reminded of something said by Ben Hogan, "Golf is a game of constant correction. The man who can correct the quickest will win most often." It follows that the man with the sound swing can correct

quickly, for such a swing will require only minor adjustments.

A positive mental attitude is indispensable, but it should be understood that golfers react to pressure in different ways. Each has his own special method of bringing out the best in himself when it is most needed. For instance, in clutch situations I tend to get so charged up that sometimes I have to give myself a pep talk "in reverse." I remind myself when faced with a tough little putt that even if I miss, the world will go on turning and I will go on eating.

Every shot should be taken as a thing unto itself. Thinking ahead, or what is probably worse, thinking behind, can divide a golfer's attention and therefore wreck his concentration.

On chipping: form precise chipping plan

A player should form a definite, detailed and precise plan before he takes his stance and makes a chip shot. He should choose the exact spot on the green where he wants to make the ball land, and he should have a clear mental picture of the bounces and rolls needed to take the ball up to the pin. I prefer a shot pattern with the ball played to land just safely past the front edge of the green. The lofted chip that lands near the pin and stops quickly may be more spectacular, but it is much less dependable.

I use my regular grip for chip shots instead of my putting grip. But many good players do use the latter, Paul Runyan and Gene Littler among them. All good chippers, I think, grip down on the club for this shot. This leaves that much less shaft between you and the ball and thus reduces that margin of error.

If you use a slightly open stance, the shot is much easier to judge. It's almost as if you are rolling the ball one-handed, under-handed toward the hole, something you couldn't easily do if you were standing exactly parallel to the intended line.

On the takeaway: always stay in motion

As anyone who has ever seen me play could verify, I am strongly in accord with remaining in motion from the time you set your stance

until you start the backswing. You cannot otherwise initiate the swing in a rhythmic pattern.

The clubhead should move away from the ball low to the ground and in a straight line extending as far back as can be managed without inducing a sway. This serves to extend the backswing, and by doing so aids a golfer in "using up" the muscles in his left shoulder, arm and side. These are the controlling muscles throughout the swing and if they aren't extended the golfer will never achieve maximum power through proper body coiling and uncoiling. Should the right side become overly active in the takeaway, it is likely that the clubhead will be picked up by the right hand and the swing's rhythmic qualities will be destroyed.

On escaping from rough: use adequate loft

The player's first thought upon getting into the rough should be to get out of it, and not to take any foolish risks.

Use a club with plenty of loft from the rough. The quicker you get the ball up, the less high grass it has to go through to get airborne. A 4- or 5-wood will get the ball up quicker than will a long iron. Also, with its smooth sole, the wood is less likely to catch in the grass. As for myself, I almost never use any club between a 4-wood and a 6-iron from heavy rough.

When grass intervenes between the clubface and the ball the clubface cannot act on the ball to produce normal backspin. Hence the need to steepen the swing arc so as to minimize the amount of grass the clubhead will have to penetrate to reach the ball. Also, your hands will get a jolt when the clubhead goes into heavy grass and encounters resistance, so a firmer than usual grip is required. ■

BETTER GOLF THROUGH SOUND PRACTICE

BY GARY PLAYER
March, 1966

There's no such thing as a "natural" golfer. The truth is, you've got to work darn hard to become a "natural" golfer. And the more you practice and work, the more "natural" your swing will appear.

Sam Snead is as natural a player as ever walked a course. But Sam Snead still spends long hours practicing—and always has.

Some beginning golfers do start with more natural ability than others—but never enough to become proficient without extensive practice. The shag bag is the golfer's—especially a beginner's—best friend. Only through practice will a golfer develop that all-important ability to repeat the same swing shot after shot. Without a repeating swing you can't expect consistent shot results.

I remember watching Dow Finsterwald swinging away on the practice tee just after he'd shot a sizzling 66 at Wilmington.

"Dow," I asked, "why in the world are you practicing now?"

"I don't want to lose it, Gary," explained Dow. "I want to keep this swing." It's sort of like being a businessman—just because he's had some success, he doesn't quit working. A good golfer doesn't quit practicing when he's ahead either.

If there is one subject that I feel particularly qualified to discuss, it is this one on practicing. During my early years in golf, I hit just about as many shots as it is possible for a human being to hit. Someone once said that probably Ben Hogan is the only golfer who has worked harder on his game than I have. I won't disagree.

The first thing about practice I'd like to stress is the importance of

hitting balls before you play a round. This pre-round workout is especially important for so-called "weekend" golfers. You can prevent a lot of pulled muscles if you warm up properly. More important, you actually improve your rhythm during a pre-round practice session. You'll be less likely to start the round with one of those bogey strings that so often puts you on the defensive for the rest of the day.

The specific pre-round practice routine I recommend is to first head for the putting green. After you've found your swing rhythm by stroking putts, then start chipping, play a few trap shots, and finally move over to the practice tee. There, start with your short irons and work up to the woods.

Some golfers prefer to work up to their driver during pre-round practice and then try to duplicate

that shot on the first tee. Others, however, like to finish practicing by recovering their short-game touch on and around the practice putting green. I think you must determine which of these conclusions to your pre-round practice puts you in best shape for the first hole.

Just as pre-round practice is vital for any golfer, so too is making your practice sessions interesting.

To build variety into my practice, I like to hit balls out of buried lies and from downhill and uphill slopes. I might try chip shots out of the rough and high shots over the trees. Then I'll practice hooking or slicing around a tree, getting the particular feel of each shot as I make it. This is good drill for the more advanced player. However, average golfers will find it better to devote most of their practice time to mastering more basic shots. In fact, novice

Gary Player was a Golf Digest playing editor when he wrote this article. He has won eight major championships and was sixth among all-time leading money-winners going into the 1975 season with $1,091,595.

players should avoid practice from bad lies. Such players are too apt to start chopping the ball and thereby build a host of bad faults into their swings.

Practicing out of rough, however, can help improve any golfer, regardless of his ability. And such practice also adds variety to your sessions. Practicing from the rough teaches you how to swing "through the ball," which you must do or you just aren't going to get much distance. Practice in the rough not only forces you to stay down on shots, but it also strengthens your golf muscles.

Regardless of where you happen to be practicing, it's extremely important to always have a target. A target sharpens your concentration, gives you a guide to judge your success or failure and, thus, helps spark your interest. Select a tree, or something in the distance, like a chimney, for your target. Or use your caddie if you happen to have one.

While failure to select a target minimizes the value of your practice, rushing shots actually hurts your game. Too often golfers throw down a bucket of balls and rapidly hit one shot after another with hardly a pause—or a thought. Rushing your swing this way on the practice tee is the best way I know to destroy your rhythm and to groove faults.

If you put your shag balls behind you, you will force yourself to actually turn around between shots. This is good insurance against rushing your sequence of shots.

To make your practice sessions truly worthwhile you must make certain that you're not just standing up there "perfecting your imperfections." When practicing to correct a fault, you should first define the problem and the correction you wish to employ.

A second person can help you overcome the basic problem that all golfers face when working on their games—the inability to see themselves swing, and thus to spot faults. So often even a good player will think he's practicing a certain movement that he's really not doing at all.

A good observer, particularly a competent professional, can often spot a fault and prescribe a solution in minutes. He can save you hours of worthless practice. How much is an hour of your time worth? I suspect you will save money—and certainly energy—by working with a pro when you have a problem.

Though I've been discussing practice area methods and techniques primarily, I should also point out that you can improve your skills immeasurably by practicing "on the course," or even at home.

Golfers who usually play the same course week after week may wish to try a practice technique I often use. It helps me develop shots I normally might not encounter during the round.

Say I'm playing a par-4 hole that usually requires a drive and a 7-iron. To improve my skill with other clubs, and to add variety to my round, I might tee off instead with a 2-iron and approach with a 4-iron.

Another way to improve on the course is to "play your partner's game." You select the clubs for your playing companion, tell him where to aim, how to play a putt, etc. He does the same for you. It's fun, and a great way to improve your own concentration.

A big problem facing the average weekend golfer is that of preserving his swing and his touch during the week. It's here that practice at home can be extremely helpful.

I know a teaching pro in South Africa who comes home at night—after spending most of the day on the course—and still practices putting on his living room carpet. He putts to an ashtray for direction. Then, for feel, he putts to a piece of string at the far end of the carpet, trying to stop the ball at the string.

I'd strongly suggest that you, too, join the legion of golfers who swing their putters in their living rooms.

Or, while your dinner is being prepared, take a club and swing a few times in the backyard. Even though you may not be swinging at a definite object, you should still practice swinging back slowly . . . and then hitting "through the ball." Some golfers favor a weighted club for their backyard swinging. It's usually a driver with a lot of lead in the head. These are readily available in most pro shops or you can "do-it-yourself" by taping lead strips on the back of one of your old woods.

This working out at home really pays off. When the weekend arrives, even though you haven't been to the course for a practice session, you will still have the feel of the club. You won't walk out on the course feeling like an arthritic grave digger trying to swing a pick-axe. ■

Practice tips from Gary Player

I. PRE-ROUND PRACTICE
  A. *Always warm up before a game to improve your rhythm, and to prevent strained muscles.*
  B. *Start by putting, then chipping, before going to the practice tee.*
  C. *On the practice tee start with short-iron shots and work up to the woods.*

II. GENERAL PRACTICE
  A. *Force yourself to pause between shots. Never rush through practice.*
  B. *Strive for a repeating swing.*
  C. *Seek professional advice, especially when correcting a fault. Don't "perfect imperfection."*
  D. *Always aim for a target.*
  E. *Spend some time during each session practicing out of rough and sand.*
  F. *Remember that photographs and movies will help you detect faults and correct them properly.*
  G. *Practice putting and club-swinging at home if you are a weekend golfer.*

SCRAMBLING: HOW TO GET IT UP AND DOWN

BY DOUG FORD
June, 1968

Scrambling, contrary to popular myth, is the art of doing the possible rather than the impossible. In recovering from the effects of a poor shot, the overriding thought should be how to return the ball safely into play.

Even if you had the strength of Jack Nicklaus and the finesse of Billy Casper, which you don't, there is no percentage in gambling. More often than not you will just put yourself deeper into trouble and ruin your

Former PGA and Masters champion Doug Ford is a master of the recovery shot.

primary objective which is to save strokes.

The real secret lies in your mental approach. The good scrambler accepts the cold logic that it is just as important to sink a bogey putt as it is to drop one for a par.

In describing some of the shots that must be a part of the equipment of an effective scrambler, I have tried to simplify the explanations of what I do down to one or two key elements which are easy to grasp and which, with a little practice, can be mastered by anyone.

CUT AND DRAW SHOTS

All good scramblers can maneuver the ball at will, beginning with the controlled cut shot which bends to the right and draw shot which turns to the left. The principal is the same on both the cut and the draw. You want to impart the correct sidespin to the ball so it will follow the flight path you have chosen (see diagram). When I want to cut the ball I merely open my stance; to draw the ball, I close my stance. I do not change my grip, only my stance. I always aim the clubface at the target (see arrows). Merely alter your stance by aligning your feet parallel to the direction in which you want the ball to start out. These stance variations will force your hands and arms to naturally swing the clubhead into the ball so it will apply proper sidespin. The swing is the same as on a normal shot.

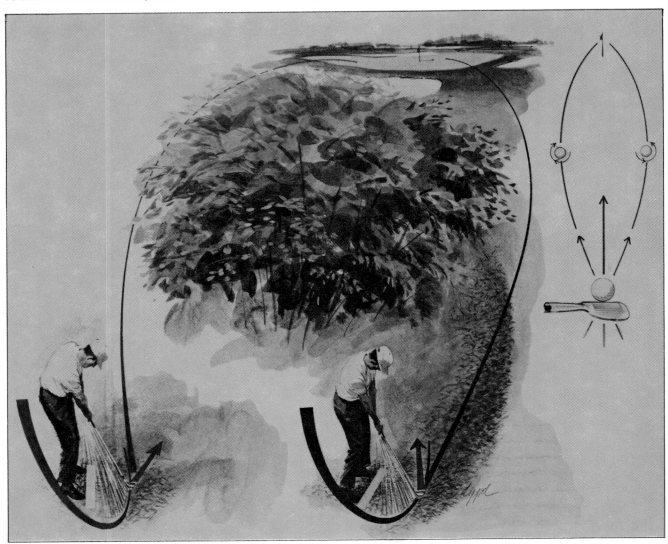

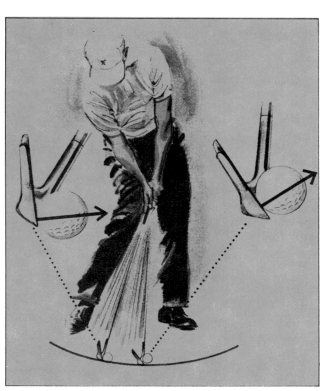

OVER AND UNDER SHOTS

Knowing how to pitch a ball high over a clump of trees or drill it low under a branch is essential in scrambling. These over and under shots are perhaps the easiest of the trouble shots to deal with.

Ball positioning is the key. It determines how much effective loft the club will carry at impact. For the high shot, position the ball an inch or two forward of stance-center. For the low shot, position the ball an inch or two back from stance-center toward the right toe. The grip, stance and swing should feel the same as for a normal shot.

COMING OUT OF THE ROUGH

The main problem to overcome when playing out of rough is the long grass which, on a normal swing, will catch between the clubface and ball during impact.

Select a more-lofted club than the distance indicates (a 7-iron, for example, instead of a 6-iron) and hood the face by playing the ball well back in your stance — either at or back of stance-center. This will automatically give you a more upright backswing and permit you to beat down and through the ball. It will give you maximum contact with the ball while cutting through a minimum of grass.

The ball will come out hooking and running because of the tendency of the grass to wrap around the hosel and close the clubface as it comes into the ball; aim about 10 yards right of target.

FIRM LEFT SIDE CONTROLS HOGAN'S SWING

BY BOB TOSKI
August, 1968

Teaching professional Bob Toski was delighted when *Golf Digest* asked him to analyze Hogan's swing in its series of Swing Studies.

"I've always marveled at Ben's ability to strike the ball with such great precision," says *Golf Digest's* Professional Panel member. "The way he controls his game on the course is also something to behold. He plays scientifically rather than emotionally. I'm sorry to say that most players, professional tour stars included, play golf in the opposite manner."

Starting from the square position, Hogan has moved the clubhead back very low to the ground with the left arm extended. This is essential if a player is to make a properly wide arc on the backswing.

Note that much can be seen of Hogan's left shoulder and left knee. His left shoulder has already started to move down and around and his left knee is bending inward (frame 1). This indicates that everything is moving as a unit.

Halfway through the backswing, Hogan's clubface is perpendicular to the ground (frame 2). This is the "square" position every golfer should emulate, for it eventually produces accuracy through a square hit.

Hogan's hands have moved back close to his body in a comfortable, free-moving arc. His right elbow is almost against his side, a controlling factor in producing a compact swing.

Although Hogan's hands have just now reached the top of his backswing (frame 3), his hips have already started back to the ball. All good players begin the downswing with a slide and a turn of the hips to the left, and this is what Hogan is doing. His right knee is beginning to kick in toward the target.

At the start of the downswing, as the lower body pulls to the left, the right forearm and elbow will begin their gradual move down and inward to the player's side. At the same time the left hand and arm should begin to pull the clubhead down to the striking position.

Now the thrust of the right side comes into play with Hogan's right knee sliding in toward the target and his right heel coming off the ground (frame 4). This is the automatic result of the earlier pulling and turning of the left side.

Although the clubhead is not yet in the immediate impact zone, his hips have turned so that a line through them would finish to the left of the target. At the same time his slower-turning shoulders are still aligned to the right of the target.

With his head steady and left arm extended, the wrist cock is retained.

Hogan's right shoulder has come down and under (frame 5) so that now a line across his shoulders points to the ball's original position.

With his lower body moving forward, toward the target, Hogan's head has moved slightly in the other direction. He is definitely "behind" the ball.

Although his wrists have uncocked, his right hand has not overpowered his left.

Although the momentum of Hogan's swing should cause his hands to finish in a lower position, this has not happened because his left arm and hand are still in control. With his left hand holding firmly and his left arm rising, Hogan's finish is relatively upright with his hands above his head (frame 6).

Hogan has finished in perfect balance; lines across his shoulders and the clubshaft are approximately level. His great, free turn through the ball has resulted in his upper body facing well to the left of the target, his hips almost as much. ∎

THE SOUNDEST WAY TO PUTT

BY BOB CHARLES
November, 1969

COMFORT COMES FIRST

My first priority in standing to a putt is comfort. The slightest tension or feeling of being out of balance tells me I will not stroke the ball correctly. I like to have my weight evenly and solidly distributed between, and on, both feet—never rocking back on my heels or teetering on my toes. I lean over just far enough from the waist to sole the putter on the ground and bring my eyes directly over the ball.

Bob Charles, history's foremost left-handed golfer, is regarded as one of the game's outstanding putters. He won the British Open in 1963.

Square alignment reduces putting to its simplest, most consistent form. To me, squareness at address means standing so that imaginary lines across my toes, knees, hips and shoulders all run parallel to the starting line of the putt I am about to play. I give great attention to this postural "squareness," especially to my feet, which I visually relate to the "line" of the putt and to my shoulders, the alignment of which, with my type of pendulum action, largely determines the path the putter will swing along.

Another important address factor, relating to my impression of "squareness," is ball location. Ideally I want to be so positioned that the club shaft is not tilting forwards or backwards, positions which, if reproduced at impact, could change the clubface loft and alignment. These postural objectives are achieved when the ball is located about two inches inside my right heel (left heel for right-handers). Possibly I *could* still properly square up the

clubface and shaft if I played the ball farther forward or back, but this would change my weight distribution by forcing me to favor either the right or left leg. For other golfers, this positioning of the ball may vary from my positioning. However, I do feel it's vital that the clubshaft be vertical for all players at address.

LIKE A PENDULUM

My conception of the soundest way to putt is that the arms and club swing exactly like a pendulum, at a very smooth, very even tempo, with the clubface square to the path of the stroke at every stage.

I often mentally visualize a pendulum action when I am putting, which helps me to make the stroke entirely with my arms, employing no wrist break or "give" in the hands whatsoever. I like to feel that the putter swings simply because it is an extension of my arms. My arms actually pivot from my shoulders, but I like to feel that a point at the center of the back of my neck is the true pivotal point

Charles compares his putting technique to the action of a pendulum. His wrists do not enter into the stroke. Clubhead movement originates in his shoulders. Note how the right shoulder lowers during the backstroke(left), then swings up on the throughstroke. He makes no special effort to keep the putterhead low but achieves this effect by eliminating the hinging of his wrists.

of the stroke.

If my putter shaft were perfectly upright at address, it could precisely reproduce the action of a pendulum and swing straight back and forth along the starting line of the putt. The putter shaft, however, extends upward toward me, which means that the head does not follow a straight-back, straight-through line. Its natural path of movement is inside the line on the backswing and inside it again on the follow-through, going straight along the line only at impact (the amount of this "inside" movement depends on the length of the swing, but is very slight with short putts). It should be emphasized that this inside-to-along-to-inside path is a purely mechanical result of making a pendulum-type swing with an implement offset from vertical, not a deliberate piece of manipulation by the golfer. If the swing is correctly made, the putter head will always be traveling squarely along the line at the moment of impact, which is

all that really matters.

Tempo is extremely important in putting. In employing the pendulum principle, theoretically one should have the same momentum going back and coming forward with the club, but in practice this doesn't always work out. Hitting *to* the ball rather than *through* it can easily lead to decelerating the clubhead before impact, the surest way I know to mis-hit putts. Thus, to ensure a solid hit, I try to swing the putter into the ball with just a little more momentum than I gave it going back. I consciously strive to produce a follow-through at least equal in length to my backswing.

"FEEL" IS NO. 1 FACTOR
I use what is known as the reverse-overlap grip, probably the most popular of all methods. It knits the hands together and enables them to operate and control the club in complete harmony.

To form this grip, I take the

club in the roots of the fingers of both hands, then lay the index finger of the leading hand—in my case, being a left-hander, the right —outside and straight down the fingers of the trailing hand. Keeping it straight and pointing down gives my grip an important sense of unity and authority. The backs of both my hands align exactly with the putter blade, and are thus "square" to the intended starting line of the putt as I address the ball.

To achieve maximum consistency I want to hold the club exactly the same way every time I putt. To reach that objective, and to promote "squareness" of alignment, all my putter grips have flat tops. This flattened surface is exactly at right angles to the putter blade, and I make a point of placing both thumbs upon it so that they lay flat and snug and point straight down the putter shaft.

Touch, or "feel," in the hands is probably the most important single

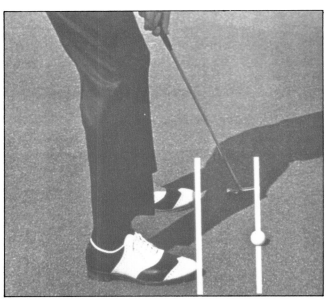
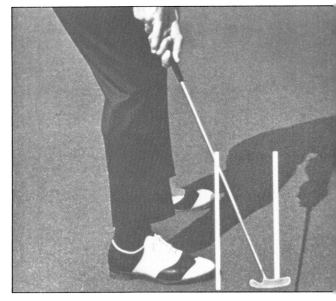

Charles feels the natural movement of the putterhead during the stroke is such that it will swing slightly inside the putt's line (above left) when it moves back from the ball, and then return along the putt line path as it strikes the ball (right).

factor in putting. Unfortunately, it is also the most elusive. In my experience it has a lot to do with the pressures exerted by the hands and forearms in holding the club. I always try to hold the club with equal pressure in each hand, though the actual amount of pressure exerted is difficult to describe. If I hold it too loosely I lose control over the putter face and length of swing. If I squeeze it even a little, my sense of "feel" diminishes. I've had my best putting streaks creating the increased momentum through the "feel" in my hands. The technique requires experience, practice and confidence in one's basic stroke, but it usually will produce much better results, I believe, than a long, uncontrolled backswing.

I do not practice putting very much if my stroke feels good. If my stroke does not feel good, I will practice hard for up to 30 minutes a day—but never longer.

Longer stints make me tired and place too great a strain on my muscles. Also, I find it impossible to concentrate properly for more than 30 minutes.

The golfer who is trying to develop a good stroke needn't worry too much about where the ball finishes everytime. He should be chiefly concerned with the mechanics and tempo of his stroke, concentrating especially on making solid, square contact with the ball.

Once you have developed a good stroke, however, I think the most important concern in putting practice should be judging distance. This, really, is what putting is all about—the development of touch or "feel," the coordination of eye and hand. To achieve this, it is best to practice putts from varying distances, always trying to roll the ball at the right speed to take it just into the cup. ■

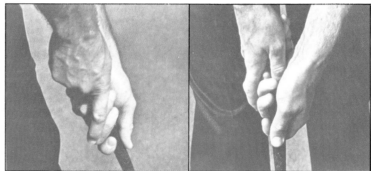

Charles strives to keep the backs of both hands aligned with the putter blade and exactly square to the intended starting line of the putt. Placing both thumbs straight down the top of the shaft helps him achieve this squareness consistently.

Charles often varies the width of his stance, but always positions himself at address so that his eyes are centered directly above the back of the ball, and toes, knees, hips and shoulders are parallel to the starting line of the putt.

TWO WAYS TO SWING LIKE A CHAMPION

BY PAUL RUNYAN
June, 1969

Gene Littler, the 1961 U.S. Open champion, and Lee Trevino, the defending Open champion at Houston this month, present an exceptionally interesting example of how golfers can achieve great success with widely differing techniques.

Gene's action, with which I have long been personally familiar, is almost 100 per cent "classical." His grip, posture, head position, the use of his body and arms, and his balance and tempo cannot be faulted. His method, like his temperament, is the kind that conserves energy.

Trevino is what is known in technical parlance as a "shut-faced" golfer. The phrase refers to the "closed" alignment of his clubface during his movement away from the ball. This derives largely from having his hands turned farther to the right (clockwise) on the club than is common among top-flight golfers. To counter-balance the closing of the clubface that inevitably results from such a "strong" grip, Lee uses stronger-than-average leg and body action in the downswing, and also restricts his wrist action more than is normal on his way down to the ball. This method, which stems partly from his thickset build, produces low-flying shots.

Although slightly taller than Lee, Gene addresses the ball with his feet fractionally closer together, and turns out his right foot more than Trevino does. Also, Littler is more upright in his stance, Trevino bending over the ball more than his short, stocky build would seem to demand (lower photos).

In photos #2, Gene has turned his body more than Lee, but Lee's club has traveled back a few inches farther. This indicates that Littler does not "work" his wrists as quickly as Trevino, taking the club back with a one-piece movement rather than predominantly with the hands and arms.

The big differences in these two swings begin to become clear in #3 and #4. Halfway back, Gene has turned his upper body through approximately 85 degrees, while Lee's shoulders have pivoted no more than 75 degrees. Even so, their clubs have reached exactly the same point in the backswing. This confirms Trevino's earlier wrist hinging, or "cocking," which goes with his lesser turn.

Golfers should also note in #3 and #4 the difference in the alignment, or plane, of the two players' left wrists. As a result of his perfect grip and "one-piece" takeaway, the back of Littler's left wrist and arm form a straight line on the same plane as his shoulders turn. This keeps a "square" relationship between the clubface and the target line that, because of its simplicity, should be the goal of all golfers. Because of Trevino's strong grip, and the type of hand action he employs, he arches his left wrist as he completes his backswing. His left wrist and arm are on a flatter plane than his shoulders are turning.

At the top of his backswing the plane of Littler's arms and club is more upright than Trevino's, because of his more erect address

position and his freer body turn. I would recommend Littler's windup to most golfers, but everyone can learn from the way both players coil against their flexed right legs.

Photos #5 and #6 show how Lee moves his hips farther and faster to the left than Gene does as he starts down. This more pronounced lower body thrust derives partly from Lee's less-than-full hip turn, but primarily from closing his clubface on the backswing. If he did not "get ahead and stay ahead" with his legs and hips at this point, Lee would find it difficult, due to his grip and wrist action, to prevent the clubface from turning over, or closing, through the ball, thus creating a damaging hook.

Although Littler also initiates his downswing with his hips and legs, it is apparent from the position of both players' clubs in #5 that Gene begins to release his wrists earlier than Lee. This is largely a reflexing result of his more upright swing plane and "square" clubface alignment during the backswing.

Photos #7 and #8 again graphically show the differences in body and hand manipulation employed by these two fine golfers in order to have the clubface meet the ball correctly. Trevino's left side is much more "out of the way" than Littler's, and his wrists are considerably farther ahead of his clubhead immediately before and during impact. Lee has considerably improved his clubface position in #7, but it is still fractionally closed facing left of his target—whereas Littler's clubface (not visible in #7) is slightly open—facing right of his target. The vibratory cycle of Gene's shaft in #8 also confirms that he releases his wrists earlier than Lee.

On the other hand, Trevino's shaft at the same point in the swing is almost straight. He seems to be almost "shoving" the clubhead out toward the target in #8.

Littler and Trevino are more nearly in the same position in #9 than at any other point in their swings. But, even here, Lee's body and arms are farther toward the target, while Gene's wrists have "released" more and his shaft is rising more sharply toward completion of the swing. Littler is definitely more relaxed.

Characteristic of the closed-clubface "puncher," Lee is "chasing" the club out after the ball with his hands, arms and shoulders, which are forced "under and through" on an almost vertical plane. This is a reflexive result of holding the clubface "square" to the target with the hands and wrists through the impact zone.

In #11 we see graphically the extent of Trevino's hip and shoulder turn going through the ball, compared to Littler's—although Gene's wrists have turned over considerably more. No. 12 perfectly illustrates the differences in the finish of a square-clubface "swinger" (Littler), and a closed-clubface "puncher" (Trevino). Lee's body has been pulled so far toward his target that his head has moved well in front of the position it occupied at address, whereas Gene has swung the club "past" his head, which has remained virtually static throughout.

As the records of these two golfers prove, both methods are highly effective. What the average golfer must beware of is trying to combine them. They are distinct techniques and whichever you prefer, or suits you best, you must go with all the way. ■

HOW PALMER HITS IT HARD

BY HENRY RANSOM
April, 1969

When I first met Arnold Palmer he hit everything hard. This intention still permeates his game. Some said he would never do well because he could not hit soft shots, but he quickly learned to finesse these.

The one thing Palmer has that has given him such tremendous success is his determination to make every shot as good as possible.

I noticed this when I first met him, at the All-America Amateur segment of the late George S. May's Tam O'Shanter tournaments in 1954. There, on the first hole I saw him play, he missed the green with his approach but almost holed out his next shot. He eventually won, six shots ahead of the runner-up, Eddie Merrins.

Palmer's technique works well for him. Though his is not a style that every golfer should follow, just the same, there are many points in his swing that any golfer could profitably copy.

Palmer is starting his swing (photo 1) with too level a shoulder turn, caused by an overactive right hand. (Note the backward bend of his right wrist.) The average player should not use his right hand this

Henry Ransom is a former tour star and member of Golf Digest's Professional Teaching Panel.

much, for he would probably pick up the clubhead too quickly and eventually lose momentum.

As a result of his extension at address, Palmer's arms are still farther from his body than would be ideal for the average player, who would tend to lose control. For most golfers using a driver, it would be better if, at this stage of the backswing, the hands were passing more or less over the top of the right foot. Arnie probably allows his extreme extension to make his backswing as wide as possible.

Look at that left arm extension! (photo 2) Arnie will keep the clubhead in a consistent path with the left arm as it is. Now his right elbow is close to the body as it should be. His shoulder tilt is desirably upright.

Perhaps the lift of his left heel is a little more than the ordinary player should permit. Arnie can keep control with his powerful body, but going up on the left toe like this would tend to make most swings too loose.

With his right leg firmly braced and his left knee pointing behind the ball, Palmer is in the position all golfers should copy. The right leg prevents a sway away from the target, while the inward bend of the left knee frees the left side.

Palmer's left arm (photo 3) is firmly in control here. His right side is following his left's commands. Although his hands and the club have moved only a few inches back toward the ball, Arnie's hips already are almost square to the target line. This demonstrates that his weight is being transferred rapidly to the left, and that the left side is ready to take the force he generates at impact.

This left-side lead is an important

source of Palmer's tremendous power. As he squares his hips, his upper body uncoils and produces top clubhead speed. If he uncoiled his upper body first and then his hips, he would lose power.

At impact (photo 4), Palmer's hips are correctly turned well around. His left side is cleared for an unhindered slash through the ball with his hands. This is indicated by the relaxed appearance of his right side, which he has completely released. He is using all of his impressive power in that side, including that in his right hand and wrist.

Too often golfers who try to hit drives hard fail to let the left arm and hand retain sufficient control. This causes the wrists to flip over too quickly at impact and a bad hook results.

Palmer's left arm and the clubshaft are in more or less a straight line. The shaft is an extension of his left arm, so to speak, which keeps the clubhead swinging along a controlled, consistent arc.

The momentum of Palmer's swing moves his right shoulder too high (photo 5), on a more horizontal plane than is desirable. He has properly used his right foot to help power the clubhead through the ball, as he is up on the inside of his right toes. Though his right knee has moved toward the target, Arnie has "stayed with the shot" magnificently. His attention is still focused on the ball's original position and there is no hint that his upper body has swayed even the slightest bit to the left. Maintaining a steady head in this manner allows Arnie to preserve through impact the terrific force he has generated with his lower body. ∎

SHORT SHOT ALMANAC

BY BILLY CASPER
May, 1971

What an advantage it is to know that you can decently play the tricky, as well as the easy, short shots. Getting "up and down" from grass is absolutely the name of the game on tour, where today winning big money is not so much a matter of shooting birdies when you are hitting every green, but scrambling pars when you aren't. That's long been my forte, and it comes from study, and practice that has developed a good "touch," and, above all, confidence. I recommend that the golfer seriously in search of improvement should not just read this article once, but keep it for repeated reference. It would be very difficult to assimilate all of the techniques presented here in one sitting or practice session. But I do promise that even the most gradual approach to mastering these shots will improve your score.

BASIC AXIOM:
PLAY THE CLUB THAT KEEPS BALL NEAREST GROUND

Under most conditions it is easier for players to execute a "roll" shot with more precision and confidence than a "flight" shot, for the same reason that they can tap the ball more squarely and solidly with the straight face of a putter than the acutely angled face of a sand wedge. It's always been a basic axiom for me, therefore, to keep the ball as near to the ground as possible on every short shot. I will putt rather than chip, chip rather than pitch-and-run, pitch-and-run rather than pitch-and-stop. I'll take the "all-air" route only when forced by some intervening obstacle or exceptional ground or weather conditions.

The clubs in the picture above

Billy Casper, a two-time U.S. Open champion, is the third leading money-winner of all time.

represent this philosophy. Reading from far to near, they are my pitching wedge, 9-iron, 7-iron, 5-iron, 3-iron and putter. They are so arrayed to roughly indicate the

distances from the green I'd use each to keep the ball as close to the ground as possible, yet still land it on the smooth surface whenever possible.

1. BASIC CHIP

Most chips are really nothing more than long putts, except that the ball starts out by going a little way through the air to miss the surface irregularities between you and the green. So keep your technique "putting simple." I stand comfortably with my weight equally distributed on both feet and the ball opposite the center of my stance. I use my normal overlapping grip and set my hands slightly ahead of the clubface, which I aim carefully at my pre-selected landing spot. My left-hand grip is firm and in control throughout.

I make the stroke by swinging my hands and arms together, with no conscious wrist break, but not to such a degree that I feel wooden-wristed. Because I always want to hit the ball cleanly, before the club touches the ground, my prime thought is:

Lead clubface through with left hand

2. BASIC PITCH

While I chip with anything from the 3-iron to the 8-iron, I play pitch shots with only highly lofted clubs. My pitching technique differs from my chipping technique in three ways. First, I play the ball a little farther forward at address, locating it from just left of center in my stance up to opposite my left toe, depending on how much height I require. Second, my hands are less ahead of the clubface at address —although they are always slightly ahead. Third, to get height and backspin by hitting down into the ball, I steepen and lengthen my backswing with a fuller wrist cock. Precise striking of the ball is essential, so:

Concentrate hard on back of ball

3. JUST OFF GREEN

Never hesitate to haul out the "Texas wedge" whenever it seems to offer the high-percentage chance of success. Unless the fringe is so rough or raggedy that you must chip, putt the ball, especially if, as in the picture where the ball is on the green-side bank of a bunker, you have an awkward lie or stance. There are at least two strong reasons always to putt the ball when conditions allow. First, roll is easier to judge than flight. Second, it is easier to make solid contact between clubface and ball. Where you really have to concentrate on this kind of shot is in judging distance, slope and grain. Thus the prime thought must be:

Compute roll with extra care

4. SHORT SHOT TO FAST GREEN

Play this delicate "touch" shot, where you're just off the green but for some reason can't putt the ball, with a 9-iron or wedge, a grip of about the same firmness you'd use to restrain a pet canary, and a chipping-type stroke. Set your weight on your leading foot, the ball in the center of your stance, and your hands ahead of the clubface at address. Hold the clubface square— "looking at" the ball— throughout the short back-and through-swing. Because of the "softness" of the shot, the tendency is to scoop at the ball or quit on the stroke, so a good prime thought is:

Swing down and through the ball

5. BALL BELOW FEET

You'll never hit a good golf shot if you're wobbling around, and this kind of lie—see picture—can most easily throw you off balance. Ensure that it doesn't by taking a slightly wider stance than normal and "sitting" on your heels and knees—which are going to have to be flexed more than usual to allow you to reach down to the ball. There is a tendency to push the ball right of target from this lie, so hood the clubface a fraction and aim a little left at address to compensate. You'll also keep the ball on line better by arching your wrists slightly to set the sole of the club flat on the slope. Play the ball from the center of your stance. Swing with your hands and arms and make your prime thought:
Keep body steady to stay in balance

6. BALL ABOVE FEET

A frequent plight, especially when you have to stand in a trap to play a ball that didn't quite make the sand. If you are standing in sand, set your feet solidly—good balance is vital on all uneven-lie shots. Choke down on the grip to compensate for your feet being so much below the ball—if you don't it's an odds-on bet you'll stub the club into the ground behind the ball. There is a tendency to pull the ball left of target from this lie. Thwart it by opening the clubface fractionally so that it aims a little right at address. Because choking down on the club diminishes power, make your prime thought:
Hit a little firmer than usual

7. UPHILL LIE

Here I'm playing from an uphill lie over a bunker—a common situation. The club to use is generally the pitching wedge, but you might go to the 9-iron if you wanted a lot of run, or the sand wedge if you had a good lie and wanted quick height but little run. Address the ball left of center in your stance, with your weight equally distributed on both feet to help you stand perpendicular to the angle of the ground. Set your hands only a little ahead of the clubface. Then swing as you would for a normal short pitch shot. The more uphill the lie, the higher—and thus the shorter—the ball will fly, so the prime thought is the same as when the ball is above your feet:
Hit a little firmer than usual

8. DOWNHILL LIE

A tough shot for most club golfers, especially when the downhill angle is pronounced. The first trick is to stand perpendicular to the slope. Keeping weight on the downhill foot helps that. Next, always address the ball to right of center in your stance, with your hands ahead of the clubface. As you get ready to play the shot, picture the clubhead following the angle of the ground. Then make a firm-wristed swing to match that mental picture. Any tendency to "flip the wrists"—let the clubface get ahead of the left hand, as happens if you are over-anxious and scoop at the ball—will make you either stub the club into the ground behind the ball, or top it. So the big thought is the same as on any chip shot:
Lead clubface through with left hand

SAM SNEAD REVEALS HIS PERSONAL KEYS

BY CAL BROWN
August, 1972

I'm self-taught and never could go back to a teacher and ask what was wrong with my swing. I just experimented a lot to find out what I could do with it.

One thing I learned was that you can't swing your hardest and be consistent. You'll rarely contact the

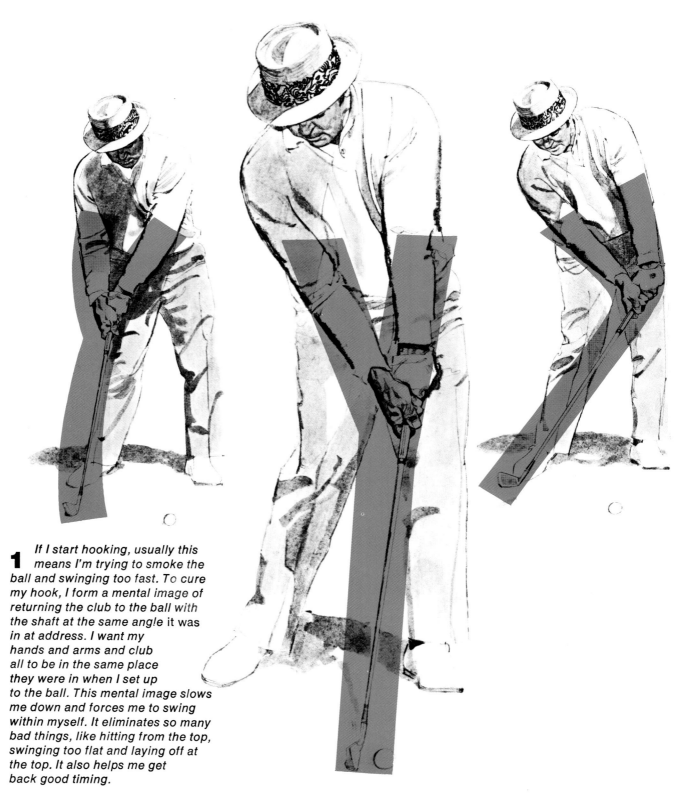

1 *If I start hooking, usually this means I'm trying to smoke the ball and swinging too fast. To cure my hook, I form a mental image of returning the club to the ball with the shaft at the same angle it was in at address. I want my hands and arms and club all to be in the same place they were in when I set up to the ball. This mental image slows me down and forces me to swing within myself. It eliminates so many bad things, like hitting from the top, swinging too flat and laying off at the top. It also helps me get back good timing.*

ball square. I learned to throttle back to about 80 or 85 per cent. This is probably the most important lesson for any golfer to learn.

When I'm really smoking the ball, I never have the sensation of hitting at all. My swing feels just like grease, as if my whole body were oiled. The key to this feeling is keeping your legs from getting tight.

Another thing I've learned is that the short game requires more practice than the long game because it requires more touch. The average golfer doesn't practice near enough on his short game.

My golf swing has become grooved over the years but still occasionally gets off track. I've worked out a few simple keys that help me check it when this happens. ∎

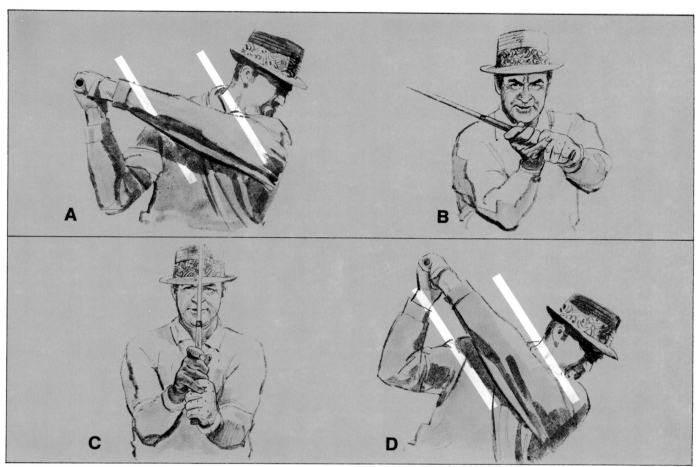

A

B

C

D

2 *If I sense I'm out of position at the top of my backswing, I swing the club back to the top and stop (A). Then I bring my hands in front of me at shoulder level with the wrists still cocked. If I'm laying off at the top, my hands and clubshaft will be tilted (B), instead of being straight up and down. To correct this, I grip the club in front of my body and cock my wrists so that the clubshaft is vertical (C). Then I simply turn my shoulders and put my left arm into what I call the "slot," between my head and right shoulder (D). Automatically I'm back to where I want to be at the top of my backswing.*

3 *If I'm pulling the ball, it's obvious that I'm swinging too flat. So I concentrate on finishing high, with my right arm between my head and left shoulder. This keeps my swing on the right track.*

KNOCK THOSE CONFLICTS OUT OF YOUR PUTTING STROKE

BY DEANE BEMAN
April, 1973

The fact that I swing the club very differently than my long-time friend and rival, Jack Nicklaus, is proof that there is more than one way to play golf. Nevertheless, I believe there are some absolutes in the game that deal with crucial areas of the swing in which golfers most commonly make mistakes.

I call my absolutes *mutually exclusive factors.* This simply means that certain moves and positions in the swing must be matched by other moves and positions. If they are, you can play well with your own particular style. But if your moves and positions do not match, if they are "mutually exclusive," your swing will be in conflict with itself and you will never play well consistently.

Now commissioner of the Tournament Players Division, Deane Beman was a player who had carved out a brilliant amateur record and a successful professional career when he wrote this article for *Golf Digest.*

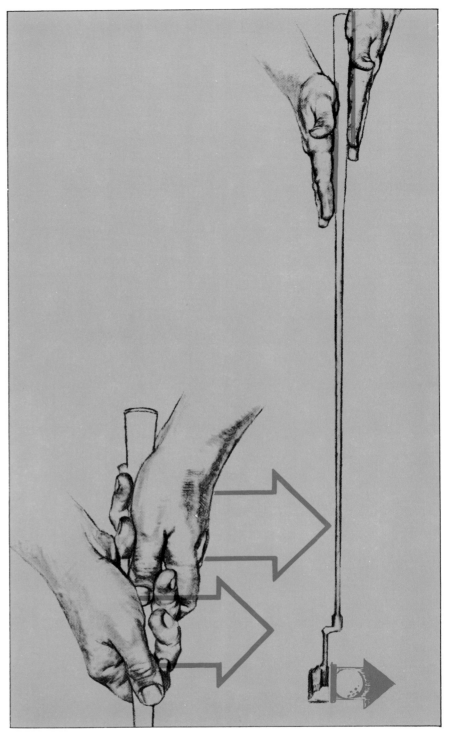

If you have a "weak" or a "strong" putting grip, you can't return the putterface square to the target at impact.
I believe that on every golf shot, from the drive through the putt, the hands instinctively return to a square position at impact. Swing at something, backhanded with your left hand and forehanded with your right, and you'll find you instinctively hit the target squarely.

The same thing happens in putting—the back of the left hand and the palm of the right naturally try to face the target at impact. Thus a golfer who grips his putter "weakly"—with his hands turned well to the left— will tend to return the putterface to the ball in an open position, or looking right of target. Conversely, a golfer with a "strong" grip—hands turned well to the right on the putter—will tend to return the putterface in a closed position, looking left of target, at impact.

This is why I believe that, whatever type of stroke is used, gripping the putter with the back of the left hand and the palm of the right square to the target line will most consistently return the face square at impact.

If you address a putt with the ball well away from your body, you can't keep the path of the putter close to the target line.

The arc of the putterhead should be kept as close as possible to your target line for the sake of consistency. To do this, you should position the ball as close to your body at address as is comfortably possible. The farther you stand from the ball on any golf shot, the more acutely the clubhead will swing inside the target line on the backswing and after impact.

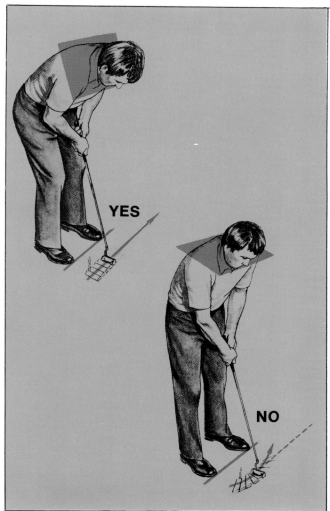

If you stand erect at address while putting with a shoulder stroke, you can't swing the putterface squarely back from and through the ball.

Keeping the putterface as square as possible to the target line is basic to good putting, irrespective of the stroke used. I believe a stroking action emanating from the shoulders, with the arms, wrists and hands locked into a solid unit, produces the least clubhead variance. In fact, although I now putt with a combination arm-and-wrist stroke, if I had it to do again, I'd change to a shoulder stroke, modeling myself after Bob Charles, the finest shoulder-stroker in golf.

If you use a shoulder stroke, your address posture has a big bearing on the "squareness" of your putterface during the stroke. If your upper body is erect at address, your shoulders must turn in a horizontal or level plane to swing the putter. If your arms, hands and club are solidly locked to your shoulders, the effect of this level turn will be to open the putterface while swinging the club inside the target line on the backswing. At impact and on the follow-through the clubhead will quickly swing back inside the target line and the face will close. This opening and closing motion is almost unavoidable with a level shoulder turn, unless you compensate by manipulating the putter with your hands.

To keep the putterface as square to the target as possible throughout the stroke, the shoulder putter should lean his upper body forward from the waist, folding his arms into his body. His shoulders then can operate in a vertical or tilted plane that allows the putterhead to be swung nearly straight back from and straight through the ball, with the opening and closing of the face kept to a minimum.

JACK'S LESSON TEE

BY JACK NICKLAUS
June, 1973

DRIVING TECHNIQUE

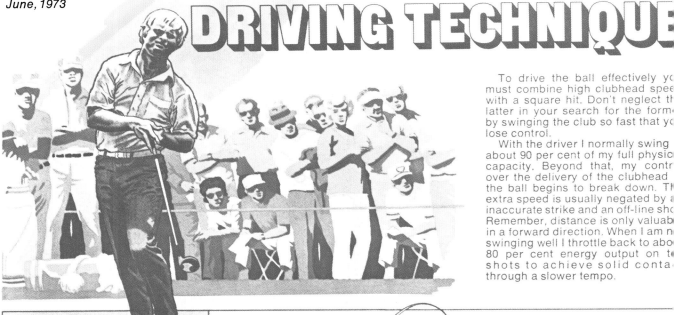

To drive the ball effectively yo must combine high clubhead spee with a square hit. Don't neglect th latter in your search for the form by swinging the club so fast that yo lose control.

With the driver I normally swing about 90 per cent of my full physic capacity. Beyond that, my contr over the delivery of the clubhead the ball begins to break down. Th extra speed is usually negated by inaccurate strike and an off-line sho Remember, distance is only valuab in a forward direction. When I am n swinging well I throttle back to abo 80 per cent energy output on te shots to achieve solid conta through a slower tempo.

Be certain you get a driver that matches your swing characteristics, particularly your tempo. Find a club with a flex pattern complementary to your timing, one that delivers the clubhead squarely to the ball without need for swing compensations. If you swing hard and fast you will normally need a relatively stiff-shafted club—too much flex will leave the clubface open at impact. For the slow or easy swinger a relatively "soft" shaft usually helps promote square delivery of the clubface.

Unless wind conditions dictate otherwise I drive for carry rather than run, whic means I hit the ball high. There are no hazards in the air and a high-flying, sof landing ball gives me maximum control over placement of the tee shot. I recommen a similar policy for golfers to whom distance isn't a problem. But if you lack lengt you're generally going to be better off driving for run rather than height. To develo this you must learn to draw the ball from right to left.

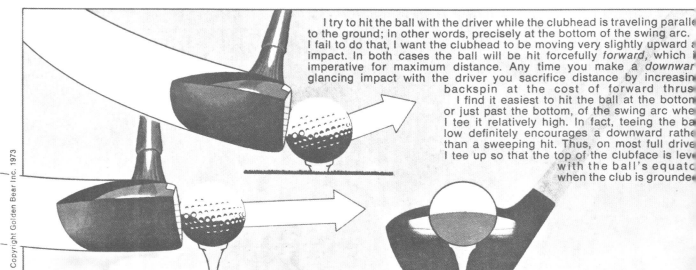

I try to hit the ball with the driver while the clubhead is traveling paralle to the ground; in other words, precisely at the bottom of the swing arc. I fail to do that, I want the clubhead to be moving very slightly upward a impact. In both cases the ball will be hit forcefully *forward*, which imperative for maximum distance. Any time you make a *downwar* glancing impact with the driver you sacrifice distance by increasin backspin at the cost of forward thrus

I find it easiest to hit the ball at the bottom or just past the bottom, of the swing arc whe I tee it relatively high. In fact, teeing the ba low definitely encourages a downward rathe than a sweeping hit. Thus, on most full drive I tee up so that the top of the clubface is leve with the ball's equato when the club is grounde

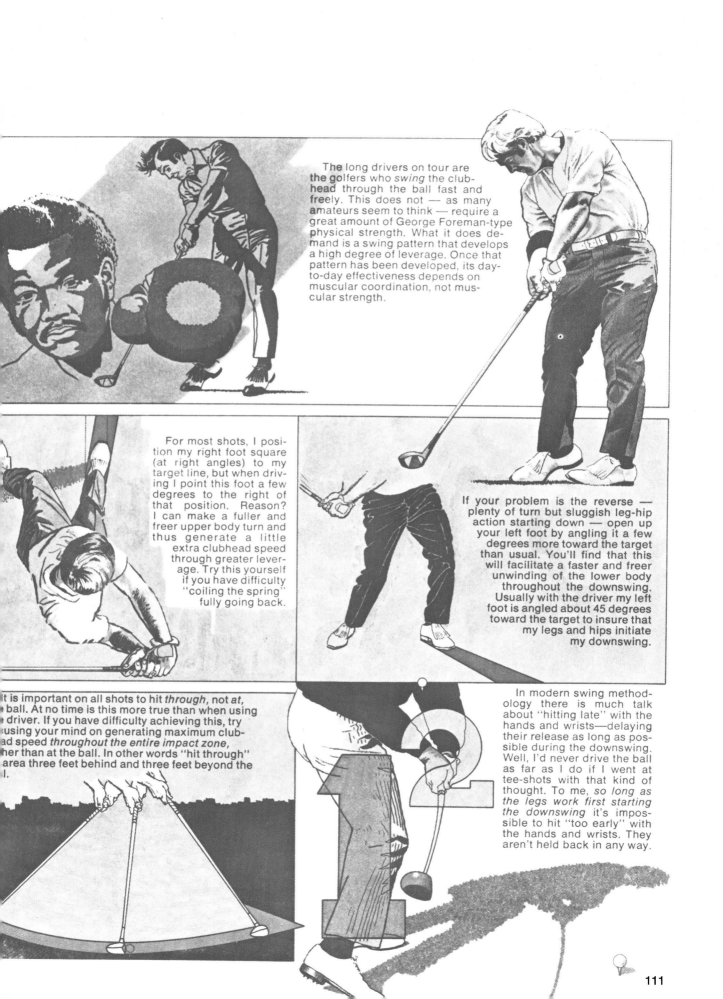

The long drivers on tour are the golfers who *swing* the clubhead through the ball fast and freely. This does not — as many amateurs seem to think — require a great amount of George Foreman-type physical strength. What it does demand is a swing pattern that develops a high degree of leverage. Once that pattern has been developed, its day-to-day effectiveness depends on muscular coordination, not muscular strength.

For most shots, I position my right foot square (at right angles) to my target line, but when driving I point this foot a few degrees to the right of that position. Reason? I can make a fuller and freer upper body turn and thus generate a little extra clubhead speed through greater leverage. Try this yourself if you have difficulty "coiling the spring" fully going back.

If your problem is the reverse — plenty of turn but sluggish leg-hip action starting down — open up your left foot by angling it a few degrees more toward the target than usual. You'll find that this will facilitate a faster and freer unwinding of the lower body throughout the downswing. Usually with the driver my left foot is angled about 45 degrees toward the target to insure that my legs and hips initiate my downswing.

It is important on all shots to hit *through*, not at, ● ball. At no time is this more true than when using ● driver. If you have difficulty achieving this, try ●using your mind on generating maximum club●ad speed *throughout the entire impact zone*, ●her than at the ball. In other words "hit through" ● area three feet behind and three feet beyond the ●.

In modern swing methodology there is much talk about "hitting late" with the hands and wrists—delaying their release as long as possible during the downswing. Well, I'd never drive the ball as far as I do if I went at tee-shots with that kind of thought. To me, *so long as the legs work first starting the downswing* it's impossible to hit "too early" with the hands and wrists. They aren't held back in any way.

On the same tack, you hear a lot of talk about ''left-sidedness'' versus ''right - sidedness.'' To me, you can't use your right side too much *so long as your left side leads and controls the swing.* For example, I hit just about as hard as I can with my right hand on full drives. Trouble only occurs if my left hand isn't leading and controlling the swing.

I have three ways of generating extra yardage when a situation calls for a particularly big drive.
1. Preparing to tee off, I consciously try to get myself into big-hit condition by letting my muscles go loose and easy. Then I am a little less deliberate in standing up to the ball, and I hit before tension can begin to build up. I use this device primarily when accuracy is not a factor and I am really intent on ''flat-outing'' a drive.

2. When both accuracy and extra distance are factors, my primary thought is to make a particularly slow and smooth ''one-piece'' takeaway. By so doing I eliminate rush — the biggest danger when you're going for a big one — and establish a smooth tempo for the swing. A deliberate start-back also insures that I'll complete my backswing before I start my downswing, which guarantees maximum leverage and clubhead speed.

3. My third means of producing extra distance is to speed up my hip action on the downswing. The way I play golf, the faster my hips turn and clear from the top of the swing the greater the leverage I generate and the faster the clubhead travels. Here the critical factor is accelerating the hip turn while keeping the whole action smooth. Any jerkiness will inevitably cause a bad shot.

Golfers who have distance problems from the tee, yet are unable to make a bigger body turn without losing swing control, might find they can increase the arc of the swing — and thus their yardage potential — by swinging their arms higher going back. I often make a particular point with the driver of ''reaching for the clouds'' with my hands. In addition to extending my arc, this also helps me complete my backswing before I start my downswing — an absolute requisite for maximum leverage.

J McQueen

JOHNNY MILLER'S KEY SWING THOUGHTS

BY LARRY DENNIS
October, 1974

Several touring professionals were talking about Johnny Miller's golf game, as they are prone to do these days.

"He says he knows where the club is at all times during his swing, and that's not too important," said Jerry Heard, facetiously. "What's important is going out and beating 300 balls and not having any idea what you're doing."

Johnny Miller, the dominant player in golf this year, does not go out and beat 300 balls on the practice tee. This is partly because when he was a boy, his swing was carefully constructed by his father and John Geertsen, then professional at San Francisco's Olympic Club. It is also because Miller is one of the tour's most astute thinkers, about his own swing and others.

"I think I understand my swing better than any of the other young pros," Miller declares. "That's one reason I don't get into slumps. If I hit it badly, it's just for a short time, because I just go back over my basic keys. It's almost always the same two or three problems, and I'm able to analyze my trouble. I don't have to go to anybody else for help.

"I'm very observant when it comes to the mechanics. I love to watch people. And I've learned from talking. If I see something interesting I talk to the player about it. Or I mark it down or I analyze it or take pictures and analyze those.

"I keep charts and records. If I come up with a key thought for my swing, I write it down. Otherwise, I forget what I'm doing when I'm playing well.

"That's more interesting than going out and beating a lot of balls. I feel I can improve my swing by sitting home at night and just thinking about what I do." ∎

Gripping lightly, relaxing body produce good tempo

"To maintain good tempo, you have to be totally relaxed," Miller says. "Also, there's no such thing as too slow a backswing. If the average player would remember those two points, he'd improve his game immediately. If you take the club back slowly, you'll start it down slowly. I even think that if you can learn to pause at the top of the swing it's a great thing. If you rush it at the top you never know where your clubface is.

"There's great timing involved in golf. You see good athletes from other sports want to overpower the golf ball, but the ideal golf swing is a very relaxed new movement. What you want to do is just get the club on the plane and let the club do the work. Learn to relax and let the left side be dominant. If you can just get a good long arc and be relaxed, letting the club go back and forward on a plane like a pendulum, you'll have an effective swing.

"Most players grip the club tightly, so their right side is tight. They always have the tendency to come over the top with that big right-side move coming down. When I'm hitting the ball at my very best, I feel I'm gripping the club about as loosely as I possibly can. The club almost falls out of my hands. And I've never talked to a long hitter who didn't tell me the same thing. They grip the club like a little bird. Your muscles are longer and react faster from a relaxed position than from a tense position. So if you grip the club tighter it shortens your muscles and makes your reaction time much slower. If you are in a relaxed, long position at the top of the swing and coming down, you will react much quicker and get more clubhead speed when you reach the hitting zone."

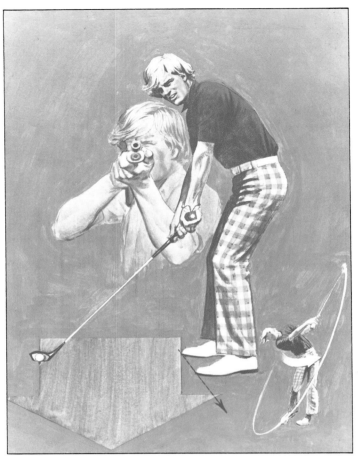

Lining up to the left leads to a better lateral move

"Apart from the mental side, which is extremely important, setup is probably 75 per cent of the game," Miller says. "My swing is dictated by my address position. It's just like lining up a gun. If you aim it at the target and pull the trigger, the rest of it is pretty elementary . . . it just flows. If I get wound up well and my head stays still and my tempo is decent, I'm going to get good shots. But if you're not lined up correctly and in a good address position, if you don't have a good firm foundation, you've got to make an almost perfect execution or correct a fault with another error to get the shot on line.

"If I were teaching a young kid, I'd have him align his body a little left of the target, which would enable him to make the good lateral move into the ball. If you set up right you can't make that lateral lead because your body blocks you out.

"The average guy sets up to the right of the target and then makes a big strong move with his right side to pull the ball back on line. This feels good . . . it's a feeling of power . . . but it makes you come over the top with an outside-in swing. Not too many guys want to set up left of the target and make the lateral shift and the slight blockout that Lee Trevino and a lot of good players do."

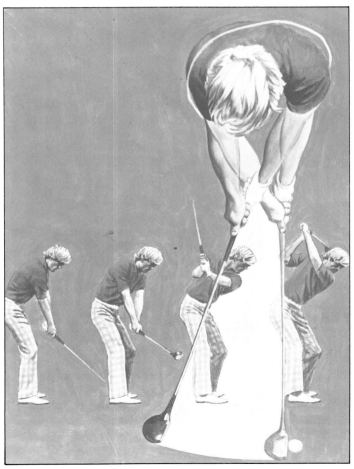

Allowing shoulder turn to open clubface naturally saves adjustments

Miller's theory is that the most important aspect of the actual swing is what the player does in the first 12 inches of the takeaway. That largely determines what happens afterward.

"So many players—I'd say 90 per cent of the pros—have a tendency to come inside and hood the club in the first 12 inches away from the ball," he says. "Now, the great swingers— like Littler, Weiskopf, Snead, Player, Ben Hogan —all do one thing . . . it looks like they're fanning the club open in that first 12 inches. In reality all they're doing is allowing the shoulder turn to open the clubface to the target line instead of hooding or closing the clubface going back.

"Ideally, you set up your left hand at address and never change the square relationship of the back of the left hand with the clubface throughout the swing. In a truly square swing, it's as if you're the hinge of a door. The door semi-opens and semi-closes, and the face of the club does the same thing.

"If you hood it going back it gives you that 'flying right elbow' . . . you're not in a power position. To eliminate having to make an extra move to compensate, let the clubface open naturally to the target line. That sets up your whole plane and your whole swing."

INSTANT LESSONS

Swing a beach pail in the sand

Many sand shots fail because of a hurried swing. Golfers who are afraid of leaving the ball in the sand, or over-hitting the green altogether, unconsciously speed up their swings. This destroys timing and causes inconsistency.

I instruct my pupils to pretend that they are swinging a bucket full of water. To swing the bucket back and forth without spilling a drop, tempo must be smooth and unrushed. As they establish this tempo through a bit of practice, they dramatically improve their control of sand shots.

By Gloria Armstrong
Professional, Atlanta C.C.
May, 1972

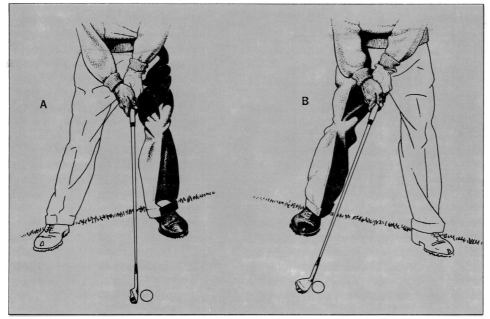

On hilly lies hit from high foot

Uphill and downhill lies needn't be a problem to a golfer if he simply remembers to "play the ball off the 'high' foot."

Because of the terrain, when playing from an uphill lie your clubhead reaches the ground a bit later in the swing—so you should position the ball toward your left foot (drawing A). On a downhill lie the clubhead reaches the ground earlier in the swing—so play the ball back toward your right foot (drawing B).

It also helps to keep most of your weight on the "high side" at the start of the swing (see drawings). This offsets the normal gravitational pull toward the lower foot which causes the tendency to hook from an uphill lie and slice from a downhill lie.

By Hardy Loudermilk
Professional, Oak Hills C.C.
San Antonio, Tex.
May, 1964

Throttle back to regain tempo

Whenever I feel my tempo and rhythm are off, and my shots begin to stray, I just make sure I'm not trying to overpower the ball. I slack off, just a little, from striving for distance. I think only of meeting the ball solidly. After a few holes of this semi-cautious play, once I'm hitting straight shots again, I'll gradually turn on the power I need to reach the par-5s in two and set up those money-winning birdies.
By Lanny Wadkins
PGA Touring Professional
December, 1972

Relax and release to cure shank

Many people have kidded me about my name, but rather than avoid me they invariably ask me how to cure shanking. One major cause of this dread affliction is tension—when the golfer worries about shot results he tries to steer the ball and fails to release his wrists and arms from their cocked position at the top of the backswing. So relax the grip and free up the muscles in the forearms, allowing the wrists to unhinge properly and the arms to roll over. If the rolling movement is done too quickly, it will cause the ball to fly to the left, but no shank will result and confidence will be restored.
By Craig Shankland
Middle Bay Club
Rockville Center, N.Y.
March, 1973

"See" the ball into the hole

The best way to help your putting is to allow your subconscious reflexes to take over by letting your eyes "tell" your fingers how to stroke the ball.

Line up your putt, take your stance, look at the hole, then look at the ball and putt without any further mental gymnastics. Trust what your eyes have seen, and you will putt well.

Try this to prove the validity of eye-finger coordination. Glance at a pencil on your desk. Look away, and reach for the pencil. Nine times out of 10 you'll pick up the pencil and you won't even have to think about it. The same thing works in putting.

By Nick Chillemi
Professional, Golden Gate C.C.
Naples, Fla.
May, 1974

Swing with ease against a breeze

When playing in wind, the tendency is to swing too hard. There is also a strong urge to "steer" the shot according to the direction of the wind. Both of these tendencies exaggerate swing faults and cause the ball to fly errantly.

The ball will stay on line much better when you swing easily and concentrate on hitting it flush. Take plenty of club to get the job done, swing with *less* force than usual, and you are sure to play well in wind.

By Johnny Johnston
Head Professional, Sea Scape C.C.
Kitty Hawk, N.C.
June, 1971

Get on the ball to stop swaying

To avoid straightening the right leg and rolling your weight to the outside of the right foot on your backswing—common faults among higher handicappers—try this simple practice-tee exercise. Place a golf ball under the outside of your right foot, just forward of the heel. This will concentrate your weight on the inside of your right foot and leg. Hit several full shots with a 7-iron in this manner, being sure to keep your right knee flexed on the backswing.

After you acquire the feeling of keeping your knee flexed and the weight on the inside of the right foot, remove the ball and hit several more shots. You'll find you will be making a better body turn and will be in a more balanced and powerful position to begin the downswing.

By Kenneth Giovando
Golf Coach, Scottsdale Community College
Scottsdale, Ariz.
May, 1974

Grip light when situation tight

A golfer has a tendency to tighten his grip when faced with a tense and challenging shot situation, such as a long carry over water.

Tightening his grip, particularly with his left hand, causes a golfer to stiffen his wrists and jerk his clubhead out of a proper plane. Mis-hit shots result.

In tense situations, consciously keep both hands relaxed and free, but firm enough to control the club, as your backswing starts. This will give you a smooth and rhythmic swing. Your left hand will tighten naturally on the downswing and your clubhead will meet the ball squarely at impact.

By Joe Novak
Professional Emeritus
Bel Air C.C., Los Angeles, Cal.
Former President
Professional Golfers' Assn
October, 1966

THE SWING OF THE FUTURE

August, 1975

No body of men in the world is better prepared to comment on the golf swing and the game than Golf Digest's Professional Teaching Panel. Collectively, the nine panelists represent more than 200 years of teaching experience and almost that many of competitive play, much of it at the highest levels.

As part of its 25th anniversary observance, Golf Digest asked the panel members to discuss the changes they have seen over the years in the golf swing and methods of teaching it and to take a look into the future. Their observations follow.

John Jacobs: As far as we're concerned in Great Britain, we've always been too dependent on too much use of the hands and wrists because we've used the small ball through the years. But because the professionals over there now have been playing the big ball for four or five years, we're beginning to see them swing much more with their arms. I personally felt very strongly about this for a long time but really wasn't able to do anything about it because the ball has had a very big influence on the game.

This has made us bad under pressure. It's important that you be able to swing consistently and have the ability to repeat it when you're scared stiff. You're much more likely to stand up under pressure when your swing is less dependent on your hands.

So, speaking from my side of the world, we're in a catch-up period. Over here, when you changed to the big ball in the late '20s or early '30s, you unwittingly made yourselves into better players. Our younger players just now are making a move to get the swing more correct, with the arms, than it's been.

Bob Toski: One of the biggest changes in the golf game from past to present is in the grip. The left hand now is facing the target more, not turned as much to the right as it used to be.

The modern player, compared to those 30, 40 or 50 years ago, simply places the club in position going back. He doesn't whirl it around his body and accentuate a big forced turn. He just resists with the lower part of his body, swings the club back into position as he coils, then attacks the ball more with the forward action of the swing. The modern player is using more arm motion, stabilizing his hand position on top and attacking the ball more strongly with the lower part of his body, getting more lash through the ball.

Eddie Merrins: The player today is beginning to use the strength of his entire body. As John pointed out, the accent in Britain for years has been on the use of the hands and the clubhead, and the better players were trained to play that way. The American player, on the other hand, has learned to play by

Gary Wiren, educational director of the Professional Golfers' Ass'n and an advisory member of the Golf Digest Professional Teaching Panel, demonstrates the pre-set position which he predicts may become integrated into the swing of the future. From this position, Wiren says, the player will make a forward press and move immediately into his backswing.

using his arms, and he's therefore able to use his entire body. I think we'll all agree this has made him a much stronger and more aggressive player than his European counterpart.

In the future, the evolution of golf instruction is going to accent this use of the arms and entire body to swing the club. This is going to erase the false idea that the golf swing is an awkward thing. I've talked to many athletes who excelled in their own sports who have told me they just can't grasp golf because they're going about it in an unnatural way. I feel they've been mistaught, and I think that golf instructors presently and in the future are going to teach a beginner how to swing a club so that he can employ his body naturally and functionally.

Cary Middlecoff: Most of the changes in the game started with the steel shaft. I played with wooden shafts as a kid and you can't take as many liberties with that kind of shaft because it has such an unbelievable amount of torque. People had to play more with their hands to be able to adjust to that and to adjust from day to day because of the change in the golf club.

So better equipment allows a lot more mistakes. As long as you keep going through the ball you'll get away with a fairly reasonable shot that you couldn't have gotten away with using the old wood shaft.

Bob pointed out the change in the grip, and that's made a big difference. With your hands facing, both square to the target line, you can beat at it with both hands. It's pretty hard to play any way but one-handed with the grip too strong. And there's a definite difference in the use of the lower body. You see the knees moving more toward the target in the downswing and helping keep the face of the club square a little longer.

But I'll tell you, take a guy like George Fazio, who was brought up in the "swing in a barrel" school. George won't play for three months and he'll go out and shoot 72 or 73. So I can't say that's the wrong way to play, either.

There are 20 times as many good athletes in professional golf now as

there were when I went on tour. We've got all kinds of kids now who were good basketball players, all-state football players, but there's so much opportunity in golf that they chose to get their college scholarships that way. They're better coordinated, they're stronger to start with and a bigger percentage of them can do the things that the good instructors try to teach.

They also know more to start with. There are more books being written all the time, and a good student of golf learns something from them. He starts out at 20 knowing darned near as much as we know now.

And our college golf here is something else. I never got to play with any good players much until I got on tour. These guys play 25 tournaments a year with good players. So all these things have meant a whole lot of progress, and it will keep getting better.

Sam Snead: Players have stressed power for the last 10 years. In the old days, they used to try to hit it 225 yards down the middle, but if you did that today you'd have to hit the next shot 245 to get it on the green. All the new courses play 7,000 yards or more.

So the swings are getting longer to get more power. Players today are finishing higher, which means they've hit through the ball more. And it looks like they're using their bodies more.

The kids today are getting bigger and taller, too. Now, a tall man doesn't have to turn his lower part as much as a short man, because he has so much from the waist up to turn. So they're making that big turn with their shoulders, which is what is making the swing longer. They concentrate on getting the left side around, because if you do that the right has to go.

I think players will improve in the future because they're starting to play earlier, and that's the way you build up your strength and accuracy. You see these skinny kids just knocking hell out of the ball because they're able to accelerate their arms, and that's the only way to get more distance. I don't think they can do anything else with the golf swing in the future unless they

run at it and swing to get more acceleration.

Paul Runyan: It's my feeling that the better swing of the future will be the same as the better swing of the past only with a better understanding of all the components. The player will more clearly understand how all the parts of the swing work together, how the legs help the arms work, how the arm swing influences the hand and wrist action and so forth. For example, a player might feel he needs more leg thrust to get more momentum in the over-all swing of the arms and club, but he won't overdo it. He'll know when it becomes a fault.

This is the marked change I see in the golf swing over the years. There is really nothing new in golf, in my opinion, but the application of the principles are much more sound today as a result of having better instruction. The good minds that are in golf today are contributing enormously to this. The young players have access to better pictures, to better ideas. The average player coming out of college now is as far along knowledgewise as the professional was years ago.

As a result, they know how to use all the components correctly. I saw this start years ago when the American professionals were dominating the British in the Ryder Cup matches. Someone said the Americans used their hands much less and the legs and back muscles more than the British professionals. In my opinion, the Americans only used their hands less by comparison. They used their hands as much, but they used their legs better. They were using their legs and hands in cooperation with each other.

Gary Wiren: The good players of today are much better, but the average player hasn't made much gain. There's a greater gap between the average player and the excellent player than there was 30 or 40 years ago.

First of all, players get introduced to golf much earlier through school programs and things like that. There is more opportunity to play. Golf is not a "society" sport as much as it was many years ago.

Secondly, there are greater incentives for them. The amount of money on tour gets an awful lot of fellows awfully interested in practicing long hours to improve. So you've got a much larger group of people who are quite good players.

And Cary's point that better instruction is available is an absolute truth—through this magazine, through better teachers, through PGA schools and that's very important. Good instruction was harder to find a few years ago unless you were lucky enough to be around a good teacher.

Why hasn't the average player gotten significantly better? Because the great player has the physical skills and he's been given a technique which is better for him. But the average player can't do it. The first thing he needs to be taught is to swing like Ernest Jones did, to feel the clubhead. If you can't feel centrifugal force, you can't play. But a lot of people aren't getting that anymore. They're trying to do it like a tour player, and they can't do it. They can't physically handle it. That's why the gap has gotten bigger.

As for the better technique that the good players are being given, there's a definite emphasis in teaching on using the left side more. We're trying to strengthen the left so it can become an equal partner with the right. There is also an important difference in leg action. Instead of the straightening-leg action, we now have the deep knee sit, more drive with the legs so you can use more muscular force. Again, that's only been made possible by the change in equipment.

As our teaching gets better, we've tried to cut out various moves in the swing. My prediction for the future is that we'll make the swing even simpler than it is now. I predict that we'll eliminate the setting motion during the swing. Instead, we'll pre-set the angle—cock your wrists, if you will—before we ever take it back.

Within the next 10 years I think you'll find the good players start with the club a couple of feet in the air, already set where he wants it. He'll set up to the ball, set the club in its position, make a little forward press to get started, then turn from there and strike the ball. That's only a prediction.

Jim Flick: I would concur with Bob's point about the grip change. We've seen how that has changed the plane of the golf swing to some degree and made it more upright.

We see a change in setup. There were more good players in the old days who set up back on their right side than we ever realized. The change we're seeing today is that the good players are out over the ball more with their upper bodies. The arms give the appearance of hanging as opposed to the extended look that we saw in players years ago, which created more arm tension. The weight now is more toward the balls of the feet.

All these changes let the swing plane get a little more upright and let the legs and body contribute, as Eddie has said, in a more meaningful way.

We see the legs assuming a different role today than in the past. They are no longer just supports for the upper body. As Bob said, they are used to achieve a position of torque on the backswing and certainly as a means of delivering the club on the downswing for the better player.

In the pictures of players in the '30s, it looks as if the body were chasing the club coming down. In today's swing, along the Johnny Miller line, it looks as if the club is chasing the body. So we're seeing a different appearance in the golf swing through this evolution. All parts of the body rather than just the hands now contribute.

I see a great evolution in the takeaway. We saw the Vardon drag and then we saw the one-piece and now we're seeing the pre-setting or early setting of the angle. I don't think it's coincidental that of the 20 leading money-winners on the tour last year, 14 of them set the angle early.

That points to the trend Gary is talking about. I don't think it will happen in the next 10 years, but within maybe the next 20 we'll see a number of players starting from the set position Gary mentioned, much as they do in baseball. I think that's why we get a better swinging action with the baseball bat. It's already set in position to return it. In golf, we're starting from a position which almost paralyzes the player in many instances. Therefore they can't get the club set. So we may see that type of thing in greater numbers, although not necessarily by the average player, who perhaps can't handle it.

That swing can be used effectively in one way right now. There are a lot of drills in every sport except golf. This is one thing we teachers have not done well. We have not used our imaginations well enough to help people develop better muscle patterns and better movement through drills and exercises. The pre-set swing is a super drill to get the average guy to break down his right side so his left side can assume equal responsibility.

As to the point Cary made about Fazio—it's going to be hard for us to draw a conclusion as to how well the modern swing will work after a month's layoff until we've used the modern swing for a number of generations. We're constantly being told that guys can't play with the modern swing, the use of the entire body, if they haven't played for a long period of time. The critics point to a player like Julius Boros, who can simply pick up a club and play so well. But that's not a fair comparison. The modern swing hasn't been in use long enough to draw any conclusions like that.

I have a feeling that 50 years from now we'll have another modern swing, so to speak, and they'll be looking upon what we're using today as the classical swing. ∎

THE PLAYERS

One of the strongest points of *Golf Digest's* editorial content traditionally has been its profiling of the prominent players in the game. During the past 25 years our editors and contributing writers have traveled virtually all over the world to interview the top golfers, professionals and amateurs, and in the process often have come to know them better than their next-door neighbors have.

It has been our policy to feature promising golfers on their way up, before they reach the crests of their careers and are extensively reported. In looking back over our old issues, we discovered articles on the young Cary Middlecoff, Arnold Palmer, Gary Player, Jack Nicklaus, Lee Trevino, Tom Weiskopf and Johnny Miller, to name a few.

Along that line, *Golf Digest* each year honors the two pro tours' rookies of the year, and the plaques hanging in our editorial offices commemorating the choices read like a Who's Who in the world of latter-day tournament golf: Nicklaus in 1962, Susie Berning in 1964, Trevino in 1967, Jane Blalock in 1969. . . .

Arnold Palmer was a rookie before we instituted the award in 1957, but his impact on golf recently was observed in another, large way by his selection as our Man of the Silver Era. In the opinion of our editors, Arnold made the strongest imprint on the game over the past 25 years, golf's richest quarter century in nearly every way.

All told, we've run a dozen and a half full-scale articles about Palmer and his game over the years, including the revealing interview in this section.

We have selected profiles here primarily about great players. It surely is no accident that they have inspired great writing, and in the following pages are some compelling match-ups of subjects and authors.

We asked of the writing that it be bright, penetrating and original. No two pieces sound even faintly similar in style, and we wouldn't want them to. Strong writing deserves better than a meat-grinder philosophy of editing that results in a droning content.

No one has achieved a greater niche in the game's history than Bobby Jones, the subject of a touching tribute by his old friend Al Laney, shortly after Jones' death.

Nick Seitz spent a week with Ben Hogan at home in Fort Worth, and his story offers illuminating insights into Ben's long-secluded lifestyle, his viewpoints on golf and his philosophy of life. Both Southwesterners, they meshed well.

We go international with an examination of the mystical hold on the Irish generated by the colorful Christy O'Connor, written by Peter Dobereiner, the distinguished British journalist, and Ken Bowden's word portrait of South Africa's unorthodox Bobby Locke.

All in all, the section on the players spans the wide panorama of the era, from Walter Hagen and Bobby Jones to "Lee Elder's Long Road to Augusta."

Preceding page: Arnold Palmer, the golfer who most influenced the game over the past 25 years, blasts from sand.

BOBBY JONES: THE MAN BEHIND THE SLAM

BY AL LANEY
February, 1972

Most people will remember Bobby Jones for the still incredible climax of his astonishing career in 1930, the original "Grand Slam" of golf, the winning of all four major championships in one year: the British and U.S. Open and Amateur titles. "The Impregnable Quadrilateral," someone called it, and time has proved that to be true. The cumulative excitement of that summer-long quest, participated in by millions on both sides of the Atlantic, has no parallel in the history of sport. But, memorable and dramatic as the achievement still appears, it is the whole record of Jones as golfer and man, not just its climax, that made his career and his life so memorable.

His story, from childhood to retirement at the remarkably young age of 28, is one of the most dramatic in sports. What Bobby Jones achieved afterward, when he became revered through long years of constant illness and suffering, is even more endearing and quite possibly more enduring. It is the story of an ancient game's greatest champion, an extraordinary human being of exceeding talents reaching far beyond his incomparable sporting feats.

From the moment when the youthful, almost childish Bobby Jones first appeared on the national scene in 1916, the outlines of both golfer and man were drawn in bold strokes, and he exerted an almost magical hold on the public. The early years of spectacular failures were never thought to be anything but transitory. Greatness was expected of him, and greatness he produced, taking the then

Al Laney covered the world's major golf and tennis events for the New York Herald Tribune. He formed an enduring friendship with Bobby Jones during the early 1920s, and was on hand for Jones' greatest golf triumphs.

No golfer in history has had a greater influence than Jones on the evolution of the golf swing. Just as he developed his superbly fluid motion as a boy by watching pro Stewart Maiden, so have millions of followers learned from movies of Jones' swing and the enlightening instruction books and articles he wrote about it.

unsurpassed total of 13 national championships in a mere seven years. And the golf course he built, the Augusta National, and the tournament he founded, the Masters, remain as achievements even greater, perhaps, than his record.

Born on St. Patrick's Day, March 17, 1902, in Atlanta, and named Robert Tyre Jones Jr. for his grandfather, a small-town businessman of Canton, Ga., he was a frail and sickly youngster. In his seventh year, his father, a prominent lawyer, moved the family to a house along the second fairway of the East Lake Country Club, five miles out of town. Just at this time, Stewart Maiden came from Carnoustie in Scotland, the town that sent so many fine golfers to America, to be professional at the club.

In later years Jones called Maiden's appointment "the luckiest thing that ever happened to me in golf." We may believe him. Because of poor health, Bob was turned loose to play out of doors instead of staying in the schoolroom, and he began to follow Maiden about the course. His own earliest recollections of himself include running about with a tiny golf club in his hand. Unconsciously, the youngster imitated Maiden as he became completely absorbed in his new pastime, but that marvelously fluid swing that was to delight thousands was inherent.

The frail boy gradually grew into a powerfully built youth with strong hands, above-normal determination and that electricity in his personality which all who knew him were quick to feel. The boy grew also into a highly sensitive person who suffered intensely from failure. At 14, in his first national championship, the U.S. Amateur at Merion in 1916, he already was regarded as one of the finest shotmakers in the world. There were to follow, however, seven long years of frustration before he won his first big tournament, the U.S. Open at Inwood in 1923.

It was a period when Jones' drive for perfection occasionally got the upper hand and manifested itself in flagrant displays of temper. He threw clubs at trees and berated himself loudly, and in the 1921 British Open he shot 46 on the front nine and played the 10th badly. After taking five strokes and not finding the cup on the 11th, he picked up his ball and, to the horror of the gallery, stalked off the course. That incident later appalled him, and led to his determined and totally successful effort to restrain himself on the course.

During the lean years, when those who were to be his main rivals were concentrating on perfecting their games, the handsome young Jones led the more rounded life of the son of a moderately well-to-do Southern family, with the emphasis on education. Golf was a game to be played when there was free time. In this respect, he was different from all other great champions.

He earned a mechanical engineering degree at Georgia Tech, went to Harvard for graduate work, and then took a law degree at Emory University. He played little golf during the school year, competing nationally only during vacations, and failing year after year to realize his enormous potential. Fishing and bridge were avocations that rivaled his golf.

It was inevitable that Jones would begin winning big tournaments, and finally the dam burst and the flood of victories came. For seven years the young amateur who played golf only as a pastime beat the best professionals. From 1922, when he finished second to Gene Sarazen at Scioto in the Open, until his voluntary retirement, sportsman Jones, playing only a few tournaments a year, never was without at least one of the four most important titles in golf.

In 1926 he won both the U.S. and British Opens, the first man ever to do that; in 1927 he was British Open and U.S. Amateur champion; in 1930 he won all four in the same year. He won the U.S. Open four times, the British Open three times, the U.S. Amateur five times and the British Amateur once. In the U.S. Open he was first or second in eight of nine years, twice losing only after playoffs. And in alternate years from 1922 on, he defeated all his opponents in Walker Cup play by such scores as 12 and 11 (over Cyril Tolley) and 13 and 12 (over Philip Perkins).

His record represents the most consistently high competitive performance in the history of golf, if not any game. It is this record, not just the Grand Slam, for which Jones should be remembered and on which he should be judged as a golfer. It was established in sport's most exciting era, the so-called Golden Age, against perhaps the strongest top-level competitive fields golf has known. Among the rivals from whom Jones won at both stroke and match play were Walter Hagen, Sarazen, Tommy Armour, "Long Jim" Barnes, Willie MacFarlane, Cyril Walker, Jock Hutchinson, Francis Ouimet, Chick Evans, Macdonald Smith, Bobby Cruickshank, Johnny Farrell, Harry Cooper, Bill Mehlhorn, Horton Smith, George Von Elm, Al Watrous, Al Espinosa, Joe Turnesa, Leo Diegel, John Golden, Ed Dudley, Craig Wood, Denny Shute, Billie Burke, Archie Compston and Aubrey Boomer.

No period of golf can show a larger or stronger concentration of first-class players, but in every tournament in which he played it was Jones against the field. The few bookmakers in golf always were willing to accept wagers on him of 2 to 1, whereas hardly anyone else was under 20 to 1. Forty years later you could get money on Palmer and Nicklaus, even at the top of their form, at 5 to 1.

And still Jones played strictly as a part-time amateur. In 1929 when he won his third Open title after a playoff with Espinosa at Winged Foot, he had found time for only about a dozen rounds of golf in the six months before the tournament. Pure amateurism, loving something simply for its own sake, probably is impossible for the champion athlete to attain, but Jones seemed very close. He never considered turning professional.

Jones was not only a good golfer but a beautiful one, an artist where others were mere craftsmen, with a style steeped in rhythm and form. Of Jones in his prime, Bernard Darwin, the British essayist, wrote, "He combined exquisite artistry with utterly relentless precision in a way not quite given to other golfers. Just to see him swing a club was a joy, and the finest tribute any golfer can receive still is to have some old-timer say 'he looked like Jones on that one'."

His hard-earned composure and grace went beyond his swing. In the days before gallery control, Jones was followed by great, rowdy, uncontrollable crowds that put an enormous strain on him, especially in 1930 when the Slam was in the making. The excitement of that long-past summer is understandable when it is realized that probably no other sports development in memory so engaged the emotions of the whole country as the climax approached at Merion in September.

Jones had begun the year by defeating all the leading professionals by the remarkable margin of 13 strokes in the Southern Open, just before going abroad with the Walker Cup team. There was talk of his winning everything. After overwhelming Roger Wethered as part of the

American cup victory, Jones won the British Amateur at St. Andrews in May, beating defending champion Cyril Tolley in the fourth round and Wethered in the finale. In the British Open at Hoylake in June, at medal play, he shot 70-72-74-75 and held off Leo Diegel and Mac Smith to earn the second leg of the Slam. Back in America, an immense ticker-tape parade of welcome up Broadway awaited him. Jones went to Interlachen in Minneapolis for the U.S. Open as the drama and suspense intensified. A sensational third round of 68 set up his 287 and a two-shot win. And then as Merion neared with its treacherous week-long stretch of 18-hole matches—only one or two shots off-line could mean defeat—millions became even more involved. The entire nation appeared to root for him to consummate the great adventure, and all this before sports results could be followed by radio. Possibly never in sport have so many been left in such an agony of day-by-day suspense as Jones teed off against a succession of new opponents, twice on some days, until Eugene Homens was beaten 8 and 7 in the 36-hole final.

It was after this summer that Jones, deciding that competitive golf was no longer bearable for a young lawyer with a family to raise, and, missing his privacy, announced that he would compete no more. It was a stunning move. But he had nothing left to prove. He had been competing at the national level for 14 of his 28 years. He wanted to go out on top.

Conditions of play have changed so greatly that it may be difficult for some younger golfers to comprehend what Jones did. Scores today are lower—but he played with wooden-shafted clubs on courses full of cuppy fairway lies, smashing long brassie shots to hard, unwatered greens as well as any man who ever lived. On any par-5 he was even money to be putting for an eagle. Jones never owned a scientifically matched set of clubs (although he put together one by "touch"); never had in his bag that marvelous little stroke-saver, the wedge.

In retirement, besides practicing law in earnest from his Atlanta office, Jones accepted contracts to make golf instructional films, write syndicated columns and books, and design clubs. Even so, he never was classed as a professional—only as ineligible to compete in amateur tournaments.

He was successful in all these activities, but it was as an author that his many-sided nature best revealed itself. Jones left a body of golf literature worthy of standing on a shelf alongside the best golf writing. The prose is vivid, clear, precisely phrased in adult terms, and warmly opinionated. And it has been remarked more than once that there was in his public speech and conversation among friends a Churchillian quality.

It was in another direction that perhaps his greatest gift to the game was to come: a golf course that embodied the ideas he developed playing the courses of the world. The result was the Augusta National, built with the help of wealthy friends on a beautiful old Georgia plantation, in collaboration with architect Alister MacKenzie. It was a course drawn out of the land itself, rather than imposed upon it, and it was improved year by year until it became one of the great courses and a model for other builders to follow.

The Masters began in 1934 as a reunion of Jones' old friendly enemies. His presence, as he made a limited comeback, gave the tournament instant prestige. Except for time out for service in World War II, he played in it each year until 1948, when a developing spinal condition forced him to withdraw. The spinal condition grew steadily worse until, in spite of several operations, he became a permanent cripple in a wheel chair. Every spring there was doubt and fear that he might not be able to make it to Augusta from his home in Atlanta, but year after year he came. Always, there was a parade of friends to his cottage near the 10th tee. He drove around the course in a golf car, letting the crowds see him, and presided with unfailing charm and eloquence at the closing ceremonies.

In recent years these appearances were no longer possible. Peripheral ailments drained his strength and dropped his weight below 100 pounds. Most men would have died several years sooner. The tournament he created goes on being golf's greatest show and one of the most important events on the yearly sports calendar. It is a fitting testimonial to him.

His appeal was universal. As captain of the U.S. team in the first World Amateur Championship in 1958, Jones had made his last visit to St. Andrews, the old gray town where the Royal and Ancient club has its seat. It was a most moving visit. Here in 1927 the crowd had swept Jones from his feet and carried him triumphantly off the final green of the Old Course after his victory in the British Open by a record score of 285. Here he had played in the Walker Cup matches and here in the British Amateur of 1930 he had gained the first leg of the Grand Slam.

Jones renewed what was called by Herbert Warren Wind in his report of the proceedings "this quite unique love affair between an athlete and a town, and a foreign town to boot." Whenever Jones' name was mentioned by speakers at the team dinner in the Borough Hall, "every St. Andrean jumped to his feet and roared his affection for his dream golfer and old friend." When at the end of the week Jones was made an honorary freeman of the Borough of St. Andrews, the first American so honored since Benjamin Franklin, the packed galleries of Scots stomped and shouted for many minutes when he was saluted as "the most distinguished golfer of his age . . . of all time." And when at the end of the ceremony Jones climbed painfully back into his electric car and steered it down the center aisle to leave, the whole hall burst spontaneously into the old Scottish song "Will Ye No' Come Back Again?"

"So honestly heartfelt was this reunion for Bobby Jones and the people of St. Andrews," Wind concludes, "that it was 10 minutes before many who attended were able to speak again with tranquil voice. Perhaps they love Bobby even better in St. Andrews than they do in Atlanta."

In both places and many others they love him still, though he is gone. ■

GOLFINGLY YOURS, THE HAIG

BY CHARLES PRICE
August, 1966

It was characteristic of Walter Hagen that he was referred to, even by himself, as The Haig, for there was something extraordinary about the man, something grandiose about the way he refused to do anything the way anyone else might. Last year, at 72, he went to New York City from his home in Traverse City, Mich., to undergo an operation for cancer of the throat. He entered the hospital by getting roaring drunk with his son and a writer friend, smacking a nurse on her bottom, and making a wry joke about Heaven to a priest as he ascended to his room in an elevator.

The Haig was the first great professional in American golf. He won 11 national championships— two U.S. Opens, four British Opens, five PGA's—and 60-odd other tournaments between 1914 and 1936. The first three tournaments of any kind he ever played in were the 1912 Canadian Open, and the '13, '14 U.S. Opens. He finished, successively, 36th, in a tie for fourth, and first. As an exhibition player, he managed to play more golf courses than the Barrymores did theatres, some 1,500 in all. His scores ranged all the way from 93 down to 58. He sometimes played as many as nine different courses a week.

The Haig was the first athlete in history to earn a million dollars. For a time he made more money than Babe Ruth, but he spent more than the entire Yankee outfield. After an exhibition tour throughout the Far East with Joe Kirkwood, the trick-shot artist, Kirkwood landed in San Francisco with $23,000. Hagen, however, was broke, his share

A veteran observer at major golf tournaments in both the United States and Great Britain, Charles Price is a freelance writer and a columnist.

having somehow not quite covered his expenses. On another occasion he once had to sit in his hotel room for three days wearing only his underwear because he had sent all his clothes to a laundry around the corner without realizing that he didn't have the money to pay the tab. When some well-off pros were renting suites at a hotel, Hagen was known to rent an entire floor. After winning his first British Open at Sandwich, England, in 1922, he gave all of the prize money to his caddie. Seven years later he won his fourth and final British title at Muirfield, Scotland. Arriving in New York, he had to borrow money from his son to tip his way off the boat.

Nobody ever knew what The Haig was going to do on or off the course—including The Haig himself. On the 15th hole of the last round of the 1914 U.S. Open at Midlothian, in Chicago, which he was winning, Hagen stepped off the fairway to ask a girl in the gallery who had caught his eye if she would like him to teach her how to play golf. Characteristically, he made the first appointment for eight o'clock that evening.

On the night before his playoff with Mike Brady for the 1919 U.S. Open, Hagen went to an all-night party with Al Jolson, got only three hours sleep, and then won the playoff by a stroke while reeling from a hangover.

The Haig won four of his five PGA Championships in a row—and then forgot that he was due to show up for the fifth. The year was 1928, and the site was Five Farms, near Baltimore. When he failed to make an appearance for practice rounds, PGA officials scouted around and found The Haig playing exhibitions in Pennsylvania. Quickly, they sent him a wire, and The Haig motored down to defend his title. When he was put out in the quarterfinals, thereby ending a victory streak of 22 straight 36-hole PGA matches, they asked him if he would kindly hand over the trophy, which he had always forgotten to bring back ever since he had won it for the second time in 1924. Sheepishly, The Haig replied that he was sorry, but he had left it in a taxi back in '25. It had never been returned. Two

years later it was discovered in a package in the basement of a sporting-goods plant in Detroit.

Despite what the public had come to believe, Hagen was not a humorist, at least not in the sense that what he said was quotable. But his timing was sometimes uncanny. Once at a party, The Haig was introduced to Ernestine Schumann-Heink, the famous contralto of the Metropolitan Opera. The Haig, who had never heard of her, took one look at Madame Schumann-Heink's disturbingly large bosom and pulled off what he thought would be an unquenchable *bon mot*. "My dear," said The Haig, "did you ever stop to think what a magnificent bunker you would make?"

Walter Hagen was born on December 21, 1892, in Brighton, a suburb of Rochester, N.Y., where his father was an 18-dollar-a-week blacksmith. From him, Walter inherited a pair of long, lean and strong hands, like a pianist's with a 12-note spread. For the rest of

his working life Hagen was to earn his living from those hands, first as a garage mechanic, then, in order, as a piano finisher, a taxidermist, a mandolin-maker, an ambidextrous ballplayer, and finally as the foremost professional golf player of his day.

Hagen learned to play golf as a caddie at the Country Club of Rochester, which was and still is the most exclusive in that city and which sat only a quarter of a mile from the cottage in which Hagen was born and raised. He was appointed head professional there in 1912. In addition to teaching golf, he also gave lessons to the members in ice skating, which he knew by instinct, tennis, about which he knew little, and croquet, about which he knew nothing.

After finishing 36th in the 1912 Canadian Open, when he was still just an assistant, he decided to play in what was to become that historic U.S. Open Championship at Brookline in 1913. Although it was only the second event of any kind he had ever entered, young Hagen, then only 20, had every intention of winning it, and said so to a number of pros he met at The Country Club. Most of them laughed, dismissing him as some fresh kid just off the boat from Scotland. Hagen was enormously disappointed with himself when, after a disastrous double-bogey seven, he tied for fourth with Macdonald Smith, Louis Tellier and Jim Barnes, only three strokes off the score of Ted Ray, Harry Vardon, and the eventual winner, Francis Ouimet. He took the first train back to Rochester. To Hagen's way of thinking, there were only two things you could do at a golf tournament —win it or lose it.

Disgusted with his golf, Hagen tried out that winter with the Philadelphia Phillies at Tarpon Springs, Fla. A semi-pro player since adolescence, he played every position on the field, including pitcher, where he performed with either hand. Pat Moran, the manager, offered him a tryout the following year as an outfielder, if he would practice his batting and lay off golf for a year. That summer, however, a Rochester newspaper publisher talked Hagen into playing in the 1914 National Open at Midlothian by paying his expenses. Although sick with food poisoning, Hagen set a course record in the opening round with a 68, to which he added a 74 that afternoon and a 73 and a 77 the following day to lead all the way. After posting his score, there was still the possibility that Chick Evans could tie him, but Hagen wasn't the least bit concerned. "Aren't you nervous?" someone asked him as Hagen, having changed into his street clothes for his date with the girl he had picked up in the gallery, watched Evans play the last hole. "No, I'm not nervous," he replied to the spectator. "Why should I be? I've got *my* score."

After the suspension of all major

Never one to do anything half-measure, Hagen wore the very best clothes and drove, of course, a Rolls Royce.

championships during the First World War, The Haig, as he was now becoming known, took his second and last National Open at Brae Burn, near Boston. With a great deal of fanfare, he journeyed to Great Britain for the first time to play in the British Open at Deal, England. In the first round, with a huge gallery at his heels, he went out in 37, then ignominiously came back in 48. He was, of course, never a factor thereafter. Playing each shot in the last round as though the championship depended on it, he eventually finished 55th. Asked by a newspaperman why he had played so meticulously with nothing at stake, Hagen replied, "I was afraid I might finish 56th!"

At St. Andrews the following year, Hagen finished sixth. In America, however, he fared better, winning the first of his five PGA Championships by defeating Jim Barnes, 3 and 2, at Inwood, on Long Island.

In '22, he won his first British Open by scoring 300 at Sandwich, perhaps the windiest championship course in the world. In '23, he lost a thrilling extra-hole final in the PGA to his archrival, Gene Sarazen, at Pelham, N.Y.

In 1924, he won his second British Open, at Hoylake, in England, with a 301. He also took his second PGA at French Lick Springs, Ind., repeating in '25, '26 and '27 at, respectively, Olympia Fields, Chicago; Salisbury, Long Island; and Cedar Crest, Dallas. He took his third British Open in '28 through the winds of Sandwich once again, with 292, and the following year added his fourth title at Muirfield, Scotland, a course that has been called the most demanding championship layout in the world with a then-record 292.

The last open tournament The Haig was to win turned out to be the Gasparilla Open, in 1935, an event for which you would have to dig deeply into the record books. By that time he had acquired a whiskey shake to his hands that he could not control even with a putter that had a 2-iron shaft and a heavily leaded head. Portly and walking with a lumber, he had assumed the look of a benign walrus.

The Haig was a "hand player," pure and simple, his good pair of hands being the indispensable tools for manipulating the hickory shafts with which he won all his major championships. With hickory —they used to say—you picked the shot to fit the club, not the club to fit the shot. And the shots The Haig picked came from a dazzling repertory: half shots, feathered fades, the longest imaginable sort of pitch-and-runs. In an effort to keep a shot under a near-gale wind at Sandwich one year, he hit the ball 160 yards with his putter. Today's players, with vastly superior equipment, score on the average only slightly better than did Hagen.

Hagen's golf form began with a very wide stance, which he narrowed a touch with each advancing year. He never placed much faith in the value of the backswing, very often repositioning the club at the top with a distinct pause. He then moved into the ball with a noticeable sway to his left, his hands flashing the face of the club into position at impact, his body barreling into the ball so that at the finish of the follow-through his weight was entirely on his left foot, which he flared out almost at his target, in the manner of Harry Vardon and the other early British pros.

Perhaps because of his pronounced sway, The Haig was the wildest first-rank player of his day and, collaterally, the best match-play golfer in history. In large part, this genius was due to his short game which, on the green, had been equaled up to his time only by Walter J. Travis, Jerry Travers, and the mature Bobby Jones. Around the greens, he had no equal.

The Haig brought a touch of showmanship to the game that it had never known before or since. He was a master of the grand gesture—showing up on the first tee at the last possible second, choosing and rejecting three different clubs before finally electing the only possible club the shot called for, handling his nervous opponents as though they were yo-yos. At a time when golf pros were still dressing in sack coats and brogues, The Haig

began wearing silk shirts, florid cravats, alpaca sweaters, screaming argyles and black and white shoes which he had had made by Oliver Moore at $100 a pair. He had his shoes broken in for him by his private caddie, Spec Hammond.

The aplomb of the man was gigantic. At Deal in 1920, during his first British Open, he discovered that the professionals were expected to eat in a refectory tent while the amateurs dined like gentlemen in the clubhouse. The Haig would have none of this. He hired an airplane and every day flew himself and some friends to a well-known inn because, as he told the tournament officials, he preferred its strawberries.

Some years after the Second World War, when The Haig had quit playing for good, his old exhibition partner, Joe Kirkwood, was making a round-the-world trip on his own when he found himself walking the streets of Rangoon. His attention was caught by a group of natives filing into a Buddhist temple, where they made meager offerings before the altar. When the service was completed and the natives had left, Kirkwood walked over to the pile of offerings and began poking through the broken bric-a-brac, old furniture, cheap beads and whatnot that made up the rubble. Suddenly, his eye fell on a framed photograph of someone he thought he knew. He picked it up. Surely enough, it was an autographed picture of a golfer, signed "Golfingly yours, Walter Hagen." One thing you could always say for The Haig. He got around. ■

LAST LOOK AT TONY LEMA

BY NICK SEITZ
August, 1967

It has been a year since Tony Lema died at the age of 32 in a fiery plane crash on, ironically enough, a golf course—a year in which to lament his passing, to remember the good times and the bad, to attempt to put him in perspective as a person.

Who was Tony Lema? He was a professional golfer, the winner of 14 tournaments including the British Open, a celebrity known to kings and Broadway columnists, but he also was a complex man never quite able to identify himself.

He was "Champagne Tony," a swinger to whom wine, women and song were a way of life. The stories of his wee-hours escapades were widely circulated. He once drove golf balls out of a hotel window, to the delight of a group of party-goers. To win his first professional championship he had to beat Paul Harney in a sudden-death playoff immediately after gulping down three Scotch-and-waters in the grill (Lema thought he had lost, and was ordering a fourth drink when he found out otherwise). On the Caribbean tour he had been known to set down a highball and demonstrate the fine art of blasting a golf ball out of the shallow end of a swimming pool while vacationing millionaires looked on in wonder.

The legend grew by bits and pieces, then by leaps and bounds. Unlike a good many legends, this one was grounded in fact. Until his marriage to the former Betty Cline in 1963, the handsome, debonair Lema fully lived up to his billing as a party boy extraordinary. "When he is playing well and getting his name in the newspapers, a touring pro can have his pick of the girls," he wrote later in a popular autobiographical book, *Golfer's Gold.* As a bachelor, Lema

took his pick, and he showed his dates the town—whatever town he happened to be in. Las Vegas, Miami and San Francisco were his favorite spas.

"Tony was a man on vacation," says Ernie Vossler, who was playing the tour when Lema, a poor youngster from the cannery section of Oakland, Calif., turned pro in 1955. "In that respect, he never changed."

Doc Giffin, then press secretary for the Professional Golfers' Ass'n tour, remembers how Lema acquired the nickname "Champagne Tony." It was in 1962, at the Orange County Open in Costa Mesa, Calif. Giffin had set up press headquarters in a small card room of the Mesa Verde Country Club. "The press corps was so small, the room wasn't even crowded," Giffin says. "We had a portable cooler of beer in there, and I can still visualize Tony holding up a near-empty can of beer after his interview following the third round and saying, 'Men, if I win tomorrow, we'll have champagne in here.' A West Coast free-lance photographer, Lester Nehamkin, told the club manager to be sure to have champagne on ice. After he beat Bob Rosburg on the third hole of a sudden-death playoff the next day, Lema ordered the champagne. The late Charley Curtis of the *Los Angeles Times,* for one, and I believe at least one of the wire-service reporters used the 'Champagne Tony' tag in their stories. I told it many times in the next few months, and it caught on nationally."

It was one of the lesser ironies of Lema's short life that he preferred Scotch to champagne. The nickname resulted in a profitable endorsement for him, but he rarely drank the bubbly stuff except for publicity purposes after a victory.

His coup in that Orange County Open, his first official tour win, was the highlight of Lema's first really fruitful season. He earned more than $28,000 in 1962 after six years of frustration. His first full year, 1956, had seen him win only $385 to rank 147th on the money list, and the ensuing five years found him winning the unimposing total of $31,000.

"I wonder," he reflected later, "how I had the nerve to start out on the tour or stay with it as long as I did. Most of the players at least got in on the ground floor. I climbed in through a basement window."

If the youthful ex-Marine was struggling during those early days as a tournament professional, he concealed the fact nicely. "I don't think he had much money," says Vossler, "but you never would have guessed it. We'd be staying at the same hotel, and I'd always see him in the barber shop getting a manicure, or having his shoes shined in the lobby, or escorting a well-dressed woman into the cocktail lounge. He traveled first class."

Vossler adds that he believes Lema's fondness for liquor was exaggerated, a feeling I heard echoed many times while interviewing people who had been close to him. "He'd take a drink or two after he finished playing a round, like a lot of other players, but he never carried liquor with him."

Tommy Jacobs was Lema's best friend. The two rookies joined forces to save on expenses, and traveled and roomed together for 18 months, until Jacobs married. "If Tony was scoring well, he didn't party," says Jacobs, "But if he wasn't playing well, he would get real discouraged and start going out at night. Actually, he didn't party all that much—he just got a little more notoriety than some others. When he got in the mood, though, there was no stopping him."

It was not untypical of Lema that he was not speaking to Jacobs at the time of his death. Lema could change moods in a moment, and not even those who knew him best ever dared guess exactly what to expect from him. A writer for a national magazine, a man who engenders strong like or dislike among the tournament golfers, was preparing an article on Lema, and he wanted Jacobs to help him. Jacobs, who does not care for the writer, declined. The writer complained to Lema, and Lema turned a cold shoulder toward Jacobs at the PGA Championship, the last tournament in which Lema played. "That would've lasted

about a week," Jacobs says.

Controlling and channelling his moodiness was Lema's foremost challenge. In his formative years in tournament golf he would shoot a bad round and, peeved at himself and the world, withdraw from the event and disappear for weeks. He was given to outbursts of temper that doubtless delayed his rise to stardom for a matter of years.

"Until 1961, he wasn't able to put together four solid rounds," says Vossler. "He often would win money because he would start fast. He led a lot of tournaments in the early rounds, but didn't win them. Later, when he learned what it takes to be a winner, he didn't get mad at himself on the course. At first he expected too much of himself. Nobody hits every shot exactly the way he wants to hit it, but Tony refused to accept that. His game was sound; he never had any bad habits."

The last four years of his life, Lema was a great putter. He would break into a delightful little jig that endeared him to the galleries when he sank a long putt. Accurate and long with his woods and a splendid scrambler around the greens, he was only mediocre—comparatively speaking—with the long and middle irons. It has been suggested that this was due to a lack of concentrated practice. "He must have worked hard when he was a kid to have that good a swing," says one veteran touring pro, "but I sure didn't see him on the practice range much. At the PGA the week he died, he didn't hit a bucket of balls all week. He played the front nine one day and the back nine the next, which is not how a Jack Nicklaus would prepare for a major championship. It looked to me as if he did naturally what the rest of us have to sweat and toil to do."

Tony Lema was not Jack Nicklaus, however, and there is another side to the manner in which he approached competition. His was the sort of swing that requires little work, and he was wise enough to realize his good fortune and leave well enough alone. The 6'-1", 180-pounder would start the downward portion of his swing with a quick return of weight to his left side (he was right-handed), so that the club always was catching up with his weight—an ideal sequence. By shifting his weight so rapidly and smoothly, he kept swing errors to a minimum.

Also, his natural mental tendency was to take the game too seriously and beat himself. After his failures of 1956-61 he finally learned to relax.

"Tony had a formula, and it worked," says Tommy Jacobs. "He had learned that he had to be loose to play well. He had come out on the tour and practiced and practiced and practiced and hadn't won, and then he changed his approach and he started winning. What would you do? Tony had to suit his game to his temperament, and vice versa. He quit letting little things bother him, stopped playing so conservatively and worrying so much, and became a successful charger, much like Arnold Palmer."

Lema charged to his high of five victories in 1964 and collected $74,000, fourth best on the tour. The next year he amassed official winnings of $101,800 to finish second to Jack Nicklaus in the money race. He had hit his stride. Before his death on July 24, 1966, the foremost instance of an athlete being killed in his prime, he had won $48,200 and was all but assured a spot among the top 10 money winners for the fourth year in a row.

His last victory was at Oklahoma City in late May of 1966 where, all seriousness, he fired 65 on the final day, missing the course record by only a stroke and holding off intense bids by Nicklaus and Tom Weiskopf. Lema's total was 271, the lowest on the tour to that point. "If I never win again," he said in accepting the first-place trophy, "I won't be so disappointed it will kill me. Golf has been good to me."

The Oklahoma City triumph was particularly satisfying to him because he had been bothered by a sore elbow and had not won in eight months, and because it was accomplished in front of his wife's family and friends in her home town.

Everyone who knew them agrees that Betty was a steadying influence on her vagabond husband, whose brief, unsuccessful first marriage had produced a son. Betty frequently traveled with Tony from tournament to tournament, and converted to Catholicism, his faith. They had met and played cards in the back of a plane in 1961 while she was an airline hostess, and they were wed two years later.

"Marrying Betty helped Tony immensely," says Jacobs. "He changed a great deal in the last year he was alive. He was far closer to being content, whereas before he was liable to be sitting in somebody's living room talking to you and suddenly he would drift off into space. He seemed at times like that to lose touch with reality. Tony was aware of this distance between himself and others, and he definitely wanted to get in step. He wanted to do things for others, particularly for people who had helped him. He just wasn't sure how to go about it. Probably Tony lacked confidence more than anything else. He never had spent much time with the other golfers. They didn't really like him or dislike him—they didn't understand him."

To repay his fellow pros and the PGA the debt he considered he owed them, Lema shortly before his death made it known that he wanted to serve on the Tournament Committee, a thankless and financially unrewarding assignment. He began, too, taking part in the give-and-take on the practice tee and in the locker room, swapping theories and jokes with players he seldom had spoken to. Bob Goalby, who made the comeback of the year in 1966, gives a large part of the credit for his success to Lema. "I don't let a bad shot bother me now," Goalby says. "I can see the value of keeping calm, and as Tony told me, you have to live a little." Less than a week after Lema talked to Goalby, Lema, his beautiful wife and two other persons perished in the wreckage of a small private plane on the Lansing, Ill., Sportsmen's Club golf course, trying to make a forced landing.

There were conflicting reports on the crash. The accepted version is that the plane had *not* landed and refueled a few minutes before crashing, but that the pilot had put it into a stall and lost control.

The final irony is that Lema originally had committed himself to play in a posh pro-am sponsored by General Electric the next day, but reneged to attend the small pro-am for which he was headed when he died.

Newspaper stories reported that Lema's suitcase contained nearly $20,000 in uncashed checks, giving rise to some wild speculation that he must have been worth well over a million dollars. The truth is that he was worth about $250,000. Early in his career he had bought up his contract following a disagreement with a backer, and the transaction left him off-balance financially for several years. Also, he was investing money with an eye toward his long-range security.

He told friends he was looking forward to starting a family. "When Betty and I have children, I'll settle down," he said. "When the kids get to the age where a father should be around, I'll probably quit playing golf for a living. I don't think this life would do for children."

Tommy Jacobs mentions that Lema had a special fondness for children, perhaps because Tony himself grew up without a father. "He would urge kids to go to college," Jacobs says. "He hadn't gone himself, but he was sure he should have. If a caddie of his was in college, and did a good job for him, he would pay him more than the going rate. Tony was getting down to earth."

Who was Tony Lema? The tragedy is that Tony Lema was just beginning to find out himself.■

IS TOM WEISKOPF THE MAN TO SUCCEED PALMER?

BY NICK SEITZ
June, 1968

The king is not dead—the king is alive and ensconced among the current leading money winners— but the king will be 39 this fall when he completes his 15th year as a touring pro. His children are nearly grown. He is passing up more and more tournaments, and soon Arnold Palmer's schedule will be only half what it once was.

To place a President of the United States in proper historical perspective might take several generations, but to evaluate the impact of Arnold Palmer on golf we need not wait. He has meant more to the game than anyone, ever, in virtually every conceivable way. His vibrant personality, aided by the world-shrinking capabilities of television, has made him the best-known athlete of this or any other age, and probably the most venerated. His gradual withdrawal poses a monumental challenge for the fur-lined world of professional golf. Professional Golfers' Ass'n official Bob Gorham puts it succinctly. "We are going," he says somewhat dolefully, "to need a new hero."

Gorham is using that four-letter word in its strictest sense. Jack Nicklaus is quite likely the best golfer of all time, powerful—which the populace finds appealing in any sport these days—and a nice fellow. But for all his victories and good manners he hasn't been able to turn on the fans as Palmer can. He does not have the flair. Everyone agrees Nicklaus is a great player but no one looks on him as a hero.

"Jack doesn't have the sex appeal," says one pro, and no doubt sex appeal is a large part of Palmer's magnetism. This is not a phenomenon reserved to golfers; the owners of hockey teams will tell you they prosper or falter with their female ticket buyers, who bring to the arena dizzyingly Freudian interpretations of what can be a simple game. Certainly as a sex symbol Arnold Palmer ranks right up there with Bobby Hull or Paul Newman. Observe the women in his galleries some time.

Tom Weiskopf has sex appeal. Granted it is a different brand. Where Palmer is older, outgoing, muscular and handsome in a rugged, outdoorsy fashion, Weiskopf is younger, rather shy, tall and slender and handsome in a smooth, semi-innocent manner. Where women daydream of being dominated by Palmer, they would rather mother the blond, dimple-chinned Weiskopf. (Often the same women are cast in both roles, for what it's worth psychologically.) In real life Weiskopf is happily married to a former Miss Minnesota.

Weiskopf hits the ball prodigious distances. He plays aggressively, charging as fiercely as Palmer when victory is within reach. The expressions on his ax-handle face mirror his desires and frustrations for the galleries and let them identify with him; and he's a winner. After four years of trying he gained his first victory in the 1968 Andy Williams-San Diego Open, and zapped on to the year's best pre-Masters record, earning more than $70,000 in official and unofficial money. He was fourth in the Bob Hope Desert Classic, and second in the Doral and Florida Citrus opens.

Close observers report that Weiskopf is attracting defectors from Arnie's Army, that he is clearly the second most popular player on the tour, and that his star is only starting on what should be a remarkable ascendancy. Tom Weiskopf, to hear his fellow pros tell it, is the next American golf hero, the man who at least will come close to filling the super void that will gape when Palmer puts his competitive game to rest.

Bert Yancey, a perceptive pro, says, "I think Tom'll go all the way. He has the game and the personality, and it's just a matter of time. All he has to do is continue to mature, and pace himself—take a week off now and then."

Weiskopf's first four years on the tour were by no means a lost cause. He made $125,000 and says you could not put a price on what he learned. But his failure to win was surprising in light of the expansive predictions that marked his first season.

Tony Lema said, "He's going to be a great one before you know it." Palmer proclaimed him the rookie most likely to succeed.

Probably Weiskopf's winless four years should be accepted as a natural adjustment period. Palmer won the Canadian Open his first year on the tour and added victories in each of the succeeding three years, but he was 25 when he turned pro. Weiskopf is 25 now.

His progress was slowed by an erratic attitude and a stomach ailment. Weiskopf is an oft-brooding perfectionist who wants to hit every shot precisely as he

has planned it. No one does, of course, but it took him a while to reconcile himself to the fact. His was not a Tommy Bolt type temper, although he admits occasional pupil-teacher sessions with Bolt have been a hindrance as well as a help. Bolt's anger boils to the surface and results in club-throwing and loud curses. Bolt is apt to blame his misfortunes on others or on golf courses. Weiskop's disgust is with Weiskopf. Bounding up the fairway with his long, splay-footed stride, he silently berates himself for a bad shot, his anger turning inward and gnawing at the lining of his stomach. In 1966 he lost 20 pounds and missed several tournaments due to a near-ulcerous affliction of the duodenum.

"I'm so darn moody," he says in an almost-tenor voice. "I can feel great one minute and sluggish the next. Gee whiz"—Weiskopf talks this way a lot—"it used to take me three holes to get over a poor shot. I got discouraged too quick. I hadn't had much experience in big amateur tournaments because I couldn't afford it, and I didn't have the patience and concentration to win out here." Now, for the most part, he does.

He calls a 66 he shot the final day at Orlando this year the finest round of his life. Yet he missed birdie putts of eight feet or less seven times. "Two years ago," he says, "I would have been so upset at missing those putts I'd never have broken 70."

Weiskopf diplomatically gives half the credit for his improved attitude to his effervescent brunette wife of 18 months. "Jeanne's wonderful. She doesn't know golf, but she knows me. She's witty and has a little streak of sarcasm in her. She can jar me out of my bad moods. She'll come up to me on the course and tell me how silly I look pouting."

Says Jeanne, "Tom is basically a lonely person. He thinks most of the time. Now he thinks about the difference between being good and great. He sits and tries to recapture the exact state of mind he had when he was playing so well at San Diego, so he can repeat it. I do most of the talking, but he's changed a lot since we were married. He's more relaxed—he's

really a lot of fun when he isn't worrying about golf."

Weiskopf says moodiness and lack of confidence are two different things, and that he never lacked confidence. As proof he points to his turning pro without a sponsor, an unheard-of move nowadays. "It wasn't because I had a lot of money, all I had to my name was the $2,500 the MacGregor-Brunswick people gave me to use their clubs, but I wanted to make it myself. I figured I'd learn more. If I had it to do over I probably would find a sponsor, but I'm proud that I made it on my own." He says winning, not making money, has always been his goal.

Weiskopf's ability to hit the long ball worked against him until recently. He was and is continually compared to the powerful Nicklaus, like Weiskopf an ex-Ohio State student (Tom did not caddie for Jack at OSU, contrary to a popular folk tale). Tom didn't want to disappoint the fans who came to see him clout the ball. "I'd get on the tee and hear some guy say, 'There's the kid who drives it farther than Nicklaus,' " Weiskopf remembers, "and I'd hit it as hard as I could." His yardage was often awesome, but his direction was often awful. Eventually he chose to forget the fans and swing easier, occasionally turning to a 3-wood or 2-iron off the tee to be sure of good position for his second shot.

He still rips into the ball, how-ever. At San Diego he averaged 275 yards a whack on the two holes where drives were measured—best in the field. Nicklaus himself calls Weiskopf the longest hitter in golf.

"I don't mind," Weiskopf says. "I'm flattered by it. But I don't think it makes that much difference. The key is that I'm hitting 14 and 16 fairways a round. I guess around 350 yards is the farthest I've hit a drive, but the wind was blowing and the ground was hard."

Weiskopf is psychically attached to a new driver, although he says it is no different from his old one, which broke. He is a superstitious man, always marking his ball on the green with the face of the coin down "so I don't get the yips" and being highly partial to yellow shirts.

Weiskopf maintains that he is not particularly strong, that he could

press no more than 200 pounds weightlifting. He attributes his power to a big swing arc and the leverage it produces, and good timing and rhythm. He says he tries to use his build (at 6′3″ and 180 lbs., he is known on tour as "The Knife") to maximum advantage, and that he never copied anyone.

"I learned more from Bob Kepler, the coach at Ohio State when I was there, than anyone else," he says. "Mainly on fundamentals." The Ohio State Scarlet Course remains his favorite. Over 7,200 yards long, it is one reason the school has given the tour such fence-busters as Nicklaus, Weiskopf, Tom Nieporte and Dick Rhyan.

Weiskopf considers the long and medium irons his best clubs aside from his driver. He considers his short-iron play adequate, his bunker play excellent, his putting good. "You notice improvement fastest in your putting," he says. "I'm not having many three-putt greens this year. I didn't have one at San Diego. I'm not doing any-thing differently except putting the ball in the hole more. I *am* doing *everything* a little more *boldly,* because I don't have to worry about money the way I used to. My pitching wedge is my worst club. I hit some real goofy-looking shots with it sometimes. And I don't handle a chip-and-run shot over 100 feet well. Actually, my fairway woods are the worst part of my game, but I don't work on them much because I can plan my shots so I don't need to hit them. Under pressure you're going to rely on what you can do well anyway."

Under pressure the excitable Weiskopf has to watch his club selection carefully. "That adrenalin gets to flowing and I'll hit the ball 15 to 25 yards farther than under normal conditions," he says. "In the third round at Orlando I was near the lead and had a 155-yard shot to the 18th green, and I knocked a 9-iron clear into the bleachers behind the green. At the Hope tournament I kept hitting my tee shots over the par-3 holes when the pressure was on. In most other sports you want to get all fired up, but in golf you have to be in control of your emotions all the time." Disciplined imagination, says

Weiskopf, is the essence of championship golf. By that he means the ability to consider all the possibilities for a shot and then to visualize it before hitting it. Ben Hogan, he believes, is the best at imagining a shot, then turning the actual execution over to muscle memory. He wishes Hogan was still traveling the tour so he could study the master.

Weiskopf's wife travels with Tom from tournament to tournament. The Weiskopfs met in the summer of 1966, and for Jeanne it was love at first sight. For Tom it was more like love at 11th sight.

"I was Miss Minnesota Golf Classic," Jeanne says, "and was handing out invitations to the pro-am party. I thought it was pretty important—I learned later most of the players never go. I had seen Tom and thought he was quite handsome, and I was hoping to be introduced to him and maybe be asked for a date. Well, I handed him his invitation, and he thanked me and just walked away! I was crestfallen. But we ran into one another on the course later in the week, and he asked me if I'd like to do something that evening. He said he didn't have a car. I told him not to worry about that, I could get a courtesy car. I took him to the zoo —can you *believe* that? But he seemed to enjoy it. He seemed so lonesome. I was sure he didn't like me. I decided I would be like a sister to him—write him letters while he was traveling to cheer him up. We didn't see each other much until we were engaged later that summer, then Tom started commuting from the tour to St. Paul—I think he was pleading non-existent illnesses and deliberately missing the cut sometimes—and we were married in October, three months after we met."

Who can tell about marriages, but the Weiskopfs appear to be the All-American young couple living happily ever after. The frequent low-key kidding between them is stimulating and quickly broadened to take in an outsider. "Jeanne's just wonderful," Tom says. "Of course she isn't too domestic-minded." This last with a grin and wink toward Jeanne. "When we first got married she washed my golf shirts with my underwear and everything came out pink."

From time to time Jeanne receives amorous suggestions from men who do not realize she is married. She has learned to take them lightly. One she took too lightly, however. This night she went to the motel ice machine, and an admirer, unbeknownst to her, was watching her from the other side of the machine. He followed her back to the Weiskopfs' room, and several minutes later the phone rang. Jeanne answered. It was her would-be suitor, who thought she was in the room alone. He said he had noticed her at the ice machine —a great line in its own right—and would like to buy her a drink. Jeanne knew Tom had been talking to fellow-pro Chuck Courtney. "Aha," she reasoned. "He put Chuck up to calling me." She affected her most alluring voice and told the caller she would like nothing better than to have a drink with him—in her room. "But don't wear orange, honey," she cooed. "It will clash with my nightie." The caller gasped at his good fortune. Jeanne hung up and giggled.

Moments later a knock at the door cut off the giggles. Tom answered it. It was the would-be Casanova, who stammered something about looking for the ice machine. "Downstairs and around the corner," replied Tom. Then Tom asked if the visitor had just called Jeanne. At that juncture the intruder did a remarkable imitation of Jesse Owens, and was gone into the night.

Jeanne plans to go around the country with her husband for four or five years. Her talent in beauty contests was interpretive jazz dancing, and she does her dancing exercises each morning, but more to maintain her figure than to prepare for a career. She revels in the tour life: the succession of trips, radio and television interviews, fashion shows, luncheons and walks around golf courses— she walks every hole with Tom. "It's so exciting," she enthuses. "I'm only 21 and Tom's only 25. We have plenty of time to settle down and have children. We do things with Frank Beard and his wife and Bert Yancey and his wife and R. H. Sikes and his wife and some other young couples making the tour— go to the movies, play shuffleboard, play cards. I'm trying to learn to play bridge, which is an obsession with these golfers. I'm taking up golf, and Tom's a good teacher. Watching Tom improve is thrilling."

Weiskopf's goal? To win the Big Four—the U.S. and British Open, PGA and Masters—an objective his new-found tranquillity and his penchant for playing well on difficult courses could well enable him to realize. Has he thought about becoming successor to Arnold Palmer? He has. "If it comes, fine," he says. "It would be tremendously exciting, but a hard life to lead . . . I'm not going to change my personality, not going to tell jokes or wear flashy clothes . . . . I withdraw into myself more than Arnold does, but I *do* have good rapport with galleries. I react to a crowd. I like to hear the noise and be in contention. At times like that I lose my shyness . . . . Boy, Arnold can do some amazing things to win. I really admire him . . . Under pressure you concentrate so hard you forget to smile at the gallery, but I'm trying to smile and stuff like that.

"What the heck, I'm the leading money winner and the only impression a lot of people will ever have of me is the one they take home from a golf tournament . . . . I'm far from reaching my peak. I learned a lot these last four years, and I expect to learn twice as much in the next four. . . . It isn't a matter of beating Arnold as much as being as good as you can be . . . . It'd be something to be in his position, wouldn't it?" ■

BEN HOGAN TODAY

BY NICK SEITZ
September, 1970

For millions of golf followers it will matter not a shred if Arnold Palmer wins the rest of the schedule, or Raquel Welch becomes a touring caddie, or the price of a hot dog on the course dives to a nickel. The year 1970 was made when 57-year-old William Benjamin Hogan, his swollen left knee squeezed into an elastic brace, limped intently out of retirement to finish ninth in the Houston Champions International and challenge briefly in the Colonial, which he has won five times.

Imagine Joe DiMaggio donning his old uniform and coming off the bench to rip a grand-slam home run before a capacity crowd in Yankee Stadium and you have some idea of the drama that drenched Hogan's performances on two of the most arduous courses in the sport.

The short return to professional golf of the man widely considered the greatest player ever, a winner of all four major championships, a national hero after he overcame the near-fatal effects of a 1949 car-bus crash, gives rise to fascinating questions. Why did he do it? What is his life like today? Has he, as some reports suggest, "mellowed?" What achievements mean the most to him? Hogan long has been the least understood of great athletes, often summarily characterized as "cold" and "aloof," and the years since he reached his playing zenith in the late 1940s and early 1950s have brought disappointingly little insight into his life style and outlooks.

Hogan permitted me to follow him for a week in Fort Worth, observing and questioning. I took up with him during the Colonial and spent two days with him afterward, as he reverted to his customary activities, which seldom include complete rounds of golf, let alone tour play. In that time, I think I came to know somewhat a Ben Hogan only remotely related to the single-dimensional, distant figure I had been led to expect.

The thing that surprised me most about Hogan was his sense of humor: droll, flavored with an earthy Southwestern spice, often evident. I remember my unsuspecting introduction to it. I accompanied him to Shady Oaks C.C. for lunch—he is the Fort Worth club's most esteemed member—and he introduced me to the manager, who personally attends him. "This guy has 15 kids," Hogan said. Expressionless, he added, *"Bleeped* himself right out of a seat in the car." I had heard dozens of stories about Hogan's dourness, and in no way was prepared for this. I nodded innocuously. After a lengthy silence, I suddenly became aware of what he had said, and burst out laughing. Hogan, who had been watching me closely, joined in the laughter. He was amused not at his own line but at my delayed response. His probing blue-grey eyes suggested: "Didn't expect that from the austere Ben Hogan, eh?"

Of his friend, Jimmy Demaret, who does not have to be coaxed hard to sing, Hogan says, "I love Jimmy's voice . . . but I don't think I can stand 'Deep Purple' again."

Hogan is no raconteur, but he enjoys hearing a good story. Golf temper stories featuring Tommy Bolt and Lefty Stackhouse are his favorites. And he enjoys, even more, spontaneous humor. Paired with Bob Goalby in Houston, Hogan burned a long drive into the wind. "Who do you think you are?" Goalby asked, "Ben Hogan?" Hogan liked that.

During the Colonial, Hogan did his warming up at Shady Oaks, 15 minutes away. The practice area at Colonial Country Club is not large, and he always has preferred to practice by himself anyway ("You don't get in anybody's way, and nobody gets in yours, and you can

137

have your own thoughts"). At Shady Oaks he hits balls from a spot between the 14th and 15th holes, across the 14th, 13th and 17th fairways. One morning, some writers covering the Colonial were playing at Shady Oaks, and "played through" Hogan's practice area. Hogan chatted with them and asked one, Kaye Kessler from Columbus, Ohio, about his swing. "It's kind of disjointed," Kessler said. "My boss told me I shouldn't take it out of town because if it broke down I couldn't get parts." Hogan chuckled delightedly. There is plenty of Irish in him.

Hogan spends several hours a day and an occasional evening at Shady Oaks, the club built by his close friend and early backer on the tour, Marvin Leonard. He is comfortable there. It is the poshest club in Fort Worth, but the members treat one another with a congenial irreverence, Hogan included. "Ben gets tired of people gettin' down on their knees when he walks into a room," Tommy Bolt says. "I've had some great name-callin' arguments with him and he loved it."

Early every afternoon, his leg and the weather permitting, he will empty an old shag bag and hit balls for 40 to 90 minutes, starting with a 9-iron and working through the set. With each club he will hit basic shots, then before putting it away will hit two different types of shots, moving the ball to the right or left, or hitting it low or high. "The basics of the swing remain the same," he says. "But I'm always experimenting, looking for better ways to hit finesse shots. I never hit a shot on the course I haven't practiced." His clear voice, neutral at first, takes on more of the drawling intonations of Texas as he warms to talking. "I'm a curious person. *Experimenting is my enjoyment.* I won't accept anything until I've worked with it for a week or two, or longer. I bring out new clubs from the plant and try them out, and I get ahold of clubs that we've sold to check them. If something doesn't work, some part of my swing or a club, I throw it out."

The scientific method. Hogan is the Linus Pauling of his field, subjecting any hypothesis to

rigorous, impartial testing. If it works, he keeps it, generalizes from it. If it doesn't, into the garbage can it goes. Gardner Dickinson worked for Hogan when Hogan had a club job in Palm Springs in his younger years. Dickinson majored in clinical psychology in college, with a minor in psychometrics—mental testing. Intrigued by Hogan's personality, he would slip IQ test questions into conversations with him. "I knew I'd never get them all past him, so I'd give him only the toughest ones from each section, knowing if he could answer those he could get the others," Dickinson says. "I calculated that his IQ was in excess of 175. Genius level is about 160. Ben didn't go to college, he regrets that, but he's a brilliant person."

One reason Hogan practices where he does at Shady Oaks is to hit into the prevailing wind. When the wind moves, so does Hogan. "If the wind is at your back, it destroys your game. You tend to try to pull the ball, swinging from the outside in, which is bad. If the temperature is below 60 degrees, you lose me. You can wreck your swing playing in cold weather, bundling all up." Each shot is aimed at a target: a small nursery building near the 18th fairway. He uses no glove. "I never could feel anything wearing a glove." Traffic is light at Shady Oaks. Such is Hogan's eminence, when strangers playing the course interrupt his practice, they often apologize.

Shady Oaks, not as long or difficult as Colonial, where Hogan formerly belonged, is nonetheless challenging, and pretty, if that term may be applied to a golf course. Hogan designed most of the bunkers. They are numerous and imaginatively and variously shaped. They are not difficult to shoot from; they are not deep and do not have high lips. "Bunkers serve two purposes," Hogan says. "They are for framing a green—to give it definition and to give the player an idea of the distance he has in hitting to the green. And for beauty. They are *not* for trapping *people.*"

Hogan holds decided views on what a golf course should be, and no one knows more about

shot values. It is his ambition to build The Perfect Golf Course, a project he has contemplated since his touring days. "I'm very close to buying the property now. The market research looks favorable. You have to know where you'll wind up before you start— otherwise you'll go broke. You have to have the right piece of land. I'm in hopes of getting a nice, rolling site with a lot of trees. That means it won't be in the Fort Worth area. I want a course that both the club member and the pro can play.

"Length isn't necessarily the key. Length has to do with climate. Where it's humid, you can't have too long a course. The greens have to be large to provide multiple pin placements and prevent their wearing out. You have to have heavy play or you're going to lose money. You give the greens character in the contouring. I like a clean course. You could grow rough for a tournament. Champions Golf Club in Houston is my idea of a tremendous course for the locale."

Hogan probably will build his course in or near sprawling, wealthy Houston. The course is sure to place a premium on driving, which Hogan deems the most important area of play. Expect the par-4s to bend slightly left or right (an equal number each way). The par-3s will call for iron shots, even short-iron shots, precisely placed. "I won't design it," Hogan says, inhaling hard on a cigarette. "I'm no architect. A person can have just so much knowledge, and there isn't enough time in the day to absorb very much and be proficient. I'll work with the architect, but not in detail. Everything takes a professional."

Hogan will build only one course.

It is common for a legendary athlete, no longer very active competitively, to sell his name— to let it be used for promotional purposes or to open doors, as the saying has it. Ben Hogan does not play the game of business that way. "I don't consider myself a businessman," he says crisply. "Once you consider yourself something, you fall flat on your face, you see." He is behind the wide wooden desk in his spacious office in front of two framed full-color maps. Several neat foothills of mail have accumulated while he was playing the two tournaments.

A high-salaried executive in the employ of AMF, with stock options and the rest, he is in full command of the Ben Hogan Company, a firm which is doing so well it can't produce golf equipment fast enough to fill the orders. He does not play golf with customers. He plays company golf once a year, at the principal sales meeting. He makes a few speeches, although he is a captivating speaker. "Some people love that sort of thing. I don't like it. If I accept a speaking engagement, I do the best I can, but I'm not comfortable."

The plant and offices are in a nondescript, outlying warehouse district. Fronted by a perfectly kept expanse of putting grass, they stand out. A visitor is asked to sign in with a receptionist, then is led to Hogan's office by Claribel Kelly, his trusted executive secretary. There are no slick public relations people around Hogan. He is not easy to see, but Claribel is his only visible shield. She went to grammar school with Hogan, and remembers him and his mother, who still lives in Fort Worth, attending a music recital she had a part in. She has worked for him for 18 years. She calls him "Mr. Hogan" as often as "Ben."

She opens his mail, but does not screen it. He reads it all, scrawling terse notes across the tops of letters for her to amplify. Hogan is sterner in his office. Trying to reach a businessman on the phone, Claribel enters his office to report that he is in a meeting and will call back. "When?" Hogan asks. Gene Sheely, the man who puts together the models for Hogan clubs, comes in with a wedge special-ordered by a tour star. Hogan puts on the glasses he wears for close work. "I found out playing in the Colonial I'm gonna need 'em to play golf, too. I couldn't see the pins. I had to ask the caddie." Hogan asks a couple of pointed questions, soles the club on the carpet. Sheely wonders if the player should be charged for the club. "Well heck yes," Hogan

Hogan is stern, but at home, with his wife Valerie and his help, a married couple that lives on the grounds, he is usually relaxed and amiable.

answers softly but firmly. The player endorses the clubs of another company. "That's one reason we don't have playing pros on our staff,". says Hogan. "Just me."

In the Hogan company's early, struggling years, Ben worked 14 and 16 hours a day to set up a system that was just as he wanted it. Walking through the plant, nodding at employees, occasionally stopping to inspect work at a particular station, he says, "I've done all these jobs myself. I like to work with my hands."

Dealing with his help, Hogan relies on direct communication. He does not phone them or send them memoranda, he has them summoned to his office and talks to them. Directly.

Today, Hogan usually will work only in the morning, and is perhaps the only executive in the country who consistently can take off at noon for his golf club and not be second-guessed. He cannot understand modern golfers—or executives—who say they do not have time for golf. "I have other

business interests that I find time for. I piddle around in the oil business. I fool around with the stock market quite a bit. I'm in the process of looking for a cattle ranch. I'll find what I want. I want it within 150 miles of Fort Worth. I keep hearing there's no money in it, but if that were true you couldn't buy a steak."

Each year Hogan is offered well-paying peripheral jobs, such as commentating on golf telecasts. Each year he declines. "Television is a different business entirely," he says. "It takes a professional to do a professional job. And I'm fed up with traveling."

He has been approached many times about involving himself in a tour event that would carry his name, but always has refused, in part because he is wary of lending his name to an undertaking if he does not have complete control over the quality, and in part, probably, because he has had it in mind to build his own course, the natural site for a "Ben Hogan Classic."

Hogan is considering writing an

exhaustive instruction book. "It would be this thick," he says with thumb and forefinger as far apart as they will stretch. "It would confuse a lot of people, but I can't help that. I get so darn tired of these bromides that don't mean anything. Explain to me the expression 'coming off the ball.' What does that mean? What *caused* it, that's what I want to know. I never see that explained. Or 'stay behind the ball.' What does *that* mean?"

Gardner Dickinson says he has seen Hogan turn down $500 for a five-minute lesson. Why doesn't Hogan teach? "You can't find anybody who wants to learn." A silence. "I did teach at one time."

Hearing Hogan speak about the formative years of the tour is a remarkable experience. "I'll tell you how the tour got started, and I've never read this anywhere," he said one noon as we ate *chalupas,* a zestful Mexican dish that is perfect by Fort Worth criteria—hot enough to make your eyes water but not hot enough to make you choke. "The wives of a handful of club professionals in the East—Bob Cruickshank, Al Espinosa, Tommy Armour, I believe—took it on themselves to book a tour in the 1930s. Their husbands were off work in the winter. Before that you just had a smattering of tournaments across the country. The wives wrote to chambers of commerce and so forth in California, and convinced several cities to have tournaments. Some of the purses were only a few hundred dollars, and we'd go to civic-club lunches to promote ourselves. The wives kept up all the correspondence and handled the books. Then the manufacturers saw what a great promotional vehicle the tour could be and hired Bob Harlow, Walter Hagen's manager, to conduct it. Later the PGA got in on it. That's how this $7 million business began.

"We'd play five exhibitions apiece to pay our Ryder Cup expenses. We got no money from the PGA. If somebody on the tour died or had troubles, we'd work out an exhibition schedule to help out. I never did make money playing the tour. It cost me more, total, than my purse winnings. I

had to do other things.

"We traveled together and ate together and sat around hotel rooms and talked at night. We were a smaller group, and invariably more closely knit. It seems to me like we used to have a more *gracious* life playing tournaments in those days. In many places we dressed for dinner, in dinner jackets. I cringe when I see fellas today walking into nice restaurants in golf clothes."

I asked Hogan which of his 60-some victories, including nine of the modern major championships, an unequalled three in the same year (1953), means the most to him. The 1950 United States Open at Merion was his answer, because there he proved to himself, in a tense, wearing, 36-hole final only a year after that horrendous car-bus accident, that he could be the best in spite of his injuries.

The past and the present were joined this spring when Hogan, away from tournament golf for nearly three years, his last victory 11 years ago, played back-to-back tournaments, and made them quite special. Each time he walked slowly onto a green with that rolling, purposeful stride, his younger playing partners often lagging respectfully behind, he was met with an ovation, an ovation very different from the usual. There was none of the raucous shouting that welcomes Arnold Palmer. This was loud, prolonged, sincere applause with an added depth. Bearing himself with customary dignity, Hogan nonetheless was moved. He frequently tipped the white cap he special-orders by the dozen. "I'm very grateful," he said in the locker room after one round. "These people are just wonderful, and I wish there was some way I could thank them."

He was, of course, thanking them merely by his presence. His huge galleries were heavily peopled with fathers in their 40s and 50s who had brought youthful sons to see a man who was the best at his profession, who elevated it to the level of aesthetics. But there were, not entirely expectedly, thousands of teen-agers on their own and young couples in their 20s. Yes, there were even a few dozen hippie

types, protesting nothing except that it was damned difficult to get a look at Hogan.

Bob Goalby counted 31 of his fellow pros following Hogan on a hot afternoon in Houston, and said they were impressed. The deeply tanned Hogan's swing appeared superb. His putting stroke, once a shambles, was smoother. His yogic concentration, a striking amalgam of intensity and composure that suggests utter transcendence, seemed not to have been impaired by the long layoff; Herb Wind's description of Hogan competing "with the burning frigidity of dry ice" came to mind.

Hogan always has said he would not compete unless he believed he could win. Possibly he has softened that stance. Why did he play at Champions and Colonial? "I don't know what in the world he is trying to prove," Byron Nelson had said. Claude Harmon said he didn't know if Ben was trying to inspire business for the Ben Hogan Company, but that Winged Foot, where Harmon is the head professional, is selling a lot of Hogan balls to guys who never bought them before.

Hogan says he expects a business residual from his tournament appearances, but that isn't why he played. "I couldn't play until I got better," he says. "Plus I was overweight, and this is a good way to lose it. I used to run in place a lot and exercise. I like to hunt, but had to quit. I was up to 175. Now I'm about 165. In the 1940s I weighed 130 to 135, then after my accident it was 145 to 150. I was curious—I wanted to see if I could walk for four days. I wanted to see if I could play some kinda decent golf hitting off my back foot. The fact it was the 25th anniversary of the Colonial had something to do with it. I've played a lot, but I've missed a lot of years. I missed three years in the service. I missed a year after the wreck. I missed two years because of my shoulder and two years because of my knee. Time's runnin' pretty short if I don't play now. I *enjoy* practicing and playing in tournaments. Besides, I haven't really done what I wanted to do."

"What is that," someone asked.

"I haven't won enough tournaments." ■

ARNOLD PALMER OFF CAMERA

By NICK SEITZ
December, 1971

As the most famous athlete of all time, Arnold Palmer has been interviewed approximately once for every golf shot he has hit. But the questions invariably relate solely to his game.

The mysterious ego essential to true greatness has not been probed. Neither have the new directions in which a graying Palmer increasingly is being pulled—including politics.

Palmer recently talked intensively about these prospects. The interview began behind the double doors of his paneled office next to his home in Youngstown, Pa., after Palmer spent from 7:30 to 9:30 a.m. answering mail. It continued through the day while an ever-restless Palmer, uncomfortable at a desk, moved to the golf club he had just purchased across the street and then to his workshop and club storage area. He took an hour out to fllm recruiting commercials for the Coast Guard. Twice Mark McCormack, his manager, called to talk business for 30 minutes.

On a warm day, he wore a deep-necked white golf shirt, subtly checkered red slacks and white loafers with no socks. The familiar voice was nasally resonant, and he proved unusually voluble.

What do you think it would take to be another Arnold Palmer? What qualities?
I never thought about what it would take to be the *original* Arnold Palmer. I just knew what my goals and desires were, and tried to work toward them. I've always been an aggressive, ambitious golfer. I had to be—when I started I didn't have much money. I've always enjoyed being around people. I wouldn't know how to start over, and you couldn't build my personality into someone else. You couldn't make a man who doesn't enjoy being with people *like* people. If you're not genuine, people sense that.

Have your attitudes changed over the years?
Not generally. I'm a provincial. I always have been.

Do you think younger people are turned off, as the saying has it, by golf?
I don't believe young people are that much different from 10 or 15 years ago, the large majority. They're better educated and more inquisitive, and that's good. I keep hearing that golf isn't exciting enough for them, that it isn't violent enough or doesn't relate to society. There's going to be a lull where we won't have the same high interest in the game, but it's only temporary. Golf is relevant today. It's a totally individual sport. Americans like to look on themselves as individuals. You can question the social significance of any sport. I think we professionals give a lot of people considerable pleasure, and that's important to me.

What goals do you hold for your two teen-age daughters?
Health and happiness. I want to let them make their own decisions on goals. Of course, I want to keep them out of trouble while they're young. I'm fairly strict. More than anything else, I want them to be realistic. They have a swimming pool in the back yard, a country club across the street and a new high school just up the road, and I want them to realize that it wasn't always this way, and if they don't do their part, someday it all could disappear. They have regular chores—doing the dishes, cleaning the pool. They go to public schools. One daughter is very ambitious, a good student. The other is not so industrious, but has more girl friends and participates in more activities.

Do you regret not having a son?
I'm sure any father would like to have a son to enjoy. But I'm happy with two girls. If I were to have a third child, I'm not so sure I wouldn't as soon have another girl.

You tried to convince Lanny Wadkins, who was going to your alma mater, Wake Forest, on a scholarship you helped fund, to stay in school instead of turning professional. What did you tell him?

I stayed in school and I suggested that he should have. I think he's turning pro too soon. Whether it's Lanny or any other young golfer, so much depends on his going to school. I know I went to Wake Forest to play golf, but I also wanted to learn whatever I could to use in later years. Lanny had only a little time to go. Whether he even got a diploma was probably not as important as his staying and maturing for another year. His approach to professional golf might be entirely different then. He'd have a better shot at the tour.

That doesn't mean a boy isn't going to be a good pro player and win tournaments. It just means that by staying in college he's giving himself a better chance. He has so many years to play. Gee, I didn't start playing the tour until I was 25.

You had been in the service and worked as a manufacturer's representative.
Yes, and I think it helped me, starting later. A young amateur plays against the pros once or twice and does pretty well, and he thinks it's an easy way to make a living. Well, there's pain and anguish that you find out about only by traveling the tour. I played in the Wilmington Open in North Carolina when I was a junior in college, I think it was, and did well. I shot 65 the first round and played like Lanny did at the Heritage Classic last year, and I thought I was pretty hot stuff, as he thinks

141

he is. But I hesitated to turn pro. I didn't have the financial means, and I wasn't sure I was prepared psychologically, so I stayed away. And very fortunately so, because it gave me time to decide just what I wanted to do. When I did turn pro, it was tough. I made it because I had matured enough to know what I was getting into.

How did the added maturity help?
We're talking about a young man who goes through high school as a star golfer and then is a star golfer in college, and in the summers he plays in big amateur tournaments where the surroundings are as nice as they can be. The country clubs are the best and the courses are all of a certain kind, very well manicured. He has status — everyone recognizes him and is attentive to him. He's staying in fine private homes with friendly people, and being entertained royally — because he's a big amateur champion.

He turns professional, and suddenly he's only one of 400 guys who travel the country trying to earn a living at golf, and hitting the ball pretty well. He's no longer famous. Golf becomes a working life instead of a game. He's spending hours on practice, and being ignored because he hasn't proved anything yet in this league. He's staying in a motel that isn't the best, and maybe eating in cafeterias. At night he sits in his room or goes to the movies, but he has a lot of time to wonder. He may have to drive hundreds of miles by himself, get to the next tournament site, and tee up and try to qualify on Monday. You think at first it will be great to travel, but there's no time for sight-seeing.

What he thought was a highly glamorous way of living isn't so glamorous. If he has ability, practices hard, doesn't let the pressure bother him, and understands the things I'm talking about, he'll make it.

Was money as big a lure to turn professional for you as it seems to be today?
The money today is greater in every way. The first few years I played the tour, the winners' checks were $1,500 and $2,000. That's a long way from $50,000, but it wasn't bad. I think working into the bigger money the way I did — winning $3,000 and $6,000 and then $10,000 and $15,000 and $20,000 — was good for me. It happened gradually, and I was able to learn to handle the money. I grew up with the purses. But my main ambition was not simply to make money — I wanted to play golf well.

Was there ever any doubt in your mind that you would reach the top?
I was always too busy trying hard to think much about failing, but in those early days on the tour I was looking around at golf courses and learning about the superintendent's job and the pro's job — in case I needed something to fall back on. I knew I wanted to be around a golf course. I grew up on one, and I always enjoyed it, working or playing. It's a healthy way to go. I knew I couldn't work indoors. In the service I spent a great deal of time in an office, and that wasn't

for me. Then when I was U.S. Amateur champion in 1954, I had a vague hope of becoming a good businessman and a top amateur golfer, too, playing in all the big amateur and open events. Then I decided I wanted to try the tour.

And yet today you have dozens of commercial involvements. How do you make an important business decision?
If I control the matter, I make it myself. I may discuss it with Doc Giffin and Darrell Brown, my assistants here. If it's a legal decision, I go to Mark McCormack's office in Cleveland. If it's a tax decision, I go to my attorneys. The purchase of the Latrobe Country Club across the street was my most recent deal, and I handled it myself, because I was familiar with the circumstances.

Are you going to retain your father as manager-pro?
If he behaves himself.

Is he still your golf instructor?
Yes. When I'm home we'll spend time together on the practice range almost every day.

What is the best business deal you have made in the past five years?
Oh, buying up some of my clothing contracts and reselling them has been quite profitable. I did that myself. That was fulfilling. I did very well buying and reselling a slacks contract.

What is the worst deal?
I don't care to say. I blame the bad ones on my advisors. I make only the good ones.

With so many involvements, the ability to pace yourself must be crucial. Lee Trevino is so ebullient and busy he has trouble developing a sense of pace. What counsel would you give him?
We've never talked about it. Oddly, I've never been paired with Lee. I thrive on a heavy schedule, but you have to know when to slow down. The question about Trevino is how he'll handle the pressure. There isn't a well-known player— me, Casper, Nicklaus, even an easy-going, fun-loving guy like Sanders — that it doesn't catch up

with. There comes a point when it is impossible for you to stay up mentally, and you have to take a break.

It's important, too, to learn how to be constructively critical. Hurting people's feelings with careless comments about their tournament or golf course, when they're giving their time for the game, doesn't accomplish anything. If you can be constructively critical, they appreciate it, and they'll probably make the improvements you want.

Nicklaus, in an interview with *Golf Digest* earlier this year, said there was no one he would rather beat than you. Do you feel the same way about him?
Damn right! We're friends, but we're strong competitors. If I beat him, it means more to me than beating anyone else.

A friend of yours speculates that from the role of world-wide sports hero you have enjoyed for so long, the only place you can go without taking a step down is politics.
I think it's part of continuing to mature that, as you grow older, you appreciate that the spotlight isn't that necessary. I might do more television commentating. I don't think that politics would be the answer. About half the people are your friends and the other half aren't. It might be the spotlight, but not the type you're interested in.

What dissuaded you?
I guess . . . politics. I might change my mind, but I have no thoughts at all of running for governor.

That sounds like something a politician would say shortly before he announces he's running.
I might become more involved behind the scenes, but I don't expect to run for office.

Some people would ask what a golfer knows about politics.
What does a politician know about politics? Who is a qualified politician? A man who studied government in college? A lawyer? Does the President know intricately every field he has to deal with? He must gather people around him who know, and he must be able to judge situations as they develop.

You have to be honest, with yourself and with others, and you have to have a feeling for what people would like. There probably are too *many* professional politicians today.

What do you see for golf on the international level?
I'd like to see the emergence of an annual tournament of champions from all over the world. If Ping-Pong can further understanding between peoples, why can't golf do more? We have a lucrative U.S. tour, but we're a little selfish and insular. We should be trying hard to get more involved internationally. Our top players often win when they go outside the country, but not enough of us go.

I would bet that there are plenty of big sponsors outside the U.S. right now for a true world tour — all they need is some indication that they could get good fields. It's very possible we're going to be losing some U.S. tournaments if the economy falls back. In those weeks we could do things internationally.

Do you plan to alter your schedule?
Yes. I found out I'm going to have to play less, because I can't stay sharp for long periods of time the way I used to. With more rest, I can play as well as ever; maybe better.

I've hesitated to cut back, because I owe the sponsors of tournaments so much. But I have to. I intend to get ready for the Masters, for example, by taking off for two or three weeks beforehand. Previously, I've usually played my way into the four major tournaments. But I've decided not to be out there every week trying to achieve something that, if I get it, doesn't mean as much as the Masters.

Also, I am going to spend more time working at my game during the off-season, at Bay Hill, the resort course I bought near Orlando, instead of spending so much of the winter at home here in Pennsylvania, where I can't play as much golf.

I'm going to do everything possible to play the best I can for as long as I can. ∎

DUTCH HARRISON'S LIFELONG PIGEON HUNT

BY JIM TRINKLE
June, 1972

It would be unkind to say Dutch Harrison loves money. He does, however, feel kindly toward it. As Dutch sees it, the only reason for being a professional golfer is to make money. He has trained every fiber in his gangling frame to detect a foolish dollar.

It was in pursuit of prosperity that he once spotted a potential pigeon too many strokes. Dutch is rarely outgamed on the first tee, and surrendering the $5 bill was a solemn ceremony for the former Arkansas cottonpicker.

"Dutch, I'm going to frame this," the man bubbled.

Harrison snatched back the $5 and snapped, "I'll write you a check."

He is wary of pronouncements from younger tour capitalists that titles are more important to them than paychecks. "Those boys," he twangs, "are stretchin' the truth a little. There ain't but one reason you're out there—to make a buck."

Such was Dutch's credo for close to 35 years as a touring pro, a stretch that produced 15 official PGA titles, a Vardon Trophy in 1954, a jillion friends—but only $19,253 in 1953, his best money-winning campaign.

Relaxing in his pro shop at Forest Hills Golf Club near St. Louis, he surveys his domain through eyes that saw the glories of Bobby Jones, the magic of Hogan, the reign of Palmer and the rise of Nicklaus.

He still can play with the young lions. He qualified for the 1971 U.S. Open at Merion at the age of 61, which the U.S. Golf Ass'n believes makes him the oldest man ever to play in the tournament proper. (Sam Snead was also 61

when he played in the 1973 U.S. Open.) By Dutch's best calculations the 1972 U.S. Open at Pebble Beach will be his 23rd if he makes it. Or is it the 24th . . .

"I reckon Sam's been in more Opens than me or anybody else," he says of old crony Snead. "I guess the biggest disappointment I ever had was at Cherry Hills in the 1960 Open. Comin' late in life as it did, it just had to be the worst disappointment. I finished the first round 6-6 for 74. Then I shot 70-70-69." He tied for third, three shots behind winner Arnold Palmer and one behind a young amateur, Jack Nicklaus.

Dutch was 50 that year. Ten years earlier, at Merion, a closing 76 had left him a shot short of joining Hogan, George Fazio and Lloyd Mangrum in a playoff. It hurt worse at Denver.

"If Dutch had the tiger in him

that Palmer has," says Tommy Bolt, "we never would've heard of some of them cats. If Dutch had thought as much about golf as the racetrack, he'd have been up there with Hogan. When Dutch was trying to win a little money to take him down the road, Hogan was trying to win the tournament."

Bolt knew Dutch when there wasn't a jaybird in Arkansas who hadn't cackled over the ex-Little Rock caddie's gamesmanship. Dutch set up his games with persuasion, patience and, if needed, a plea for the aged and infirm. Once he showed up for the Odessa (Tex.) Pro-Am with a young, unknown amateur, and waltzed through the field. The amateur was George Archer.

"We used to kid Dutch because he'd always get a game with a couple of new players in practice rounds," recalls Byron Nelson. "He

Jim Trinkle of the Fort Worth Star-Telegram is a familiar figure in the press rooms of major golf tournaments, and has won several national writing awards.

didn't practice with Hogan or Snead. He'd say 'Those kids need some seasonin'.' "

Bolt remembers, "He was a master of the soft shot. It'd look like he knocked the blood out of a 1-iron and it'd flutter out there 165 yards and die next to the hole. He made it look so good the guy he was playing would bust a 2-iron, and he'd have to call a taxi to take him to his ball."

Fables of his trickery amuse Dutch, who, as a one-time companion of Titanic Thompson, got to observe a legendary gamesman at work. "Aw, I'd never heckle a man or anything like that," he says. "I might *dee*-coy him."

It was and is a game of wits. "To win, you got to get every break, then somebody's got to kick it away," he says, rearing back in his chair. Ernest Joe Harrison at leisure could pass for one of the millionaires whose names he has carried for 62 years.

Titanic Thompson says he and Dutch once played Paul Runyan, later the PGA champ, and club professional Julius Ackerbloom for $6,000, which in the early '30s was a prince's ransom. Titanic was banking Dutch and himself. An Arkansas syrup executive was staking Runyan's team.

"We were 2-up with two to play," Thompson recalls, "but Runyan came out of the boonies for a birdie on 17 and Ackerbloom holed a 40-footer on the last hole to tie us." Years later in his 80s, Titanic still sputtered at the way the pigeons got away from him and Dutch."

"They wouldn't play no more," Dutch says. "That Karo surp man took his surp and got outta there."

There followed years when Dutch and others like him scuffled for quarters and half-dollars any place they could make gasoline money.

"In 1935, me and Bob Hamilton had been playing a couple of schoolteachers at Pinehurst," he recalls. "Those teachers just donated around $9 a day to us to have somebody to play with."

One morning as they waited for the teachers they noticed a stranger sitting at the first tee. He was nattily dressed. They eyed him warily.

"You fellas got a game?" the stranger asked. They mentioned their prearranged foursome. "Will they let five play?" he persisted. Dutch and Bob, who didn't want anybody riding shotgun on their game, didn't think so. But the teachers asked the stranger to join them.

"We play 50-cent syndicates and carryovers," Dutch said, figuring that since the stranger had crashed their party, he might as well buy some of the cake. The stranger, who said his name was Snead, casually inquired, "Y'all play any side bets?" and Dutch's suspicions were stirred.

"When he set his club on the ground—he had an old whippy-shafted Willie Ogg—and took his stance," Dutch says, "I knew we had a bear by the tail. I coulda made birdies on the first and again on the third hole, but Bob said wait and catch a carryover."

Hamilton and the teachers all hooked into the rough on the par-5 sixth hole. Bob told Dutch it would be a good one to win.

"Those days I had a hook I could control, so I curled mine down there about 260 yards," Dutch says. "Goin' down the fairway I saw a ball about 40 yards ahead of mine, and I figured it was one of the teachers' second shots. But this Snead just kept walkin'."

Snead said, "My ball must've hit a rock." Dutch's eyes rolled back in his head. The only rocks at Pinehurst were in the 19th Hole, surrounded by bourbon.

"I hit a 3-wood about 20 feet from the flag," Dutch says. "I thought, 'Let's see what he does now.' He pulled out a 4-iron and knocked that thing six inches from the flag. That was how I met Sam Snead. We didn't win a single syndicate. He won 12. He said, 'You all got a game tomorrow?' I told him I was booked up from then on, for him to work his side of the street and we'd work ours."

Harrison won the 1939 Crosby and Texas Opens and later won them again. He almost won the Texas tournament again in 1964, which would have been a quarter-century after his first San Antonio victory.

Dutch always has admired the way a nice set of odds can pump up a bankroll. He figures the return is worth the risk.

"After the war, the Reno Open was one of the first $25,000 tournaments," he remembers. "They had me 30-1 in the books there, so I borrowed $100 from Bob Hamilton to bet on myself. Bob said 'I'm 5-1. Don't you want to bet on me?' I *knew* I was gonna beat Bob."

Perhaps it was a combination of Reno's fleshly pleasures—which Dutch spurned—and Nevada's gamy atmosphere, but the field fell so far behind he was able to coast in.

"I never had a bigger thrill in golf than that. I could've six-putted the last hole and won," he says. "I was playing with Herman Keiser and Jimmy Demaret. You know how dusty-lookin' it gets out there? That desert just turned green to me. I was in a daze, really enjoyin' it, and Keiser said, 'Ain't you gonna putt. Let's get this thing over

Golf's panorama from Hagen to Hogan, Aaron to Ziegler, has passed before Dutch's eyes. He says, "My top five now, on any course, are Nicklaus, Palmer, Trevino, Boros and Gardner Dickinson. Nicklaus is like Hogan in his prime—by himself.

"In my day, Hogan, Snead, Nelson, Henry Picard and Demaret were just as good as the modern stars. They could play with anybody out there now."

Three months into his 63rd year, Dutch plays infrequently. There's a buck to be made around the shop.

His wife Thelma pays the bills. Dutch counts the money, which is what a guy's in the business for.

Jesse Barge is one of Dutch's assistants at Forest Hills. Jesse is 23 and has no ambitions to be a tournament professional. He would like to be a good club pro, like Dutch Harrison, who has been both. He watches and listens.

"What's so great about working for Dutch," he says, "are all the things I learn about golf. It's not that he's just a great technician. He teaches you the traditions of golf."

It's a nice endorsement by one of golf's youngsters of one of its patriarchs. So go the days of one of the saber-tooths from an earlier golf jungle. Dutch isn't running any more footraces, but nobody's gaining on him. ∎

SHUCKS, I MAY JUST GO ON FOREVER

BY CAL BROWN
August, 1972

Sam Snead's longevity is probably unmatched in the history of American sport. No athlete has performed so well for so long.

Snead, 60 this year, has captured a record 84 tour events and has been second 59 times. No one knows how many lesser tournaments he has won—he figures the total is somewhere around 60.

Ben Hogan, Byron Nelson and Ralph Guldahl also are 60 in 1972 —it was a very good year for golf births in 1912—and all were wonderful players. But Snead is the only one still playing top-level competitive golf.

How has he persisted so successfully?

Some of the answer can be found in his unusual physical gifts, but more crucial is his compulsive need to win—the flaming competitive urge he has not lost.

During a practice round last year at the PGA Championship, Snead, Bob Goalby and Jerry Barber were approaching the 17th hole, a par 5 that requires a long, straight drive. I was riding in Snead's golf car gathering notes for a story and on the way to the tee I casually asked him how much distance he had lost on his drives.

"Thirty or forty yards," he said, although he thought he could still pop it when he had to. Snead then teed up his ball, reached back for all the hardware, rolled mightily over the shot and hit a squirty-looking snap hook that finished in the trash about 200 yards off the tee. He teed another ball—and did the same thing. The third swing was perfection, the ball soaring gracefully for 260 yards.

Snead returned to the car satisfied he had made the shot he wanted to make, but growling petulantly about the first two swings. There was a fair piece of change riding on the match. I decided to walk up the fairway with Goalby. Snead jumped in the golf car and tore after his ball up ahead.

"A lot of guys lose their desire to play after they reach a certain age, but not that old man," Goalby said admiringly. "He knows he can't win with his putting, but he still has that desire to compete. I still get nervous playing with him and I must have played 40 rounds of golf with the man."

Later, after Snead had struck a glorious recovery shot and collected all the bets on 18, as he was driving me away from the PGA National club we talked about desire.

"Well, when that goes, it's all over," he said. "Desire is the most important thing in sport. I have it. Jeez, no one has any more than I got. I admire a guy with will and drive, the kind who will beat you 10 and 8 if he has a chance. Pour it on. I think you got to be that way in sport.

"A lot of guys on the tour are nice guys, but that's the trouble with them—they're too nice. They'll never win with that attitude. I wouldn't hurt a chicken crossing the road, but if I got a man in trouble on the golf course I'd kick the hell out of him. I don't care if he's my best friend."

Snead's competitive juices began flowing at an early age. His brother Jesse told me a revealing story about the young Sam. Jesse, seven years older than Sam, is the father of touring pro Carlyle (J. C.) Snead. He has lived in Hot Springs, Va., all his life and recently retired as janitor at The Homestead.

Jesse said. "He had a real competitive urge. He used to drive our momma's brother, Ed Dudley, crazy. We called Ed 'Unk.' Sam used to bet Unk on anything from golf to horseshoes. One day Dudley showed up with a new set of used clubs. Sam had a few ratty castoffs he'd nailed together. Sam said, 'C'mon, Unk, let's go over to the goat course and play for ice cream.' Afterward, I saw them eating ice cream at the store and asked Unk how he did. 'I can't beat that little bleep no matter what I do,' Unk groaned.

"Well, we all came home and pretty soon Sam invited Unk up the hill to pitch horseshoes. Dudley was good at horseshoes and said he'd get Sam for sure this time. Off they went. On the last pitch, Unk threw a ringer. Sam looked at him and said, 'You know, Unk, if I throw one on top of yours that's a double score for me.' Unk nodded. Sam threw a ringer and then fell down on all fours, holding his sides with laughter. Unk grabbed Sam and scrubbed his hair like a washboard. That's why Sam hasn't got any hair—Unk scrubbed his head so much.

"Finally, Unk thought he had a way to get Sam. He had a fishing hole all scouted and he suckered Sam into a bet on who could catch the most fish. Ice cream stakes again. Unk went straight for an old rock beside the fishing hole where he knew the fish was hiding. He dropped his hook and brought out a couple of fish in no time. Sam was on the bank a ways off and wasn't catching anything. He watched Unk for a few minutes, then hauled over an old sunken log and got on it. He pushed it toward Unk, fishing all the way, and when he got near he kind of slipped off, accidental like. Sam climbed up the rock and said, 'Hey, Unk, that ain't no way to catch fish. You got to jiggle the line more, like this.'

"Sam dropped his hook, bent over and started jiggling his line up and down and pretty soon he had landed three fish. Then he cleaned Unk's fishing pole. Unk was so mad he scrubbed Sam's head again and then chased him home. When they came in the house, Momma asked Unk who won. Unk just glared and said, 'I come as close to knocking

his little tail over the railroad car as that little bleep will ever get.' Sam whipped Unk at marbles, too. Sam's a great marbles shooter, even today."

The competitive instinct, the need to win, the reluctance to let a ripe pigeon off the hook all are part of the Snead personality. There are other sides, too, such as his well-publicized regard for money and reluctance to part with it.

Not long ago, I asked Jimmy Demaret if Sam really was as tight-fisted in the early days as people have claimed he was. Jimmy paused for a moment, then said, "Yes, he was tight, all right. You knew, didn't you, that he threw a birthday party for his father, who was about 90, in Walgreen's Drugstore? Sam had the party there because his closest buddy, Johnny Bulla, had a deal with Walgreen's and could get a discount there."

Fred Corcoran, until recently Snead's manager, says Sam still counts the balls in his bag, even though he can get all he wants from Wilson.

The reason for Snead's failure to project a friendly public image lies in his wariness. He is at ease with people who want nothing from him but his company, but if he senses a phony or sycophant his eyes narrow, looking for the nearest escape route.

Even today, Snead walks swiftly to the first tee and back to the clubhouse. He signs autographs quickly. When someone approaches him and says, "Hey, Sam, remember me from Akron?" the Snead guard flies up. "Nope," he may say coldly.

His guardedness is understand-able to those who have known him throughout his pro career. He was admittedly gullible as a young man coming on the tour from a backward environment, although he never buried his money in the backyard as some of his friends have suggested. Snead lived in the limelight from the start, thrust into a starring role because of his enormous talent. His first year on the tour, 1937, he was picked as the favorite to win the U.S. Open. Even though he won 30 tournaments in his first five years on tour, he was being called "The Great Runner-up" by some writers because he had not captured any

major titles. He never forgot that.

He has had very little private life, yet he craves solitude more than most people. He has the mountaineer's instinctive suspicion of strangers and is, in a sense, allergic to the adulation of the public. He never has been a man to hang around the tour too long at a time; he has to return to the Virginia hills.

"I've never been anywhere that somebody didn't recognize me," Sam says, "even in foreign countries. Once the guide on an African safari told me he was in my gallery once at Tam O'Shanter in Chicago. Can you beat that?"

Sam never smoked and, until recently, never drank. Now he will drink beer after a round of golf and an occasional daiquiri, very sweet, before dinner. His pursuit of earthy enjoyment has nonetheless always been major league.

A love of music comes from his family, all of whom played an instrument or sang. Snead still plays trumpet and says he misses the jam sessions he used to have with tour compatriots Lionel Hebert, Jimmy Demaret, Errie Ball, Dick Mayer and Claude Harmon. An FM system constantly pipes music into every room of his Florida home.

When Sam is not playing in tournaments, giving exhibitions or hunting, he can usually be found at The Greenbrier, the stately resort bastion of propriety and elegance where he has been pro since 1936. Snead has a fine two-story, five-bedroom house on 130 acres in Hot Springs, Va., an hour away, where his wife Audrey spends the summer. A big, blonde woman he met in the first grade and married in 1940, she sees little of him.

Sam lives in a large suite at the hotel. His position in the dining room is as fixed as the white paint on The Greenbrier buildings. He always sits in the same chair, at the same table just inside the entrance, from where he can scan the entire room.

During the winter, Sam and Audrey move to their comfortably luxurious home overlooking the ocean in Highland Beach, Fla., a short distance from the Boca Raton Hotel where Snead used to be winter pro. The handsome, white-pillared house has a two-story entrance hall, two living rooms and the largest walk-in closet I've ever seen off Sam's bedroom. A magnificent game room downstairs is equipped with pool table, eight-stool bar and most of Sam's golf and hunting trophies. One is a 15-pound bonefish he caught on a six-pound test line—still a world's record.

The Sneads have two sons. The oldest, Samuel Jackson Jr., is 27 and manages Sam Snead Enterprises, a diversified corporation that includes Sam's many golf, business and financial activities.

The younger son, Terry, 23, has been retarded since birth. He lives in an expensive private hospital, and comes home to Hot Springs for visits each year. Normally, Sam does not speak of this, but he thinks about it a great deal, he admitted wistfully one night. He seems to have accepted the inevitable but it has affected him more deeply than he is willing to let on.

There is a strong sense of family loyalty about the Sneads, but the relationships are peculiarly aloof. The other members of Sam's family are Homer, the eldest brother who runs a driving range in Florida and from whom Sam learned to play; Lyle, dead; Wilfred (Pete), recently retired from the Pittsburgh Field Club pro job; Janet, married with six children, and Jesse.

In 1939, Sam's swing started giving him trouble in Florida and he told Bobby Jones he was going home for a lesson.

"My brothers are the only ones who know what I'm doing," he said to the great amateur. Snead drove all night to reach West Virginia and looked whipped when he arrived. He called his brothers together.

"Boys, let's go to the golf course. You got to tell me what I'm doing wrong," he said.

On the first swing Jesse and Pete hollered at the same time, "Stop there.

"You're laying the club off, and swinging flat," they choroused.

Sam looked up at his backswing.

"Damn, that's it. I'm going right back to Florida."

He jumped in his car and drove back and when Jones saw him the next day, he said to Sam, "I thought you were going home for a lesson."

"You just watch me," Sam replied.

He teed one up and struck a drive about 320 yards down the middle of the fairway and went on to win three straight tournaments. Afterward, Jones said, "I guess I'll go up to West Virginia and get a lesson from your brothers."

Snead still is an amazing physical specimen. His walk is springy and alive and he dances with the grace and rhythm of a young Astaire. Contrary to popular myth, he is not magically double jointed. The reason he can bend his left thumb back so far is that he broke it playing football and the thumb healed crooked.

Snead has never been very cerebral about the golf swing. Most of what he has learned has come by trial and error. He rates concentration highly. "You must concentrate intensely, if for only a few seconds, before each shot, but it must be total concentration."

Like most great drivers, Snead believes putting is most important in golf, with driving second. (Most of the great putters believe the reverse, of course.) When it comes to building a golf swing, Snead is refreshingly candid.

"You're not going to get it from someone else. You have to find the stroke within yourself. You can't buy it at the drugstore. It just doesn't come that way. I've been up all those lanes and byways. You take away a man's personal mannerisms, you kill him in any sport.

"Golf is the only sport where a man 60 can play with the best. That's why golf is such a great game. And no one has ever licked it."

"Sam has played more golf than any man who ever lived. He just loves the game," says Demaret.

Snead and his accountant once estimated that he had hit over 1.6 million golf balls in his career. He still plays about 250 rounds a year and in his younger days played even more, which adds up to something over 100,000 rounds of golf in 40 years.

Snead believes his putting problems date from the 1948 U.S. Open at Riviera which Hogan won when Sam stuck an iron shot three feet from the hole with a chance to tie—and blew the putt.

Snead has had physical problems not many fans know about. He has

suffered from a bad back for 20 years. An affliction called spinal othesis of the fifth lumbar vertebra hits the sciatic nerve in such a way that his left leg won't move properly. He also has a form of tendonitis in his left hand that forces him to loosen his grip occasionally. When that happens he either snap hooks the ball or leaves it dead right. To cut the pain in his hand, he takes butazolidin, the drug that disqualified Kentucky Derby winner Dancer's Image. Snead rarely mentions these chronic ailments.

When the great Open mystery is mentioned, as it inevitably is any time Snead's career is discussed, Sam is philosophical. "I don't know whether it's a jinx. I know I've thought a lot about it. I've finished second in the Open four times, more than anyone else except Palmer (who also has finished second four times). I guess where there's a human element there's human frailty. It's the same with Arnold and the PGA. Each year it gets tougher and tougher. When you win a major tournament once, it seems like it's easier to win it again. But I'll live with or without the Open title."

Snead, whose various business ventures (including the golf shop at Greenbrier, a golf consulting service, contracts with Wilson Sporting Goods and other investments) bring him more income each year than the leading money winner makes on tour, has no financial worries. "I've got everything I want. As long as you got three squares a day, drive a Cadillac car, don't have to worry about bills, and go to bed and wake up when you choose, what else do you want?"

I asked Snead if he ever considered quitting competitive golf. He looked at me strangely.

"Well, there's no substitute for being young. The old guys don't like growing old. I don't like it, but we gotta give way. The trouble with old people is that they keep everything in. They ought to just draw it back and let it go—in golf and in life. That'll keep you young. Your muscles are as good as the way you use them.

"I'm lucky. Shucks, if my health holds up I just may go on forever." ■

GOLF'S MOST UNLIKELY CHAMPION

BY KEN BOWDEN
December, 1972

Undoubtedly, Bobby Locke was the oddest golf champion this land has ever seen. He was, however, truly a champion, winning 13 U.S. titles of one sort or another, the Open championship of Britain four times, of France twice and of Canada, Mexico, Australia, Germany, Switzerland, Holland, Ireland and Egypt each once. In seven attempts at the U.S. Open, he finished third twice, fourth twice and fifth once.

When Locke left his tiny hometown of Vereeniging near Johannesburg and boarded a plane for his first visit to America, he had just beaten Sam Snead in 12 of 16 head-to-head matches in South Africa. But no more unlikely tournament golfer had ever crossed the Atlantic.

As an 18-year-old winner of the 1935 South African Amateur and Open championships, Locke was a svelte, good-looking, fair-haired young man. Even when upsetting Henry Cotton and his crowd in England over the next four years, Locke was the orthodox "young comer." He had a good, strong, straightforward swing, and he wore pants like everyone else's. The most remarkable thing about him then was probably his magnificent putting touch. But there was no doubt about his over-all golf ability, at least by European standards. Cotton, then Britain's best, flatly refused to meet the South African in a big-money head-to-head match, despite repeated challenges and much adverse publicity.

When Locke arrived here in 1947 he showed the marks of a hard war —he had flown 1,800 hours as a bomber pilot—in his thickening frame, darkening hair and jowly, weather-beaten face. At 29, he looked 40.

But it was his *outfit* that really got

to the U.S. pros and the few fans at his first tournament, the Masters, who went looking for the "guy from Africa." For golf, the post-war Locke almost always wore knickers — big, baggy, hot, flapping bloomers—and up above them a white, business-type shirt. And around the collar of the shirt was a tie . . . yes, a *tie.* "When the temperature climbed over 90," he says, "I rolled up my sleeves."

Probably only two people remember Locke's actual performance—rather than his appearance—in his first U.S. tournament, the 1947 Masters. One is Locke. He shot 289, one over par, to finish eight strokes behind winner Jimmy Demaret. As he had

wanted to go to Britain in 1947, not America, Locke was pleasantly surprised by his debut. But his main reason for remembering this particular tournament is that he played with Bobby Jones, of which more later.

The other person who remembers Locke's debut is the man mainly responsible for his coming here in the first place, Sam Snead. Sam by then knew more than enough about Locke to see an omen in the South African's almost immediate mastery of American golf conditions at Augusta. "The others guys thought I was nuts, but I wouldn't have bet one red cent against him in any tournament," says Sam.

Following his Masters debut,

Locke proceeded to capture four of five tournaments from this country's best. He won the Carolinas Open and at Houston with a 277 total, lost his putting touch temporarily at Fort Worth and merely tied for third, then rebounded to win the Philadelphia Inquirer's tournament and the Goodall Round Robin. At Philadelphia he carded two 70s on the final day to make up 10 strokes on Ben Hogan, and in the Goodall he birdied three of the last four holes for a point total of plus-37.

Locke did not stop there. Ever convivial and increasingly confident by the day, he placed sixth in the National Capital Invitational and fourth in the U.S. Open, won the All-American Open, the Canadian Open and the Columbus Open, tied for second in the Western Open, placed seventh in the Denver Open and lost a playoff to Dutch Harrison in the Reading Open. When he departed at the end of summer he was richer by $24,327.50. At the year's end he was second to Demaret on the money list—and Demaret had played the full 12-month tour.

America was stunned. It was stunned first by the apparent effortlessness with which this unathletic-looking "African guy" beat golfers whom America had been told were the world's finest. It was stunned by his bizarre haberdashery. It was stunned by his "cool"—his unhurriedness, his concentration and his unshakable composure in adversity or success. Perhaps most of all, the golfers of America were stunned by his method.

By the time he got to America, Locke had developed and refined to perfection the most individualistic swing of any big winner in history—Hagen with his sway and Palmer with his crashing, flourishing follow-through are models of orthodoxy by comparison. Locke hooked everything, including, it seemed, his putts. Not drew, hooked . . . whipped it around in a high, wide, swinging half-circle.

At address, he aimed his entire body somewhere right of first base, with his right foot pulled back a couple of feet behind the left. Going back, he swung the club sharply inside with a huge upper body turn and a lot of flippy wrist

action. At the top he had the club pointing into the right bleachers. Coming down, his shoulders rolled and spun like a wallowing whale. Every shot would start way right, then curl slowly back to centerfield. Very few failed to finish on target. And even fewer of Locke's approach shots failed to finish pin-high. He never stepped off a course in his life, but he was as good a judge of distance as today's pros are measurers.

Today, at 55, laughter is very close to the surface in Locke. He has a dry, British-type wit, a good-natured sense of put-down, and an almost Pickwickian love of verbal and practical jokes. It is a light approach that carried him through some tough patches during the nine summers he visited in the U.S. Once his novelty value wore off and it was obvious that he was going to move large sums of money across the ocean, Locke took some hefty verbal punishment on the U.S. tour—some of it to his face, most behind his back. His rapid appreciation of his own value and his determination to capitalize on it off as well as on the course didn't help.

He actually was banned from playing here in 1949, after he won his first British Open, on the grounds that he had failed to keep commitments to play in U.S. tournaments. The facts are that U.S. sponsors wanted him to play but didn't want to pay him the appearance money they paid U.S. stars. Locke thus decided to stay in Britain for the rest of that summer, and it would seem that he gave U.S. promotors ample notice of this decision. Nevertheless, the U.S. PGA suspended him until the spring of 1950, when his drawing power prompted some rethinking.

Humor helped Locke ride through or above most of this. A lot of the snide comments and criticisms he simply answered with a joke. His style of play was the easiest target, and one of his best lines came in answer to a damning remark about his weak left-hand grip. "Yes, you're probably right about the left hand," he said, "but the fact is that I take the checks with my right hand." Another great line answered the crack—repeated a thousand times—that he had a

buggy-whip swing. "Actually," he'd say, "I'm a singer. Golf with me is a sideline."

Despite his great ability to concentrate, Locke never found it necessary to be a sourpuss, even on the golf course. While others made tournament golf a deadly serious thing, Locke appeared to be having a genuinely good time.

Locke bears no malice to any of his critics from that era. His achievements in America helped to set him up financially. He met and courted his wife here, and although he loves South Africa first and Britain next, he likes and enjoys and is grateful to America. He developed a close friendship in the nine years he played here with the late and universally loved Ed Oliver, but he retains no deep associations with other contemporaries. "I hit them in the pocket, and that's where it hurts most," he says.

The near-exception is Sam Snead. Locke has a deep respect for Snead's achievements and a great regard for his golf swing. Like a lot of people who know Snead well, Locke also enjoys Sam socially. They dined together last summer when Snead visited Scotland to play for (and win) the World Senior championship, and Locke relished the time with his old rival.

The American Locke admires most, however, is unquestionably the late Bobby Jones. One reason for this is the quality of Jones the man—Locke always has striven to be considerate, polite and modest and aware that there is more to life than can be found in winning golf tournaments, and he deeply admired these traits in Jones. An equally strong reason is that, at the behest originally of his father, Locke modeled his entire game on Jones'. Locke was very close to his father, an Ulsterman who emigrated to South Africa just before the turn of the century, became a successful sports-outfitter, started his son in golf and encouraged him to play the game professionally. (Locke's parents lived into their late 90s in an apartment Locke bought for them that he has kept empty and untouched since their deaths.)

Locke recalls, "When I was 13,

my dear old dad gave me Bobby Jones' book on golf, and he said to me, 'Son, here is the finest golfer in the world, and I want you to learn how to play from his book. A lot of people are going to try to help you, but just let it go in one ear and out of the other. You just model your game on Bobby Jones and you will be a fine player.' So that's what I did when I started, and what I have done all my life. So you can imagine the respect I've had for Bobby Jones.''

America always has been a pragmatic country, and as Locke continued to zap its superstars, much of the golf populace stopped snickering at his swing and started to study it. Everybody recognized, of course, that Locke was a phenomenal putter—but he had to get the ball on the green in pretty much the right number of strokes before he could start waving his rusty old wooden-shafted wand. He did so with what he believed was the natural golf swing, one which didn't have to be kept constantly tuned with hours of practice, as opposed to the more artificial action developed by the American professionals. Locke carefully guarded against over-practicing, an attitude which sprang from more than his desire to play as naturally as possible. He wanted to conserve himself as much as possible, to give of his resources on each occasion only that amount necessary to win, so that he could go on giving—and winning—for a very long time. Record scores meant nothing to him; statistical measurement of his play—fairways missed, greens hit even less. The object was victory as effortlessly as possible. He was the antithesis of Hogan and the strongest challenger to Hagen for the title of the golf champion who "played badly best."

The older he grew, in fact, the more conservative Locke became. In Britain, where he played most of his golf and had his greatest victories—the Opens in 1949-50-52-57—Locke got into endless trouble about his speed of play. He was not like Jack Nicklaus, who careens along the fairways, then takes aeons over the shot. Locke had just two speeds for everything —leisurely and slow. Once he

actually got to the ball, he played his shots with dispatch. But getting there was the problem. Week in, week out, the writers would record how he took 20 minutes to put his shoes on, 10 minutes to collect his scorecard, five to get a ball from his bag. He had his pace and nothing would shift him from it. Large gaps would open on the course ahead of him, his playing partners would grow red-necked and fiery-eyed, officials would threaten, but Locke remained immovable. Since the war, at least, nothing—but *nothing*—has ever hurried him.

There was one very strong foundation to both Locke's composure and the limited amount of "oiling" he had to give his swing. He had a fantastically fine short game—putting, pitching, chipping, bunker play, the lot. "I learned very early in life," he explains, "that, as Bobby Jones said in his book, the real secret of success in golf lies in turning three shots into two. If you miss a third of the greens in every round, but turn three shots into two four times, you save four shots a round. If you do that in every round of a tournament you save 16 shots. Thus, once I had my long game in reasonable shape as a young man, I worked for many, many hours—many, many days and weeks and months—on my short game. And it paid very well by taking the pressure off my long game. I always felt confident that I could make pars when I was playing well, a few birdies might come my way."

In the final analysis, though, it was Locke's putting that enabled him to take America by storm. He was the greatest—many still believe the greatest ever. And the U.S. tour pros never got over it. There was more to Locke's magical putting than technique. He never changed his putter, and although his stroke was influenced by Walter Hagen during The Haig's tour of South Africa in 1937, his basic approach to the putt was regimented . . . a ritualistic inspection and cleaning of the line, a long look from behind the ball, two practice swings and a simple, easy strike at the ball with no further ceremony.

In 1959, Locke was traveling in a

car that was hit by a train on a level-crossing in South Africa. Unconscious for days, he was lucky to live. Locke has not won a major tournament since, but today he loves golf as much as he ever did. At home in Johannesburg, he attends in the mornings to the management of the apartment block he owns. Most afternoons he plays golf, usually at one of the local clubs; he will play quite happily with anyone, for a modest Nassau or the sheer fun of it.

Locke loves Britain—the countryside, the people, the easy-paced lifestyle, and the hundreds of friends he has made there—but it is the Open that draws him most. Five years ago the R and A ruled that any previous champion may play without pre-qualifying. Locke says, "I will go on playing in the Open as long as I can walk."

Of his game today, Locke will say only that "the fairways get longer and the holes get smaller." But the game is still there—the big, high hook, the wonderful judgment of distance, the inevitable choice of the percentage shot over the gamble and the masterly touch on the short strokes.

A few days after he had won the Vermont Open, on the evening before he left America, the members at the Rutland Country Club gave Arthur D'Arcy Locke a party. They got him a ukelele, and they got a few Pabsts inside him, and they got him singing and telling his jokes, and it was a big night.

"And, Maastah," said Rutland pro Hank Vergi, "We shall sure miss him." ■

THE RETURN OF FLASH GORDON

BY WILLIAM PRICE FOX
April, 1973

In the press tent during the 36th Masters the only problem confronting the gentlemen of the fourth estate in filing their stories was not who would win or how or why, but how to describe the No. 2 man, the cherubic Jim Jamieson. Portly, stout, merry, massive . . . how about awesome? In New York City the ad men were facing the harder facts—the tape measure facts. If he won, could he fit in the Masters jacket? What products could he endorse? None of his clothes came off the rack. There was no way on that full profile for hip-huggers and double knit shirts or the new look in belts. Maybe shock aborbers, mufflers, transmission work, oil products, STP . . . a younger Andy Granatelli?

The Augusta greens which Cliff Roberts had baked out and shaved down took care of the situation; Jamieson began to fade. Later his voltage moved up again but it was like the overnight trickle charges at battery shops. There weren't enough holes, there wasn't enough time.

Growing up with John Wayne, Gary Cooper and James Stewart, most of us still want our heroes looking like heroes. People like Casper, Jim Jamieson and Trevino can be sidekicks like Gabby Hayes, supplying the comic relief around the horse trough, but never the silver-spurred soft-talker who rides into the sunset, leaving the love stuff behind for lesser mortals. But reality has a harder edge and the old Randolph Scott oranges and the primary colors of the funnybooks have begun to fade. Palmer loses, Snead tires, Hogan is absent, Nelson is old and Jones is dead

William Price Fox III teaches creative writing at the University of Iowa. A native of South Carolina, he grew up just across the river from Augusta, Ga. His first novel was *Ruby Red*.

. . . . "Where Have You Gone Joe DiMaggio?"

Finally after the cheeses and during the brandies someone mentions a country and western nasal song riding low on the charts, "One Man's Trash Is Another Man's Treasure." We talk ourselves into Coody, Rosburg, Mason Rudolph, Boros, Casper, who if surprised in a steambath would look like Nero's ward bosses. We talk about the new anti-hero. And then we change the subject. But later on when the fire is banked and the crickets are telling their secrets to the night we realize we are all still waiting for the White Knight, the flaxen-haired, bronzed, blue-eyed darling of Dale Arden's eyes, Flash Gordon. He should be tall, blonde, Nordic, with clear blue eyes and slim honest loins. We want Flash Gordon back, or Brick Bradford, or one of the square-jawed Steve Canyons of yesterday.

Palmer's long, thrusting strides, his hunched shoulders and aggressiveness still pack the galleries. We still want him to win, but when the long groans rise up from behind the hidden greens as they did at the Augusta National we know he's whistled a skulled shot from the trap into the rhododendron or missed another 14-incher. Snead's long swing and beautiful turn are still with us but he can't putt. Time passes, the dogwood drops, the azalea browns. Palmer keeps losing, Snead misses the cut, Hogan doesn't show and Player's fine edge seems dull. Soon they will be joining Lorne Green and Arthur Godfrey selling mobile homes and Geritol or grinning from the backs of dog food mixes. Maybe the hero is dead. Can you see Bob Rosburg squinting into the sun and stalking the streets of Dodge City? Casper lying out under the stars? Or Jim Jamieson leaping from roof to roof to horse and galloping off flat in the saddle under the singing bullets? It takes a lot of bourbon.

But hark, who's this striding down the center of the fairway? His ball is out beyond the long Weiskopf's and they say he hit it with a spoon. The hair is right, golden; the long stride is right and the look in the clear blue eyes is of eagles and St. Andrews and Carnoustie. It's Nicklaus, Jack Nicklaus. Steel-eyed, square-jawed, faster than a speeding bullet, more powerful than a locomotive, as deadly as the sliding cobra. Nicklaus born in the center of the country, tall, cool, strong, right . . . But does he fit the lead hero mold?

A lot of us never personally liked him. He was the bully on the block who owned the bat and the ball, had the first car, got the first girl and when he sliced off tackle for 12 yards it always took three of us to drag him down. He was too much . . . too aggressive, trained too hard and said dumb things to the press, but worst of all he was fat. He had to buy from the stylish stout rack. "The Golden Bear" fit him like 100 pounds of chunk coal in a crocker sack.

Some nicknames work, some don't. Ben Hogan was "The Hawk." Joe DiMaggio was "The Yankee Clipper" and Sam Snead is still "The Slammer." "Larrupin' Lou" didn't catch Lou Gehrig. "The Splendid Splinter" just laid there for Ted Williams and now as Jack Nicklaus took charge of the Masters on the first day at the first-hole ball-washer and he's moving down the road to wherever they build the Golf Hall of Fame saddled with "The Golden Bear," attention must be called that it fits him like a blue tutu and pink pantyhose. The bear whether he's grizzly, brown or black is sluggish and known for his low comedy of pushing over garbage cans and begging for Fig Newtons. He sleeps four full months of every year and, if pressed, can survive on roots and berries with only small side dishes of meat.

Jack Nicklaus has changed, slimmed down and wears his hair between a Ringo Starr and a Billy Graham. He's easier to talk to. Funnier. He wished his caddie, Willie Peterson, didn't have such fast hands pulling the ball out of the cup. ("Once he almost grabbed too soon. But Willie is super on the greens, super. He kept telling me, 'you can make it, you can make it.' Those greens were tricky, tough.") Cliff Roberts' greens had been shaved down, starved down and dehydrated and when the wind dried them even drier they became greased and hard as stone. Putts slid by and took off like slot car racers. ("I said, let me hear it again and he did. And I made it.") Nicklaus is looser now, more open. At one poignant moment he forgot when his father had died. ("He missed the last three Masters.") That seemed to be the calendar he used. There can be no question about it. He's golf, all golf and he's why the ranks are thin at the top.

Watch him on the practice tee. While others are chirping away with the gallery about the price of greens fees in Arkansas and the infield chatter between the pros and amateurs runs through 12-cent hamburger franchises to steaks to women, Nicklaus keeps out of it. He works. Even after a good round he goes back to the practice tee to make sure he's ready for the next day. Watch his head, his eyes, his jaw and neck. The concentration is incredible, predatory. One caddie described his full turn. "Man, he goes beyond the point of pain and then some . . . . He has an I-beam for a spine . . . Listen! It's like a damn 12-gauge."

Trevino said it even better. "I said two years ago that he's the best the game has ever seen. He's a freak. He's so strong. He might even beat two people. Beat their best ball. Nobody'll beat him." Nicknames have a tough way of clinging on. Sixty-year-old federal judges still wheel around when someone shouts "Blinky" or "Four Eyes." In the hard South it's even tougher, closer to the bone. "One Eye," "Snake," "Pig," "Frog," "Crip." But these names at least have a ring to them. You can hear them and you can say them. How can you chant "The Splendid Splinter" or "The Golden Bear?" If ever a man was begging for a better nickname this is it.

If not The Golden Bear then what? "Big Jack" sounds like a cheap ale; "The Lion" too shaggy, sleepy; "The San Andreas Fault" too clever. In his yellow sweater and beltless blue double-knits, his towhead catching the slanting light, there can be no denying he is the predator. And when he reaches up for the big one and catches it and hooks his jaw in affirmation we know there are no roots and berries in his diet. It's fresh red meat which he kills and renders himself. He is the cat who prowls alone, who waits until he's hungry then kills the finest. In Mexico he would be "El Tigre."

Most galleries watch the flight of the ball, but not Nicklaus'. They don't look up and out until he does. They watch the hands, the jaw, the big turn, the high finish and then the flight of the sizzling ball. Some watch his leg action, others his long extension but most the concentration. Maybe Hogan had the same quality. Maybe Snead was so natural he didn't need it and maybe Palmer can still turn it on when everything is working for him. But now today, April 1973, Jack Nicklaus has it—on the practice tee, the first tee, the 72nd . . . and with it he has the hands, the legs, the turn, the everything. And so while we love listening to Trevino and watching Arnie scramble, when we put the long green down it's following the advice of a man far wiser than most of us, Jimmy the Greek, who once uttered, "If David were fighting the giant tomorrow, the smart money would be on the big man."

Great, how great? Greater than Jones, wiser than Hogan, longer than Snead? If Old Tom Morris were with us now and 25? If Sam Snead were 20 years younger, Bobby Jones in his prime? If Sugar Ray Robinson had been white, 40 pounds heavier and born at the turn of the century he could have taken Dempsey, and if a frog had wings there would be some readjustments in the trees. The hard cold fact is Nicklaus is here now, today. His tee-to-green game and putting have never been better; he's stronger, wiser, smarter, better. He will play and he will win and unless something like a brick wall or a subpoena server gets in front of him there will be no stopping him.

One press sage after the first 36 holes at the '72 Masters said they were giving it to Nicklaus on a TKO to prevent him from murdering the field on Saturday and Sunday, which he could have done. Instead, he eased up and coasted in. Had he turned loose he could have broken it wide open. But like the Bengal tiger who kills only when he's hungry and leaves the tougher cuts, the chitlins and the bones for the jackals and the small creatures

of the night, he loped in cool and calm and slid into his fourth Masters jacket. If ever it fit the right man at the right time, this was it.

In a flight of ripe and mellow fantasy Tom Weiskopf said that asking a man to beat the Augusta National course under the present conditions would be like asking the reporters to write a Hemingway short story in two weeks. The greased simile slid by like wet soap on wet tile but it pointed up the hard fact that the course under perfect skies stopped everyone but Nicklaus. His scores across the top of the leader board began and stayed in under-par red while the rest of the field were in the protective green coloring of second and third place. There were two tournaments going on. Nicklaus was playing the course and himself, the others were playing each other. He won going away and the smart money in Vegas stayed smart.

Downtown in Augusta a church on the main pike caught the heavy commerce in the air: "When Christ Arose God Placed the Masters Jacket on Him" . . . The townspeople near the course rented their places for $700 to $1,000 for the week and fled to Valdosta, Macon and Muscle Shoals. One store sold Masterburgers with sides of fries for $1.35. Green jackets, hats, belts, shoes and sweaters were shipped in from 7th Avenue New York by the car load.

Despite the hustle and the hard sell on the road shoulders, once inside the course that Jones built and where Roberts' Rules of Order prevail this is the best run, best organized and most beautiful tournament in the country. Roberts, who knows every blade of grass, the evils of poa annua, and the underside of every rhododendron and magnolia, is a master host. In his summit meeting with Lee Trevino at the clubhouse they both emerged victorious, which is the hallmark of true politicians.

And so at the 36th Masters it was Jack Nicklaus from the first tee to the 72nd. At no time did any of us doubt he would coast in. Why then do we resist him and still root for Palmer? It's simple. Palmer is a nice, easygoing guy; he's easy to like, Nicklaus is not. The stories of

his rudeness to caddiemasters, pros and the general public are leveling off and declining but an honest accounting would put him in the Ted Williams red on public relations. We prefer our heroes modest, self-effacing, smiling and laying off a large measure to the other guy and lady luck. We expect men like Snead, Hogan and Nicklaus to go smiling through every interview and confrontation like Art Linkletter and Ed McMahon . . . Maybe it's because we've been conditioned by Jack Armstrong the All-American Boy and the smiling pole-vaulting chaplain on the back of Wheaties boxes into playing the game for the sake of the game. No one warned us of the killers out there in the tall grass and their singular ways. I personally don't want to like Nicklaus, to have him over for my wife's barbecue and see my home movies. I want him to be remote, a loner. If he wants, he can read Classic Comics and nothing else, kick dogs and kill cats and fish in brooding silence. I don't want him thanking the lighting men, the press and all the little people who made it possible, or volunteering to sell Girl Scout Cookies on the weekends.

In one of Sugar Ray Robinson's fights his second-round victim let out the sad lament, "I never knew the ring could be that small." Against a killer the ring is always that small. That's the way it should be. You feel your strength draining as the suspicion hardens into the ice-cold fact that you're not going to be admired for being there, but merely and humiliatingly handled. This is what Dempsey, Louis, Jones, Snead and Hogan did in style for years. And that's what Nicklaus is doing today. Like the tiger he should be left to roam alone, accounting to no one, respectful of none. He should not and cannot be the one who's grateful. We should. ■

IRELAND'S GOLFING SAINT PLAYS LIKE THE DEVIL HIMSELF

BY PETER DOBEREINER
October, 1973

At a recent golf tournament in Ireland a visitor took up his position behind two priests. As a matter of incidental intelligence you always take up position behind priests at Irish tournaments. They have a highly developed technique (compounded by exploiting the natural deference due to their cloth with some brisk work with their elbows) of insinuating themselves to the forefront of galleries.

Anyway, this visitor was startled to hear one priest ask of his companion, "Who's that playing with Himself?" The visitor looked down the fairway in shocked surprise. With his ear not yet attuned to the native idiom, he had not immediately understood that the question was merely an inquiry as to the name of Christy O'Connor's playing partner.

In Ireland, in a golfing context, it is unnecessary to use the name of O'Connor. It is Himself. That is enough to denote the most famous sporting hero the Irish nation has produced and one of the few overseas players to make an impact on the American sporting public without actually joining the U.S. tour. This has been done mainly with a long string of Ryder Cup appearances. He'll be playing with the British squad for the 10th time this fall when the U.S. team invades Muirfield. This will be a record number of appearances in the cup matches for either side.

At home, Himself is held in public esteem as a secular saint. The volume of gallery support is

One of England's best known golf correspondents, Peter Dobereiner is the author of the book, *The Glorious World of Golf*. He is a frequent contributor to *Golf Digest*.

generally reckoned to be worth two shots a round to O'Connor. And the weight of prayers for his short putts, in the opinion of opponents, puts him at risk of a penalty for outside assistance.

People see O'Connor differently. To some he is a quiet, shy man. To some, a hell-raising extrovert, eager for a fist-fight. To some, a moody boor. To some, a warm and witty companion.

Everyone agrees that he is a superb golfer, but as to the man himself there are as many O'Connors as there are people who think they know him. O'Connor does nothing to clarify this situation. He is a very private person and takes the rather old-fashioned view that while he may be a public figure on the golf course, everything else about him is entirely his own business.

In a literal sense there are two Christy O'Connors on the golf circuit, which makes life tiresome in reporting tournaments. There is Himself and his nephew, with the same name, the same darkly handsome appearance and—dare I predict?—the same potential for golfing success. But we are concerned with Christy senior—and that is quite enough O'Connors to try to unscramble.

The most important thing about O'Connor is that he is Irish, and that condition implies more, much more, than a straight label of citizenship. To be Irish is to ingest the tormented history of that race with your mother's milk. You are weaned on the Orange repression and thus rebellion (against authority in all its forms) is instilled in the cradle; Cromwell's repression cauterizes those areas of the brain which deal in logic, the Easter Rebellion puts fire into your heart, and the potato famine puts a chip on your shoulder.

Other factors work their mischief in the making of an Irishman. County Galway, which is O'Connor country, is a dark and mysterious area of inhospitable mountains where to till the land the coastal folk first have to create the very soil by mixing sand from the beach with seaweed and waiting for the rains to wash away the salty sourness. Poverty is, then, another chromosome in the genetic chain of the Irish. The simple struggle to survive has left its mark. So has religion. And so, above all, has the native Gaelic imprint of mysticism and feckless joy. Irishness is both a blessing and a curse.

The Irish, who dearly love a myth, are content to accept that Christy sprang onto the scene as a young professional, full-grown and with a God-given swing, and immediately began to win fortune for himself and fame for his race.

The prosaic truth is that Christy, born some 48 years ago, learned the rudiments of golf while caddying in Galway and subsequently moved, via Killarney, to Royal Dublin Golf Club. O'Connor's swing was far from natural. People who watch his smooth rhythm, with the minimum of fuss in assessing the shot, are led to believe that his swing is an inborn talent, requiring neither thought nor practice. The notion is absurd, although these days O'Connor's pre-match routine consists of hitting no more than half a dozen shots to capture the "feel" of his swing.

As a young man it was his habit to take himself off to Dublin Bay and hit golf balls off the sand for hour after hour. If you have ever tried to hit a golf ball off seawashed sand you will know that there is only one way to do it: by clipping the ball cleanly off the surface. Try hitting down and through, in the way you take a divot off grass, and you break a wrist. Here was the genesis of the O'Connor swing and the technique which earned him the nickname of Wristy Christy. Here too, no doubt, was implanted the seed of unpredictability which has made O'Connor such an in-and-out player all his life. When his immaculate timing is slightly off, O'Connor's game suffers more than most.

The so-called modern method, with a long extension down and through the ball, gives a golfer some margin of error when his timing is astray. But when O'Connor is firing sweetly, flicking the ball away with a combination of power and artistry, he is a match for anyone.

O'Connor's early reputation was based on his inordinate length. As a young man he gloried in the strength of his athletic frame and there is hardly a club in Ireland where they do not recall an example of tremendous hitting.

With maturity came wisdom. "Nowadays I drive for position and I don't mind that I have to sacrifice a bit of length." Today, as he approaches 50, O'Connor's shoulders are rounded in a "golfer's stoop," permanently hunched into the address position. He occasionally suffers from arthritic pains in the joints. Even so, on his day he still plays better than most. Pros look for his name on the leader board with apprehension, knowing that he can win any tournament.

He is feared less for his strokemaking than for the intangible—but far more important—qualities of his character. His record is impressive enough, with several important victories every year of his competitive career. He won the first four-figure check in the history of British golf and, much later, won the first five-figure check. But dig a little deeper into the statistics and the essential hardness of O'Connor emerges. Nearly all his triumphs have been achieved with a low last round when the pressure is making the others falter.

If the wind blows—they call it O'Connor weather—the pros recognize that the dice are loaded in favor of Himself. Where others are fighting the elements and slogging at full-bore with a 6-iron, O'Connor will take his 3-iron and outwit the gale. The harder it blows the more quietly he seems to play his shots.

On a windy day in Ireland, before his home crowd, O'Connor is reckoned to be virtually unbeatable—given two other conditions. The first premise is that his putting must be in good order, and that is totally unpredictable. Some days he holes everything with an inspired flair,

other times he cannot putt worth a cuss.

The other pre-condition, possibly related to the first at times, concerns the sensitive subject of how he has spent the previous evening. There is an Irish tradition that drinking is not so much an aid to conviviality as an end in itself. The idea, not to put too fine a point on it, is to get plastered.

It matters little that O'Connor is reasonably temperate by nature. He enjoys a social drink as much as the next man, but no more than that. The point is that every Irishman wants to buy Christy a drink. It is a national ambition, a duty. And since there are even more Irishmen abroad than there are in Ireland he can never escape.

Americans may ask: if this O'Connor is such a hell of a golfer why isn't he up there with Palmer and Nicklaus? It is a valid question and deserves a rational answer, if one can be found. The answer lies partly in ambition. O'Connor prefers a modest life-style. He still lives in the same house he bought when he first moved to Dublin as a young man. By Irish standards he is wealthy enough. He has all the fame he can handle.

But there is another reason and it resides in a dilemma which every talented golfer must face and resolve. The Bitch Goddess of Success is a demanding mistress. For every bounty she bestows she demands a sacrifice.

You want to make a million? Very well, you may. But in the process you must cut yourself off from your friends and the warm associations of your social circle. You must subjugate your family to your career. You must wander the world and make speeches and live among the kings and mandarins of commerce. You must, in short, deny your birthright. To an Irishman, a *real* Irishman, the proposition is unthinkable.

Christy O'Connor, the private man, has settled for a more modest but happier way of golf—and life ∎

PERSISTENT PLAYER GAINING ON GOAL TO BE THE GREATEST

BY NICK SEITZ
February, 1975

Phil Ritson, his early teacher, remembers sharing a room with a 16-year-old Gary Player and waking in the morning to find Player staring into a mirror and declaring, "I'm going to be the greatest golfer in the world! I'm going to be the greatest golfer in the world!" He must have said it 50 times, Ritson remembers, and then he went out and practiced sand shots by the dawn's early light.

Twenty-two years later, Player is one of a very few golfers who could be ranked great, and he has lost none of his zealous determination. It is easy to imagine him today in front of a mirror repeating his vows or out slapping sand shots as the rest of us slumber heedlessly through the pre-breakfast hours.

Depending on the day you ask him, he speaks with iron resolve and eyes that burn with the intensity of automobile headlights of one towering goal or another. He wants to win more tournaments than anybody else ever, he wants to complete a second cycle in the four major championships, he wants to strike the ball as purely as Ben Hogan. And he continues to compete around the world week after week in his unwavering quest for immortality.

"Of all of us," observes David Graham, the bright young touring pro from Australia, "he most deserves his success. Sometimes he carries his positive thinking too far—he's the only guy I know who can shoot 80 and say he hit the ball super—but then he's a great self-promoter. He's a credit to the sport, and his record is better than people realize. The man won a major tournament 15 years ago and he won two more majors in 1974."

I buy Graham's assessment. We have had enough lightweight debate over Player's sincerity in matters of physical fitness, race relations and international diplomacy. There is no denying that his enthusiasm can overflow the banks of thoughtfulness and spill out into ridiculous overstatement. For instance, he says with revival-tent fervor, "I know I've worked harder than any human being up to age 38, not just at golf but at developing my body, my public relations, my mind." A truly well-developed mind might not make a claim like that. A course on which Gary has just shot 67 always seems to be the toughest he has ever overcome. An almost compulsive competitor, Player has to have a test of character. If he doesn't have an obstacle to clear, he will erect one to keep up his interest, and at positive thinking he should give Norman Vincent Peale two a side.

But we should appreciate that Player is essentially a golfer and should be judged by us, as golf followers, essentially as a golfer. It is on the course, single-mindedly confronting—almost embracing—his next problem, that the real Gary Player reveals himself.

In 1974 Player was overshadowed by Johnny Miller, who almost forgot how to lose. Miller deserves the honors he got, including the PGA Player of the Year Award, but Player deserves more acclaim than *he* got. Certainly the PGA should re-evaluate its somewhat specious points system for determining a player of the year when Player finishes sixth.

Player in 1974 might have come closer to winning the Grand Slam than anyone has. In 1953 Ben Hogan won three of the four major tournaments but didn't enter the fourth, the PGA Championship. Six others have won two majors in a season since the Masters began in 1934: Craig Wood, Sam Snead, Jack Burke, Arnold Palmer, Jack Nicklaus and Lee Trevino. Did any of them come as close to the slam as Player? He won the Masters from behind and the British Open from in front (his seventh and

eighth majors over-all), was tied for the lead in the U.S. Open after two rounds and was never more than five shots from the top in the PGA, matching the tournament record of 64 in the second round.

Player also won at Memphis in this country and took six titles abroad to go over 100 for his pro career. He capped the year by winning the Brazilian Open where he shot a shocking 59. "It was my best year," he says, "and maybe the best year anyone ever had." All this the year after major surgery, more serious than most of us realized, took him out of action and out of our field of attention.

As usual, Player came back from adversity with redoubled desire, in one case flying for two solid days and nights and disembarking from the plane to go straight to the course and win another tournament. He says he has traveled a total of four million miles to play golf, and that is one record that should outlive us all. Unlike the other superstars, he still practices as much as he plays, devising competitive games to make himself concentrate. He might hit chip shots, for example, until he sinks three dozen, come hell, high water or darkness.

Where does he get his dedication? How does he sustain it?

To reply, Player flashes back to his boyhood. We are eating in a New York restaurant, Player with the meticulousness he applies to everything, cutting his steak into uniformly small bites, drinking warm water laced with lemon juice to aid his digestive processes. He talks of his mother's death when he was eight and the insistence then and thereafter of his father, a good golfer who worked in the South African gold mines, that affirmative thinking is the only response to a challenge. That was his first exposure to positive thinking.

An older brother, Ian, further influenced him at an early age to try harder than the rest, Player says in his now book *Gary Player: World Golfer*. Ian, who refused to be held back by a chronically bad knee, laid out a five-mile track where the two ran together. One day the young Gary wearied and went to his knees, wheezing that

158

he couldn't finish.

He writes, "My lungs felt as if they would burst. Without any warning Ian yanked me to my feet and cuffed me on the side of the head. 'What do you mean you can't make it, man?' he exploded, his face flushed red with anger. 'You can do anything you want to. Remember that. There's no room for *can't* in this life.' I'll never know how I did it, but even though my feet felt like they were weighted down with lead and my leg muscles were knotted with pain, I ran the rest of that five miles without stopping for anything. Believe me, I was cured of ever threatening to quit in front of Ian again."

It was Ian, Gary says, who gave him his first golf club, which he had whittled from a stick.

Soon after Player devoted himself to golf he made Ben Hogan his hero. He still reveres him, although there has been friction between the two. Hogan's example convinced Player that a small man without great natural athletic ability could construct a winning golf game.

"I promise you Hogan knows more about striking a golf ball than any man who ever lived," Player says. "If I could just ask him five questions and get his answers I'd be a lot better player than I am."

You no doubt have heard the story about Player calling Hogan at his equipment plant from overseas for help with his swing. The conversation is supposed to have gone something like this:

"Mr. Hogan, this is Gary Player. I would like to ask you a question about the swing."

"Gary, who do you work for?"

"The Dunlop company."

"Well, call Mr. Dunlop." Click.

Many experts suspect Player has always fought a pull-hook shot pattern because he wants to swing shorter and flatter like Hogan. Player periodically proclaims victory over his roundhouse hook; after winning the '74 Masters he announced he had found The Secret. *Golf Digest* instruction editor Larry Dennis pried it out of him—Player said he was holding his head more upright so he wouldn't block his natural back-swing turn—but going into the 1975 season Player was still hooking dramatically at times.

The fact is, the tense-looking Player's game invariably is less imposing on the face of it than that of any other top player, what with his hooking and finishing his swing off-balance and using unorthodox strategy. He can shot 68 and appear to be shooting 15 strokes higher. But he frequently brings off daredevil recovery shots. It doesn't hurt him to be off balance at the finish of his swing as long as he's in balance when he contacts the ball, and his strategy has a way of working out.

Says Phil Ritson, "Gary has the willpower to completely blot a bad shot out of his mind. He forgets it immediately and begins planning the next one. Every shot is a separate little game with him."

Perhaps most crucially, Player gives every shot his utmost respect and concentration whether it's a trouble shot or a tap-in putt. "The thing I admire so much about him," says Byron Nelson, "is that he just never wastes a stroke, not once in a year. He plays each shot for everything it's worth."

There is a story about Player emptying a shagbag on the practice green and making one-foot putts for an hour. A fellow pro asked him what in the name of Harry Vardon he was doing. "I'm getting used to sinking putts," was Player's answer.

At 38, we see no indication that Player's awesome dedication is flagging. He reminds us when we compare all-time greats that a player really should not be evaluated until his career is done, and implies that his is far from ended.

Says Jimmy Demaret, a peer of Hogan's, "Player is self-disciplined and physically fit, and I think he can be a super player for five more years without exhausting himself. When he gets into his 40s, his legs will get weak and then his nervous system will go. He won't be another Sam Snead, playing top golf at 62. He isn't big enough. But in my time Player and Hogan are the most dedicated golfers I've ever seen, and I've seen a few."

If the next five years are anything like 1974, Player might not have to play longer than five more years to satisfy even himself. ∎

LEE ELDER'S LONG ROAD TO AUGUSTA

BY DWAYNE NETLAND
April, 1975

Oct. 28, 1974—Lee Elder boards a commercial flight at Washington National Airport with Deane Beman, commissioner of the PGA Tournament Players Division. They fly to Atlanta, and step into the private plane of J. Paul Austin, chairman of the board of the Coca-Cola Co., and continue on to Augusta. A chauffeured car is waiting at Daniel Field. It has been sent out by Clifford Roberts, chairman of the Masters Tournament. The driver turns off Washington Road and proceeds slowly down Magnolia Lane to the elegant white clubhouse. Elder gazes quietly out the window. He is about to play his first round of golf at Augusta National where he will become the first black ever to compete in the Masters.

May 10, 1946—Lee Elder, 12, is caddying at Tenison Park in Dallas for Dick Martin, an accomplished golf hustler. Elder watches in fascination as Martin accepts and doubles the press on the 18th hole, a tricky par-3. Lee is learning how these thing are done. Martin wins the press and the match, and offers

to sell the young caddie a second-hand set of clubs with the comment, "Pay me later, when you have the money." Twenty-two years later, Dick Martin, by then a wealthy businessman, encounters Elder and his wife at a tournament. Smiling, Martin opens a tattered little black book, noting the unpaid account. Rose Elder laughs, and writes out a check for $40.

Oct. 28, 1974—In the Augusta National locker room the game is arranged. Elder and Jim Gabrielson, the British Amateur runner-up from Atlanta, will play Beman and Austin. Clifford Roberts comes in to wish them well. Elder thanks him and Roberts says, "Keep swinging." On the first tee Elder slices his drive into the woods. "Take a mulligan, Lee," says J. Paul Austin. "We'll all take one."

Elder reloads, and splits the fairway with his next drive. He hits a 6-iron to the green and gets down in two putts. Henry Brown, a 1-handicap player who has caddied for Roberto de Vicenzo and Art Wall in the Masters, hands the ball to Elder with an easy grin. Brown

knows he will caddie for Elder in the 1975 Masters.

July 10, 1953—Titanic Thompson is trying to set up his mark for a game in Tulsa, Okla. The mark is reluctant. He's aware of Thompson's reputation as a hustler. "Tell you what," Titanic sighs. "Tomorrow you and your friend play me and my caddie here and give us two a side. The kid can't play worth a nickel, but at least we'll have a game." The mark nods. That night Thompson takes his caddie out to a lighted driving range and works him for two hours. The next day they slip the pro $10 to allow the 19-year-old black to play. "Ti and I dusted those guys pretty good," Lee Elder will recall years later.

Oct. 28, 1974—At the nine-hole break, Paul Austin's foursome has lunch in the office of Clifford Roberts at Augusta National. Elder has shot par 36, with a birdie on No. 7 and a bogey on No. 8. "I'm impressed with this golf course," he tells newsmen. "It's everything I ever heard about it. But it's also a course I feel I can play well. I'm anxious to have a look at the water holes on the back nine."

Aug. 27, 1954—Titanic Thompson and his partner have just closed out their opponents in a match at Pierre, S.D. "Ease off into the car and wait for me, Lee," the old man says. I'm going to play these fellows a little cards. I'll be along."

Oct. 28, 1974—The match at Augusta National is over. The team bet is even. Elder, with his 74, pays off his individual bet to Beman, who has shot 73. Elder has bogeyed the 10th after a short approach, the 12th with a 5-iron into the back trap ("way too much club") and the 16th with three putts. He reached the 475-yard 13th in two for a birdie. "The hardest holes on the course are five, 10 and 11," Elder says. "They favor the big hitter. I may have trouble with them. A man can lose a lot of strokes back there in the corner of 10-11-12. I'll have to hit the ball higher to play these elevated greens. I'm going to get me a new set of irons by spring. But the treatment I received here today was fantastic."

May 2, 1956—Titanic Thompson and Lee Elder are enjoying a hefty breakfast of grapefruit, bacon and eggs, hotcakes and coffee at a truck stop in Topeka, Kan. Thompson insists upon eating well each morning. They have a match two hours later, which will consume much of the day, and Thompson has a hunch he can scratch up some extra money afterward by betting that he can throw a quarter from 15 feet and stick it into a potato at least once in seven tries. The sucker takes him on, and Titanic spears the spud on the fourth throw.

Nov. 27, 1974—Lee Elder has a problem. He counts the number of requests he has received from close friends for the Masters and the figure is over 200. He calls Clifford Roberts and explains his dilemma. He is told that the Masters will cooperate in every way, but tickets are scarce. Lee and Rose Elder study the list of applications again and again, tightening it here and there. Rose Elder writes out a check for $2,070, covering 69 tickets, and mails it with a note. Rose has no idea how many tickets she will receive. The Masters office lets it be known that it does not disclose any ticket allocations. The situation is almost certain to become an issue before Elder finally tees off.

June 4, 1958—On his final swing with Titanic Thompson, Lee Elder returns to Tenison Park. Ti is slowing down a little, but the pair is traveling in a Cadillac now and the pickings are still good. Elder looks around at the familiar old course, named after E. O. Tenison, a Dallas banker who donated the land to the city with the understanding that "it would be perpetuated as a municipal recreation area for men of all persuasions." Once located in a wealthy section of East Dallas, the neighborhood is deteriorating. There are more of the jukebox bars where Clyde Barrow, the badman, once hung around. Erwin Hardwick is still there, in the pro shop, and he greets Elder warmly. Lee is a skilled player now, his reputation as Titanic's partner known widely among the hustlers.

Jan. 9, 1975—Lee Elder's preparations for the Masters are proceeding smoothly. He has arranged to play Augusta National with Bob Menne, another first-time Masters entry, during the third week of March. He hopes to get in two more rounds on the Monday and Tuesday preceding the Sea Pines Heritage Classic at Hilton Head. He will play at Greensboro the week before the Masters, then fly to Augusta Sunday night in a private plane obtained by Burl Bowen, director of the Old Dominion golf tournament at Norfolk, Va. Elder will be accompanied in Augusta by a traveling party of 10, and needs two houses to accommodate them. He will play a Masters practice round on Monday with Jim Colbert, Lee Trevino and John Mahaffey. Tuesday is set with Bob Menne, Vic Regalado and either Jack Nicklaus or Gary Player. Wednesday he will take part in the par-3 contest. He is concerned about the hounding of the huge press corps. He knows he is in for a week of microscopic scrutiny.

June 11, 1962—Elder's apprenticeship with Titanic Thompson is over. He is on his own now, trafficking in the world of the Fat Man, Nassau Nick, The Fly. You calculate the odds and squeeze for any advantage, "catching policy," as the hustlers say, at just the right time to send the other fellow home c.o.d. At the Pipe o' Peace course near Chicago, a man agrees to play Elder nine holes, providing Elder hits every shot standing on one leg. Elder shoots 41 and wins the match by a stroke. The man asks for a rematch the next day, stipulating that Elder wear a rubber rainsuit. Elder insulates the rainsuit with cold, wet towels, shoots 35 and wins again by a stroke.

Dec. 1, 1974—Rose Elder is sitting at her desk, in the paneled attic of the Elder home on a tree-shaded street in Washington, D.C. As her husband's business manager, she is studying some contracts. Lee has kept his longtime associations with Faultless, Foot-Joy, Munsingwear and All-Star gloves. He has a newer endorsement policy with Oldsmobile. A Washington radio station is negotiating to have him do a daily 10-minute report from the tour in 1975.

That night Rose will sit at the head table at a testimonial for Lee at the Washington Hilton. Nearly $10,000 will be raised for Elder's scholarship program, currently benefiting over 500 underprivileged youths in the District of Columbia. Among the dinner guests will be President Ford, who will say, "People won't remember 1975 as the first full year of Gerald Ford's presidency; they'll remember it as the year Lee Elder first played in the Masters." A month earlier, Elder had played golf with Gerald Ford at Congressional Country Club, shooting 71 while the President shot 96. "The trouble with President Ford," Elder had said, "is that his left hand is turned too far toward his right shoulder. But he's a great putter." Rose Elder chuckles at the memory of that quote. A bright, attractive woman with a warm sense of humor, she is the 1974 recipient of Tuesday Magazine's "Woman of the Year" award.

July 20, 1964—Weary of hustling for a living, Lee Elder has joined the United Golf Ass'n tour, composed predominantly of black players. The purses aren't much, ranging between $3,000 and $5,000, but it's still competitive golf. At the Langston Golf Club in Washington, where the UGA tour has stopped, Elder is chatting near the clubhouse with his good friend Ted Rhodes when a black woman on the driving range catches his eye. "That's Rose Harper," Rhodes says. "She's in the first flight of the women's amateur division. Want to meet her?" Elder does indeed. They marry in 1966, and settle in Washington, Rose Harper's home town.

Jan. 9, 1975—Lee Elder is recalling his memorable invitation to compete in South Africa four years earlier with Gary Player. Elder's admiration for Player is unbounded. He talks of the apartheid policy then in effect in South Africa, Player's constant demonstrations of friendship ("I can't say enough about Gary; he's all man") and of Lee's victory on that trip in the Nigerian Open, against a field containing eight members of the

British Ryder Cup team. Elder still thinks that should have qualified him for the 1972 Masters. He recalls writing for an invitation on the basis of that victory, and being told that a foreign championship would provide entry to the Masters only to a foreign-born player.

Oct. 4, 1967—After two days of postponement by heavy rains, the rookie qualifying school is about to open on the East Course of the PGA National Golf Club in Palm Beach Gardens, Fla. Among the 111 players who will compete over 144 holes to determine the 30 qualifiers are some big names: Deane Beman, Tony Jacklin, Marty Fleckman, Bobby Cole, Orville Moody, Ron Cerrudo, Bob Murphy, George Boutell, Bob E. Smith and Ed Sneed. Lee Elder is also on hand. He shoots 76 the first day, played from the front tees because of the weather conditions. Rose Elder is worried. Lee's next seven rounds are very steady, between 70 and 74. Bobby Cole is the qualifying medalist of the class of 1967, with a 572. Sharing 15th place, with 586, are Elder and Moody. Elder has taken his first step toward the Masters.

Jan. 10, 1975—Lee Elder, in a moment of reverie, is reliving the most decisive moments of his life. On April 21, 1974, with two holes remaining of his final round in the Monsanto Open at Pensacola, Elder trails leader Peter Oosterhuis by two strokes. Elder birdies the 71st hole with a three-foot putt. On the 72nd hole, Elder hooks a 6-iron shot around a tree and lands within five feet of the cup. After Oosterhuis drops a six-footer for a par, Elder makes his birdie putt to force a playoff. Because the tournament is not being televised, the playoff starts on the first hole. Oosterhuis misses a birdie putt of 2½ feet on the first hole. They continue on, halving the second and third. On No. 4 each hits a 7-iron to the green. Oosterhuis is 19 feet away and Elder 18 feet, in the same line. Oosterhuis rolls his birdie putt dead at the hole, but it stops six inches short. Elder watches carefully, then lines up his putt and knocks it in. Rose Elder is not there to share his

triumph. She is at home, working on tax papers. But she receives a telephonic report of the playoff from Hubie Green. Elder's first reaction to his victory is, "My God, I've finally won." The realization that he has at last qualified for the Masters comes a few seconds later. Clifford Roberts, hearing the news of Elder's win, telephones the Pensacola Country Club to issue Elder a verbal invitation to Augusta. Elder tarries momentarily, saying he will think it over. Rose Elder calls Lee, and advises him to accept immediately. He does. The Masters is 51 weeks away.

Sept. 4, 1972—At the Greater Hartford Open in Wethersfield, Conn., two graduates of the Tenison Park School of Hustling, Lee Elder and Lee Trevino, share the 72-hole lead at 269. On the first playoff hole Elder has a birdie putt of 19 feet, in the same line as Trevino's from 18 feet. Elder misses. Trevino spits on his hands, hunkers over his putt and rolls it in. There will be no Masters for Lee Elder in 1973.

Jan. 20, 1975—Opening his tour season in the Tucson Open, Lee Elder is already thinking about the Masters. It is closing in on him. "I'd like to be able to think I can win, naturally," he says. "But my next goal is finishing among the top 24, so I can qualify for it again next year."

May 19, 1974—At a nursing home in Euless, Tex., Titanic Thompson dies at the age of 81. He has lived long enough to hear that his one-time caddie will play in the Masters, and now he probably is making celestial book, at 3 to 1 odds, that Lee will finish among the top 24. ■

THE PERSONALITIES

There is no better way to appreciate the broad scope of golf than to consider the diverse roles of three such dissimilar men as Joseph C. Dey, George Low and the late Titanic Thompson, who are featured in this section. The first is a virtuous rules authority who administered amateur golf and later the professional tour in this country for a total of 40 years. The second is a putting genius better known for his enormously successful living off opulent friends. The third was a gambler who hustled unsuspecting victims in any form of endeavor ranging from a round of golf to betting on the number of watermelons contained in a passing farmer's wagon.

They symbolize the varied personalities of golf, the notable figures who have walked with the Ben Hogans and the Arnold Palmers in and out of the limelight through the years, often leading the way. *Golf Digest* has always kept an eye peeled for them, realizing the potential of their behind-the-scenes "people" stories.

It has to be a special characteristic of golf that it attracts, in so many unusual ways, so many distinctive personalities. There would seem to be something in the game for everyone—and something in everyone for the game. Although they have manifest it in incomparable ways, the people in this section share a common love for the sport.

The writers are often as interesting as their subjects. Dan Jenkins is internationally known today as the author of the best-selling novel *Semi-Tough* and a brilliant writer for Sports Illustrated. When he did the piece, "George Low, America's Guest" for our September, 1960, issue, he was the lesser-known sports editor of the Fort Worth Press and just emerging as a writer of national stature. He knew George Low from amiable encounters on the tour, knew him as a delightfully consummate artist in the ancient game of freeloading, which Jenkins, as a veteran newspaper man, had to respect. Jenkins is known for his cool and his great ear. Writers who have known him for years cannot recall him ever taking a note during an interview.

Also proving that the offbeat can be at least as interesting as the onbeat are pieces by two members of the *Golf Digest* staff, editor Nick Seitz with a whimsical portrayal of trick shot artist Joe Kirkwood and associate editor Cal Brown with a warm look at Freddie McLeod and Jock Hutchison, the lovable old Scottish pros who for many years hit the first shots at the Masters Tournament.

It's a package bristling with good reading about men who may not have mastered the short irons, but who have given the game great substance and color.

THE INCREDIBLE TITANIC THOMPSON

BY LOUIE WHITSITT
June, 1958

A small gallery following the golfers hushed noticeably as they learned the high-stakes twosome had just wagered $10,000 on success or failure of the next shot —a challenging 25-foot putt.

The nerveless Manhattan gambler, Nick "The Greek" Dandolos, a consistent high-70 golfer, took the putter from a caddie and, poker-faced, knelt behind the ball to study its lie. Walking to the pin, Dandolos further surveyed the terrain, then confidently returned to fall into an effective putting stance.

Titanic Thompson eyed his opponent's action from just off the green. An artist of gambling odds, the tall, sinewy, suavely handsome son of Little Rock was noted for plunking down tall stacks of folding green on any type of bet—if the proposition originated in his clever brain. Intimates of this incredible personality, a left-handed player, rated him one of the nation's best gambling golfers and likened this fat wager to myriad others which made Titanic, born Alvin C. Thomas in 1893, an incomparable legend of the fairways.

Nick addressed his ball, expertly swung the putter and swept it cupward at a calculated speed.

The crowd edged forward. Expressions of awe sliced the silence as, true on course, the big-money shot sped up and over a tiny rise. Losing momentum, though, it threatened to falter inches short of paydirt. Then, as if propelled by an invisible hand, the sphere crawled those final inches to drop exhaustedly into the cup!

Titanic dismissed his loss with the offer of another wager.

"Bet you double or nothing I can hit a silver dollar with my pistol eight times out of eight, from 15 feet."

Thus another fabulous bet was made—one reminiscent of a time Titanic Thompson recouped severe losses suffered in a dice game one wintry afternoon by betting a player $2,500 he could drive a golf ball 500 yards. Before the gamblers headed for a Long Island course of Titanic's choice, he found the proposition quite popular, with over $8,000 covered by doubting parties.

Titanic picked a tee set atop a hill, fronted by a wide water hazard 200 yards off. His drive, accurately aimed at ice covering the hazard, bounced off the ice and rolled nearly half a mile before stopping!

This day, Dandolos paced off the specified 15 feet. Titanic pulled a small pistol from his golf bag. Eight perfectly aimed shots hit the target. He retrieved the silver piece and gave it to "The Greek" for a souvenir.

From the late 20s through the early 50s, Titanic Thompson beat fairways from Dallas to Duluth and New Orleans to New York, meeting amongst a variety of opponents some of golf's best, including Ben Hogan, Dick Metz, Len Dodson, Bobby Locke and Toney Penna. Hogan voiced praise for Thompson's rare ability to play under pressure the day he linked together close to 50 sidebets to come out of a Galveston match winner by $12,000.

"If Ti had devoted half as much time to serious concentration as to just baiting and outwitting his opponents, he'd have been a Bobby Jones-Ben Hogan combined," Penna once said.

While top professionals were straining to carry home $25,000 annually, Titanic, touring the countryside, picking his marks, called it a rough year if he didn't bank a cool 100 G's. Some of it was accrued from dice and card games or occasional bizarre bets.

In 1928 Leo P. Flynn, boxing promoter and ex-manager of Jack Dempsey, introduced Titanic to Grassy Sprain C.C. members.

"I'd like to pit Mr. Thompson against your club pro, George McLean," Flynn announced.

A match was arranged. Flynn got down a bet of $2,500 on Titanic when several members pooled their money to back McLean. Titanic's game was wobbly. McLean won handily. Flynn argued for a rematch. The unknown Titanic helped with, "I'm not in your class, George, but I can play better than I did today. Give me a reasonable handicap, and I'll bet you good money."

The match didn't make sense. How could an amateur hope to beat a good pro? Ti's handicap was set at eight strokes. "Good money" began to show, with Flynn and "Big Bill" Duffy, an Owney Madden henchman, pushing club members to cover $13,000.

Titanic played according to script. At the end of 16 holes, he had dissipated his eight-stroke handicap. McLean, pressing for the kill, was soon to learn a new betting wrinkle — that of "fixing a game upwards."

McLean's drive from the 17th tee stopped six feet from the pin. Titanic placed his shot four feet closer. Unnerved by this action, McLean blew his easy putt, giving Titanic the match when they halved the final hole in par!

Titanic posted many a zany fairway bet. He once bet a Tulsa golfing star, noted for his driving power, he could let him make three drives per hole, playing the longest ball of the three, and beat him. Playing the best of his three drives, the Tulsan won six of the first nine holes. But on the back nine, the star became arm-weary and Titanic swept on to victory!

Key to Titanic's incredible success, however, was his dead-earnest application when big money showed. ∎

163

GEORGE LOW: AMERICA'S GUEST

BY DAN JENKINS
September, 1960

It just isn't like George Low to turn down a free meal, a free drink or a free anything for that matter.

Thus, it was a jolt to everyone at the Colonial Invitation tournament last May when Low bypassed Jerry Barber's invitation to buy lunch.

Barber, one of the leading money winners on the 1960 PGA tour, was noticeably stunned at Low's refusal. Then the method in George's madness became apparent.

"How much did you win last week at the Tournament of Champions?" Low asked Barber.

"$10,000."

"Well, I'm saving you for bigger things," Low explained.

This is a typical demonstration of the free-loading prowess of George Low, the leading character on the men's professional tour and the fellow that the pros will not putt for money on the practice green.

"My yearly income averages about $10,000, but I spend $50,000 more of my friends' money," George admits with a touch of pride.

Low, a hulking Scot who wears a solemn, jowly, bronzed face behind dark glasses and carries a can of beer, is as much a fixture on the PGA trail as Cary Middlecoff's hay fever or Tommy Bolt's flowered sport coats. No tournament is really complete without him.

It was Paul Grossinger, the New York resort fellow, who tabbed Low "America's guest."

"You gonna use Grossinger's name in this story?" George asked at a recent PGA stop. "Good. That ought to be worth a freebie."

Few, except those on the inside of pro golf, realize that Low is

Now a senior editor with Sports Illustrated and author of the best-selling novel, *Semi-Tough,* Dan Jenkins was sports editor of the Fort Worth Press when he wrote this article for *Golf Digest.*

probably the game's finest putter —and putting instructor.

Giving putting lessons is Low's primary method of making a buck —"this way and that," as he says. He doesn't hustle the business, however. That would be too much like work.

"I was born energetically lazy," he explains.

Low's reputation as a putter has been growing since about 1946, the year of his last fling at trying to play golf for a living.

He wasn't good enough to match the Byron Nelsons week after week, so he quit playing—except on the putting greens. There was also the matter of an old back injury, traced to a private plane crash in the 1930s. He never fully recovered.

However, Low is in the record books—in a most unusual place.

He was the first pro to break Nelson's fabulous streak of successive victories in 11 official and 12 unofficial events. It was at the 1945 Memphis Open where

Freddie Haas, then an amateur, won with 274. Low was second at 275 and Nelson third at 276.

"I seen that Nelson was getting out of hand," he quips today.

Notoriety is something George doesn't really care about, but it suddenly became unavoidable after Arnold Palmer won his second Masters championship last April.

Within earshot of about 100 golf writers, Palmer credited Low for helping him this season. Talking about the putts that netted him a torrid birdie-birdie finish, Palmer said,

"I kept thinking what my old friend, George Low, always says, 'keep your head down and don't move.' "

Low refuses to take any credit for helping Palmer, however.

"If I've helped him it was with his confidence. I think he was just giving me a plug because that's the way he is, a great guy who likes to help out his friends.

"It's like the doctor who sits and smiles at the patient and then hands him some sugar pills—and the guy thinks he's got some miracle drugs that will cure him."

Palmer did not need any technical help, according to George.

"He does everything right," Low said. "In putting, he has the quick left wrist that makes you take the clubhead back on the inside. He has most of his weight on the left foot —where it ought to be for balance. And his action is concentrated from the elbows downward."

Low recommended another thing for good putting: Keeping both thumbs squarely on the shaft for proper feel.

"When you reach in your pocket for a coin," he explains, "the last thing that touches the coin is your thumb. You use it to pull out the coin. Right? It's the most sensitive finger. That's why you grip the putter with both thumbs on the top of the shaft."

Consistency is the key to Low's putting proficiency. That is the reason the pros shy away from engaging him in a putt-for-money session. He can out-putt some of them using a sand wedge.

"The reason I beat them is because that's all I've done for 15 years," George points out. "They

got other worries, like getting on the green. I'm already there. I hit it the same way every time with the putter. You can putt me for 30 minutes and maybe you'll have a hot streak and win. But if you stay with me for an hour or so, you got no chance because I'm going to keep hitting it the same way and you're not."

Byron Nelson has been around golf for a while. Is what George says true?

"Don't ever try him," Nelson warns.

After all of these gypsy years, Low is proudest at the moment because a George Low putter is coming on the golf market. Eight different models will bear his name.

Old-timers may remember that George Low Sr., another big Scot, was runner-up for the U.S. Open title in 1899. They may also recall that this George Low was pro at Baltusrol for 27 years where he tutored some early-day White House hackers named William Howard Taft and Warren G. Harding.

That was George Low Jr.'s father. And George was born at Baltusrol, as a friend suggested, probably in the 19th Hole, the only one he ever parred. He was indeed a child of golf.

Baltusrol acquainted Low with wealth, for an adjacent cottage belonged to the Henry Toppings.

"I thought we was rich, like everybody else," George says. "Later on, when I knew I could never afford an overcoat, I had to work it out so's I spent my winters in Florida and Palm Springs."

Through the years George has become good friends with more wealthy people than any resident of Wall Street. Golf was his entré, along with a sharp humor, a talent for needling people and making them like it, and a basic honesty that makes people like him.

It was Bob Johnson of New York's Roosevelt Raceway who made a classic statement about George that comes close to summing him up.

Low was in a party with Johnson and others one evening and George kept asking the host for another $100 to buy drinks for everyone in the place. Finally Johnson confessed, "Just to associate with

Low is better than having a high Dun and Bradstreet rating."

There are no official statistics on it, but Low is sure to have seen more tournaments in his lifetime than practically anyone.

He will average about 30 a year, but he has to get away occasionally to see how things are going with such friends as jockeys Eddie Arcaro and Willie Shoemaker. If golf is his business, then the ponies are his hobby—or vice-versa. Also, he likes to spend some time with Jimmy Demaret in Houston—he Christmases there—and with San Francisco Giant owner Horace Stoneham in Phoenix.

If Low has a home base at present it is Delray Beach, Fla., where he keeps an apartment and a Cadillac. His office?

"I don't have to be back to the office for 30 more years," he'll tell you.

When last seen by this writer, George was on his way to another tournament, driving Arnold Palmer's car. In the trunk were most of his belongings, including some scrapbooks.

The scrapbooks contain photos of George with almost every big name golfer and celebrity and wealthy sportsman who has ever stepped on a putting green. One of the pictures shows George with his hand in the pocket of Wilbur Clark, the Desert Inn impressario at Las Vegas.

It's the closest George Low has been to big money since he moved out of the Topping's neighborhood at Baltusrol. ■

DOES YOUR SWING GO *SHHOOO?*

BY NICK SEITZ
May, 1970

It is Paul Hahn's crusading ambition to convince the club golfers of the world that their game should be an enjoyable leisure activity, and that they should be more realistic about it. The 51-year-old trick-shot specialist has given 4,000 exhibitions at country clubs from Maine to Mandalay, making his point by turning golf into rollicking entertainment.

Hahn will drive the ball 200 yards with a clubhead attached to a garden hose, or while standing one-legged on a chair swinging with one hand, or while on his knees; he will step brisky through a line of 10 balls with a middle-iron in each hand and crack out soaring shots alternately with his right hand and then his left; he will swat two balls at the same time, making one slice and the other hook.

He overlays his hour-long show with a slick patina of jokes and commentary that gives it a dimension of humor surpassing that of any other comic sports act. His verbal humor is inspired by Bob Hope, who occasionally sends him material, and it is aimed squarely at the collective solar plexus of his golf-playing audiences. His imitations of the duffer determinedly keeping his left arm straight are classic, as are his pointed jibes at the country club set ("the businessmen who drive in air-conditioned cars from air-conditioned offices to air-conditioned clubs to take saunas").

Hahn is grateful for Hope's help, but really needs no contrived material. "The peculiarities in golfers today would give 10 writers hundreds of scripts," he says. "You can take the human situation, magnify it, and have a heck of a routine."

Hahn's show is based, in addition to comedy, on a knowledge of golf that goes beyond that of many touring and teaching professionals. The PGA recently awarded him the Horton Smith Trophy for outstanding work in golf education. Top teaching professionals customarily win it. Hahn has pronounced views on how the club player can lower both his handicap and his frustration quotient.

"First of all," he says, sinking back with a beer into a striped couch in his Manhattan apartment, "you have to realize that you shouldn't expect more than is reasonable. If you play golf once or twice a week and you think the few good shots you hit are more indicative of your ability than the many bad ones, you aren't being realistic.

"This game can make you very unhappy if you tackle it that way. It's just like when I went across town to have lunch at Toots Shor's at noon. If I had expected that taxi to make every light and avoid all the traffic, I would have been frustrated, because he hit every red light and got caught in the Park Avenue rush to boot. I wasn't frustrated because my expectations were more realistic than that.

"This is true of anything, and yet otherwise intelligent people look on golf differently—they expect to play this one game well without much practice. I've been on my tour for 20 years now, and I still hit at least a thousand balls a week to stay sharp. I used to hit that many every day. Either spend as much time on the practice range as the pros or

166

don't expect to play well and don't lose your temper on the course."

Hahn believes most of us could become better golfers merely by assuming his basic outlook. "My trick shots evolved from thinking of alternate ways to do things," he says animatedly, "and the greatest lesson I could give anyone that he probably hasn't already heard a million times is to think of the many ways you can hit the ball or play a shot. The more you think, the better you play—up to a point. That point comes when you stop analyzing the shot and hit the ball. Then you let your subconscious take over.

"But think about the action of the clubhead across the ball, what kind of spin you want to apply and what you want the ball to do. Think of where to play the ball in relation to your feet. On sidehill and downhill lies you have to use one more club than usual. If the ball's below your feet you're going to slice it and it won't go as far. If its' above your feet you have to choke down on the grip and swing on a shorter arc.

"Before you get set to swing, visualize the plane you want to swing in. Draw it in your imagination, through the ball, then visualize making a good swing on that plane. But, again, don't be worrying about these things while you're actually swinging. Put the picture in your mind before you move the club. Good golfers never think about how to hit the ball—they think about *where* to hit it. They have a picture in their minds of the ball in flight and the target. Someone once asked Sam Snead how he sliced the ball and he said 'I think slice.' Isn't that beautiful?"

Hahn has a further word for those of us who *unintentionally* slice: "The toughest thing in the world is to get a person to aim himself to the right if he's having trouble slicing. Instinctively he feels he must aim more left to stop the ball from finishing to his right."

He pauses, but only to catch his breath. The runaway monologue resumes. "Of course, you have to remember that the critical point in a golf swing is the first move in the downswing. There is no exception to this rule. I have studied every great golfer in the world, and they all start the downswing by return-ing the bulk of the weight to the left side. That move puts you in balance and into a position that lets you use all your energy in hitting the ball. You can tell a good player by *listening* to his swing. A good player's swing goes SHHOOO and a poor player's goes UH . . . . UH. I pantomime that in my act."

Hahn's act was born when, as an impoverished assistant professional at a Chicago club, he found that in experimenting with off-beat shots to amuse himself he also amused the members, who demonstrated their appreciation by passing the hat. Hahn had arrived in Chicago in 1948 after a brief and unspectacular whirl on the PGA tour. He "earned barely enough money to mark my ball" as a touring pro, but gained an insight into his personality that was to have a striking effect on his future.

"I'd done some radio and Little Theatre work, and I knew I had a lot of ham in me. On the tour I discovered that the fans respond more emotionally to a putt that just misses than to one that goes in. I suspect that I subconsciously was putting to leave the ball just short so I could hear the ooos and ahhs of the galleries. I wasn't competitive enough, and so I got out and went to work in Chicago."

The season in Chicago ended on Labor Day, and Hahn moved to Los Angeles, where he went to work at a driving range. On the side he began developing a full-blown trick-shot routine. He met and played golf with a number of movie people, including Bob Hope, who began feeding him material, and then was befriended by a golf-crazy coffin distributor. The coffin man booked him for exhibitions at area high schools.

By now, Hahn, 30 and married, was thinking seriously about taking his act on tour for a living, and he decided to start in the Pacific Northwest. "Bob Hope told me if you could make 'em laugh up there you could make 'em laugh anywhere, so off I went. I got a hundred bucks for my first three shows. As I drove from place to place I'd think about the show and each day it got a little bigger and better, and here I am, getting ready to go around the world again—for a thousand a show."

Often flying his own plane ("People keep looking up and mistaking me for Arnie's caddie") his travels have not been without incident. He has driven a ball across the River Thames, over mine fields in Vietnam and into the pyramids in Egypt with no untoward repercussions. But in Ceylon he once swung and opened an underground ant bed, and out roared what seemed like millions of flying ants. In his excitement he grabbed the first thing he could reach to try to smother them. Unfortunately, the first thing he could reach was the sari, or outer garment, of one of the local female caddies helping with his show.

Naturally he talked his way out of that one. "I've never had trouble with language barriers," Hahn says. "Out of the country I rely more on pantomime." He changes his act enough from year to year to give it a fresh look, although most of the millions who have seen him perform return to chuckle again at the staples. Seeing Hahn six or seven times, like seeing the Harlem Globetrotters over and over, is pleasurable almost to the point that knowing what's coming enhances the enjoyment.

His most famous trick used to be "The William Tell Shot," in which a pretty buxom blonde would lie on the ground with the ball teed in her mouth and Hahn would belt it crisply with a 5-iron. He dropped the shot from the show when he heard that youngsters around the country were trying it with gullible girl friends—and when Ben Hogan warned him that everyone misses a shot once in a while, adding candidly, "Even me."

Though he is trim and tanned and looks more in his 40s than 50s, Hahn is phasing himself out of the demanding day-in, day-out tours, traveling now less hectically and only to parts of the world he especially enjoys visiting. His son, a newly turned trick-shot performer, recently toured the world with his father, and the plan is for Paul Jr. to follow in his dad's spiked footsteps. "He's a super striker of the ball," says the elder Hahn, "but he doesn't have my gift of gab yet." But then few do. ■

HASTE YE BACK, HAGEN

BY NICK SEITZ
October, 1970

"I'm sorry," said Joe Kirkwood, the most imaginative shotmaker golf has known, "I'd love to tell you some Hagen stories, but my publisher wants me to save them for my book." His Australian accent was edged with regret. Kirkwood traveled with Walter Hagen for 25 years, taking golf to the world, and the two were fun-seeking confreres whose exploits defy embellishment.

We were sitting in the pro shop at Stowe Country Club in bucolic Vermont where he is head professional, surrounded by a vast melange of memorabilia—a rock collection, inspirational signs, some of his own verse—and incidentally, golf equipment.

Kirkwood apologized for not being able to relate any Hagen stories—and then told a string of them. There was the one about Hagen at Leo Diegel's funeral. Hagen and Diegel had been fierce but affectionate rivals in the 1920s. Remorseful over Diegel's death, Hagen imbibed at some length, and led Kirkwood into the wrong church. The pair sat through the longer part of a funeral service for someone else before realizing their error. Later they caught up with the Diegel ceremonies at the cemetery. Hagen told the minister he would like a word with Leo.

He approached the closed casket and knocked on it loudly. "You in there, Leo?" he rasped, tears in his eyes. "See you soon, old buddy. How in hell'd they get you in there anyway with your arms stuck out?"—a reference to Diegel's unorthodox putting style. Kirkwood says, "It was one of the most touching things I've ever seen."

And there was the time irrepressible story-teller Kirkwood and Hagen, tiring of hitting golf balls out of their New York City hotel window at the bums in Central Park below, walked several blocks and launched a contest to see who could play his way the fastest back to the hotel, through the lobby, up the elevator, across the room, and into the toilet bowl. They played this game several times and Kirkwood defeated Hagen consistently. An infuriated Hagen always was first back to the room, but was inept at chipping his ball into the toilet, while Kirkwood never missed.

For Kirkwood, chipping into a toilet bowl was nothing. The first great trick-shot performer (a designation that he does not like but that he raised to the level of legitimacy), he could do more with a golf ball than anyone before or since. He could tee two balls and, with a 7-iron, hit them simultaneously and cause them to cross in mid-flight, one hooking and one slicing; he could pound a ball into the ground so that only the top was visible, and crack it over 200 yards with a 4-wood; he could play left-handed with right-handed clubs; he could demonstrate his unparalleled touch by taking identical full swings with a 2-wood to pantomime the development of a novice player, and barely topple the ball off the tee, then dribble it a few feet, then hit it 50 yards, and eventually 275 yards. Or he could flail at it and pop it harmlessly into the air so that he caught it without moving.

He could tee six balls in a row and, in quick succession and without looking, move down the line and cleanly strike one after another, making them alternately hook and slice.

"The most difficult shot was the one where I'd hit backward out of a bunker and the ball would finish close to the hole," he says. "I kept my hands low and didn't come up with my swing. The ball flew right over my shoulder. Grantland Rice made a Movietone short of that shot, and after I saw in slow motion how close I was to getting hit I didn't do it often.

"I used to swing a lead shaft that would wind around my neck, and one day I hit myself in the shoulder on my backswing and spit out all the teeth from one side of my mouth. People thought it was part of the act and I was spitting out corn. There was a time when I'd do anything for money."

Money was something only other people had when Kirkwood was young in Australia. He left home at nine, encouraged, he says, by his parents, and dropped out of school. "Three of the happiest years of my life were in the second grade," he jokes. He became a boundary rider (cowboy) for a sheep ranch, in his free time playing golf on three makeshift holes with a gift club.

"There was nobody to copy, so I had to use my imagination," he says. "I never intended to be a showman, but I wanted to do something the other fella couldn't do." In his early 20s he won the Australian Open Championship and, too young to fight in World War I, made a patriotic contribution by entertaining disabled troops. "I tried to show them what could be done even though they were amputees," he says. "I would hit a ball with one hand, or standing on one leg. That's how I got started."

Fifty years ago, Kirkwood came to America. A good player, he won several tour events and the Canadian Open, and finished high in the British and U.S. Opens, but decided he could not live well enough on the skimpy purses of the day, and threw in with Hagen as a trick-shot pioneer. The two men were an immediate success around the world, the penurious, better organized Kirkwood complementing the carefree Haig. They played exhibitions in places golf had never been, on islands without names. The story goes that they once stopped a war in China because no one wanted to miss their act.

They entertained loin-clothed natives, presidents or convention-goers, but they also entertained each other. In Scotland, Hagen wanted a lesson from an old teaching pro. So he concocted a scheme. He and Kirkwood passed themselves off as Canadian cattlemen just taking up golf, and for an hour the old Scot grappled with what he doubtless considered the two oddest swings he had ever come upon. As they left, he called after them, "Haste ye back!"

Five years ago Kirkwood settled in Stowe. He says he was fishing in nearby Bethel, fell in fighting a big trout, and was washed downstream to Stowe. The club had no pro, Kirkwood was tired of a schedule that often called for three shows a day and a long overnight drive, and he figured he would never find a more attractive, relaxing environment. He stayed.

He kept his game in shape, occasionally going on the road to give exhibitions, and breaking par on his own championship course playing with members and using only a 5-iron, In 1960, at the age of 63, he fired a 62 at Deland (Fla.) Country Club to become the youngest man ever to receive a certificate from *Golf Digest* for shooting his age, the golfing feat of which he is proudest. Actually, there is some uncertainty about Kirkwood's age. He says he is presently 74, but his son Ron who helps him operate the Stowe pro shop, says Social Security records show 78 (another son, Joe Jr., was a competent tour player and played Joe Palooka in the movies).

The once husky Kirkwood has cancer of the liver and has lost 70 pounds since a year ago, and his doctor has told him bluntly that he will not live another year. The irony is that liver ailments are popularly associated with excessive drinking and Joe never drank. Medicines keep him out of pain, and, while he spends much of his time resting, he can still be lucid and entertaining, his sense of humor as lively as ever.

When a local doctor shot himself with a pistol, someone remarked that it had to be due to one of three reasons: love, money or illness. Said Joe, "Or a very bad slice." Always a bit of a dandy, he continues to dye his hair, and even now is attractive to women. On the summer weekend that I visited him, a pretty woman in her 40s was in town trying to ingratiate herself with Joe. "She's gotta be crazy," Joe growled later. "A harem would do me no good."

He is determined to finish his book, with a woman writer who belongs to the Stowe club.

"The only thing I regret is that I can't play golf," he says. "I love the game. But I've played 8,000 courses and been able to go everywhere I wanted to go. I've had a full life; plenty of money, good friends. I've bought a little plot of land to be buried on here, and I don't want any fanfare or crap when I go. I'd just like to think the boys will drive by and say, 'Hi, Kirkie.' " ■

Editor's note: Joe Kirkwood died Oct. 29, 1970, at age 73 after a long illness.

JOCK BE NIMBLE, FREDDIE BE QUICK

BY CAL BROWN
April, 1972

Two aged figures move slowly across the freshly cut lawn in front of the Augusta National clubhouse. The warm Georgia sun splashes through the early April morning, releasing the faint, familiar smell of pines and flowers. A sweatered gallery has already begun to drift away from the putting green toward the starting box where officials in trim green blazers and white slacks wait quietly inside thin yellow ropes for another Masters Tournament to begin.

One of the two old men is Freddie McLeod. He won the U.S. Open in 1908. He is 88. The other is Jock Hutchison, winner of the 1920 PGA Championship and 1921 British Open. He is 86. McLeod and Hutchison are the honorary starters at each Masters Tournament, a ritual they have enacted every year since 1963. McLeod competed in the first Masters in 1934. Hutchison first competed in the tournament in 1935.

They are native Scots, Hutchison of St. Andrews and McLeod of North Berwick, friends of half a century, and two of the last surviving links to the original Scottish invasion of American golf. They also are the last survivors of the days when all past U.S. Open and PGA champions played here. Now, because the touring pros demanded more spots, only the Masters champions are forever eligible.

Hutchison and McLeod are led inside the ropes. They pose for photographers. Behind them their white-uniformed caddies hold aloft signs bearing their contestants numbers. The numbers are their ages.

Hutchison wears brown trousers, a white cap and yellow turtleneck jersey with matching sweater.

McLeod is turned out in a bright orange sweater over a white button-down shirt with red, white and blue striped tie, grey cuffed slacks and a brown fedora. He wears thick eyeglasses.

There is a momentary lull, and Hutchison asks a man in the gallery, "Do you know how much a Scotsman can drink?" He waits craftily. When the man shrugs, Jock cackles "Any given amount." The crowd smiles.

McLeod and Hutchison are wired for sound by two technicians for a movie being shot on the Masters. One of the technicians demonstrates how the microphone works and fumbles while putting the battery unit in Hutchison's hip pocket.

"Well, alright, laddie, but don't take my dollar," says Jock in a Scottish brogue.

The first hole at Augusta is a par-4 that sweeps up a long hill and curls to the right around deep bunkers. McLeod is first to hit and drives his ball straight down the center about 160 yards. There is applause and he doffs his hat. Hutchison's turn. He addresses the ball, pauses and then licks his hands.

"I'd rather my wife hit this one," he says. He hits an acceptable drive which lands on the right side of the fairway and asks, "Where did it go? I can't see where the ball goes, that's the hardest thing now."

The pair sets off, McLeod walking with short, careful steps. Hutchison walks with a limp caused by arthritis of the right hip. Someone calls from the gallery, "We hope you make the cut." McLeod looks around vacantly and snorts, "Make the cut? I'm more concerned about making the hill."

A small group separates from the crowd and strings out along both sides of the fairway to follow them.

On the green, Hutchison misses a short putt and grumbles. McLeod then leaves a putt short. "That's the trouble with you little, light fellows—you can't hit it," Jock says.

At the second tee, Hutchison scrapes his tee shot low and straight. It just clears the ladies' tee. He makes a face. McLeod reassures him.

"It's okay, Jock. You can find

your ball. That's all you can expect now." After their third shots on this long par-5, McLeod is 40 yards ahead of Hutchison. Jock argues with his caddie, who wants him to hit a wood, and finally selects a 5-wood. The shot disappears into a bunker in front of the green.

"I should have taken the damn 3-iron," mutters Hutchison.

When he reaches the bunker, Jock peers at his ball and says he wishes he had a drink. He makes a fine recovery, and then realizes that he is himself trapped in the steeply banked bunker. He crawls up the side and painfully claws his way past the protruding lip. After holing out, he looks at his ball and says, "Well, I've still got the same ball."

McLeod chides him for dawdling with the spectators between green and tee. Despite their ages, they play surprisingly fast. Not as briskly, though, as some tournament officials once thought.

"We used to play six holes and then cut over to the 16th, skipping the rest. No one ever knew why we finished play so quickly," McLeod confesses. They have not played

more than nine holes for many years.

Now they are back at the clubhouse, tired but happy with finishing nine holes before an appreciative gallery.

They walk into the white plantation clubhouse and up the winding, green-carpeted staircase to a small changing room beside the bar. Both order Scotch and water.

A friend comes in to congratulate them on their round.

"I thought Freddie was good, but I was lousy," Jock says.

"You were," Freddie agrees. The banter between them begins to perk up as they talk about the old days.

"Freddie got all the good-looking women, and those he didn't want he gave over to me," Jock reminisces.

Both deplore the elimination of the stymie rule.

"Jock, you could'na lay me a stymie no matter how hard you tried," Freddie says.

"I just want you to know I'm two years older than him," Freddie remarks to a reporter.

"And you look 10 years older,"

Hutchison replies. They order another drink.

McLeod lives in retirement at the club he once served as professional, the Columbia Country Club, Chevy Chase, Md.

Hutchison, retired, still receives a salary from Glenview (III.) Country Club where he became professional 38 years ago.

Neither man seems anxious to end the reunion. They met in 1908 at Myopia Hunt Club, Hamilton, Mass., where McLeod won the Open and a purse of $300. They look around the room in vain for old friends.

"Jock is all that's left," says McLeod. ■

JOE DEY'S 40 YEARS OF SHAPING THE GAME

BY HUBERT MIZELL
January, 1974

Reach inside Joe Dey's traditional blue blazer and you will find two pocket-sized books. One is the Rules of Golf, the other The New Testament. Joe always carries them . . . they govern his life. He even helped write one of them.

Dey is a man of exemplary moral fiber, totally devoted to God, family and golf. Strikingly forceful at age 66, he retires in February after 40 years as golf's most accomplished administrator. Perhaps no major sport has been so positively and indelibly marked by a non-competitor since Judge Kennesaw Mountain Landis ruled baseball with unquestioned authority a half century ago.

Dey spent the final five years of his career as the first commissioner of America's professional golf tour, trail-bossing an $8 million business effectively and with unfaltering dignity while dealing with some of the most individualistic athletes anywhere. For 35 years prior to joining the Tournament Players Division, Dey was executive director of the United States Golf Ass'n. He became the most powerful figure in international amateur golf and the ranking rulesmaker of the world.

There may never be another Joe Dey.

"If there are two things of which I am proudest," he says while preparing to step down, "they would be the establishment of a standard code of rules and the forming of the World Amateur Golf Council." The council, which consists of 60 countries, operates the World Amateur Team Championships for both men and women.

Although so many of his fondest memories are from his USGA days, Dey should not be short-changed

Hubert Mizell is sports editor of the St. Petersburg Times. He has been a member of the Associated Press staff in Florida and New York, and an associate editor of *Golf Digest*.

when credit is given for the incredible prosperity the pro tour now enjoys. He became commissioner at the tailend of a feud between touring players of the Professional Golfers' Ass'n and the club professionals who control the organization. It appeared the fight might lead to the establishment of rival tours, but that was averted when the PGA formed a new wing known as the Tournament Players Division. The TPD needed a strong commissioner. When the decision was announced, Jack Nicklaus perhaps said it best . . . "Joe Dey is the only man for the job."

When it comes to the pros, Dey has to be especially proud that a Tournament Players Championship will be conducted at Atlanta over the Labor Day weekend. That was one of his prime goals, a fitting climax to the summer championship season. Perhaps the award for this event, which could become the world's fifth major championship, should be the Joseph C. Dey Jr. Cup.

Still, those recollections of so many U.S. Opens linger on. Five years with the professionals cannot dim those 35 with the amateurs.

"Joe loves to referee great tournaments," says Frank Hannigan, assistant executive director of the USGA and a man who worked under Dey for many years. "He talked often of walking the final 18 holes of the 1951 Open with Ben Hogan when he shot 67 at Oakland Hills on one of the toughest setups an Open has ever known. Joe also likes to recall 1964 when he walked alongside a weary, heat-sapped Ken Venturi during his Open victory at Congressional."

Dey took pride in setting up tough courses for major championships such as the Open and U.S. Amateur. He practically wrote the book on it along with former USGA President Richard Tufts. Joe even enjoyed rising at 5 a.m. to go out and supervise the placing and cutting of the cups for the day's round.

You often recall individuals in certain ways, in certain garb. Lincoln in that stove-pipe hat . . . Groucho Marx with the waggling cigar . . . Hogan in that little white golf cap. You remember Joe Dey as a stately figure in a long-sleeved white dress shirt, a conservative necktie and an armband that said either "USGA" or "Rules Committee."

Dey and his USGA committeemen made many memorable decisions involving rules over the years. During the final round of the 1940 Open at Canterbury, he announced the decision that Ed "Porky" Oliver and five other golfers had been disqualified for teeing off ahead of schedule. The two threesomes jumped the gun when hearing reports that thunderstorms were moving in from Lake Erie. Oliver and the others were told of their fate after the round and Porky was stripped of a chance for the championship since his score had tied Lawson Little and Gene Sarazen. Little beat Sarazen in a playoff the next day. In another decision, Dey had to tell roundish Jackie Pung of Hawaii that she was

being disqualified after apparently shooting her way to victory in the 1957 U.S. Women's Open at Winged Foot. Mrs. Pung had signed an incorrect scorecard.

People who have bargained with Dey will recall him as a well-mannered but stubborn and tough negotiator. A frugal person, he has a rare ability to generate financing for golf projects, as evidenced by the 50 per cent growth in purses since he became the tour's commissioner in early 1969.

Dey was born in 1907, the son of a Norfolk, Va., businessman who himself had a niche in sports history. "Dad played on the first football team at North Carolina State University in the 1890s," Dey says proudly. The Deys moved to New Orleans in 1910 where Joe did so well in school that he qualified for scholarships at Tulane and Louisiana State University. His family was moving north, however, and Joe decided to enroll at the University of Pennsylvania.

You know Dey had to be an Ivy Leaguer, a fellow who wore the school tie to pep rallies and sang every word of the alma mater. But it's a little-known fact that he was a college dropout . . . a man loaded with determination to become, of all things, a sports writer. "I left school to write for the old Public Ledger in Philadelphia," he recalls. "After five years I shifted to the Philadelphia Bulletin." Joe covered football and some of Connie Mack's Athletics baseball teams. He also developed a fondness for golf and became co-owner of a sideline publication known as the Philadelphia Golfer.

"Newspapers covered golf in more depth back then," he says. "We had a reporter walking the course with players and sending play-by-play copy back to press headquarters by messengers. I recall the record 28-hole playoff between George Von Elm and Maurice McCarthy in the 1930 U.S. Amateur. Alan Gould was sports editor of the Associated Press and devised a system with one of his helpers. The guy was supposed to run onto a roadway where Gould could see him from afar and raise one hand if Von Elm won and the other if McCarthy won. The kid lifted the wrong hand and Gould sent out an erroneous bulletin to the world that Von Elm had won the match."

Dey remembers covering the 1930 U.S. Amateur at Merion when Bobby Jones was completing the Grand Slam. Joe's final tournament as a sports writer was the 1934 Amateur at The Country Club in Brookline, Mass., when Lawson Little thrashed David Goldman 8 and 7. Frank Hardt, then secretary of the USGA, was scouting around for an executive director and recommended Joe for the job. Dey went to work for the USGA with one secretary and a small office on 42nd Street in New York about 100 yards from a building where he would rule the professional tour two generations later.

Dey was a great theater buff in those days. He had acted in Philadelphia in a group known as Plays and Players. After becoming the USGA's operating chief, he studied scripts and lyrics with all the enthusiasm of a youngster collecting bubble gum baseball cards.

"Joe is great on theater trivia," says Hannigan. "I'm not bad myself and we used to play games when traveling together for the USGA. He always beat me. Joe can recall lyrics from the most obscure plays and he knows playwrights and composers almost as well as he knows former winners of U.S. Opens." Dey has drifted from the theater in recent years, largely because of the trend to obscene language on the legitimate stage.

Now that he's retiring, Dey may get to play more golf himself. He has never been a low-handicap player—usually shooting in the high 80s—but he has always found time to be strong in club operations at The Creek Club on Long Island. He plans to keep his home in the New York suburb of Locust Valley while spending time writing articles and doing religious work. After breaking in the new commissioner, he may remain as a consultant to the pro tour. That all seems fitting since it is almost impossible to think of golf without Joe Dey . . . or vice versa. ■

THE PLACES

Inseparable from nature at its most resplendent, golf's settings give the game a unique appeal. In no other sport does the battleground so vividly project its own personality. Golf is man against course, and the latter often is capable of upstaging the former.

Golf Digest frequently conveys in words and pictures the demanding beauty of the world's finest courses. Biennially it carries a carefully researched listing of "America's 100 Greatest Tests of Golf," a feature that has become the hallmark of course assessment in this country.

Not that greatness is our only concern. Our writers and photographers have crisscrossed continental boundaries to explore the wildly disparate history and flavor of courses ranging from exclusive Augusta National to nine-hole public layouts with sand greens to Tenison Park, a municipal course in Dallas that long has been a haven for resourceful hustlers from Titanic Thompson to Lee Trevino.

The results of this pursuit have appeared, over the years, in various forms. They include travel features on areas such as the Monterey Peninsula, reprinted here.

Then, one of our most popular sustaining features on golf courses has been Places to Play, a monthly review of interesting courses, usually new, that are open to the public.

The high point of this quarter century of golf course journalism was the vast, colorful hardback volume, *Great Golf Courses of the World.* Edited by William H. Davis, president and editor-in-chief of *Golf Digest,* it was published in 1974 to enthusiastic acclaim.

Inevitably, exposure to these courses vividly affects our writers and their methods of expression.

Cal Brown was so overcome by the rugged beauty of the Monterey Peninsula that he had to restrain his emotions—in the manner of a critic reviewing a play he had hopelessly fallen in love with—to produce the touching tribute that appears here.

Jim Murray, on the other hand, employs a more facetious approach in his delightful sketch of Los Angeles golf. He writes irreverently about the misadventures of the movie crowd and the tinseled snobbery of some LA clubs.

Only in golf does the playing field rival the contestants in personality, and it does so in uncommonly captivating ways. They are captured for you in the following.

HUSTLE PARK: WHENCE THEY SHIP THE PROS HOME C.O.D.

BY GARY CARTWRIGHT
June, 1969

There is a large pecan tree on the crest of a hill beside Tenison Park's No. 12 fairway. That is where they first saw him that Sunday afternoon eleven years ago.

This foursome consisting of ex-big league baseball player Davy Williams and three other action lovers were about to play their second shots on 12 when *The Redeemer* (as some would call him later) appeared from behind the pecan tree. He must have been a fearsome and sobering sight: dressed all in black, they say, and holding a Bible in one hand, his arms raised so high that his bushy black beard seemed to grow from the neck of his frock coat, eyes burning like the windows of hell.

"Repent!" he shouted. "Lay aside the sticks of the devil!"

Well, they should have known better. After all, this was Tenison Park, the garden spot of East Dallas, the flower of fortune and fate, a sort of municipal casino-on-the-green where, if a man sticks around long enough, someone is sure to make it even money that the sun will set in the south. Tenison Park, "where they go home C.O.D." Tenison Park, where the resident Robin Hoods have names like Fatman and Dogman and The Fly, where the legendary gambler Titanic Thompson keeps hours as solicitous and regular as your downtown bank president, where in days past a Mexican urchin named Lee Trevino would offer to beat your best-ball using a Dr. Pepper bottle off the tee.

Tenison Park; they should have known better. And they did. "They say you can't hustle an old hustler," observes a hanger-on in Tenison's flagstone clubhouse with the

A former Dallas newspaperman, familiar with the characters who frequented Tenison Park, Gary Cartwright is now a freelance writer.

Virginia steeple. "Hell! That's exactly who you *can* hustle." So it was that Sunday afternoon eleven years ago.

After about two minutes of ideology mixed with some praying and cussing under the pecan tree, they got it on. The Redeemer, who swore then and there he had never taken grip on a "devil's stick" (in that case, a 3-wood) in his life, made an exception right then.

"He played just good enough," Davy Williams recalled later. "There was a lot of hallelujahing and 'Lord, put the right club in your servant's hand,' but if we hit a fat one he hit one a little fatter, just to build up the money."

When it was over, the original foursome was several hundred dollars poorer but wiser. Nobody ever saw The Redeemer again, or if they did they didn't recognize him.

There is not a golf course in the civilized or savage world which has failed to attract its share of sports, but since the late 1920s Tenison has been known in select circles as a free port of open action. Such famous names as Jack Carson, Audie Murphy, Ted Lewis, Kyle Rote, Mickey Mantle, and Dizzy and Paul Dean have tested their various skills at Tenison. Two U.S. Open champions, Trevino and Ralph Guldahl, played here in their formative years.

Just after World War I a Dallas banker named E. O. Tenison purchased 128 acres of wooded, rolling land a few miles east of downtown Dallas. What old man Tenison had in mind was a memorial to his son who had died in the war. He donated the land to the city with the understanding that it would be perpetuated as a municipal recreation area for men of all persuasions, and that is an accurate description of what Tenison Park has become. (Later, the city purchased an additional 160 acres and commissioned Ralph Plummer to design a second 18-hole course.

Years ago this was a wealthy section of Dallas. Stately old mansions and high ivy-walled estates still grace the Lakewood area just north of Tenison, but the backside of the park is pocked by slum neighborhoods and tough

bars that seem forever situated next to railroad tracks. Richard Speck, convicted killer of five nurses in Chicago a few years ago, grew up around here. Clyde Barrow sometimes hung around the joints on East Grand. In this climate, where the have-nots were constantly mingling with the haves, the almighty dollar had the capricious allure of frost on a window pane.

"I guess a lot of us were pretty hot-blooded way back there, back in the late 1920s, through the Depression years," says Erwin Hardwick, who has worked at Tenison more than 40 years, at least 25 as head professional.

"But that's water under the bridge. They used to play for $100 a nine, $10 a hole with presses. That was when a man was working his tail off for $35 a week, too. But now I'd say there is less betting at Tenison than at any country club in town."

Hardwick says that he put a stop to the heavy gambling in 1953, about the same time two FBI agents came around asking after a certain fellow. The agents first flashed this picture of a bald-headed man: nobody recognized him. Later they produced a picture of the same guy wearing a wig. "Why that's old Nassau Nick!" Hardwick gasped. "He ought to be on about 17 right now." The last time anyone saw Nassau Nick they were leading him off in handcuffs. It turned out he was an ex-FBI man using his old identification card to cash checks to finance his growing golf hustling empire.

"It was hard to tell how much big money changed hands," says Hardwick. "There was a lot of big talk, you know, and there was plenty of side action. It got so bad that they were using cars to follow the players around the course. I put a stop to that, and I started charging greens fees for anyone who wanted to watch. What really made it bad, the kids from Woodrow Wilson (a nearby high school) took to coming over and following the action. They'd hear all that big talk, and they'd think: why go to school if money is that easy? It was bad for golf."

Trevino recalls, "I didn't really play Tenison much until after I came out of the service. There

wasn't a lot of hustling going on that I could see, just the hustlers hustling the hustlers. Shoot, I didn't have no money to hustle. We'd play a dollar medal and quarter skins. I'll say this—there were a lot of good players around Tenison. They're still there, too."

The best of them is Dick Martin, a frail, skittish little man in his 50s. Far as anyone knows Martin has never worked a day in his life, unless you call golf work. "Somebody asked me one time why I didn't turn pro," says Martin. "Man, I can't afford it." Trevino prudently avoided matches with Martin for years; now Martin avoids Trevino.

To men such as Martin, golf is a business not unlike the stock market. They calculate the odds, study the charts, squeeze for advantage and risk less than they can afford. Tenison birds recall the afternoon Trevino was playing best-ball against three regulars, including Arthur Corbin, a fellow who had been known to bring Dick Martin and others to their knees. Martin was watching from a secure distance.

"Hey, Dick," Trevino called to the lean little man on the clubhouse steps, "You're not gonna let this one get away, are you?"

It happened that an hour before Martin had stumbled on an old acquaintance who owed him a pile. Martin had thought the gent was dead. Money from providence scorching his pocket, Martin wagered $25 on each of Trevino's opponents. There are some who remember it as $25 a *hole*. Anyhow, Trevino closed out all three of them quickly. That was the day he shot a record 63 on the East Course (par 72). The defending U.S. Open champ, who learned his fundamental skills at Dallas' Glen Lakes Country Club on rainy days using a left-handed club that he found in the weeds ("People ask how I could be accurate with a left-handed club. With a left-handed club you *have* to be accurate!"), also holds the record of 64 on Tenison's par-71 West Course.

Martin's betting style, however, is normally less passionate. "The secret," he says, grinning like a fox in a hen house, "is handicapping." Martin once played five high-handicap players' best-ball, with the added stipulation that they would play their second shot from where his tee shot finished. Naturally, Martin could outhit any of them, but on this particular day he developed the most fantastic hook. Every tee shot hooked into the woods, except a couple that barely dribbled off the tee. Martin won the nine-hole match in five straight holes.

Tenison's reputation for being "where it's at" permeates golfdom's more adventurous souls like the song of the sirens. Frequently, though not invariably, the music is sweeter than the reward.

Cynical as pawnbrokers, Tenison regulars maintain a state of readiness. Your standard gypsy hustler in the Texaco uniform with Billy Frank stitched over one pocket will stick out like a gold tooth, yet this fails to explain what happened not long ago when a stranger from Mississippi put the touch on them for several bills.

"He was a real charmer," says Dutch Boyd. "He claimed to be an ex-All-American football player from Ole Miss who was on his way to Hollywood to be a movie star or something. In one afternoon he made a half-dozen guys for a hundred bucks each. The boys are still waiting to see him in the movies."

More in character is the case of the well-known pro who took a leave of absence from the tour four years ago and headed for Tenison where he understood that quick money was laying around like pecans. Call him Roy. He hit town, according to Dutch Boyd, with "thousand dollar bills stuffed in his watch pocket." And he went back, as they say, C.O.D.

Typical of Roy's misfortune was the day he played a rather harmless-appearing retired Air Force officer named James. His reputation as a long hitter preceding him, Roy agreed to let James, a 3-handicapper, hit two balls to Roy's one. In other words, if James blew a six-foot putt, he got a second chance to sink it.

Predictably, James won every bet, even though Roy scored in the low 60s that particular day.

"After about 10 days he (Roy) was on his knees," Dutch recalls. "He was crawling around yelling,

'Hell's just a block away from this place!' Ti and some of the big bettors decided that Roy was business, so they took him to El Paso to play Trevino (who was relatively unknown at the time). Roy couldn't bring him, either. I don't know what it was with Roy, no matter how good he played he was always against someone that would catch policy when he had to."

To "catch policy" is to deliver when the odds are appropriate. Then and not a second before. More than one Tenison tourist has gone home to brood on the fact that a golf match can indeed be fixed—"fixed upward," as Titanic says—if the fixed one is talented enough to hide the symptoms until the price is right. Roy could not see how an amateur such as James could beat a good pro. It may not have occurred to him that for thousand dollar bills James was not, strictly speaking, an amateur.

Dizzy Dean and some of his high rent pals from nearby Lakewood played Tenison until two monumental examples of bad luck convinced them to look elsewhere. The former baseball star always requested a special caddie, a veteran named Bud. It was a well-known fact that Bud bet against Dean, but this failed to shake the famous Dean confidence until one day in a tight situation Bud handed Dean a 4-wood where a 5-iron would have been more than enough. On another afternoon and in another financial crisis Ol' Diz came to the 18th tee dead even with his opponent, home pro Erwin Hardwick. Eighteen is a short par-3, blind and tricky. Both men hit good tee shots, but as they approached the green only one ball was in sight. It rested less than six feet from the hole.

"Man alive!" Dean chirped, "I believe that's *my* ball!"

"I hope so," cracked Hardwick, " 'cause if it is, mine's in the hole." And it was indeed.

The games people play at Tenison depend as much on imagination as skill. They tell of the day that Fatman was $600 down to The Fly when a hijacker stepped out of the woods near No. 3. (This is not as uncommon as you might suppose. Titanic Thompson once shot and killed a robber on a

course in Tyler, Tex.)

"Your money or your life!" the robber is supposed to have said to Fatman and The Fly, at which time Fatman took out his roll, peeled off six bills and handed them to The Fly, thus settling up before subsequent transactions commenced.

When there is nothing else to do, Tenison natives amuse themselves with such games as Tunnel of Love or Screaming Willies.

An elevated railroad crosses the course behind the 17th green, necessitating two tunnels about 200 yards apart. The game is to tee off at the clubhouse, play under one tunnel, back through the other, and end up on the 18th green. Par is 12. Screaming Willies is a game of nerves and concentration. Under the rules a golfer is allowed to shout, sing, whistle (Titanic has been known to shoot his pistol in the air) or otherwise distract his opponent's attention as the mood demands.

"The thing about playing here," says Luke Adams, an assistant pro at Tenison, "is you earn what you win. No matter how good or how smart you think you are, somebody is just as good and just as smart. Most matches go off 50-50. There's no rocking chairs here."

Don Cherry, the singer-golfer, is another celebrity who owes much of his maturity to Tenison Park. Some years ago when Cherry was still playing a small supper club, The Chalet, in Lakewood, Titanic Thompson was giving lessons in the art of blasting out of a trap with a 7-iron.

"I remember it well," says Dutch Boyd. "Ti let Cherry use a sand wedge. Now Cherry was a damn fine golfer, but Ti made him pull up. Yes sir, he made him pull up. I remember it well 'cause it was just before Cherry made his first hit record, *Prisoner of Love.*"

"That wasn't his first hit record," argues a sharp-nosed man who is sitting at the snack bar putting away a 60-cent bowl of Tenison chili. "No, his first hit was *Vanity.*"

"I've got 10 that says *Prisoner* of *Love,*" Boyd snarls. Boyd ought to know. He looked it up a couple of years ago, winning the identical bet he is now prepared to risk in the memory of all that is good about Tenison Park.■

PINE VALLEY: MONU- MENTAL CHALLENGE TO ACCURACY

BY CAL BROWN
October, 1969

Tucked away from public view down an anonymous country road near the small town of Clementon in southwestern New Jersey is Pine Valley Golf Club.

This magnificent—some say fiendish—creation, hewn from the pine-covered sand hills that eons ago formed the ocean floor, is as good an argument as you will find that backbreaking length is not essential to a great test of golf.

Pine Valley's full length of 6,765 yards (6,442 from the regular tees) does not strike fear into anyone's breast—not until one steps to the first tee. There one catches a glimpse of the two principal design features that give Pine Valley its stern, intimidating character—vast,

sandy wilderness and thick forest. There is no "rough" at Pine Valley. Instead, desert-like scrub surrounds every fairway and most of the greens, which are immaculately conditioned and appear, in contrast, as islands of green velvet.

One must play to these "islands" from start to finish. Tee shots must carry expanses of up to 175 yards of unkempt dune on every hole to reach safe ground. The careless, wild or indifferent shot is dealt with severely. Since rakes are forbidden on the course, the sandy soil expanses are pocked with foot-prints, mounds, holes of burrowing animals, roots and ragged clumps of scrub, heather, Scotch broom and Poverty grass. If you can find

The hapless player who fails to arch his second shot far and high enough on Pine Valley's 367-yard second hole will see it fall back on the mountainous dune that rises 40 feet above the fairway.

your ball in this or in the woods (which Pine Valley caddies are devilishly adept at doing) you play it as it lies, for there is out-of-bounds on only one hole.

The all-male club is strictly private. Its president for the past 40 years, John Arthur Brown, has assiduously guarded its sanctity and the comfort of its members owing to the fact that Pine Valley is widely discussed wherever genuine golfing spirits gather and has more requests for visits than can possibly be accommodated. It is widely regarded as the toughest golf course in the world. This is certainly not true for the fine player who can strike the ball consistently and truly. It may well be the most testing for the average player of, say, seven handicap or more, whose shot-making is less reliable. Handicap records of Pine Valley members tend to bear this out. For the low handicapper, three or under, there is no difference between his handicap at Pine Valley and other courses he plays. As handicaps increase, however, the player's handicap at Pine Valley tends to be two or three shots greater than his handicap at another course; in some cases the difference is four or five strokes.

One or two mistakes is all it takes to hike your score dramatically at Pine Valley. There is a story about one gentleman who needed a bogey 5 on the 18th hole for an 84 to win a substantial bet that he could break 90. He finished with 97. The late British golf writer Bernard Darwin is said to have played the first seven holes in even par. Following a good drive, he proceeded to take 16 strokes on the short eighth hole and returned to the clubhouse. It was this kind of thing that could lead Darwin to remark later, "It is all very well to punish a bad stroke, but the right of eternal punishment should be reserved for a higher tribunal than a Greens Committee." On another occasion, Bob Hope stepped to the 130-yard 10th flushed with relief after a 43 on the front side; he finally holed out with an 11.

It may be adventures like these that inspire poets and writers to describe Pine Valley with adjectives like heroic, majestic, monstrous, sublime, deadly, beautiful and one or two uncomplimentary terms of Anglo-Saxon origin. One would be hard put to soften any of these epithets. It also has been called a penal golf course which is true only in the sense that it so ruthlessly penalizes poorly struck shots.

The truth is that Pine Valley is eminently fair. The landing areas for tee shots are very wide. Alternate routes to the greens are provided on at least nine of the 14 long holes, although a safe routing will not get you to the green in regulation figures. There is little margin for the player who chooses to risk everything, a feature upholding the principle that a risk is not worthy of the name if one can get away with an error, however slight. The course demands that if you accept challenge you must be prepared to execute.

It is no secret that a number of professional players, particularly long hitters, do not rate Pine Valley among the great challenges in golf. One suspects the reason for this is that Pine Valley is not the place for raw power. It is a place where subtlety and a well-positioned tee shot will pay rewards, where brute strength is tolerated only if accompanied by great control and nerve. The professionals, who are accustomed to letting it fly to get all the advantages of length without severe penalty, do not like the idea of laying up with an iron or 4-wood. Yet, there is ample room for power at Pine Valley, with sufficient tests of strength for even the heaviest hitters on six holes.

"It is only penal if you are not playing well," says George Fazio, the former touring pro who now is designing courses himself, and who was once the professional at Pine Valley. "I think it has been proved over the years in competition, both amateur and professional, that the best player will win at Pine Valley. You must play the course, not necessarily your own game. The player who does not possess all the shots would not thrive there." It is, in short, a golf course for the man who relishes the game above his own individual prowess.

What sets Pine Valley apart from all but a handful of courses is not only its unusual terrain, but also the number of absolutely first-rate holes it throws at you. It probably has more classic holes than any other course in America.

There are but two par-5s and both are superb. The 15th is surely one of the greatest in the world. Some of the best (and longest) players in golf have surveyed its 603-yard length—Nicklaus, Snead, Harney, Souchak, Bayer, Thomson—and none has ever reached it in two, not even from the middle tees which cut its distance to 584 yards. It is that rare, totally honest hole that hides nothing and yet will succumb to nothing short of perfection. The tee shot must carry over a lovely lake to a wide landing area which slopes lazily uphill and around a gentle bend to the right to a tiny green, perched like a sentinel in the distance. The closer one approaches to the green, the tighter the fairway becomes as woods and sand converge on a narrow neck that is not more than green's width across. The fairway tilts to the right near the green to send any half-hearted approach careening to disaster. The hole yields par with three adequate shots, but even with a drive of 300-plus yards one would have to hit a career second shot absolutely straight, all carry, to get home in two.

The 585-yard seventh hole boasts Hell's Half Acre, considered the largest sand trap in the world, an acre and a half of the most unholy-looking territory this side of the Badlands. It stretches across the entire fairway from about 270 to 370 yards out, and men have been known to disappear here for hours. Once across, the golfer must contend with an approach to a peninsula of putting surface that juts out into a huge estuary of sand.

Pine Valley's four par-3s, collectively, are unmatched for variety and pure splendor. Any one would be the showcase of most courses. Except for No. 5, they provide no safe tee shots except onto the green. The long-iron third hole is surrounded by a sea of sand. The 10th, a 9-iron pitch, features Satanic bunkering. The 14th, a middle-iron shot, nestles between forest and lake.

The fifth hole is one of the most dramatic one-shot holes anywhere. One aims over a narrow lake to an open green 226 yards away. The terrain slopes sharply down to the

The only safe escape from the fiendish bunker above, nicknamed by those who play the course after part of the Devil's anatomy, is straight back. One of the most destructive holes in captivity is Pine Valley's 185-yard 14th (right), where a good player once took 44 shots.

water about 100 yards from the tee, and then the far slope rises to fearsome bunkers 50 yards in front of the green. Forest closes in on all sides. Standing on the tee with a 1-iron or 3-wood can be the loneliest experience imaginable. The hole has no tricks, and even allows a generous margin of error to be short. But don't hit it off line.

One of the popular refrains at Pine Valley is that at the fifth, "only God can make three." The Almightly has company, to be sure, but all of Pine Valley's par-3s have brought good men to their knees. Gene Littler, in a televised match with Byron Nelson, caught one just a little off line at the fifth, watched his ball tumble down the steep ridge at the right of the green, and eventually scrambled for a 7. The 14th was the scene of the most catastrophic shotmaking in Pine Valley's 56-year history. It was there that John Brooks, a low-handicap player, took 44 blows to negotiate its mountainous, jungle-bestrewn, lake-guarded 185 yards, a score that stands as the single-hole record, if you go for that sort of thing.

Pine Valley is not really the demon it is made out to be in these yarns, however. A great course, believes Pinehurst's respected president, Richard Tufts, should yield to a great round of golf. Scores would indicate that Pine Valley is such a course. The record in competition is 67, by club member George Rowbotham, while the four-round mark is 286 (71-69-71-75) set by Craig Wood. Nicklaus and Ted Turner, the club's professional before Fazio, have posted 66 in informal rounds when tee and pin positions were at less than maximum severity. But the record shows that no one has ever given Pine Valley's par 70 a battering.

There have been some sensational starts, the most recent made in 1968 by Major Tom Fotheringham, then captain of Great Britain's Royal and Ancient Golfing Society. Forced to start at the short 10th because the course was crowded, the Major put his first shot at Pine Valley straight in the hole. "Of course, you will keep the ball as a memento of this historic ace," a friend suggested afterwards.

"Oh dear, no," the Major replied. "I put it in the water at 16."

The best round by a first-timer was 67, scored by a British naval officer who was warming up for the club's annual Crump Memorial Tournament, named after the late George Crump who created Pine Valley. In the competition next day, he was unable to break 90. The most popular piece of local folklore has J. Wood Platt, a gifted amateur of the Bobby Jones era, opening his round with 3, 2, 1, 3—two birdies and two eagles—and then repairing to the bar. He failed to emerge to finish the round.

One must play Pine Valley the same way a porcupine courts its mate—very carefully. In a professional tournament, Ed Dudley shot 68 in the first round and followed with 77 and 85. One player, who scored 79 his first time around, came back the next day with 98. "I was fine until I found out where all the trouble is," he wailed. Bill Campbell, the former National Amateur champion and Walker star, tells of his first experience in the Crump tournament. "In one match, I scored seven 3s in 10 holes and closed out my match on 13. I thought I really had Pine Valley's number. The next day, Bill Hyndman beat me 7 and 5. We walked in from the same place I had won the day before, but if I had finished the round I would have scored in the mid-80s. Pine Valley tests the mind as well as the stroke. You must think well, and you can never make the mistake of trying to steer the long shot."

This demand for mental exercise is not the only reason Pine Valley is celebrated. Its quality and character stand as a bastion against the "mischievous tendencies" of modern course design that tradition-minded architects warned about years ago. The notion that length and huge greens make for testing golf has spawned a rather dreary assemblage of courses of little distinction, monotonous replicas of one another. If it is true that life rebels at conformity, it is not hard to see why we react with interest and excitement to a golf course that is imaginative, thought-provoking, appealing to the eye and challenging. A truly testing course should demand consideration, not

merely muscle, on every shot, and will offer the opportunity of testing every club in the bag and every type of shot.

From beginning to end, Pine Valley can hardly be faulted on any of these counts. Its greens are large and true, and not so fast as to discourage bold putting. Yet they present varying degrees of slope that demand correct reading and stroking. Visually the course stirs the blood; there is scarcely a hole that does not present a memorable image.

The first hole is a splendid opener, a 427-yard dogleg that allows absolutely no wayward flighting of the approach shot. It is a shade tougher than one might prefer, but it properly sets the tone for what is to follow. The 424-yard 18th is a solid finishing hole that looks from a high plateau across the barrens to the fairway below, guarded by water and sand on the right and thick woods on the left. The approach must clear water and a series of bunkers gouged in front of the huge, raised putting surface where three-putts are as regular as the sunrise.

A great test of golf should be a little like an honest judge: no bribes accepted. Pine Valley is like that. For all of its lurking danger and uncompromising retribution, it is a course one plays with relish, where pars are collected gratefully and where birdies are small treasures to be hoarded against one's next visit. ■

GOLF'S DIFFERENT SISTERS

BY CAL BROWN
September, 1970

They sit like two restoration pieces, about a driver and a 2-iron apart, amid six full-length golf courses in the Appalachian Mountains— The Greenbrier and, its 175-foot clock tower rising high above the trees, The Homestead. Encrusted with more wealth and tradition than the annual meeting of the United States Golf Ass'n, these two grand old resorts (dating back to 1776 and 1790, respectively) have stood for many years as a kind of barometer of social and economic success. Most executives have, at one time or another, attended meetings at either The Greenbrier, in White Sulphur Springs, W. Va., or The Homestead, in Hot Springs, Va., although surprisingly few seem to have visited both, even though they are only 40 miles apart by car. If you have been to one, it is said you're successful, but you're a little more "in" if you've been to both.

Despite the large volume of expense-account dollars that circulates at the two resorts, Sam Snead, the host professional at Greenbrier, moans over the loss of "action" on the golf course. "I used to could pick me up a match for a grand or fifteen hundred most any day," he says wistfully, "and now all we got coming down here are these bright young executives in their $90 suits, and they can't figure no way to get more than a $10 Nassau on their expense accounts." A playing lesson with Sam costs $100, and he'll tee it up with anyone who has a bankroll. He can still shoot any of The Greenbrier courses, when the ante is right, in under 65.

Snead, who began his golfing career at The Homestead and then moved to The Greenbrier in 1936, is involved in more local folklore than Abe Lincoln in Illinois. He was

born in Ashwood, a few miles from Hot Springs, in country so steep, Snead says, "that the dogs only have room to wag their tails up and down." Many of the stories they tell of Snead can't be repeated, although a lot of the rest have made their way into golf legend.

At The Homestead, each of the three courses has its own identity, clubhouse and golf professional. The Upper Cascades layout, which was built in 1923 by William Flynn, is one of the best courses in the country. Located about three miles from the hotel in a setting of pastoral, mountain beauty, it unfolds with a marvelous assortment of shots. Snead believes it is the finest training course he knows. "There isn't any kind of hill you don't have to play from, or any kind of shot you won't hit there," Sam drawls. "If you could train a youngster to play on that course, he'll play anywhere." Right out the side door of The Homestead is its oldest course, dating from 1892, which winds through the hills behind the hotel. It is easy, pleasant golf with a heavy dose of scenery. John D. Rockfeller used to enjoy pitching dimes into a brook on the first hole and watching the caddies scramble for them. The newest course, laid out in 1962 by Trent Jones, is long and tough, and almost never crowded, partly because it is six miles from the hotel, and partly because you can't walk it — the distances between green and tee are so long. However, it is one of the most scenic experiences you will ever have in a golf car, as much from green to tee as from tee to green.

At The Greenbrier, all three golf courses fan out from the yellow-awninged Golf and Tennis Club which is just a short walk from the hotel and is the hub of all day-time social and athletic activity. All three are well-conditioned, but less demanding layouts than the Cascades courses. The best of them is The Old White, which was built in 1910, and has since been remodeled twice.

The Greenbrier course, built in 1925, was the scene of Snead's remarkable 59, scored in the third round of the Sam Snead Festival in 1959, the lowest known round of tournament golf in history. In that round, Snead played the last seven holes in 21 strokes, seven under par. The third course, the Lakeside, was added in 1962 and has become well known among lesser golfers for some of its ball-hungry water hazards.

Not far from The Greenbrier, at a private estate called Oakhurst, five Scots began playing golf with imported sticks and gutta percha balls in 1884, four years before John Reid and his "apple tree gang," credited with having started golf in America, began golfing on a farm in Yonkers, N.Y.

By appearance and age, The Greenbrier and The Homestead are anachronisms in this day of slick, impersonal, automated resorts. Until recently, they were even hard to reach. You once had to own your own railroad car to get to either White Sulphur Springs or Hot Springs. And if your name wasn't Vanderbilt, they generally put you up in a stable.

But times have changed these spas which grew up around the mineral springs that guzzle forth all over the region. Both resorts still maintain therapeutic bath clinics, and at Greenbrier there is a diagnostic clinic for visiting executives who want checkups, where the examinations are fitted around golf starting times. In the early days the resorts were hang-outs for Southern aristocracy, from Thomas Jefferson to John C. Calhoun to Robert E Lee. When Henry Clay visited The Greenbrier in 1817, his bill for three days came to $16.51½, including room, board, grog, laundry, a dozen cigars and lodging for three horses and a servant. Today you spend that in tips. Each day. The average daily tab for a golfing couple these days totals around $130, but no one seems to mind paying it, for what he gets.

There is a good deal of rivalry between the two for convention and group business—as an important source of revenue for resorts of this size—but it's all very gentlemanly. An unwritten code exists between them that says neither will try obviously to steal clients from the other. The rivalry may have started in 1890 when J. P. Morgan and his syndicate acquired the Chesapeake & Ohio Railroad and, since it was on the rail line anyway, decided to buy The Greenbrier. But during an inspection visit, the story goes, one of Morgan's partners found that his white shoes had become mildewed by the West Virginia mists. He wanted no part of owning a hotel where such an inconvenience could occur, and vetoed the deal. The syndicate instead bought The Homestead, ran a spur into Hot Springs and canceled trains to White Sulphur Springs, a move which didn't appeal a whole lot to people at The Greenbrier. The Chesapeake & Ohio, which later did buy Greenbrier, still runs two trains a day into White Sulphur Springs, but most visitors arrive by car or plane. A new jetport is now open 12 miles from Greenbrier, and there is a small-craft airstrip next to the golf course. An airport that takes turbo props is 17 miles away from Homestead. The Homestead is now owned by a corporation whose chairman, Daniel H. H. Ingalls, is head of oriental languages at Harvard and a specialist in Sanskrit.

The two resorts possess thousands of acres of land devoted to all kinds of recreational activities besides golf. The variety of sport available is probably as much a factor in drawing guests as is the high level of the cuisine and service at the two establishments. If you're looking for evening entertainment, though, you could do better in the Chagrin Falls Public Library. On a big night there are movies (rated G, of course) in the comfortable theaters downstairs at both resorts. At The Homestead, the band is called an orchestra, and the beat at best is a fast waltz or a slow fox trot, by Meyer Davis— before, during and after dinner. At The Greenbrier, the after-dinner combo swings a little harder—but hardly enough to rock with.

At Greenbrier the only place on the premises where drinking is allowed, other than at the Golf and Tennis Club, is called the "Old White," an amiable "clubroom" with a modern combo. Things are a bit wetter at The Homestead since Virginia loosened its Blue Laws about a year ago, and cocktails are now permitted in the dining room, for the first time since 1912. Drinks are also served in The Homestead Club, a cocktail lounge, at the golf clubs and in the hotel's plush grill. Virginia has had a history of peculiar behavior over the subject of alcohol and other social disgraces. When Daniel Webster visited the place, he attended a "wine frolic" and observed to his host, "I am told that I am not popular in Virginia, and I cannot well account for it, for I am very Virginian in all my tastes and habits—I drink, I fail to pay my debts and I am not overscrupulous of my marital relations. Such qualities, I think, ought to make me very popular with Virginians."

The style at both places has always been very much ladies and gentlemen. Even today, dozens of uniformed attendants seem to lurk behind the pillars in the over-sized, well-stuffed lobbies and hallways. The places became, in time, a favored marketplace for eligible young ladies, most of whom rode side-saddle, sipped colored ice through a glass straw, and looked on the game of golf as a mild form of idiocy.

But not all of The Greenbrier ladies were so sedate. There was Alva Smith, who married a Vanderbilt and a Belmont, and was as good a choice as you could find for any women's liberation movement. (She once advised a fellow feminist, "Brace up, dear, and pray to God. *She* will help you.") There were the Langhorne sisters, one of whom, Irene, married Charles Dana Gibson and became the original Gibson girl. Nancy became Lady Astor and was on the receiving end of at least one Winston Churchill classic. "If I were your wife," spat Lady Astor, "I should put arsenic in your coffee." Growled Churchill, "And If I were your husband, madam, I should drink it."

Nor was The Homestead denied an occasional display of spirit. When Mrs. Cornelius Vanderbilt led her summer armada to Hot Springs, a New York newspaper considered her parties so vital to the national interest it sent along a writer just to cover these moving social events. At one of the parties, the American ambassador to Germany was so moved he tore off his clothes, jumped naked into the pool and had to be carried away by the bemused attendants.

If the portraits of Greenbrier and Homestead seem vaguely indistinguishable, it's not surprising. They are very much alike. The Greenbrier, with 650 rooms, is slightly larger than The Homestead, with 530 rooms, but both are huge, quiet, luxurious fortresses where people are polite, friendly but aloof; where the word service actually means something, and where the food is very, very good.

The difference is one of degree rather than kind. The Greenbrier, with its white collonades and rotondas, where Bing Crosby claimed the maid cleaned his room with a mink mop and checked for dust with a lorgnette, might be a bit grander, more ornate and blue-blooded. The Homestead, despite its colossal main lobby and bright casino club, a little more subdued, gentle and reserved. Put it another way: During World War II, when both resorts were used by the government as holding camps for enemies, the authorities, respecting if not understanding differences, put the Nazis at The Greenbrier and the Japanese at Homestead.

In the lobbies and expensive shops on the ground floors, you still see old ladies who, in much larger numbers, used to spend a month or two tottering about the hallways and sniffing the rich mountain air. Maybe they remember how it was, maybe they come back to re-live some half-remembered romance of their youth, or maybe they just don't know where else to spend the rest of their money. They look slightly confused by all the changes, and disapproving of the fuss about golf and things. And maybe, like the two resorts whose walls have stood for so long, resembling, as someone once said, a couple of great ocean liners beached among the mountains, they wonder if they are the last of their kind. ∎

GOLF IN LOS ANGELES: PART ROYAL AND ANCIENT, PART DISNEY

BY JIM MURRAY
January, 1973

Golf in and around Los Angeles tends to be—like the rest of the landscape—unreal . . . part Royal & Ancient, part Disneyland. The Good Ship Lollipop with 4-irons. You expect a director to come walking out of the woods on 18 in puttees and with his cap on backward yelling, "Cut!"

The stuffy types at Blind Brook or Old Elm or The Country Club would never understand. There's a gaudy impermanence to Golf Hollywood that would shake the walrus mustaches right off the portraits in those staid old clubs. Remember, we're talking about an area where a chain-saw manufacturer bought the London Bridge and had it shipped over to provide a crossing over desert sand. They bought the Queen Mary and turned it into a chop house. They could buy St. Andrews and stick it up at La Quinta.

You get a running start toward understanding palm-tree waterpipe golf if you listen to that old joke about the sport in Los Angeles. Seems a man named Frank

Jim Murray, one of the country's best-known and most widely read sports writers, is a syndicated columnist with the Los Angeles Times.

Rosenberg, a Texas oil man, wanted to get into Los Angeles Country Club, the West Coast version of the stodgiest and most exclusive club in the world. It is said eligibility for membership is a Hoover button, a home in Pasadena and proof-positive you never had an actor in the family. Once, when a member proposed Jimmy Roosevelt for membership, they not only blackballed the Roosevelt, they kicked out the member.

Rosenberg was rejected out of hand and the membership committeeman politely suggested he try Hillcrest. Hillcrest is a golf course which was founded by a movie man who was snubbed at a Pasadena course because of his religion. It has fewer gentiles than a kibbutz.

Rosenberg was stunned to be rejected by L.A.C.C. and he so confided to a friend. "Oh," suggested the friend, "they probably thought you were Jewish. The club is restricted."

So Rosenberg applied at Hillcrest. "Fine, we'll take your application and wait for the first opening," he was told. "Fine," said Rosenberg, "but there's one other thing I want you to know—I'm

not Jewish."

The committeeman looked at him and said softly, "Oh dear, I'm sorry. We don't admit gentiles." "Well, I'm an s.o.b.!" exploded Rosenberg. "If you can prove that," the committeeman told him, "you can get in Riviera!"

Riviera may be the most beautiful of the L.A. area courses. But it's a monster. It is the *only* Southern California golf course ever to host the Open. Hogan won it there in 1948. It's a demanding 7,100-yard, par-71 track no weekend player should be abroad on. Its rolls list mostly ruthless golfers, not card-players, not social members, but guys who can shoot in the 70s anywhere in the world.

It used to be a hustler's paradise. The stories are legendary (also libelous) of the dentists, Philippine generals, European counts, carefree movie stars and moguls who got fleeced on its not-so-broad fairways. It was Titanic Thompson country. You could get a bet on the color of the next dog coming up the fairway. It is Dean Martin's happy hunting ground as this is written and Dino is usually marauding on its tees and eucalyptus trees in division strength. It looks like Hitler's armor coming down the back side. Martin usually has three or four foursomes (or fivesomes) of pals, usually including one name pro (Devlin, Floyd, Bayer or Bolt), and the bets flow two or three holes back. Barry Jaeckel, French Open winner and son of a movie star, used to *caddie* for Dino, who has a reputation for having lost a fortune at the game. If so, he did it some time ago. Dean now is recognized around Riviera as a guy you give strokes to at your own peril. All the same, the trading is livelier among those golf cars than it is on the Paris Bourse. I know a lot of people who would like to cut 10 per cent of it and retire to the French Riviera after one season.

So, if golf is your bag, get in Riviera. They don't care what your religion or background is there. But they hope you have money and are willing to risk it. Mac Hunter, the pro there, was once considered a better prospect than Arnold Palmer and may hold the record for a club pro making cuts in the U.S. Open.

His dad won the British Amateur and his son just won the California Amateur at Pebble Beach. If a guy says he's from Riviera, be sure to say, "We'll adjust at the turn," or you may go home in a barrel.

L.A. Country Club, apart from its exclusivity, is noteworthy because it sits athwart what must be the most expensive cluster of real estate in the world. It is almost in the center of Beverly Hills and its two golf courses have nearly a mile of front footage along Wilshire Boulevard. It is a 2-iron from Saks Fifth Avenue, I. Magnin, Tiffany's and the most expensive furriers and jewelers and boutiques in the world. The Beverly Hilton Hotel hangs over it. Imagine a golf course on either side of Fifth Avenue from 38th Street to the 80s and extending for 250 acres in all directions, and you have a notion of the Big Rock Candy Mountain that is L.A.C.C. Some *countries* couldn't afford to buy it.

If Riviera is the club for golfers and L.A. the club for oil, orange and railroad barons, Bel-Air attracts the management end of the broadcast and movie media. There are more station managers, network West Coast brass and their satellite advertising agency account executives (with a sprinkling of used-car dealers) at Bel-Air than at any other club in America.

It once was a club for L.A. Country Club rejects. It, too, sits astride some of the world's richest real estate, and it used to be a sandbox for the movie rich. Bing Crosby once belonged here. Fred MacMurray, Ray Bolger, Andy Williams play here and the Show-Biz types, the *talent,* shower downstairs. The upstairs locker room is, fittingly, the executive suite. The talent *handlers* — directors, agents, press agents, producers, ad men and network veepees shower up here.

Dean Martin was a daily communicant at Bel-Air until a greens committeeman cut up the greens to "improve" the course, a venture that was to prove long and, therefore, costly, because Dino had dozens of others quit in protest at having to play temporary greens. The departure of a Dean Martin from a golf club is comparable to a nearsighted millionaire leaving a

crap game in a smoky room.

Lakeside has a charisma all its own. Here, in the salad years, the movie greats gamboled . . . Laurel and Hardy, W. C. Fields, Crosby, Hope, Jack Carson, Dennis Morgan, Gordon MacRae and Johnny Weissmueller drank here. Across the street from Warner Bros., it was a happy hunting ground for Warner's stars, who were not of the same magnitude as MGM's in those years but were a whole lot more festive. A requirement at Lakeside was that you be able to hold your booze. This was the club of the hard-drinking Irish and, the gag was, a standard for admission was that you had to be able to kill a fifth in nine holes.

Disc jockeys, industrial press agents, radio announcers *(radio!)* still dot Lakeside's membership rolls. The Old Guard is almost all gone (Buddy Rogers and Richard Arlen still play, for you trivia buffs). Only Bob Hope remains and fits in a fast nine holes on the infrequent occasions he is at home. Crosby keeps a locker but hasn't used it in years. The hard core of Lakeside is made up of guys who made it in the Big Band Era. It's THE club to belong to if you live in the lace-curtain sections of the Valley. Like Bel-Air, it has a slightly more modern step to it, as reflected in its clubhouse and dining areas. It's a golf course for the well-heeled suburban types. Unlike the mutton-chop sideburns courses like L.A., it has no trouble making the bar and restaurant pay off but, like them, its club flag is at half-mast too often these days.

Wilshire Country Club is almost in downtown L.A. This makes it accessible to judges, lawyers, business executives, railroad and bank presidents. Color it dull gray.

The city's most celebrated golfers long were Hope and Crosby. Crosby in his prime was a solid 2, but he has drifted away from the grand old game in favor of bird-shooting and game-fishing. But not before he was hitting a few practice shots off the 10th tee at Bel-Air one afternoon (Bel-Air has no practice range) and a member of the greens committee came out and stuffily ordered Der Bingle to cease and desist. Crosby looked at him with that cold look a friend once described as "Arctic blue," the look that could stave in the bow of the Titanic. And Crosby gravely packed his clubs, emptied his locker—and has not been seen at Bel-Air since. He occasionally shows up at the more raffish Lakeside (which has a practice range), where the members don't much care where or for what purpose you hit the ball. W.C. Fields was fond of playing the course sideways with his pal, Oliver Hardy. He liked being in the trees where he could drink without scandalizing the natives.

Mickey Rooney holds the unique distinction of being thrown out of Lakeside. The Mick was a solid 3 in his best days, but he was not only a club-thrower, he threw whole sets. He once played the front nine with a new set and, at the turn, junked them and bought another new one for the back nine.

Playing with Mickey is like playing in the middle of a rehearsal for a Broadway musical. Mickey will sing the score, act the parts. He will do Judy Garland and Professor Labermacher (an old Jessel routine). He showed up on the first tee one day proudly announcing that Jack Nicklaus, no less, had straightened out his swing. As he moved flawlessly through the first three holes, he purred with praise for the new set of stiff shafts he had purchased. He dispensed tips with a lavish hand for the rest of the foursome. By hole 5, the swing began to disintegrate. By hole 9, the Mick was looking darkly at his new set of clubs and beginning to question Nicklaus' credentials to be teaching golf. By the back side, Mickey was holding the clubs aloft to anyone who would listen and demanding, "I ask you! Just look at these things! Look at the hosel! How can a man play with implements like these!" If you're a Mickey Rooney fan, you're rolling behind the trees, helpless with mirth. Mickey's funnier when he's not trying to be. But the members got tired of ducking in the showers when Mickey came through looking for a game, and they told him to empty his locker.

At Hillcrest, the game is "Can-You-Top-This?" and I don't mean a golf ball. There is a table at Hillcrest that is a shrine of Show Business. George Burns, Jack Benny, George Jessel, Eddie Cantor and Al Jolson used to lunch in a shower of one-liners. Every noon was a Friar's Roast. Danny Thomas represents the Catholics at Hillcrest. In the days of the Dusenberg-Bugatti-leopard-on-a-leash Hollywood, more picture deals were set here than at neighboring Twentieth Century-Fox, which is just across the street and is gradually giving way to a high-rise subdivision. The opulence of Hillcrest is Hapsburgian. The chandeliered dining room makes the Queen Mary foyer look like a lunch counter. The Marx brothers (save for Groucho, who disapproved of golf courses because there weren't enough girls) were the best players in the comedians' flight.

Brentwood, referred to as "Hillcrest East," plays host to the newer crop of comedians—Joey Bishop, Don Rickles, Don Adams (who also belongs at Riviera) and the generation of stand-up comics who came along in the television-Las Vegas era. Brentwood is not as severe a test of golf as L.A. C.C.'s North Course or Hillcrest, but successive renovations have given its clubhouse more and more of a Taj Mahal look.

Brentwood is important historically, because it was to have been the site of the 1962 PGA. The California attorney general threatened legal action because of the PGA's "Caucasian only" clause, and the PGA in 1961 jerked the tournament to friendlier climes at Aronomink in Philadelphia. But later in '61 the offending phrase was removed from the by-laws and the way was paved on tour for the Charlie Siffords, Lee Elders and George Johnsons.

Los Angeles probably has more "celebrity" tournaments per square foot than any golfing area in the world. Any golfing actor worth his marquee value would rather be caught without his makeup on camera than without a favorite charity. As Jerry Lewis once complained, "By the time I arrived, all the diseases were taken." George Jessel once observed that all that was left for the newcomers was gonorrhea. Chuck Connors has

a tournament. A Tim Conway, a Bob Stack and even character actors have tournaments of their own. Even the tour fixtures have reached out to embrace celebrities. The venerable L.A. Open was the last to capitulate and become the "Glen Campbell L.A. Open." The slightly less venerable San Diego Open is now the Andy Williams SDO. The celebrities trade guest appearances at each other's tournaments, and the star power attracts the Kansas City wheat merchant to pay out a grand to tee it up with some crooner or TV tough guy in the pro-am.

Humphrey Bogart, it may surprise you to know, was very nearly a scratch golfer. Once a journalist drinking buddy of his put this reputation down to side-of-the-mouth braggadocio. Bogey, who rarely made one, took his pal down to Tamarisk and proceeded to rip off an impeccable 73 after not playing for two months.

It's a game for all seasons in California. You can play golf 365 days a year. Every private club is awash with entertainment giants and sports greats. You might bump into a Jerry West (but not in the rough) at Riviera or a Jim Brown at Western Avenue (a flat muni-type club where the membership is largely black). The Dodgers' Don Sutton will be at Oakmont in the off-season, as will half the franchise. The Rams are addicts.

It's not a game uniquely suited to a community famed for its happy endings. John Wayne ducked the game throughout his career, even though his whole stock company, including Grant Withers and Ward Bond and Forrest Tucker, was scattered around Lakeside, where Wayne had a membership. The official reason was that "a golf ball just isn't Duke's size." The screenwriter, James Edward Grant, had a better explanation: "How could a guy who won the West, recaptured Bataan and won the battle of Iwo Jima let himself be defeated by a little hole in the ground?" ∎

MONTEREY: HOW I WAS SEDUCED BY A PENINSULA

BY CAL BROWN
January, 1971

In the Bible it says that God made the world in six days and on the seventh, rested. But I think that on the seventh day he created the Monterey Peninsula. There cannot be another place on earth quite like it, nor another place that has three golf courses of such quality in so small a space.

It is as though every thundering emotion, every subtle line had been withheld from the rest of creation and then dumped in this one place to test our understanding of the superlative. One's response to this angular chunk of land, shaped like the snout of a rhinoceros and jutting into the Pacific about 90 miles south of San Francisco, is instant and elemental. Even on a gray, overcast day or during a winter storm, it is compelling and seductive.

Hills and craggy bluffs tumble into the sea which ebbs and crashes against copper-brown rocks, casting huge white plumes and mist into the air above dozing seals and an occasional solitary beachcomber. Gray-boled and winter-green cypress trees cling to the soil in clumps or in stark individuality, bent and twisted by the wind and spray. Here and there the headland splashes down into uneven, white-faced dunes. Surmounting everything is a sense of quiet, a curious intimation of settled spirit on the raging coast.

Here are three of the world's greatest golf courses, and how could they be otherwise? Their names alone stir the juices—Pebble Beach, legendary and rugged; Cypress Point, shy and mysterious, a splendidly proportioned and artful mistress; and Spyglass Hill, diabolical, controversial and maddening in its newness.

Within 5,200 acres of private land

known as the Del Monte Forest, the late Samuel F. B. Morse founded and developed some of the most expensive real estate and one of the most magnificent resorts in the world. The Del Monte property is encircled by a 17-mile drive over which visitors may travel, at $3 per car. No overnight camping is permitted, and no plant or animal may be "disturbed, injured or removed." Deer roam freely through the forest and across the golf courses.

There are signs of stress on this priceless plot of ground. One hears grumbling about pollution in Monterey Bay, and about segregation in public accommodations (including golf courses). Someone at Del Monte has allowed a house to be built behind the fifth green at Spyglass Hill which, while architecturally impressive, intrudes on the natural beauty of the hole. But with few such exceptions, there is little to remind one that life is anything but a succession of esthetic fulfillments and magnificent golf holes.

PEBBLE BEACH — Rugged

Like many of our greatest courses, Pebble Beach was designed by amateurs. Jack Neville and Douglas Grant, both California amateur champions, laid out the 6,777-yard course in 1919. It has held three national amateur championships, the first in 1929. That was the year Johnny Goodman, then an unknown, came out from Omaha to beat Bobby Jones in the first round. The winner was unheralded Harrison Johnston of Minnesota, who bested a field that included Francis Ouimet, Chick Evans, Lawson Little, Chandler Egan and Cyril Tolley. In 1947 the cast included Dick Chapman, Bud Ward, Smiley Quick, Bob Rosburg and Frank Stranahan, but the winner was Skee Riegel who walked like a fighter and played like a machine, smoking two packs of cigarettes per round, to beat Johnny Dawson in the finals. In 1961, Jack Nicklaus took the second of his amateur crowns here, beating Dudley Wysong 8 and 6 in the final.

Pebble Beach opens like a lamb, with four easy, very ordinary holes. The fifth is a short, quick thrust up

through a sliver of light between the trees and then, suddenly, you are upon the ocean riding two terrifying shots along the crest of a massive bluff to the sixth green. To the right, nothing but emptiness and, far below, thrashing surf and rocks.

The sixth hole, a 515-yard par-5 that Byron Nelson thinks is the toughest hole on the course, begins a stretch of five of the most spectacular holes in golf, three of them on a narrow, craggy spit that overhangs the ocean. The seventh is a tiny, 120-yard downhill pitch that looks almost like a miniature golf hole. But when the wind blows, it can require a solid 4-iron into the gale. The eighth is a marvel, one of the great two-shotters in the world. After a blind tee shot to a plateau, you are faced with hitting 180 yards over a sheer cliff, across a chasm that resembles a shark's maw and to a green that is pitched into a depression and completely surrounded by bunkers.

The ninth stretches 450 yards along the ocean, its right margin eaten away by the surf. When the wind is up, the biggest hitters cannot get home even with two wood shots. During the 1963 Crosby, Dale Douglass took 19 blows here after landing on the steep bank, an even worse place to be than the rocky beach below.

There are many who believe the inland stretch from 11 through 16 is inferior and not at all in keeping with the hair-raising ocean holes. This is only partially true. Certainly 11 and 12 are routine holes, but 13, a straightaway par-4 of 400 yards, is perhaps the most underrated hole on the course. The second shot must fly true to avoid bunkers and trees guarding the green.

The 14th is a marvelously deft par-5 that curls away from the sea to the right and has been the scene of a few miserable encounters. Here Arnold Palmer, who has never won the Crosby, came a cropper in 1964. In going for the green on his second shot, Palmer hit a tree on the right and went out of bounds twice. He made nine on the hole and dropped from contention. The next day, a storm knocked the tree down.

The 17th, a par-3 surrounded by

sand and ocean, looks more beatable in real life than it appears on television—until you play it. The 18th, a journey that ends happily only after three very strong shots and two good putts, is among the most ballyhooed finishing holes in golf, and quite rightly.

SPYGLASS HILL — Maddening

Spyglass Hill is a Robert Trent Jones layout that opened in 1966 and ever since has been the target of strong words. Most of the abuse comes from touring pros, who are not accustomed to shooting in the 80s.

Spyglass, in its youthful striving for greatness, is too new to be finally judged. Several things about it are evident, though. It is ruthlessly tough and on windy days almost impossible. In 1970 it was rated at 76.1 from the back tees (6,972 yards) but it has never been played in competition over its full length.

The course record is 70, two under par, made by Forrest Fezler, a California amateur who played the ball "as it lies." The best professional score in competition was also 70, made by Bob Murphy in the 1968 Crosby. But he played from the middle tees (6,609 yards, which carries a rating of 74.1), and was improving his lies.

"People can't believe it's so tough," chortles Spyglass Hill's home professional, Frank Thacker. "The first five holes are more a case of fright than anything else." The first hole sweeps 604 yards through the pines down to the ocean, and the next four holes are played on the dunes from one island of grass to the next. The second, though a lay-up hole, is nevertheless an appealing two-shotter that wants a thoughtful golfer and is, for the medium hitter, a fearsome journey past waist-high spikes of pampas grass. The third and fifth are land-locked par-3s sandwiched around the par-4 fourth, a partially blind hole.

These psychological thrillers are among the easier holes. Once the course turns inland it gets narrower and longer, and your breath and shoulder turn get shorter. Spyglass Hill's greens are huge, and you can three-putt all day long. Putts of 150 feet are possible. A lot of the criticism of the course centers around the greens, which have since been remodeled. The first time the course was used in the Crosby, on the 14th hole, a gem of a par-5 with an angled green perched on the left above a pond, one of the contestants putted off the green and into the water. On the same green, Jack Nicklaus

once four-putted from 14 feet.

Is Spyglass tougher than Pebble Beach? Probably. Not long ago two doctors teed off at Spyglass Hill with three dozen golf balls between them and had to send the caddie in for a new supply after six holes. But though Spyglass is rated a stroke tougher, it lacks the wild, undisciplined spirit of Pebble Beach. Spyglass is a more refined article, with a harder, more sculptured look than either of the other two courses here. Jones was not given the kind of elemental terrain with which to work that is to be found at Pebble and Cypress, yet he has made a great deal of what he was given. One suspects that it is a course whose character is exposed more deeply the more it is played.

CYPRESS POINT — Artful

"If I were condemned to play only one course for the rest of my life, I would unhesitatingly pick Cypress Point."

So says Joe Dey, former executive director of the USGA and now commissioner of the Tournament Players' Division of the PGA. Dey, no mean judge of golf courses, is not alone in this choice. Golfers fortunate enough to play this little masterpiece more often than not come away feeling that Cypress

The early morning rays on the 18th hole at Pebble Beach set an irresistible mood of golf on Monterey Peninsula.

Point is more fun to play than any other on the peninsula.

Its length alone—6,464 yards—makes it the easiest of the three Crosby courses. Still, the course record is the same as at Pebble Beach, 65, set by Bill Nary in the 1949 Crosby. Ben Hogan shot the course in 63 during a practice round in 1947 for the unofficial mark.

The course was conceived in 1926 by Marion Hollins, the women's national amateur champion of 1921, and Roger Lapham, who was president of the California Golf Ass'n and a member of the USGA executive committee. They bought property from Del Monte and commissioned Alister MacKenzie to design the course. MacKenzie, a Scot and former doctor in the British Army, later did the Augusta National course in Georgia with Bobby Jones.

Cypress is strictly a golf club, and its members are *golfers*. There are no pools, tennis courts or other distractions. Non-members are not permitted in the clubhouse, even during the Crosby tournament. For years the pros had to change their shoes outside. Now a separate room has been added for this purpose.

The use of golf cars is discouraged as are other modern frills. The caddies here—many having plied the trade for 40 years—are considered by some visitors the best in the world. When you tee it up at Cypress Point, the game is on.

The first hole is a lazy dogleg to the right and, at 407 yards, long enough to loosen the muscles. Until recently the tee shot had to negotiate an old, dead pine tree that blew down in a storm and had been called "Joe DiMaggio"—it caught everything. The second is a properly menacing par-5 of 544 yards that angles left and thus courts the gambling tee shot. The third is a slender one-shot hole, no more than a middle iron, the fourth a shortish par-4 that carries you deep into the woods past little bands of deer and half a dozen beautifully placed bunkers. The fifth, a short par-5, 490 yards, swoops left abruptly up a hill literally covered with bunkers to a tiny green on top.

By the time you reach the sixth hole you are caught up in the pure joy of the place. You feel that every shot is just what you always knew golf should be. Soon you are heading toward the distant ocean over the rugged dunes from holes eight through 13. At 15, a mere 139 yards, you play across a narrow gorge where the water boils angrily as it cuts its way into the cliff. The ball must reach the putting surface, for there are trees, sand and clutching ice plant all around. The ice plant, thick, fleshy stuff, is like trying to escape from a vat of marshmallow.

Then comes the 16th, which has been called the ultimate test of golfing courage. From the back tees it is 233 yards of carry across the Pacific to a large green on the tip of the point. The average golfer must lay up short to the fairway on the left and then pitch to the green. Only on windless days do the pros try for it. The late Porky Oliver made 16 after going in the water four times, and Henry Ransom picked up after 16 attempts to move his shot from the beach up the sheer cliff to the green. Another pro, Hans Merrill, has the all-time record of 19. He made it all on the same ball, going from ice plant to ice plant for nearly half an hour.

The 17th is another heroic hole, a par-4 that runs along the cliff for 375 yards to a green that lurks behind a fat, sprawling cypress tree. The tee, set next to the 16th green on the point, looks into the cliff and you can take as much of the barrier as you like. Once in the fairway you must play either left or right of the tree and stop the ball very quickly. You can easily hit over it—and just as easily into it. Jimmy Demaret once played this hole in the wind by hitting two drives; he aimed the second out over the ocean and let it blow back.

After the excitement of the ocean holes, the 18th is a soft dissolve swinging gently up through scattered trees to a flagstick silhouetted against the sky next to the clubhouse, of simple Spanish California style that looks so natural on the site it seems to have grown there among the cypress trees.

Opinion about a golf course can be a fragile thing. But taken all as a

The heroic 17th at Cypress Point (above) plays from the tee, center foreground, across the ocean 375 yards along the cliffs to the green, framed in the distance by two bunkers and jagged rocks. Right, the cleverly fashioned second hole at Spyglass Hill (seen from the tee) is, for the average hitter, a short but menacing prospect.

piece, the Monterey Peninsula and its golf courses are something to behold. There is enough variety to sate the most demanding golfing spirit. It is a special place where the tendons and mind can stretch on equal terms. In fact, if Heaven isn't like Pebble Beach, I won't be going. ■

THE COURSE JACK BUILT: IT'S ALL DOWNHILL

BY LARRY DENNIS
August, 1974

"Golf," says Jack Nicklaus, "is a much better game played downhill than uphill. It's more visual and more fun."

A downhill golf course, then, is what Nicklaus has constructed at Muirfield Village in the rolling woodlands of central Ohio. Because of elevated tees and deep valleys, there are only three uphill drives on the course—and they don't seem to be uphill.

Built specifically for tournament golf, the course winds through deep woods with an amazing variety of trees, including the second largest bitternut in the state of Ohio. Occasionally it breaks into the open with flattish holes that pitch and roll, reminiscent of a seaside links. Three streams run through the property, bringing water into play on 15 holes and forming the valleys which helped Nicklaus create a course that is virtually an 18-hole amphitheater.

Spectators can view almost every hole from the hills above. Jack contends, "This course can accommodate more people and provide more viewing opportunities than any course I've ever seen." On the 18th, for example, 20,000 can see the action from the surrounding hillsides.

When necessary Nicklaus gave nature a hand. "You elevate an area and fit the green into it. You get instant background and maturity. It takes more money and dirt, but you don't have to wait 15 years for a golf course."

Instant maturity he has achieved, and with it perhaps instant greatness.

The idea was born during the 1966 Masters on the veranda of Augusta National, where Nicklaus was sitting with Ivor Young, a

The gorgeous over-the-water 12th hole, Jack Nicklaus' own favorite, is shown at top from the horseshoe-shaped member's tee (it plays at 141 yards from there and at 158 from the elevated championship tee). The delightful 15th below is a short (482 yards), straight par-5 with a narrow fairway running up and down over hills and through valleys. A dry creek bed, heavy rough and huge bunkers guard the green's front and make going for it in two a calculated risk.

long-time friend from Columbus. "I thought the Masters was a great thing for golf and I'd like to do the same thing in Columbus," Nicklaus recalls. "I wanted the finest course we could have, to house a major tournament and to be of service to the game. I told Ivor to go back and buy some land."

Indeed, Muirfield Village Golf Club may become home to the Masters of the North. There will be a tournament, beginning in 1976, probably during Memorial Day week. "I don't want just another tour tournament." Nicklaus says. The gods of tournament golf frown on invitationals, but it is safe to assume that Nicklaus will get his Masters.

"I hope this course is to Jack Nicklaus what Augusta National was to Bobby Jones," Nicklaus says. "The course is a reflection of what has happened in my life, of what golf means to me. I guess you'd have to say it's my mark, or at least closer to it than anything I've ever done. I don't like the word 'monument,' but it's my showplace, what I feel the game of golf should be."

Nicklaus deliberately did not name the course itself, hoping it will earn one by reputation. It likely will. It is a par-72 layout, at its inception 6,983 yards from the back tees (6,466 from the member tees) but playing shorter because of the elevated teeing areas. There is more premium on placement than strength, although strength is sometimes required. "It's not necessary to have to stand and beat it all the time," Nicklaus says. "Golf is played with the head as well as the swing."

The fairways of Seaside and Astoria bent grass are wide enough in most cases so the drive is not severely threatened by the thick bluegrass and fescue rough. The second shot makes stricter demands. The greens artfully twist, redan fashion, into hillsides and behind streams and man-made lakes, and they are guarded by some of the 72 traps that dot the course. The Toronto bent putting surfaces range in size from about 3,000 to 7,000 square feet ("They're not turf nurseries," Nicklaus smiles) and are subtly contoured and sloped.

Muirfield is a fair course; blind situations are few and there are no gimmicks. Nicklaus believes there always should be an option, a way to go other than the most dangerous.

All the par-5s can be reached in two shots—including the 549-yard seventh with a trailing wind —but not without flirting with water and heavy rough that will penalize a mis-struck shot. The most delightful hole on the course might be the 482-yard 15th, straight as an arrow but narrow, up and down hills to an elevated green protected by traps and heavy grass.

The set of enchanting par-3s is relatively short, ranging from 158 to 200 yards, but each hole is testing. The 174-yard eighth, completely surrounded by sand, and the 12th are particularly charming and treacherous.

The first, second, 17 and 18th holes are laid out to play with the prevailing wind, on the theory that a player is entitled to a chance at a good start and a good finish. When the wind does not blow that way, about one day in four, only the fittest will survive.

The course is not without faults. Nicklaus thinks there may be too much water and may eliminate some. Because of the elevated tees, some of the par-4s came up too short for the long-hitting tourists. But there is room for more length, and it will be added where needed. Nicklaus makes thousands of dollars worth of changes every time he comes to town, and it is safe to assume this course never will be finished.

"No great golf course was ever right at the start," Jack declares. "Golf courses aren't built . . . they evolve."

Nicklaus brings to course design the same qualities of insight, concentration and determination that have made him perhaps the greatest player in history. His Golforce, Inc., team works by a concept that blends design, construction, maintenance and management under one roof. He is spending more time at this than any other activity except playing— a couple of days every week or so building Muirfield alone. It is plainly his bag.

"I love it," Jack declares. "My golf game will be here only a certain number of years and then it will leave me. I've always dreaded the day I'll be finished, with nothing to do. I've seen other athletes in that situation, and I don't want to be there. I don't want to be a club pro, but I've always wanted to stay in golf."

Nicklaus admits to admiring and being influenced by several course designers—by Donald Ross, who built the Scioto course in Columbus on which Jack grew up . . . by Alister Mackenzie who did Cypress Point, Augusta National and the Ohio State University courses where Jack played college golf . . . by Dick Wilson . . . and by Pete Dye and Desmond Muirhead, with whom he has worked. But Nicklaus by all accounts is his own man with his own theories.

"You use what you have, taking advantage of natural beauty when you can," he says. "Most people don't realize you build a course for a purpose. You must consider the property, the type of play the course will have, and the budget. It's not hard to build a great golf course on land like this—on good property with an unlimited budget. The key is the routing of the holes. But if you take bad land and a half-million dollar budget and can accomplish what the course is supposed to be, then you're a great architect."

Nicklaus also believes it's important to build a course the members can enjoy. Challenging the tournament player, accommodating the spectator and keeping the member happy were his goals at Muirfield. Nicklaus succeeded, although not without considerable cost. When he and a club member named Tom Weiskopf officially opened the course with a Memorial Day exhibition, a total of $1.6 million already had been spent on the golf course alone. That makes it probably the most expensive golfing playground ever built, and even Nicklaus admits, "We've gone a little past practicality."

Just to keep everything in perspective, when Nicklaus the player challenged Nicklaus the architect in the opening-day exhibition, he went around in an immaculate 66, unclawed by his own tiger. ∎

THE LIGHT TOUCH

Good golf humor is a rare literary achievement, delightful to read but difficult to write. What seems amusing when it happens on a golf course often falls flatter than a double bogey when set down in words or artwork. But not always. *Golf Digest* has been fortunate over the past quarter century to present a number of humorous essays, verses and cartoons that not only have tickled the readers but have stood the serious test of time.

We have called upon distinguished authors such as Henry Longhurst of Great Britain, whose discourse on the putting yips is reprinted in this section and whose work is spiced with a droll British humor, tempered by an obvious devotion to golf. And we have asked for and received a more jugular approach from Don Rickles, the night-club and television insult specialist, who roasts the touring pros with a tongue-in-cheek putdown.

Some of our best material comes unsolicited. Over 1,000 pieces of mail arrive in our offices each year bearing humorous (sometimes) fiction, parodies, verses, cartoons. Usually they are sent to share personal experiences with us and other readers, rather than for the express purpose of making money. All are read. Often they see the light of print.

Such an over-the-transom success was Ted Barnett, who was just out of Dartmouth when he brightened our year in 1952 with the fable of Slamming Suki Sukiyuki, reprinted in this section. Barnett wrote under the pseudonym of Lawrence Theodore Jr. (you'll have to ask him why). His essay was accepted as a hilarious spoof by us and most of our readers, but later that year we received a harrumphing letter from an official of the Royal and Ancient Golf Club in Scotland, questioning its authenticity.

Barnett, or rather Theodore, followed a few months later with the tale of Pieter Van Schuyler, the gorilla trained to hit a golf ball 400 yards. Pieter's only problem was that he hit it 400 yards whether he was on the tee or on the putting green. The story became so popular that Jack Paar related it a decade later on his network television show. And only this year, TV comedian Flip Wilson brought it out again on *his* show.

Inevitably, the best of the outpouring of humor into our offices wound up in two bound volumes. The first one, in 1957, was called *Fun in the Rough,* edited by Howard R. Gill Jr., publisher of *Golf Digest.* Fifteen years later, contributing editor Larry Sheehan edited the book *Best Golf Humor From Golf Digest,* which included artistic representation from two of our most durable cartoon contributors, David Harbaugh and Ed Lepper, both featured in this book.

Golf is, after all, a game, meant to be enjoyed and give pleasure (it isn't an exercise in advance calculus or World War III). We trust that the articles reprinted here will rekindle the warm glow of laughter that greeted their initial appearance.

SLAMMING SUKI SUKIYUKI

BY LAWRENCE THEODORE JR.
July, 1952

There was a Japanese golf professional at the swank Hamilton Country Club in Bombay, India, who caused more of a furor in international golfing circles, until his untimely death in 1924, than any Bobby Jones or Walter Hagen.

Suki Sukiyuki Jr., known to his fans as "Slamming Suki," was probably the only golfer in history to win a major golf championship right-handed one year, and left-handed the next. He accomplished this remarkable feat in capturing the British Open in 1919 and 1920.

The bright star of Suki's fame faded, however, when his unparalleled triumphs were disallowed by the sacrosanct Royal and Ancient Golf Club on the grounds that he had employed to his own advantage a type of follow-through not sanctioned in British play. This follow-through, not uncommon among Asiatic golfers, consisted of striking the ball twice in a single swing, but with such great speed that to the unaided eye it appeared to be but a single stroke. Slow–motion movies brought the fact to light, however, and thus Suki's record-smashing 275 in 1920, his left-handed year, was actually 550.

Born the son of well-to-do peasants in the Honshu province of Japan, Suki spent his early childhood in the Honshu tradition—breeding goldfish and skiing the slopes of Mt. Fujiyama. Suki Sr., however, soon realized that his young son was in need of schooling of a more formal nature than was then available in Honshu, and sent him post-haste to a private school in Tokyo. One day a group of boys from the school went out to the Imperial Links to see a golfing exhibition by the famous Duncan MacPhee, who was then on a world-wide barnstorming tour. From that day forward Suki was a slave to gutta percha and hickory. His wealthy parents had him outfitted and arranged to have him take instruction from Tama Shanti, the dour Japanese champion. This was unfortunate in that Shanti was an exponent of the aforementioned illegal follow-through. Suki, for his part, was an apt pupil and within nine months had officially taken Shanti to the cleaners, becoming the new champion of all Japan—a title he never relinquished.

Seeking new fields to conquer, Suki entered the Chinese Closed, at Hong Kong, in 1910. It was there that he inadvertently discovered his amazing ambidexterity. On the 18th hole of the final round, and needing but a triple bogey to win, Suki was in trouble. He had hooked his drive into a rice paddy, blasted out and into a small forest of yew trees, and, on his third shot, rolled up tight against the right side of a small ornamental pagoda. His cushion was fast deflating. The hot Chinese sun was pouring down. Suki took off his pith helmet and mopped his sloping brow. What to do?

He assayed the impossible lie, his grinning opponent, and the green some 290 yards away. Smiling thoughtfully, he drew from his bag an adjustable club which some admirer had given him after the Japanese Open the year before, as a kind of good luck piece. Now was certainly the time for it! Setting it for a left-handed driving-iron position, he wound up and struck. The shot was one of those low screamers, straight as a chopstick, that begins to rise slowly and then almost ascends to the heavens. The direction was true, the distance was perfect, and Suki had holed out, left-handed, from almost 300 yards away. This became the famous "Pagoda Shot" and heralded a new era for "Slamming Suki" Sukiyuki.

After Hong Kong, Suki dropped out of competition for six weeks, bought himself a set of left-handed clubs and practiced intently. He found that left-handed he was just as proficient as right-handed, if not more so. He decided to enter the Shanghai Open and play strictly left-handed. He won, going away.

After garnering every conceivable Far Eastern trophy, Slamming Suki made plans to sail for England where competition was stiffer. This project was, however, postponed by World War I.

With the close of the War, Slamming Suki made good on his plan for a tour of the British Isles. He arrived in England early in 1919, just in time for the Ulster Open. Suki immediately became the darling of the galleries. He was physically unprepossessing, but his toothy grin, owl eyes behind thick, black horn-rimmed glasses, and of course his booming shots with either hand, captivated the golfing public.

1919 was a year that will not soon be forgotten by those who know golf. It was, of course, the year of Suki's "Big Sweep" of British golf. He won the British Open right-handed, the Irish Sweepstakes left-handed, the Scotch Lowball right-handed, and, to cap everything, the Welsh P.G.A. Championship alternating left- and right-handed strokes.

Suki's fame was unparalleled. He was feted in all of the golfing capitals of the British Isles.

Soon after the 1920 Open, however, the shocking truth of the "double hit" technique which had led to Slamming Suki's amazing successes was bared to the world via the slow-motion camera. After returning his many laurels to assorted second place winners, Suki packed his bag, took his two sets of clubs, and set sail for Bombay, India, and the Hamilton Country Club. He was disillusioned and vowed never again to set foot in the Western World.

Suki remained at Hamilton, as professional in residence, until one sad day in 1925. He was in the Bombay station waiting for a train to Karachi, where he was to defend his Indian Invitational title. Becoming impatient, he stepped on the track to see if the train was coming. He was instantly struck on the left side by the incoming express and hurled to the next track where he was struck on the right side by an outgoing local. Thus Slamming Suki Sukiyuki died as he had lived —ambidextrously. ∎

Lawrence Theodore Jr. is the pseudonym of a creative man whose affection for golf has endured many facets of his career. Formerly an advertising agency executive on the West Coast, he is now in the real estate business in suburban Chicago.

GOOD OLD DAYS AROUND THE CADDIE SHACK

BY AL BARKOW
September, 1965

My introduction to golf began on a warm, motionless, lonely, school's-out summer day when I was 13. A pal said I could make some money carrying someone's golf clubs. Fine, I thought. I'll make enough to buy a pair of baseball spikes and a fielder's mitt.

On that summer day I found my way out of the brick and stone of Chicago to suburban Tam O'Shanter C.C. and entered a world of unbelievably clean green grass on which men walked wearing red pants and white shoes, and little white caps with the tops cut out of them. It was a polite, gentle world where, if you were in someone's way, they shouted "fore," instead of "look out, buddy." Soon after, Ben Hogan replaced Stan Hack in my idol room, and the money I made went for golf clubs, shoes, tees, balls, greens fees and entry to amateur tournaments.

On that first day I was directed to a tall, stern, white-haired man called the caddiemaster.

"What do you want, son?"

"I want to caddie."

"Ever caddie before?"

"No."

"No, sir."

"Nosir."

"You're a little small, but I'll give you a try. Go wait up at the caddie shack until you're called."

He pointed to a white house on a hill overlooking a creek. Up there fellows were swinging golf clubs and chipping golf balls towards a hole someone had dug with a heel of his shoe. A branch was sticking in the hole. They were betting on who could get closest to the hole in one shot, and talking in terms of fade, and hook, and Texas wind

Al Barkow is a freelance writer, and author of the book, *Golf's Golden Grind.* He was first exposed to golf as a caddie at Tam O'Shanter Country Club in suburban Chicago.

ball, like Demaret, whoever he was.

Soon, myself and a few other sunstruck neophytes were herded down to the second green, where the caddiemaster was waiting. It was the first golf green I had ever seen, and I couldn't believe it was made of grass. Fresh from the city streets, the only grass I knew was those strips of chained-off straggle that separate the apartment buildings from the asphalt street; those little havens for the neighborhood's dogs. This soft, smooth surface I was kneeling beside was a rug. I was afraid to touch it for fear I'd make it dirty.

But there was the caddiemaster, walking all over it, with spiked shoes yet.

With the caddiemaster was a deeply tanned fellow of 15 or 16, wearing a neat white cap and a very confident half-smile on his face. He was a regular caddie, and as the caddiemaster instructed us on golf course behavior, this fellow demonstrated. How calm, poised and easy he was as he walked all over that fine carpet. He must have remembered to wipe his feet.

"The caddie whose player gets the ball on the green first must take the pin. . . . Never walk in a player's line. . . . The man furthest from the hole putts first. . . . Hold the pin and flag together so the flag doesn't flutter. . . ."

Some touchy guys, these golfers.

"Stand on the same side of the hole as your shadow. . . . Clean the club off before putting it back in the bag. . . . Keep the balls clean. . . . See that white box with the stick in the middle?"

We looked towards the first tee.

"It's got a brush and water in it. You wash golf balls in it. It's a ball washer."

Ahhh, that's what it is.

"Never make a sound when your player is hitting. . . . Always keep up with your player. . . . Never fall behind. . . . All right, lad, pick up that bag and carry it to the clubhouse."

He was looking right at me. I jumped up, hugged the bag of clubs to my chest with both arms, and began to waddle away like a duck. I didn't get very far.

"You expect to walk four miles holding a golf bag like that?"

The lean, bored, regular caddie took the bag from me with one of those grins the experienced have for their inferiors.

"Take the underside of the long strap in the bottom of your right hand. . . . Swing the bag up and lay the strap onto your right shoulder. . . . Move the bag horizontally along your backside. . . . Hold the clubheads so they don't bang against each other. . . . Don't forget it."

I didn't.

So now there was a new order in my life. I didn't even know how much money I would be paid when I did caddie, but every morning, early, I was out of the house and off to the course. Under my arm was a brown paper bag filled with two or three thick sandwiches, an apple, a peach, and some raisins. My mother never fully understood what I was doing on a "gulf" course, but she understood hunger.

A singular, special delight on an early summer morning is the quiet of the city, and the cool morning air that tickles your skin. A kid on a new adventure, alert to new sensations, enjoys it, and remembers it well. I was off to the golf course. The bus would get me to the end of the line, and I would hitchhike the rest of the way, aided by a new golf cap, wide, baggy, nonadjustable, and oversized. What fear could a grown-up driver of an automobile have for the likes of an 80-pound bag of small bones wearing a hat that flopped over his ears like a generous portion of whipped cream?

Each caddie had a number, the size of which was in direct

proportion to his experience. My first number was 395. Out of 400. The number was on a badge, bought for 50 cents and was worn on the shirt. It marked your standing in the society of caddies clearly, and without hesitation. I was suddenly a "flytrap," a caddie who can't find the ball, steps on it when he does, and usually walks through a sand trap instead of around it. How else could I be classified as No. 395?

But I made progress. I memorized words like "flange," "hit it stiff," "looper," which is a caddie, "birdie," and "hit it on the toe." Good words, and bad ones. And as soon as I heard them I tried to use them. I wanted to belong. Occasionally, I left myself open for a hail of criticism.

I found that my player was two up with two holes to go. Flushed and cocky, I told my fellow loopers, three wise, experienced 17-year-olds, that "my man is stymied in his match."

Did they give it to me good. I was laughed at and derided, sneered at and smirked upon. "He's dormie, flytrap. Stymie is when he has a tree in front of his ball, or a dumb caddie like you."

I learned.

It wasn't very long before the inevitable happened: I became a golfer. A neighbor gave me some old wooden-shafted clubs and one of those stiff, narrow, round canvas bags.

I couldn't put the clubs down. In the house I was making shreds of the family rugs while "working on my swing," and spotting the ceilings with thin black streaks. Now, along with the brown bag of sandwiches and fruit every morning was included a golf club and a pocket full of Po-Dos, Air-Flights and Cincinnati Tool Steels. Waiting time at the caddie shack was now spent "hitting shots towards that makeshift hole."

I hit balls down the long rough of the second hole, and entered the contest, and lost, to the other caddies. At the end of the day's caddying I was back up to the shack for more practice.

There were very few jocks, loopers, bag-rats, and flytraps who didn't play the game. Often, after caddying all day, we would walk down the road to a public course (a housing development, now) and play nine holes, sometimes 18, before the light went out. Many times we putted out on the last green with the hole illuminated by matches.

We always made sure we caddied over the weekend, the busiest days, because that qualified us to be in on the most important day of our week, Monday—caddie day.

What an opportunity! We didn't mind that we had to be off the course by noon, or that the markers were positioned way ahead of the regular teeing ground, or that the pins were set way in front to save the biggest part of the greens. We had a chance to play off impeccable turf amid the rich splendor of the country club. Enough!

Some of us dressed to the teeth for the occasion. Despite the soaking dew, we wore our best slacks, and if we had to roll up our cuffs, so what, we could show off our new argyle socks, bought in the pro shop for the price of a round of caddying. We were playing at the country club, after all.

And if the shoulders of our finest white golfing shirt became black-striped by the end of the day because we had to carry our own bag, it was ignored. Ma could wash it out.

The next day, or even that afternoon, we shucked off the fancy clothes, put aside the golf clubs, and returned to work.

"Who's bag you got?"

"Big John O."

"How come you always get the good bags?"

"I happen to be a very good jocko."

"I got two ladies."

"See you next week."

Who were some of these caddies? Some were my peers, contemporaries who caddied and earned money and scholarships to go to college and become engineers, metallurgists, salesmen, professional golfers. Others were older men, professional caddies, who travelled north and south, as the weather dictated, making their living toting golf bags.

The professional caddies were a colorful crew. There were men like Swede, an amiable, sleepy-eyed hulk who got the best bags at the course. A huge, rotund man, his abdomen swelled out from just below his Adam's apple, reaching a point in space that denied him sight of his feet, then curved gracefully back in to join the top of his thighs. He always held his head high, Swede did, perhaps to keep himself in balance. He caddied every day of the season, made a ton of money, and used it all to drink a tun of beer every night. Swede never had a harsh word for anyone. So long as he got his bags during the day, and bagged at night, he was happy.

A caddie at Tam O'Shanter during the '50s was double lucky. He was in on the ground floor during the years of the Tam All-American and World's Championship of Golf tournaments. As thousands of people stormed the gates, paying hard cash to get in, we caddies walked in free, our ticket the white tee shirt with "Tam O'Shanter" written across the front. We had "open sesame" to the wildest, most exciting two weeks of the golfing year.

The World was the first of the really big money tournaments in professional golf. Actually, there were four tournaments at once, each at 72 holes of medal play. There was a men's and a women's pro event, and a men's and a women's amateur tournament. It was an extravaganza in the real sense of that overworked word. It was carnival time. Everybody was there trying to knock over the prizes. There was Joe Switzer, the licorice king, who handed out his product to one and all, and played a pretty fine game of amateur golf at the same time. There was a mystery golfer, who played with a hood on, and pros with strange names such as Ugo Grappasoni and Flory Van Donck. And of course there was Babe Zaharias and Patty Berg, and Vic Ghezzi, and Johnny Bulla, and Sam Snead, and Byron Nelson, and Bobby Locke, and it went on and on.

There was George May, the promoter, who walked around the course betting the pros a hundred dollars they couldn't hit an open green with a wedge from 10 yards out, and paying off on the spot when they made the easy shot. And, of course, there were the people. A huge, moiling mass who roared mightily at the play, and left behind an ocean of hotdog wrappers, broken umbrellas, scorecards, and smashed grass.

While the galleries raced for position to watch the shots, we caddies walked to the front, right next to the very ball that was being played, and talked with, worked for, and advised these stars of the show —these pros. The caddies with the most rounds, or loops, got first choice of bag, and so on down the line. Those who worked hard all year and took no time off to play a little golf of their own got the top bags. They snapped up Snead and Demaret, who were always in the big money, or Joe Louis, the Bomber, who was an amateur but paid off as though he had won the top pro purse.

One kid made up his mind early in the spring of one year that he was going to caddie for Ben Hogan. He wanted nothing better out of his life than to pack the sack of the Hawk. He began his climb to high office during the cold, wet days of late March, piling up loops early. He worked hard right up to pick time, and was first in line. He knew all along that Hogan didn't always come to Tam, even if the prize money was the biggest in golf, because Hogan and George May didn't always get along, but this kid was determined, and willing to take a chance.

Hogan still hadn't committed himself at pick time. If the kid chose Ben, and the little man didn't come, the kid would probably end up with some pro who might not make the cut. All the other top bags would have been gone. He picked Hogan anyway.

And Hogan came, and Hogan won, and the kid was vindicated.

After the tournament the kid began to look like his man, so great was his love. He wore white caps, and plain tan slacks, and brown leather shoes. No fancy Demaret styles for him. He smoked a cigarette, and kept it rigid in his mouth as he squinted down fairways, or ball washers, or wherever he squinted. He walked like Ben, and he talked like Ben,

and he even tried to play golf like Ben—which was a mistake. Only Hogan can swing like Hogan, and the kid, who was not a bad player before Hogan, had a tough time getting it in under 90 after Ben left.

Most of us caddies were a simple, mercenary crew with a mild streak of idealism. We wanted a player who would place well in the money so we could share his winnings, but we also wanted a man who was respected as a shotmaker.

We spent a lot of time on the practice fairway when the tournaments were at Tam. We ducked and dodged while in the stream of fire, never really able to follow our player's ball. But we always came up with some golf ball —they were dropping around us like hailstones. A pro may have been on the Wilson Co. staff, but by the end of the two weeks at Tam he might have had more Spalding Dots in his shag bag than anything else.

There were five years of tournaments for me. I caddied for Ed Furgol, an extremely talented golfer with a high temper, and I spent two weeks pulling golf clubs out of the turf after Ed fired them in like darts from the top of his high follow-through. Those were years when Lloyd Mangrum won everything—twice—because he worked for George May, representing Tam, and when he won the first prize, May doubled it. Those were the years when Bobby Locke needed a par on the 18th green to win it all but, because he couldn't hit a cut shot from the right side of the fairway, made a six and lost. On that same hole, another time, Lew Worsham rolled in a wedge shot from 110 yards out for an eagle that beat Chandler Harper out of $25,000. Poor old Chandler, the look on his face after that.

But those were years, too, when I spent near-idyllic summers out of the city, making a bit of money and learning a game I would never forget—or forgive. Quiet days in July when I would get to caddie for Mr. Horlick, the malted milk man, who played nine holes and decided it was a nicer day for flying than golfing, and gave me 10 bucks for nine holes of work.

Ten bucks!

They were good days, those caddie days. There were interesting people, and interesting events, and an entirely new society I never knew existed. I found out about fresh air, and trees, and grass . . . and sand. I was tanned by the first of May and only got browner as the year went on.

And I became a walker, which is the best way to see the world, be it a golf course or a foreign city you're visiting. When you walk you have time; time to look around you and see things, time to think about what you're seeing. You're not concerned with mechanical things —controls. All you need control is yourself. In your golf game, the time it takes to walk up to your ball is just enough to settle you down, and for you to figure out how you want to play the shot. And with a caddie to carry your clubs you're absolutely free to pursue the game and enjoy yourself.

A caddie is an extra pair of eyes to follow your ball, the rooter for your big shot that will win the match, the fellow who knows every blade of grass on the course, and shares his knowledge with you. He's the boy who puts back the golf course for you after an iron shot; who rakes smooth what sand is left in the bunker once you get out of it. He's an integral part of the game. He always will be. ■

ARNIE, YOU'RE GREAT, BUT...

BY DON RICKLES
August, 1971

Rickles, master of the hilarious insult, is a left-handed 21-handicap golfer who is as awed by the stars on today's pro tour as he is demoralized by his own attempts to play the game. He suspects the touring pros have supernatural powers, but for a while, we got Rickles to treat them as if they were material for his act:

Jack Nicklaus is fine, but they ought to put a cord on his backside and make him a cannon. Who is he kidding with this diet jazz? I saw him walk on a green in Las Vegas once and a bunker gave way. He's a real live-wire. His idea of fun is to sit home on a Saturday night with a glass of hot cocoa singing Ohio State fight songs.

Arnold Palmer is fantastic if you like to see a guy try on slacks all day. I call him Harry Hitch. I can't figure out whether he's looking for his belt or has trouble finding pants

that fit. Arnold is the kind of guy who stands in a room alone a lot combing his hair and humming to himself. He looks in the mirror and says, "I'm an idol! I'm an idol!" He doesn't exactly light it up at a New Year's Eve party. Meanwhile, he's got the ranch and you and I are looking for Friday.

Tom Shaw is a wonderful kid, he really is. With his cute blond hair and trick-or-treat shirts, he belongs with Spanky and the rest in "Our Gang" comedies. He wants to take

Ryan O'Neal's part in "Love Story." Tom runs through the grass a lot yelling, "Gee, we won the game." When they ask him his age, he stands around by the lake looking at the ducks.

Gardner Dickinson is one of my favorite guys, but he has one big problem. He needs a hot meal. We

went into a health club once and the man became a pole. When the Lord gave us bodies, he skipped Gardner and left him with only a hat and ears. A lot of guys will tell you that Gardner's the finest shotmaker on the tour today. Who cares?

Orville Moody is a beauty. You know what he does for fun? Once he took me to his house and showed me how he imitates a boat whistle with a beer bottle. He keeps telling me he was a sergeant in the Army; I fire a gun and then he feels relaxed. He came up to me one day and said, "I'm Orville Moody." I gave him a cookie and he went away.

Gary Player is all right if you like to see a grown man dressed up like Black Bart all the time. He walks around like a dwarf cowboy. All he needs is a number on his back and a roller derby helmet. He sent away for a Charles Atlas course when he was 15, but they forgot the decoder and he ate a tree. Gary's a million laughs, but don't look for me herding sheep in South Africa.

Tom Weiskopf—With a name like

that, he ought to get a German helmet and see if he can get the Army back together again.

Bruce Crampton—I just found out who he is. For years I was using him on turkey.

Bob Goalby—He must be fantastic, but what type of work is he in?

Charlie Coody—He's okay if your dog died in some little town and you need a sheriff.

Ben Hogan—He was good in the movie, but I always thought he was Glenn Ford.

Frank Beard—He looks like a bad doctor from Elko, Nev., whose chemistry set blew up and he's golfing for a penance.

Doug Sanders has a lot going for him. Emmett Kelley picks out his clothes. Smart outfits. Doug looks like he took a bad trip through a paint factory. He's a fabulous guy socially, though. He always goes to the cocktail parties, and then shows up the next morning at the tourna-

ment crying, "Please. Let me suck the ice."

Lee Trevino is a tremendous golfer except during the lettuce festival. Then he falls apart. I saw Lee once at a railroad station outside El Paso, and he sold me a souvenir. He put a Band-Aid over his eye and said he had to go practice his putting.

Dave Hill ought to get together with Dave Marr and Dave Stockton and try to get their names printed in the Daily Gazette in Wilkes-Barre. Hill is a lovable guy, but whenever he makes the cut he goes into shock. He stands on the tee and hopes his name is called so he can go play with the grown-ups.

Julius Boros is a marvelous person if you like marlin fishing. He's great on the back of a boat, but on the golf course he dozes off. He's Perry Como's kid by another marriage.

AM

BY LARRY SHEEHAN
January, 1971

One of golf's most talked-about topics in 1970 was the book, PRO, Frank Beard's diary-treatment account of life on the pro tour. Beard "wrote" the book with a tape-recorder which he carried with him throughout the year. Much-praised for its candor and wealth of detail, PRO was also criticized in some quarters for what was claimed to be its preoccupation with trivia. But that was not the reaction of writer Larry Sheehan. He was so inspired by PRO that he rushed off and produced a companion volume, AM, in one afternoon.

December 25—Woke up this morning to something special. My son was standing on my stomach. He was saying "Up time." I got up. "What the heck's going on?" I said.

"It's Christmas morning," my wife said. Sophie was in her bathrobe, eyes half closed, looking swell. I don't know what I'd do without her. Behind every man is a woman. All of us out here on the country club circuit owe a lot to our wives. Shucks.

"Let's go back to bed," I said.

"It's Christmas," she repeated. "O Come Immanuel. We Three Kings."

"All right, all right," I said. The whole family went downstairs, the eight children, the dog, the cat, the damn Mynah bird, me.

The kids started tearing into their presents. I mixed myself a nog. I hate egg nog so I went heavy on the bourbon. Sophie thrust a

Few authors have covered a wider gamut in golf writing, in a comparatively brief time, than Larry Sheehan. Formerly the managing editor of *Golf Digest,* he spent his idle hours turning out humorous articles. Since becoming a freelance writer, he has authored the Doug Sanders book, *Come Swing With Me,* and *Sam Snead Teaches You His Simple "Key" Approach to Golf.*

gift in my hand. It was fairly heavy. "You shouldn't of," I said. I ripped off the wrap. It was a dozen brand new golf balls. I was touched. I tried to kiss her, but I tripped on one of my kids, spilling nog all over. "Sorry," I muttered. Already I was mentally cutting myself adrift from all the confusion and noise— such was the magical effect of my gift. As I fondled my dozen brand-new golf balls, I thought of my weight—165 pounds—and I resolved to get down to my playing weight of 155 pounds within a month, by going on a special diet I had heard about, where you eat nothing but bacon and grapefruit and drink lots of club soda at room temperature.

I started thinking how golf and I had been together for a long time, our relationship totally unimpeded by progress. "All I need is confidence," I thought, sitting there, spilling a bit more of the nog on my lap. The pressure on a 24-handicap golfer is tremendous. I kept fondling the bright new golf balls until my eye caught a slip of paper in the box. I picked it up and read it and found out that the balls my wife had picked out for me, the big Am in her life, were specially constructed to float in water.

Confidence.

March 14—Spent the morning at the driving range. I hit two buckets of balls. At $1.50 a bucket, that's a lot of money. Actually, $3 plus 15 cents for coffee after the first bucket. But I managed to collect an additional half-bucket at no cost by venturing out into the range.

My practice session went okay. Generally, I start by missing the ball altogether, then gradually work up to hitting part of the ball, usually the top part. Finally, I get myself into a groove where I'm working the clubhead firmly into the back of the ball, and putting a little hook spin on it. Putting some of that old Larry Sheehan hook spin on it.

April 3—Rooney, Big Cliff and Anxious Louise were at the range today, trying to get their games together. They all wanted to know what I've been eating lately. I'm up to 170 pounds and I've got to get me a diet that works. I may try one a friend suggested, where you eat sukiyaki four times a day.

I love Rooney dearly, but he is a

cad and a fool. Big Cliff, probably my best friend on the amateur tour, is a cheater, a fake and a tightwad. Anxious Louise, a nervous putter as the name implies, and I spend a lot of time together. But off the record, Anxious is a jerk.

It was really great to see my pals again.

April 19—Anxious and I teamed in the Spring Member - Member qualifying round. I was imparting a little too much business to my drives. Who was it said the woods are lovely, dark and deep?

Shoulder's a bit weary tonight. I'm about the only guy at the club who carries his own bag all the time. It's not that I'm cheap. My friend, Big Cliff, is the tightwad. It's that I believe I am serving the best interests of the game and its traditions by doing so. Caddies get $4.50 a loop at my club.

May 23—I have a problem out here on the amateur tour. My invisibility. I'm a retiring, impersonable chap. The only thing I can do well is play golf badly. As a result, my image is a bit weak around the edges. Today, for instance, was the Men's Member-Guest. I brought one of the younger fellows from the office. Wanted to impress him, and so we're walking past the pro shop when the caddie master bolts out and says, "Mr. Ferlinguysen, your wife's on the phone."

"I'm not Mr. Ferlinguysen."

Minutes later, one of the boys who works the snack bar strolls past and says, "Hi, there, Mr. Hollinghast."

"I'm not Hollinghast! I'm Sheehan, I tell you. Larry Sheehan! Sheehan!"

"Easy, Pete," said my co-worker. "Easy, big fellow."

"Pete?" I demanded. "Pete?"

June 6—First round for the Member-Member Handicap Trophy took place today, but don't look for my picture in the papers. I started out trying to blank the flag with my wood shots. When that failed, I tried to blank the flag with my long irons. Then with my short irons. Then I tried blanking the flag with my putter.

Felt bad about coming home to Sophie with the same old story. So I didn't. Me and Big Cliff went down to John's Fairly Good Pizza and tied one on.

June 15—Picked up some calories somewhere, somehow. I now tilt the scales at 184, which is no joke for a man of my size—I'm barely 5′2″. But I'm beginning a new diet—eating nothing but dried fruit and pancakes made from whole wheat flour. Let's see what happens. Hope to restore that old gamma globulin in the near future, which is Latin for thinness.

June 26—Spent a while at the club this afternoon, brushing up for the Governor's Cup. Determined to make a dent in the standings with this one. Down the range from me was old Junior Jefferson, the club champion. Really wonder about Junior. He'll nod hello to me, and all that, and even shoot the breeze if we happen to be stuck next to each other, as in neighboring shower stalls or in an elevator. But I honestly wonder if he knows my wife's name, or the names of my eight children. I felt his eyes on me watching me blank the practice range flag with my long irons.

Well, I'd like nothing better than to knock off old Junior in a match. Unfortunately, the occasion won't present itself during the Governor's Cup. He's in the championship flight. I'm in the fourth.

June 27—It's murder to be out of the running so early in a tournament. What do you do during the next three weekends? Some young kid beat me 7 and 6. Normally I wouldn't mind getting beat in the first round of the fourth flight in the Governor's Cup, but this young kid I was playing used a ball that was grass-stained, lop-sided and gashed in 15 places. He had what we call on the amateur tour an unfair disadvantage.

July 4—Since I'm out of the Governor's Cup, I decided to forego the game altogether on this national holiday except for hitting a bucket of balls at the range, for $1.50, and in the evening I took six of my children to a Walt Disney movie at the drive-in.

July 18—Teamed up with Sophie in the Mixed Foursome Championship Chapman System Match Play 50% Combined Handicap Flights of 8 According to Handicap, and we did poorly. I was swinging well, but missing the ball.

Sophie thought it was wrong for me to practice for two hours after we came in off the course, while everyone else was sitting around soaking up the booze and receiving awards. She claims that I am the laughing-stock of the club for practicing my game so often, even though I can't break 100. She thinks I should be more sociable.

I have only one comment. Since when is the amateur tour a popularity contest?

July 30—Spent four hours on the practice tee, prepping for the Club Championship. Junior Jefferson came over.

"How are you hitting them, Marv?" he said.

I figured he was trying to rattle me. I replied quietly, "Putting a little hook action on them all right, George." Then I swung and hit about six inches behind the ball. Dirt sprayed my white ducks. "Little overcompensation," I cracked.

August 1—I'm riding a wave tonight and the bourbon's on me. Call me Bourbon Larry. Took Rooney in the first round, 3 and 2. My irons were crisp as crackers and had a nice little amateur tour hook action in their tails.

After absorbing my victory bourbon and watching TV for a few hours, I hit the hay. Athletes have different opinions about sex—that is, about its value just prior to an important contest. Generally I've favored restraint, but that's because I'm the kind of guy who will sacrifice almost anything for achievement on the playing field. But tonight, after wrestling with the question for many minutes, I perceived that sex is not in itself evil and that, for instance, I could have it tonight and not lose my sharpness tomorrow morning.

"I've changed my mind about avoiding sex the night before important matches," I said to Sophie. "Hey, I changed my mind, did you hear?"

For crying out loud. Sophie was sound asleep.

August 2—I was defeated by Anxious Louise, 7 and 6. My folks are expecting a phone call from me tonight. I honestly don't think I'll be able to make that call, for it would require me to report on my performance in the most important golfing event of the season. In

fact, I'm planning to remain in this linen closet until tomorrow morning.

September 12—Suddenly I weigh 210 pounds. I'm on a new diet— eating nothing but peanut butter and camomile tea—but already I look like an advertisement for the local thrift shop.

No big surprise that we lost in the first round of the Member-Member Championship, then. Big Cliff, my partner, didn't help much, either. He borrowed a tee from me on the third hole and never did give it back to me. That's the kind of thing that really bugs an Am.

October 18—Well, today was the Turkey Shoot Shotgun Mixed Chapman System 50% Combined Handicap Sign Up by October 4.

I signed up on October 6 so I couldn't play.

Just as well. I now weigh 370 pounds, and other members are beginning to stare. Maybe it's just nerves.

November 3—I finally gave in, and bought two new pairs of pants. Bought them at Big Men, Inc., the only store in town that had my size. Can you imagine paying $24.50 for two pairs of trousers? $24.50!! Why, I could have bought a whole new set of clubs for that.

November 12—Thought I'd try to get one more round in today before winter sets in firmly. Junior Jefferson was out, so he and I played nine, pitching and chipping on the temporary greens. At the end Junior said, "I really enjoyed playing with you, Max," and I thanked him.

December 25—Sophie gave me a dozen golf balls and, oddly enough, the present has set me to thinking about next spring, and some of the competitive events scheduled early at the club. I honestly believe that with a little more practice and a little less bad luck, I can make my mark on the amateur tour this coming season. But I know I must make my move early—strike my irons while they are hot, as we Ams like to say.

Of course, I probably thought the same thing last Christmas, when, as I recall, Sophie also gave me golf balls for a present. But last year, I didn't weigh any 445 pounds. That's got to shake up my foes out at the club, when I step up to the first tee again. ∎

FROM LAKE HOPATCONG WITH LOVE

BY CHARLES BROME
June, 1972

The first hole at the Lake Hopatcong Public Golf Course, in Landing, N.J., stretches a sheer 264 yards over hill and dale. Mostly hill.

It is a hole of remarkable versatility, playing sometimes as a dogleg right and sometimes as a dogleg left, depending on whether you hit your tee shot on the heel of the club or on the toe. Should you somehow manage to hit one down the middle, the hole still plays as a dogleg. This time a dogleg *down,* over the hill.

Thus, it is practically a twin to the first hole at the Merion Golf Club (East Course) in Ardmore, Pa., site of the 1971 U.S. Open Championship. Except that the first at Merion is 91 yards longer, has considerably more grass and not nearly so many rocks, plays as a dogleg right only, and was eagled by Arnold Palmer during the second round of the 1971 Open.

Arnold Palmer has never in his life eagled the first hole at Lake Hopatcong. Nor, so long as the USGA persists in its bias against short, hilly, rocky, nine-hole public courses, is he likely to remove this blot from his record.

Moreover, the obvious question —which course presents the greater challenge, Merion or Hopatcong?—remains unanswered, one of the great enigmas of our time.

I speak with authority on Lake Hopatcong because that is where I play golf with jolly old Ken Waterman, every Sunday morning when it isn't snowing too hard. And I know everything there is to know about Merion because the editors of *Golf Digest,* desperate for really sound coverage of the last Open,

A self-admitted golf addict, Charles Brome is a weekend player at Lake Hoptacong, N.J., who spends his working hours in the promotion department of Scholastic Magazines in New York.

turned to me for help.

Merion on the first day of the Open is something special. You park your car, if you are a Member of the Press, not just a peasant, in a green and pleasant area just off the 16th tee. Nice spot for a picnic. By the time you have found your way to the press tent near the 18th fairway you are ready to fork over your million dollars and sign up as a member.

The fairways are perfection. Merion bluegrass (a strain specially invented by Mother Nature for fairways, and she first planted it at Merion) makes a tight, firm turf.

The rough is perfection, too, deep and thick and lush enough to break anybody's heart. "I wasn't more than six feet off the 14th fairway," Orville Moody said later, brokenheartedly, "and I took a sand wedge and hit it as hard as I could hit it, and I didn't advance the ball 20 yards."

The greens, as you'd expect, are like velvet. Maybe just a trifle too much like velvet. On my way to the press tent I stopped to examine the 17th green. It was cut to somewhere around a millionth of an inch, and had apparently then been rolled 30 or 40 times, waxed, and polished to a high gloss.

The Merion and Open people were still nervous about the 269 Jack Nicklaus shot there in 1960. They were determined to make sure their golf course would not be "humiliated" by a flock of low scores in the Open. It wasn't, you will recall—Nicklaus and Trevino finished four rounds at even par 280.

To accommodate the swarm of newspaper, magazine, radio and television people (I estimated about a million) who come from all over the world to cover the Open takes considerable doing. The hub of it all is the press tent, an enormous (80' x 100') spread of canvas with a wooden floor perhaps four feet off the ground. It is surrounded by a cluster of lesser tents—caddie headquarters, scorers' headquarters, marshal headquarters, transportation headquarters, ecology headquarters (trash collection), first aid headquarters and such.

But for a high class *Golf Digest* correspondent, these tents don't

really count. What really counts is the press tent. That is where famous writers like Red Smith and Herbert Warren Wind hang out. And that is where you must go to get the real genuine press credentials you have been promised.

Unfortunately, that is also where a burly Burns Detective man is standing, ready to spot you in an instant as an intruder in the realm of Red Smith and Herbert Warren Wind. "Just a minute, there, buddy," he will probably say in a very loud, hoarse voice. And Red Smith will turn to stare at you and Herbert Warren Wind will start to laugh.

The press tent can wait.

I walked on past, giving the Burns man a cold and hostile look. I hurried on toward the Merion clubhouse, the first tee, the 18th green and the practice green, all clustered in one lump. On the way I encountered my first real golfer. It was Tom Weiskopf. He was walking along talking with another man about shoes. I assumed the other man was president of the world's largest shoe company. "If you will wear our shoes during the Open we will give you a million dollars and you can keep the shoes afterward." That sort of thing.

On to the practice green.

AND THERE THEY WERE! All those people you see on the CBS Golf Classic and via satellite from places like Great Britain or Augusta really do exist! Not just as tiny little figures on a TV screen or lines of type in a newspaper, but as actual people—arms, legs, eyeballs, whiskers—the works.

There was Billy Casper, looking chubby. There was Tony Jacklin, looking dapper. There was Deane Beman, looking grouchy . . . . and Tom Shaw, looking semi-teenagey . . . . and Orville Moody, looking anonymous . . . . and Bob Charles, looking left-handed. And even Arnold Palmer, looking just great.

They were standing around on the practice green putting two or three balls at holes, even as you and I, and watching them trickle off at the end, each man looking very much the way he looks on the TV, only about 20 per cent more so. Damndest thing you ever saw.

After the first excitement wore off

(fortunately, I had resisted the initial impulse to turn excitedly to the people beside me and shout, "Look! Look! There's Whatshisname"), I looked around for Sam Snead and Ben Hogan.

Neither of them was there. Another black mark against the USGA. Greatest tournament in the world and two of the greatest players in the world missing. Inexcusable.

I know there was some foolishness about Snead's entry papers, and Hogan's knee was not all it might have been. Not relevant. They should have been flown in on special planes, packed in ice if necessary, and given a bag of gold each for standing around and existing.

The experience of standing right there watching Arnold Palmer miss 10-foot putts was somehow comforting. Arnold hadn't spotted me and called a policeman—maybe Red Smith wouldn't either.

So I strode masterfully back to the press tent. A curt nod to the fake Burns guard. Boldly up the steps and straight to the registration table. Rather well done, if I do say so.

I was armed with a letter from Jim Gaquin, USGA Tournament Relations Manager, telling me how happy he was that I was coming to the Open and promising to give me some real genuine press credentials. There to accept my letter was Lois Gaquin (wife of Jim Gaquin), who turned out to be one of those nice ladies who specializes in putting oafish people at their ease. In a trice she had supplied me with a red badge (number 275) that said "Press A" on it (that's as high as you can get, I would imagine—Red Smith probably had a badge that said "Press A" on it, but with a lower number) and an armband possessed of magical powers. With it, you can go inside the gallery ropes and no marshal can say you nay.

Meanwhile, out on the golf course, the finest players in the world were competing for the U.S. Open Championship. So I went out to watch.

Surrounding the first tee was an enormous crush of people. Rich folks on the clubhouse verandah to the left, already drinking daiquiris and nibbling on hummingbird tongue sandwiches; peasants on the right, drinking beer and cokes and stuffing themselves with hot dogs.

Together, they formed a frighteningly narrow funnel of people down the first fairway. Best not try that at Lake Hopatcong. Affable old Ken Waterman and I would carpet the hillside with corpses.

Only the first two or three layers of people can actually see anything, of course. The rest are watching by ear. A man with a public address system says, "Next on the tee, the likeable Ken Still, of Tacoma, Washington!" There is a spattering of applause, a moment's silence, a crash (not a click—a smashing, bashing CRASH that makes you wince), an "oooh" from the crowd, and that's it for likeable

Ken Still.

Once you've heard one crash, though, you've pretty well heard them all. My plan to watch every player hit every shot on every hole, every day, apparently needed revising.

I had wisely prepared a secondary plan—a list of specific players I had to see play a few holes, at the very least. Bruce Crampton and Gene Littler, because they have such lovely swings . . . . Doug Sanders and Miller Barber, because they have such odd swings . . . . Tom Weiskopf because he hits the ball so long and Deane Beman because he hits the ball so short . . . . Tony Jacklin because he is from England and so is Henry, of the Lake Hopatcong Henrys . . . . Arnold Palmer and Jack Nicklaus and Lee Trevino because they are Arnold Palmer and Jack Nicklaus and Lee Trevino.

Crampton and Sanders were playing together the first two days and the starter tossed in J. C. Snead as a bonus. I picked them up on the first hole. Snead shambling down the fairway, a portly Gomer Pyle. Sanders with a kind of debutante slouch and socks that glow in the dark. And Crampton marching—head up, chest out, arms swinging, like Alec Guiness looking for a good place to build a bridge.

Sanders, as usual, was dressed up like the third chorus boy from the left in a 1933 musical. Bit long in the tooth for the Playboy of the Western World, I thought. But it's his life. All I cared about was how he manages to hit the ball so well with that great wide stance and that inconsequential little backswing.

He takes a few practice swings first—and they are very long and graceful, very smooth and classic-looking, not unorthodox at all. Then he hits his shot, using exactly the same swing except that this time he moves his feet way to hell and gone apart and doesn't take any backswing worth mentioning.

Bruce Crampton? In my next incarnation I don't want to come back as an international jewel thief. I want to come back as a golfer. And if I can't have Sam Snead's swing (he will probably still be using it himself for another 40 or 50

years) I'll settle for Bruce Crampton's.

I came across Tony Jacklin, another player on my special "must" list, mostly by accident. "Come on, little Tony!" I happened to overhear a lady pleading, in very much the same tone Jane would use if Tarzan had been stepped on by an elephant and Had Lost the Will to Live.

I couldn't blame the lady. Jacklin is small and slender and boyishly handsome, with enough curly headed innocence to arouse the mother instinct in a much grumpier woman than she appeared to be. He is also a former U.S. and British Open champion whose slight frame is constructed largely of steel springs, and there is enough wickedness mixed in with the innocence to interest younger females, too. Poor devil is probably chasing them out of the closet all the time.

When Miller Barber addresses the ball he does almost everything wrong. On the backswing he continues to do everything either upside-down or backwards. But Barber is very careful not to actually hit the ball with either his address or his backswing. What he hits it with is his downswing, a smooth, flowing, vicious, whistling arc. The moral is that you can fool around with your backswing if it makes you happy, but be sure to use Miller Barber's downswing when it comes time to hit the ball.

Playing with Barber was an amateur named Jimmy Simons, a solidly built boy of 20 or so. He was playing very well indeed, splitting fairways and hitting greens like clockwork—and then missing his birdie putts by the most infinitesimal of margins. He didn't even seem to notice that Barber was ready to go off like a volcano, and that Weiskopf already had.

I followed the same group again the next day, out of curiosity. Same story.

On the third day, as every schoolboy knows, Simons shot 65 and led the Open by two strokes. The only difference was that his putts were falling. That's always the difference.

Following players around the course is fine, and that's what I did for most of the first two days. But

after the first few thousand miles, even my remarkable physique was beginning to develop body and tender squeaks. I also was having trouble making my legs move.

Fortunately, by that time I had discovered the 16th tee. For some reason, although there would be hundreds of people around every other tee and green on the golf course, there rarely seemed to be more than a handful at the 16th tee. I spent a good part of the third and fourth days there.

I learned many things of great interest at the 16th tee. Here are some of them:

—Bobby Nichols has the biggest, most powerful hands I have ever seen. They just sort of swallow the club, even though he has the grip built up to the diameter of a water main in a city the size of Casper, Wyo.
—Ben Crenshaw has a solid swing, and Jimmy Simons had best keep a close eye on him.
—Jack Nicklaus cannot possibly hit the ball as hard as he does. It violates all the laws of nature. Even if he could, the ball would never stay on the fairway.
—Arnold Palmer may very well be the most personable man in the world, with Al Geiberger a close second. Either of them is welcome to join me in a casual knockabout at Lake Hopatcong.
—The world's finest players are also the world's slowest players.

I didn't stay for the playoff. There would be only two players to keep track of—one short and dark, with a flat swing and a rubber snake; the other tall and blond, with an upright swing and no rubber snake. It was too easy a test.■

THE YIPS— IF YOU'VE HAD 'EM, YOU'VE GOT 'EM

BY HENRY LONGHURST
September, 1973

There can be no more ludicrous sight than that of a grown man, a captain of industry perhaps and a pillar of his local community, convulsively jerking a piece of ironmongery to and fro in his efforts to hole a three-foot putt. Sometimes it is even a great golfer in the twilight of his career, in which case the sight is worthy not of ridicule but of compassion. He will battle on for a year or two, but twilight it is, for "once you've had 'em, you've got 'em." I refer, of course, to what Tommy Armour was the first to christen the "Yips."

When he wrote a book called *The ABC's of Golf,* Armour had no difficulty with the letter Y. The Yips drove him out of tournament golf. On a somewhat humbler level they drove me out of golf, too, and a long and agonizing process it was, ending on D-Day, 1968, the anniversary of the invasion of Europe. On that occasion I put my 25-year-old clubs up into the loft with the water tanks, where they remain to this day because I am too mean to give them away.

Armour wrote graphically of "that ghastly time when, with the first movement of the putter, the golfer blacks out, loses sight of the ball and hasn't the remotest idea of what to do with the putter or, occasionally, that he is holding a putter at all." This confirms the description of that most distinguished of all sufferers, Bob Jones, who recorded that just before the moment of impact the ball "seemed to disappear from sight." Jones also recorded how he once was partnered with that sterling character of the late 1920s and

early '30s, Wild Bill Mehlhorn. Poor Mehlhorn! He was only three feet frm the hole, said Jones, but gave such a convulsive twitch at the ball that it shot across the green into a bunker. He then had the humiliation of exchanging his putter for his niblick, and, we may assume without being unkind, that was the last seriously competitive round he ever played.

Contemporary with Jones and Mehlhorn was Leo Diegel, whose extraordinary spread-elbowed putting style put a new phase into the golfing vocabulary—"to diegel." I watched him on the 18th green at St. Andrews in 1933 when, from some yards above the hole, he had two to tie for the British Open title. While his partner holed out, Diegel paced up and down, much as an animal in its cage, repeatedly taking off his felt hat and mopping his

brow. When his turn came, he charged the ball down the slope, several feet too far, chased after it, and, almost before it had come to rest, yipped it a foot wide of the hole. Everyone knew, as I am sure he did, too, that Diegel would never win an Open now.

Armour wrote, "Yips don't seize the victim during a practice round. It is a tournament disease." Here the great man was certainly wrong. My mind goes back to a conversation at Augusta with Craig Wood, who was robbed of the 1935 Masters by Gene Sarazen's historic double-eagle. Craig told me that he even got the Yips on the practice green, all by himself and with nothing at stake. Again, Armour says, "I have a hunch that the Yips is a result of years of competitive strain, a sort of punch-nuttiness with the putter." Wrong again,

The author considers this photo of Arthur Lacey, the one-time English golfing great, the ultimate classic example of the Yips. The left hand has flown off the club, the stance has become shaky and the short putt squirts wide of the hole.

Familiar to golfers and golf followers on two continents, Henry Longhurst is a columnist with the London Times and *Golf Digest.* He also appears frequently on television as an analyst at major tournaments in the United States.

surely, for you will see any number of compulsive yippers, though many may not admit it, in Sunday foursomes whose members never play serious competitive golf at all.

In winning the 1931 British Open Armour, having perpetrated a most frightful Yip to miss from two feet on the 71st hole, found himself faced with a three-footer to win. "I took a new grip, holding the club as tightly as I could and with stiff wrists, and took a different stance . . . From the instant the club left the ball on the backswing I was blind and unconscious." Next day that greatest of golf writers, Bernard Darwin, recorded in the London *Times* that he had never before seen a man so nonchalantly hole a three-foot putt to gain a championship!

Who, would you guess, wrote the following, and in what book?

"As I stood addressing the ball I would watch for my right hand to jump. At the end of two seconds I would not be looking at the ball at all. My gaze would have become riveted on my right hand. I simply could not resist the desire to see what it was going to do. Directly, as I felt that it was about to jump, I would snatch at the ball in a desperate effort to play the shot before the involuntary movement could take effect. Up would go my head and body with a start and off woud go the ball, anywhere but on the proper line."

That was written by Harry Vardon, winner of six British Opens and one U.S. Open, indisputably the greatest golfer that the world has yet seen. And the book was entitled *How to Play Golf!*

Americans sometimes refer to the Yips rather unkindly as "whisky fingers," and sometimes no doubt they are. Perhaps the last word on "whisky fingers"—and almost my favorite golfing quotation—was uttered by Vardon to a lady who was trying to persuade him to sign the pledge. "Moderation is essential in all things, madam," said Vardon gravely, "but never in my life have I been beaten by a teetotaler."

Sam Snead, whose fluent style has lasted longer than any other man's in the history of the game, was reduced to putting between his legs, croquet-fashion—and he was a total abstainer for years. The croquet putter gave many a golfer, myself included, an extended lease on life and the banning of it was an act of cruelty to many hundreds of miserable wretches for whom the very sight of a normal putter set their fingers twitching. The ease with which you could line up one of these croquet putters to the hole was quite remarkable. By holding the club at the top with the left hand, thumb on top of the shaft, and loosely lower down with the right arm stiffly extended, the most inveterate yipper could make some sort of stroke at a four-foot putt which would not expose him to public ridicule. We did not ask to hole it; all we wanted was to be able to make a stroke at it, and this we could do. The United States Golf Ass'n not only decided to ban a method which had brought peace to so many tortured souls but the group let its decision become public before the Royal and Ancient Golf Club of St. Andrews had time to consider it, thus putting the latter in the impossible position of either banning the club or falling out with the USGA. So they banned the club.

Further proof that the dread disease is not traceable to a dissolute way of life was furnished by the "Iron Man" of golf himself, Ben Hogan, who of all the men who have played golf since the game began would have seemed most likely to be immune. The rot set in, so eye-witnesses have assured me, on the 71st green at Rochester in 1956, when he was well placed to win a record fifth U.S. Open. Not only did he miss the three-footer, which anyone could do, but he yipped it, and that was the beginning of the end. At any rate, my last memory of Hogan in competitive golf is at the Masters some years ago. Every green, as usual, is surrounded with spectators and, as the familiar white-capped figure steps through the ropes, everyone spontaneously rises to give him a standing ovation. And a moment later he is stuck motionless over the ball, as though hypnotized, unable to move the ironmongery to and fro.

Is there any cure for this grotesque ailment? Few people can have made a more penetrating research than myself. The first led me to a psychiatrist-cum-hypnotist, who solemnly tried through my inner self to talk the ball into the hole. This, of course, was ridiculous since all I was seeking was that, on surveying a four-foot putt, a massive calm should automatically come over me instead of the impression that I was about to try to hit the ball with a live eel.

Better hope came from an Austrian doctor, who wrote to say that he knew the solution and would be willing to reveal it to me. Within a matter of hours I was visiting him in his rooms in London. "It all comms," he said, "from ze angle of ze right ell-bow." Something in that, I thought, recalling how, with the right arm stiffly extended, one could at least make some sort of stroke with the croquet putter. The theory seemed to be supported by the fact that, if you have difficulty in raising a glass to the lips, it is when the arm bends to approximately the putting angle that your drink is most likely to make its bid for freedom.

Innumerable "cures" for the Yips have been tried and passed on from one sufferer to another. Looking at the hole instead of the ball; putting left-handed; putting cross-handed with the left hand below the right, and putting with the hands wide apart (probably the best bet of the lot). A friend of mine has had his hands about a foot apart, with the left below the right, and then pulls down as hard as he can with the right—and he a one-time runner-up in the British Amateur.

As an ancient and finally defeated warrior—three putts from a yard on the 18th at St. Andrews, and only as few as three because the third hit the back of the hole, jumped up, and fell in—I listen politely to all their tales. But the bitter, inescapable truth remains. Once you've had 'em, you've got 'em. ■

MUNY GOLF TAKES GUTS

BY JAY CRONLEY
November, 1963

I requested a tee off time at 10:00 a.m. on a Saturday that was promised lovely—temperature between 70 and 80 and a fast track. Wind: none. Moisture: in Coors cans.

"No."

Well, yes, I see. Let's make it 9:00 a.m. Should be able to shake it up by then.

"No. Full."

Eight? No. Seven? No. Noon? No way. One? Ha-ha. Two? You a comedian? Three, four, five p.m.?

Jay Cronley, a columnist with the Tulsa Tribune, is a frequent contributor of freelance articles for magazines, including *Golf Digest.*

Three no's. Six a.m.? Out of the question. When then? Which is where 5:30 a.m. comes in.

It comes in quickly. It is not completely light at 5:30 a.m. It is not anything, except mighty still—still dark, still before the newspaper, still stiff. Any false hopes you had about feeling heavenly vanishes between squints. If you are not the son or daughter of the pro, chef, parking lot guy, mayor, or keeper of the greens, you are out of luck, Mac. Municipal players are best characterized as Macs.

We drink beer, clonk around in any number of stripes and dots,

stand in line and get wicked sunburns.

Don't feel all that sorry for us. We get to play golf without shirts. The men. We can find from one to 20 golf balls per 18-hole round. The country club player pays for the right to shoot a quick comfortable, fashionable 90. We do it furiously, for maybe $10 total, if we get the bounce.

There are those who have never played a municipal golf course, the Esquires and III's and Van-Some-things, and it is to them that I dedicate this material. While you are scratching your toes on rich carpet in the men's lounge, we are trying to hit an 8-iron off bare dirt that is nourished by spilled pop.

Now, I have played some splendid municipal golf courses, one in Albuquerque with fairway grass thick as welcome rugs, and one in Ireland that played through castle ruins. The difference then is psychological. You must summon inner courage to tee it up with a man dressed in sneakers, an ascot, and a glove on the wrong hand, who says, "Mind if I play through?" on the No. 1 tee.

It is my contention that anybody, with proper money, can play a country club golf course. It requires I'll-lead-us-to-Omaha-Beach-boys, why-don't-we-step-out-back, race-you-around-the-block guts to play a municipal golf course.

Down the No. 1 fairway at shortly after 6:00 a.m., as the sun pulls away from the horizon, displaying the hole in pink glow, there is still some fog, but you can see 14 guys trying to tee off. There is an official "starter," a retired gentleman with a microphone who says, mostly during backswings, "Mr. Snodgrass next on the tee." If you venture forth alone you are paired with other jokers who generally range in handicap from four to 30. I got a used truck salesman and his buddy who sold books, a 17 and an 18, and one of the oldest men I have ever seen upright. During a splendid round last year he shot 134, about his age.

Hello, glad to meetcha. Me, oh, I'm an eight handicap or so. The old guy and I will play them for two bucks a side, lowball. The old guy can't hear for beans. YOU AND ME. PARTNERS. TWO BUCKS. DOLLARS.

The tee area is roped off, like a bullfight. Behind, the thumps of practice swings echo off the asphalt. My partner had four clubs. Can he use my putter? Sure. SURE.

Mulligans—hitting drives, machine-gun style, until one finds the fairway—are as common as elm trees. The theory of mulligans at a municipal course is that 11 mulligans are no worse than one. If you are going to violate the Rules of Golf you might as well go ahead and violate the heck out of them. Golf balls are flying from the tee. I promise you that for the briefest of moments, both our opponents were teeing off at the same time.

The law of averages once again prevailed and they are down the middle.

My partner nudges it dead left into the driving range, and he plays one with a stripe around it.

It is not unusual to find strange objects in municipal sand traps, even bones. Some players think the rake by the side of the trap is a hazard itself, and that it is a two-stroke penalty if you touch it. Putting out of a trap was invented on a municipal course. Also, throwing it out of a trap. Also, leaving it in a trap.

There are many reasons why play tends to be slow on a municipal golf course. A main one is that a golf ball, however wounded, is a sacred object, and when one is hit into wood, over road or into water it is searched for. Other people's balls also are searched for. A view of the public course from above must look like the biggest Easter egg hunt of all time.

Another reason for slow play is inferior play. When you seven-putt a green, it takes time. When you forget where the green is, it takes time to find it. When you stop to climb a fence and get a Coke from an adjoining supermarket, it takes time.

You are always hearing, "Excuse my buddy here, he is just learning."

Another reason is that nobody lets you play through, as if it were a sin. You ask to play through, then put 'em up and get ready to fight. Hit into them, they will hit back, and pretty soon it will be just like volleyball. It is as if letting somebody play through means

you are a sissy.

As we completed No. 9 at 10:00 a.m. there was much teaching activity on the practice tee. It takes a real man to give lessons at a municipal course. You must spot improvement in a series of flailing arms, you must iron out slices, fade hooks and keep a straight face because no, Mr. Whomple, it isn't like croquet.

A municipal golf course is two parts, the front nine and the back nine. It is not a whole. There were six groups on the ninth tee, one of which should have been there, five of which had sneaked on when the back nine attendant, age 16, ran off after a girl from the pool.

We waited a six-pack worth, 35 minutes. My partner napped. I read half of a 200-page novel, and our opponents went to practice putts on the 18th green, which was near. When I looked up there were nine golf balls on the green, and the group coming up the 18th fairway was only a sixsome. Illegal, but fun.

The 18th is appropriately uphill, and, as the most logical placement of all, the bar and grill is just behind. You could fly one there and remain. The grill is what it is all about, the place where competitors fret over the scorecard as if it were Form 1040, shoes off, bag lumped in a corner, beer frothing, body still rippling like you just drove Kansas City-Las Vegas, non-stop.

This is where you add the eights and nines and discover where the $4 is headed. The money is handled, gently, like a Masters' jacket. Losers crumple the proof, scorecard, as if it had been a poorly selected ticket at the $2 window. The sandwiches are the greatest, the beer the coldest, the companionship the best.

Sometimes you have to go as far back as No. 2 to find that one crisp shot that will bring you back. My partner is exhausted, pale. I get some beer in him and he wants to go nine more. We make a game for next week and we are good friends.

To hundreds of thousands who go to drive-in movies, shop sales, buy golf balls at the drug store and putt from 10 yards off the green this is the only game in town. ■

RUB OF THE GRIN

Casual water: any temporary accumulation of water which is not one of the ordinary and recognized hazards of the course. This includes melted ice cubes.

———

There's nothing extraordinary about a long hitter. The woods are full of them.

———

Man blames fate for other accidents but feels personally responsible when he makes a hole-in-one.

———

A round of golf is like taxes,
Both try a strong man's soul,
Drive hard to get up to the green
Then wind up in the hole.

———

You can sometimes tell the quality of a golfer by the size of his divots. A good golfer replaces the turf. A bad golfer returfs the place.

———

Frank Russo, who has his name stamped on his golf balls, was playing at the Merill Hills course in Milwaukee. Russo sliced a shot in the vicinity of a young woman in a parallel fairway. As he walked toward his shot he saw that she was preparing to hit his ball.

"I think that's my ball," he called to her.

"No, it isn't," she replied before whacking away. "I always play with a Frank Russo ball."

———

Two golfers were enjoying them-selves at the 19th hole.

"My wife says she'll leave me if I don't stop playing golf," said one.

"Gee, that's too bad," said the friend.

"Yeah, I'll really miss her."

———

When the dedicated golfer passed on and reached heaven, he found a paradise beyond his wildest dreams. The golf courses were glorious. Approaching the first tee, he noticed a lanky gentleman about to hit his tee shot, and stopped to watch.

The man swung and sent a long, high drive arching across a little dogleg and a cluster of bunkers guarding the green some 410 yards away. The ball struck the flagstick and dropped a foot from the hole.

The newcomer shook his head and turned to St. Peter. "That's unbelievable. That guy must think he's Jesus Christ."

"That *is* Jesus Christ," said St. Peter. "He *thinks* he's Arnold Palmer."

———

Golf is a game in which you fork over $400 for a set of clubs and then spend your weekends trying to use them as little as possible.

———

You've criticized my stance and
   swing,
My drives and every tee shot.
From tee to tee, you've helpfully
Improved my game a lot.

Now one more item needs your clear
And analyzing brain.
Please tell me how you like my
   grip—
Around your jugular vein.
        —Catherine Lavarnway

———

For sale: Large size dog house,
set of golf clubs, reasonable.
    —Rockville (Conn.) Journal-Inquirer

———

I smashed my patented slice off the tee at a Wichita municipal course and watched it flutter over the green of the par-3 and disappear. Red-faced, I followed the flight of the ball and met a foursome trudging off the green I'd just eclipsed.

"Sorry 'bout that," I apologized. "Did you see an errant ball flying overhead?"

"I saw a ball land over there," grumbled one of the golfers, pointing toward a clump of trees, "but I don't know what brand it is."
        —Max Seibel

———

Fred shaved his score so many times
To look more like a hero,
He finally made a hole-in-one
And gave himself a zero.

———

A chap who frequently leaves the office early to play golf instructed his secretary this particular day to tell all callers he was "away from his desk for the afternoon."

After he had left the office a member of his golfing foursome who had forgotten which course they were playing that day called for the information. The loyal secretary only replied that her boss was away from his desk.

"Just tell me," the golfer persisted, "if he's 20 miles away from his desk or 30 miles."

———

The club had scheduled a husband-wife Scotch four-ball and the club champion appeared at the par-4 first hole with his wife, a notoriously poor player.

He hit a beautiful drive 275 yards down the middle. She hooked the second shot deep into a clump of trees.

Unperturbed, he played a brilliant recovery shot which rolled to within three feet of the pin. She in turn jabbed at the ball and sent it 18 feet past the hole.

Without a murmer, he lined up the long putt and managed to sink it. As they walked to the second tee he remarked, "We'll have to do better. That was a bogey 5 you know."

"Well, don't blame me," she snarled. "I only took two of them."

———

Show me a golfer
   Whose takeaway's low,
Whose backswing is
   Always inhumanly slow,
Whose balance is flawless,
   Whose pause at the top
Is absolute beauty,
   Whose rhythm won't stop.

Show me a golfer
   Whose weight shift is sure,
Whose line to the target
   Is true, sweet and pure.
Show me a golfer
   Whose head doesn't move,
Whose contact and follow
   Are all in the groove.

Show me this golfer
   And (pardon my pique)
You've shown me the guy
   I'm playing next week!
        —Dick Emmons

———

Her words in accents calm and clear
Weren't those, alas! I'd longed
   to hear.
She told me, while my hopes fell flat,
Just what was what . . . and that
   was that.
Enough! Too much! With bitter groan
I stilled the crackling telephone.
This afternoon no golf I'll play.
The weather girl said: "Rain all day."
        —Mike Mitchell

CARTOONS

"Bite!"

"OK, Bruno, lemme have four more."

"How'd it go, Randy?"

"...and I'd like to thank my wife
who kept me from getting overconfident."

"No, I'm not stalking the wild asparagus!"

"Let's go, Fred, the first tee's open!"

"Well, well, what's-his-name is getting to be quite a big boy."

"There's nothing like a good steady rain to make you really appreciate this game."

"Too bad you're not 112—you'd have shot your age."

"Honey, I'm home!"

"If he took an X on the last hole,
give him two X's on this one."

"Hassim, your golf course came today!"

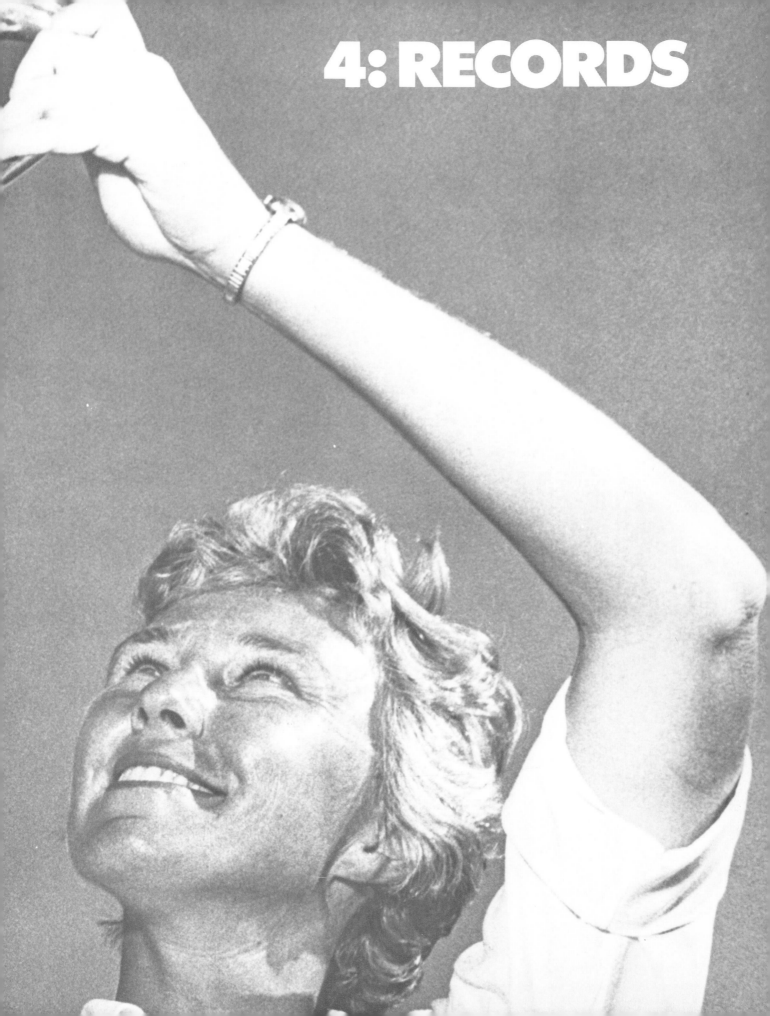

RECORDS

Statistics, *Golf Digest* has always believed, give golf continuity and a basis for comparison. A tournament golfer is on his own, and his performance can be meaningfully measured in black and white, or whatever colors are found on the scoreboard this week.

We have always given record-keeping serious attention, especially since our first Annual issue in 1956. Our readers enjoy studying past and recent performances. We know the Annual serves as a vital reference work for the nation's golf writers—we see it in use in the press rooms at tournaments large and small.

Until *Golf Digest* initiated its awards program in the 1950s, professional golf did not honor competitors who compiled outstanding first-year records or who showed marked improvement. Our Most Improved and Rookie of the Year awards are important to professionals on both the men's and women's tours. Established stars are recognized through our Byron Nelson and Mickey Wright Tournament Champion awards, which go to the players on the two tours who win the most tournaments during the year.

The nation's amateur golfers are not ignored. Once a year we list almost 4,000 club golfers who win Most Improved awards (January issue) and another 6,000 who win their club championships (February issue).

Our own unique statistics are the Performance Averages. Cary Middlecoff, a contributor to the magazine since its formative days, in 1954 pointed out that the money

Preceding page: Mickey Wright, U.S. golf's winningest player in the past quarter century with 82 victories, hefts the 1964 U.S. Open trophy.

list did not truly reflect a competitor's performance. Middlecoff helped us develop the Performance Averages, which rank players relative to the showings of fellow competitors in the fields. As it happens, Cary was the leader in the 1955 Performance Average list. During the past 25 years Kathy Whitworth and Jack Nicklaus have won six Performance Average championships apiece, more than any other players.

Ben Hogan's feat of winning three of the four major professional titles in 1953 stands as the competitive highlight of the past 25 years. Hogan won the Masters, U.S. Open and British Open but did not play in the fourth of the modern Grand Slam events, the PGA Championship. That year the PGA ended July 7 and the British Open began July 8. Hogan had gone to the British Open site, Carnoustie, more than two weeks ahead of time to prepare for the competition.

Golf's purses rose dramatically during the past quarter century to over $8 million today, and the period spawned the tour's first millionaires. Arnold Palmer made a million in prize money before anyone else, going over the magic number in the 1968 PGA Championship. Since then, Billy Casper, Jack Nicklaus, Lee Trevino, Bruce Crampton, Gary Player, Tom Weiskopf and Gene Littler, in that order, have achieved million-dollar status. Nicklaus also became the first and (so far) the only golfer to win $2 million on tour when he won the 1973 Walt Disney World.

Women's professional golf also has advanced rapidly, although at a slower pace than the men's. Kathy Whitworth has passed the $500,000 mark.

Two other women own the distinction of having won the most professional tournaments during the past 25 years. Mickey Wright

leads with 82, while Miss Whitworth is second with 71. Arnie Palmer's 61 is a relatively distant third, Sam Snead having won a goodly share of his record 84 before 1950.

In 1973 the total purses offered on the women's tour first passed $1 million. That is a whopping increase from the less than $50,000 in 1950.

Because most successful young men amateurs turn professional, no one dominated the field. Only three players won more than one U.S. Amateur: Harvie Ward, Deane Beman, and Nicklaus taking two each. On the women's side, JoAnne Gunderson Carner swept five Amateur championships before she turned professional. Anne Quast Sander was next with three, and she has remained an amateur.

The statistics on the following pages, figured especially for this volume, cover a cornucopia of achievement that nostalgia can only enhance—but that needs no help.

216

CHRONOLOGY

BY JOHN P. MAY

1950
Ben Hogan returns to competition for first time after near-fatal traffic accident in 1949, ties for lead with Sam Snead at Los Angeles but loses playoff. . . . Snead wins 10 titles. . . . Stymie ruled out. . . . LPGA is formed. . . . Marlene Bauer, 16, makes debut as professional golfer.

1951
Clubs with movable heads ruled illegal. . . . Ben Hogan wins U.S. Open at Oakland Hills ("I brought the monster to its knees," Hogan says after finishing with a 67).

1952
Dwight Eisenhower elected President, becomes symbol of golf boom. . . . Stroke-and-distance penalty declared for out-of-bounds (was distance only before). . . . Louise Suggs sets U.S. Women's

Open record score of 284 at Bala G.C., Philadelphia. . . . Jack Burke wins four consecutive tour events.

1953
Ben Hogan wins Masters, U.S. Open and British Open but declines to try for "modern" Grand Slam when he does not enter PGA Championship, saying latter's match-play format too rugged for his physical condition.

1954
Arnold Palmer wins U.S. Amateur, then turns professional. . . . Fairways in U.S. Open roped for first time. . . . Sam Snead beats Ben Hogan, 70-71, in great Masters playoff.

1955
Mike Souchak scores 257 in winning Texas Open, setting all-time tour 72-hole record.

1956
Harvie Ward wins second straight

U.S. Amateur, becomes first repeat champion since Lawson Little in 1934-1935. . . . Babe Zaharias dies after long battle with cancer. . . . Practice strokes prohibited between holes, from hazard and on or to any green not yet played.

1957
Jackie Pung apparently wins U.S. Women's Open but signs scorecard which shows a 5 instead of the 6 she actually made on the fourth hole in the last round and she is disqualified; Betsy Rawls wins.

1958
PGA Championship changes format from match play to stroke, and Dow Finsterwald wins. . . . PGA tour's total prize money reaches $1 million for first time. . . . "Current" and "basic" golf handicaps abandoned; now there's only one handicap.

1959
Billy Casper wins U.S. Open, sets 72-hole tournament putting record of 114. . . . Art Wall birdies five of last six holes to win the Masters by one stroke. . . . Bill Wright becomes first black to win a USGA title when he takes the Publinx.

1960
Arnold Palmer shoots 30-35—65 in last round to win the U.S. Open, establishes reputation as a charger; he wins eight tournaments during year.

1961
PGA drops Caucasian clause in its constitution, so for first time blacks can become members. . . . Number of golfers in the United States reaches five million. . . . Merchandise prize value an amateur may accept is raised from $100 to $200.

1962
Jack Nicklaus, in first year as a professional, wins the U.S. Open. . . . Arnold Palmer sets new British Open record of 276 in winning title at Troon.

1963
Mickey Wright wins 13 Ladies PGA titles, most ever won on the women's tour. . . . PGA tour total purses exceed $2 million for first time.

1964
Ken Venturi beats the heat and the field to win a dramatic U.S. Open at Congressional. . . . Tony Lema wins the British Open at St. Andrews without a practice round

Always one to clear time for a round of golf in his hectic schedule, the late President Eisenhower symbolizes the golf boom of the '50s.

Peter Thomson grins elatedly as he holds the trophy of his fifth British Open victory in 1965.

and with Arnold Palmer's putter (Arnie didn't enter).

1965
Jack Nicklaus sets Masters scoring record of 271. . . . Peter Thomson wins fifth British Open. . . . U.S. Open format extended to four days. . . . PGA establishes qualifying procedure for tour applicants. . . . U.S. Amateur format changed from match play to stroke play.

1966
Tony Lema, his wife and the pilot die in an airplane crash. . . . Billy Casper makes up seven strokes on last regular nine to tie Arnold Palmer in U.S. Open, then wins playoff. . . . Solid golf ball appears.

1967
USGA handicaps now based on best 10 of last 20 (instead of 25) and 85 per cent (instead of 80) of differential. . . . Ben Hogan, 55, shoots 66 in the third round of the Masters, including a record-tying 30 on the back nine, ties for 10th. . . . Lee Trevino bursts on scene with tie for fifth in the U.S. Open.

1968
Bob Goalby wins the Masters when Roberto de Vicenzo, who had actually tied for the top spot, signs a scorecard that shows a 4 instead of a 3 on 17 in the last round. . . . Croquet putting ruled illegal. . . . Arnold Palmer becomes first to reach $1 million career earnings. . . . PGA tour reaches $5 million

plateau. . . . JoAnne Gunderson Carner wins fifth U.S. Women's Amateur. . . . Tournament players form own division within PGA.

1969
Joseph C. Dey leaves USGA after 34 years, becomes commissioner of men's tour. . . . Tony Jacklin becomes first Briton to win British Open since 1951. . . . British achieve unexpected tie with U.S. in Ryder Cup. . . . Walter Hagen dies.

1970
JoAnne Gunderson Carner joins Ladies PGA tour, predicts she will win (it took awhile). . . . It's now OK to lift and clean your golf ball after any putt; continuous putting is out.

1971
Bobby Jones dies. . . . Astronaut Alan Shepard hits a 6-iron shot—on the moon. . . . Lee Trevino wins U.S. Canadian and British Opens within four weeks. . . . Number of U.S. golfers reaches 10 million.

1972
Ladies PGA attempts to suspend

Jane Blalock for alleged cheating during play, but court disallows suspension and she countersues organization for $5 million. . . . Graphite shafts make their appearance.

1973
Jack Nicklaus wins PGA for 14th major championship, breaking Bob Jones' all-time mark of 13; he also becomes first to exceed $2 million in earnings. . . . Johnny Miller's fourth-round 63 sets U.S. Open 18-hole record and wins him the title. . . . U.S. Amateur format changed back to match play.

1974
Johnny Miller explodes with victories in tour's first three events, the first to accomplish this, and goes on to win eight titles and all-time record $353,021. . . . Kathy Whitworth becomes first woman professional to exceed $500,000 in career earnings. . . . Deane Beman succeeds Joseph C. Dey, retired, as tour commissioner. ∎

Kathy Whitworth—the first woman professional ever to surpass the $500,000 mark in pro golf winnings.

UNUSUAL FEATS

BY JOHN P. MAY

1950

Lee Mackey Jr. scores a 64 in the first round of the U.S. Open at the Merion Golf Club, Ardmore, Pa., setting an 18-hole Open record that was not to be broken for 23 years. . . . Ralph Blomquist, a professional, shoots 28-30—58 Dec. 5 on the 6,327-yard, par-72 Oakmont Country Club course in Glendale, Calif.

1951

Cary Middlecoff staggers to a 14 on a 321-yard hole during the Greensboro Open, the tour's highest single-hole count of the year. Cary walks in after this disaster.

1952

Charles Konkowski, a fireman from South Orange, N.J., wins the New Jersey state driving contest with a wallop of 299 yards. Konkowski describes himself as a "driving range golfer"—he never actually plays a round, just hits at ranges.

1953

Lew Worsham strikes a blow for himself and televised golf when he

Lew Worsham generates great enthusiasm for the game when he shoots the first dramatic shot seen on television in 1953.

holes a wedge for an eagle on the last hole in George S. May's World Championship to edge Chandler Harper by a stroke. It was the first exciting golf shot seen on TV. . . . Jimmy Self, a professional, sets a world marathon record for the number of holes played afoot within a 24-hour period by traversing 265 at the Conway (S.C.) Country Club.

1954

Amateur Frank Strafaci is stopped at a North Carolina highway roadblock and questioned by two officers looking for a criminal. They refuse to believe he's playing in the North and South and ask him to hit a shot. Strafaci tees one up—and tops the ball. At that the policemen guffaw; they knew who he was all the time.

1955

Dick Shawn, the comedian, gets a tongue-lashing from the owner of a home off the 13th hole at the Englewood (N.J.) Country Club. Shawn had sliced his ball into the yard. In not too long a time, however, the resident calms down. No wonder—he sold his house to Shawn for $50,000.

1956

Golf Digest picks Cary Middlecoff to win the U.S. Open championship —and he wins.

1957

Young Tony Lema takes his stance in the rough off the 12th fairway at Pebble Beach during the Bing Crosby, grits his teeth and swings. Then he disappears. The force of Lema's swing had caused him to slide down a nearby embankment. "Tony is probably the only golfer in history," quips Bob Hope, "who traveled farther than his ball on the same shot." . . . Jim Williams of Marietta, Ohio, carded eight birdies in a row in scoring 28-35—63 at the Selma (Ga.) Country Club. It was an amateur under-par record string that held up for 12 years.

1958

Joe Dobson Jr., six-year-old Enid, Okla., golfer, becomes the youngest in history to score a hole-in-one when he holes out his tee shot on the 115-yard fourth hole at the Meadowlake Golf Course, Enid. Joe's record held up for 10 years.

1959

W. E. Jackson, playing a lighted par-3 course at Jacksonville, Fla., is startled on the fourth tee as a wild

hog snorts out of the woods. When the beast charges, Jackson stands his ground, whacks the hog between the eyes with his 9-iron—and suddenly has 200 pounds of tough pork on his hands. . . . James J. Johnston Jr., Fort Worth, Tex., sets an all-time record for the number of holes played afoot within a 24-hour period on a course of at least 6,000 yards. He plays 363 at the 6,101-yard Abilene (Tex.) Country Club Oct. 14-15.

1960

Joe Kirkwood, the trick shot star, becomes the youngest ever to match or beat his age on a course of at least 6,000 yards when at age 63 he scores a 62 on the 6,320-yard Deland (Fla.) Country Club course.

1961

Former baseball pitcher Lou Kretlow sets an all-time distance record for a hole-in-one when he aces the 427-yard 16th hole at the Lake Hefner Golf Course, Oklahoma City. His record was later eclipsed. . . . Judy Kimball sets an 18-hole Ladies PGA putting record by taking 20 in the last round at the American Women's Open, Minneapolis. . . . Bob Goalby establishes a PGA record by scoring birdies on eight consecutive holes during the fourth round of the St. Petersburg (Fla.) Open.

1962

Dr. Joseph O. Boydstone, Bakersfield, Calif., scores 11 holes-in-one on regulation courses during the year, the most aces ever made before or after (so far) within a chronological year. Dr. Boydstone's aces were all on different holes which measured from a minimum of 123 yards to a maximum of 210.

1963

Mr. and Mrs. George Gordon, Ayr, Scotland, become the first and only husband-wife tandem ever to score holes-in-one on the same hole on successive shots. Margaret makes her first, from the women's tee, 135 yards from the green on the fifth hole at Scotland's Turnberry course. George then holes out from the men's tee, 145 yards.

1964

Norman Manley, Saugus, Calif., scores holes-in-one on the 330-yard seventh and the 290-yard fifth at the Del Valle Country Club, Saugus, to become the only golfer in history to have aced successive par-4 holes. . . . Paul Dobrowlski, Norbeck, Md., glances up as he waggles over a tee shot on the 15th hole at the Manor Country Club, Norbeck. He spots a bucket in the middle of the fairway, 220 yards out. "Impossible," Dobrowlski thinks to himself, and lands his ball in the bucket.

1965
Bob Mitera, 21, Omaha, Neb., scores history's longest hole-in-one on a straightaway hole when he sinks his tee shot on the 444-yard 10th hole at the Miracle Hills Golf Club course, Omaha. A 50-mph wind helps propel the big shot.

1966
Henry H. Zeckser, Seattle, ties the all-time record for fewest putts during an 18-hole round on a regulation course when he putts only 16 times at the Jackson Park Municipal Course, Seattle.

1967
Katherine Murphy, a Los Angeles nurse, establishes a new marathon record for women by playing 156 holes afoot within 24 hours at the San Luis Rey course in Bonsall, Calif. The record still stands. . . . J. R. Ables, a student at Ohio State University, wins two club championships in one day. In the morning he plays the second round of a 36-hole tournament at the Hiawatha Golf Club, Mt. Vernon, Ohio, and wins the stroke play event with a 139. Then Ables hustles to the Mt. Vernon Country Club, where he defeats O. W. Stanley in the finals of that club's match play championship. . . . Cynthia Sullivan ties the 18-hole Ladies PGA putting record by taking 20 in the third round of the Amarillo (Tex.) Open.

1968
Tommy Moore becomes the youngest boy ever to score a hole-in-one on a regulation course when he aces the 145-yard fourth hole at the Woodbrier Golf Course, Martinsburg, W. Va., at the age of six years, one month and one week. Tommy, from Hagerstown, Md., aces the same hole again later in the year. . . . Bill McNair, 24, and Bud Thornton, 46, both of Akron, Ohio, playing together, sink their second shots for double eagles on the 550-yard 12th hole at the Turkeyfoot Lake Club, Akron, for a rare "double" double eagle. . . . A. C. Brown, 62, Chattanooga, Tenn., scored a 62 at the 6,529-yard Rivermont Golf and Country Club course, Chattanooga, to become

220

Mrs. Joan Harrison, 72, in 1972 becomes the first women ever to shoot her age on a regulation course.

the youngest ever to match his age on a course of at least 6,000 yards.

1969
Jimmy Smith, 22, Nashville, Tenn., sets an all-time record for amateur golfers when he scores nine consecutive birdies during a tournament at the McCabe Golf Club, Nashville. Smith's streak comes on holes four through 12, which includes two par-5s, five par-4s and two par-3s.

1970
George Henry Miller, Anaheim, Calif., at 93 becomes the oldest to ever score a hole-in-one when he aces the 116-yard 11th hole at the Anaheim Municipal Golf Course. . . . William Diddel, 86, Naples, Fla., sets an exceptional record for the most number of strokes shot under a golfer's age (12) when he scores a 74 at the 6,289-yard Country Club of Naples.

1971
Tom Doty, 23, an assistant professional at the Brookwood Country Club, Wood Dale, Ill., sets an unsurpassed scoring record of 26 for nine holes of at least 3,000 yards at Brookwood's front nine. Doty is 10 under par on the 3,300-yard nine. He cards 33 on the back side for a 59 with a total of 16 putts, which also ties the all-time putting record.

1972
A vintage year: Dick Kimbrough, 41, North Platte, Neb., sets two all-time records. He plays 364 holes afoot at the 6,068-yard North Platte Country Club course for a marathon record (holes played within a 24-hour period). Later on the same course, Kimbrough plays 18 afoot in

30 minutes, 10.3 seconds, a speed record. . . . Mrs. Joan Harrison, 72, Clearwater, Fla., registers the first and only (so far) age-matching score by a woman when she scores a 72 at the 5,388-yard Hound Ears Lodge course, Blowing Rock, N.C. (age rounds for women count only on courses of at least 5,250 yards). . . . John W. Eakin, San Jose, Calif., scores history's longest double eagle when he makes a two on the 609-yard 15th hole at the Makaha Inn West Course, Hawaii.

1973
Raymond Lasater, 43, Lebanon, Tenn., sets an all-time record for the number of holes played consecutively when he covers 1,530 at the Hunter's Point Golf Course, Lebanon, in 62 hours and 20 minutes.

1974
Professional Roberto de Vicenzo, Argentina, establishes a record when he goes under par on 10 consecutive holes (one through 10) at the Villa Allende Golf Club, Province of Cordoba, Argentina. He opens with six birdies, eagles, then birdies three more. De Vicenzo eventually scores 61. . . . Gene McNamee and Robert Glosier score another "double" double eagle when each hole out their second shots on the 505-yard ninth hole at the Bogey Hills Country Club, St. Louis. . . . Rosemary Thompson, Amarillo, Tex., sets a record for amateur women golfers when she makes nine birdies in one round, at the Ross Rogers Golf Course, Amarillo. Mrs. Thompson, 32, also matches her age for nine holes with an outgoing 32. ∎

WINNERS

MEN'S MAJOR CHAMPIONS

YEAR	U.S. OPEN	MASTERS	PGA	BRITISH OPEN
1950	Ben Hogan	Jimmy Demaret	Chandler Harper	Bobby Locke
1951	Ben Hogan	Ben Hogan	Sam Snead	Max Faulkner
1952	Julius Boros	Sam Snead	Jim Turnesa	Bobby Locke
1953	Ben Hogan	Ben Hogan	Walter Burkemo	Ben Hogan
1954	Ed Furgol	Sam Snead	Chick Harbert	Peter Thomson
1955	Jack Fleck	Cary Middlecoff	Doug Ford	Peter Thomson
1956	Cary Middlecoff	Jack Burke	Jack Burke	Peter Thomson
1957	Dick Mayer	Doug Ford	Lionel Hebert	Bobby Locke
1958	Tommy Bolt	Arnold Palmer	Dow Finsterwald	Peter Thomson
1959	Billy Casper	Art Wall	Bob Rosburg	Gary Player
1960	Arnold Palmer	Arnold Palmer	Jay Hebert	Kel Nagle
1961	Gene Littler	Gary Player	Jerry Barber	Arnold Palmer
1962	Jack Nicklaus	Arnold Palmer	Gary Player	Arnold Palmer
1963	Julius Boros	Jack Nicklaus	Jack Nicklaus	Bob Charles
1964	Ken Venturi	Arnold Palmer	Bobby Nichols	Tony Lema
1965	Gary Player	Jack Nicklaus	Dave Marr	Peter Thomson
1966	Billy Casper	Jack Nicklaus	Al Geiberger	Jack Nicklaus
1967	Jack Nicklaus	Gay Brewer	Don January	Roberto de Vicenzo
1968	Lee Trevino	Bob Goalby	Julius Boros	Gary Player
1969	Orville Moody	George Archer	Ray Floyd	Tony Jacklin
1970	Tony Jacklin	Billy Casper	Dave Stockton	Jack Nicklaus
1971	Lee Trevino	Charles Coody	Jack Nicklaus	Lee Trevino
1972	Jack Nicklaus	Jack Nicklaus	Gary Player	Lee Trevino
1973	Johnny Miller	Tommy Aaron	Jack Nicklaus	Tom Weiskopf
1974	Hale Irwin	Gary Player	Lee Trevino	Gary Player

MEN'S PROFESSIONAL TOUR LEADERS

YEAR	MONEY		PERFORMANCE AVERAGE*		VARDON TROPHY		TOURNAMENTS WON	
1950	Sam Snead	$35,759			Sam Snead	69.23	Sam Snead	9
1951	Lloyd Mangrum	26,089			Lloyd Mangrum	70.05	Cary Middlecoff	6
1952	Julius Boros	37,033			Jack Burke	70.54	Sam Snead	5
1953	Lew Worsham	34,002			Lloyd Mangrum	70.22	Mangrum, Hogan	4
1954	Bob Toski	65,820	Gene Littler	.696	E. J. Harrison	70.41	Bob Toski	4
1955	Julius Boros	63,121	Cary Middlecoff	.659	Sam Snead	69.86	Cary Middlecoff	5
1956	Ted Kroll	72,835	Ed Furgol	.550	Cary Middlecoff	70.35	Ted Kroll	3
1967	Dick Mayer	65,835	Dow Finsterwald	.643	Dow Finsterwald	70.29	Arnold Palmer	4
1958	Arnold Palmer	42,607	Billy Casper	.611	Bob Rosburg	70.11	Ken Venturi	4
1959	Art Wall	53,167	Gene Littler	.603	Art Wall	70.35	Gene Littler	5
1960	Arnold Palmer	75,262	Arnold Palmer	.706	Billy Casper	69.95	Arnold Palmer	8
1961	Gary Player	64,450	Arnold Palmer	.725	Arnold Palmer	69.82	Arnold Palmer	5
1962	Arnold Palmer	81,448	Jack Nicklaus	.601	Arnold Palmer	70.27	Arnold Palmer	7
1963	Arnold Palmer	128,230	Gary Player	.864	Billy Casper	70.58	Arnold Palmer	7
1964	Jack Nicklaus	113,284	Jack Nicklaus	.875	Arnold Palmer	70.01	Jack Nicklaus	4
1965	Jack Nicklaus	140,752	Jack Nicklaus	.828	Billy Casper	70.59	Jack Nicklaus	5
1966	Billy Casper	121,944	Billy Casper	.791	Billy Casper	70.16	Billy Casper	4
1967	Jack Nicklaus	188,988	Arnold Palmer	.739	Arnold Palmer	70.18	Jack Nicklaus	5
1968	Billy Casper	205,168	Billy Casper	.803	Billy Casper	69.98	Billy Casper	6
1969	Frank Beard	175,223	Dave Hill	.643	Dave Hill	70.34	Dave Hill	3
1970	Lee Trevino	157,037	Dave Hill	.673	Lee Trevino	70.64	Billy Casper	4
1971	Jack Nicklaus	244,490	Arnold Palmer	.737	Lee Trevino	70.41	Lee Trevino	5
1972	Jack Nicklaus	320,542	Jack Nicklaus	.801	Lee Trevino	70.91	Jack Nicklaus	7
1973	Jack Nicklaus	308,362	Jack Nicklaus	.894	Bruce Crampton	70.69	Jack Nicklaus	7
1974	Johnny Miller	353,021	Jack Nicklaus	.841	Lee Trevino	70.53	Johnny Miller	8

MEN'S AMATEUR CHAMPIONS

YEAR	U.S. AMATEUR	NCAA	NATIONAL PUBLIC LINKS	USGA JUNIOR	USGA SENIOR	GOLF DIGEST #1 RANKING
1950	Sam Urzetta	Fred Wampler	Stan Bielat	Mason Rudolph		
1951	Bill Maxwell	Tom Nieporte	Dave Stanley	Tommy Jacobs		
1952	Jack Westland	Jim Vickers	Omer Bogan	Don Bisplingoff		
1953	Gene Littler	Earl Moeller	Ted Richards	Rex Baxter		
1954	Arnold Palmer	Hillman Robbins	Gene Andrews	Foster Bradley		
1955	Harvie Ward	Joe Campbell	Sam Kocsis	William Dunn	J. Wood Platt	Harvie Ward
1956	Harvie Ward	Rick Jones	James Buxbaum	Harlan Stevenson	Fred Wright	Harvie Ward
1957	Hillman Robbins	Rex Baxter	Don Essig	Larry Beck	J. C. Espie	Hillman Robbins
1958	Charles Coe	Phil Rodgers	Dan Sikes	Buddy Baker	Tom Robbins	Charles Coe
1959	Jack Nicklaus	Dick Crawford	Bill Wright	Larry Lee	J. C. Espie	Jack Nicklaus
1960	Deane Beman	Dick Crawford	Verne Callison	Bill Tindall	Michael Cestone	Jack Nicklaus
1961	Jack Nicklaus	Jack Nicklaus	R. H. Sikes	Charles McDowell	Dexter Daniels	Jack Nicklaus
1962	Labron Harris	Kermit Zarley	R. H. Sikes	Jim Wiechers	M. Carlsmith	Labron Harris
1963	Deane Beman	R. H. Sikes	Bob Lunn	Gregg McHatton	M. Carlsmith	Deane Beman
1964	Bill Campbell	Terry Small	Bill McDonald	John Miller	Bill Higgins	Bill Campbell
1965	Bob Murphy	Marty Fleckman	Arne Dokka	James Masserio	Bob Kiersky	George Boutell
1966	Gary Cowan	Bob Murphy	Monty Kaser	Gary Sanders	Dexter Daniels	Gary Cowan
1967	Bob Dickson	Hale Irwin	Verne Callison	John Crooks	Ray Palmer	Bob Dickson
1968	Bruce Fleisher	Grier Jones	Gene Towry	Eddie Pearce	Curtis Person	Vinny Giles
1969	Steve Melnyk	Bob Clark	John Jackson	Aly Trompas	Curtis Person	Steve Melnyk
1970	Lanny Wadkins	John Mahaffey	Bob Risch	Gary Koch	Gene Andrews	Lanny Wadkins
1971	Gary Cowan	Ben Crenshaw	Fred Haney	Mike Brannan	Tom Draper	Gary Cowan
1972	Vinny Giles	Ben Crenshaw / Tom Kite	Bob Allard	Bob Byman	Lew Oehmig	Ben Crenshaw
1973	Craig Stadler	Ben Crenshaw	Stan Stopa	Jack Renner	Bill Hyndman	Ben Crenshaw
1974	Jerry Pate	Curtis Strange	Charles Barenaba	David Nevatt	Dale Morey	Jerry Pate

*Exclusive Golf Digest method calculated by dividing number of possible points (50 per tournament entered) into points earned (50 for first place, 49 for second . . .)

WOMEN'S MAJOR CHAMPIONS

YEAR	U.S. OPEN	LPGA	TITLEHOLDERS	WESTERN OPEN
1950	Babe Zaharias		Babe Zaharias	Babe Zaharias
1951	Betsy Rawls		*Pat O'Sullivan	Patty Berg
1952	Louise Suggs		Babe Zaharias	Betsy Rawls
1953	Betsy Rawls		Patty Berg	Louise Suggs
1954	Babe Zaharias		Louise Suggs	Betty Jameson
1955	Fay Crocker	Beverly Hanson	Patty Berg	Patty Berg
1956	Kathy Cornelius	Marlene Hagge	Louise Suggs	Beverly Hanson
1957	Betsy Rawls	Louise Suggs	Patty Berg	Patty Berg
1958	Mickey Wright	Mickey Wright	Beverly Hanson	Patty Berg
1959	Mickey Wright	Betsy Rawls	Louise Suggs	Betsy Rawls
1960	Betsy Rawls	Mickey Wright	Fay Crocker	Joyce Ziske
1961	Mickey Wright	Mickey Wright	Mickey Wright	Mary Lena Faulk
1962	Murle Lindstrom	Judy Kimball	Mickey Wright	Mickey Wright
1963	Mary Mills	Mickey Wright	Marilynn Smith	Mickey Wright
1964	Mickey Wright	Mary Mills	Marilynn Smith	Carol Mann
1965	Carol Mann	Sandra Haynie	Kathy Whitworth	Susie Maxwell
1966	Sandra Spuzich	Gloria Ehret	Kathy Whitworth	Mickey Wright
1967	*Catherine Lacoste	Kathy Whitworth		Kathy Whitworth
1968	Susie Berning	Sandra Post		
1969	Donna Caponi	Betsy Rawls		
1970	Donna Caponi	Shirley Englehorn		
1971	JoAnne Carner	Kathy Whitworth		
1972	Susie Berning	Kathy Ahern	Sandra Palmer	
1973	Susie Berning	Mary Mills		
1974	Sandra Haynie	Sandra Haynie		

*Amateur

WOMEN'S PROFESSIONAL TOUR LEADERS

YEAR	MONEY		PERFORMANCE AVERAGE**		VARE TROPHY		TOURNAMENTS WON	
1950	Babe Zaharias	$14,800					Babe Zaharias	6
1951	Babe Zaharias	15,087					Babe Zaharias	7
1952	Betsy Rawls	14,505					Rawls, Suggs	6
1953	Louise Suggs	19,816			Patty Berg	75.00	Louise Suggs	8
1954	Patty Berg	16,011			Babe Zaharias	75.48	Suggs, Zaharias	5
1955	Patty Berg	16,497	Patty Berg	.894	Patty Berg	74.47	Patty Berg	6
1956	Marlene Hagge	20,235	Patty Berg	.882	Patty Berg	74.57	Marlene Hagge	8
1957	Patty Berg	16,272	Patty Berg	.830	Louise Suggs	74.64	Patty Berg	5
1958	Beverly Hanson	12,639	Mickey Wright	.819	Beverly Hanson	74.92	Mickey Wright	5
1959	Betsy Rawls	26,774	Louise Suggs	.905	Betsy Rawls	74.03	Betsy Rawls	10
1960	Louise Suggs	16,892	Mickey Wright	.883	Mickey Wright	73.25	Mickey Wright	6
1961	Mickey Wright	22,236	Mickey Wright	.891	Mickey Wright	73.55	Mickey Wright	10
1962	Mickey Wright	21,641	Ruth Jessen	.798	Mickey Wright	73.67	Mickey Wright	10
1963	Mickey Wright	31,269	Mickey Wright	.907	Mickey Wright	72.81	Mickey Wright	13
1964	Mickey Wright	29,800	Mickey Wright	.838	Mickey Wright	72.46	Mickey Wright	11
1965	Kathy Whitworth	28,658	Kathy Whitworth	.862	Kathy Whitworth	72.61	Kathy Whitworth	8
1966	Kathy Whitworth	33,517	Mickey Wright	.900	Kathy Whitworth	72.60	Kathy Whitworth	9
1967	Kathy Whitworth	32,937	Sandra Haynie	.826	Kathy Whitworth	72.74	Kathy Whitworth	10
1968	Kathy Whitworth	48,379	Kathy Whitworth	.883	Carol Mann	72.04	Kathy Whitworth	10
1969	Carol Mann	49,152	Kathy Whitworth	.855	Kathy Whitworth	72.38	Carol Mann	8
1970	Kathy Whitworth	30,235	Kathy Whitworth	.831	Kathy Whitworth	72.26	Shirley Englehorn	4
1971	Kathy Whitworth	41,181	Kathy Whitworth	.740	Kathy Whitworth	72.88	Kathy Whitworth	4
1972	Kathy Whitworth	65,063	Kathy Whitworth	.782	Kathy Whitworth	72.50	Kathy Whitworth	5
1973	Kathy Whitworth	82,864	Judy Rankin	.668	Judy Rankin	73.08	Kathy Whitworth	7
1974	JoAnne Carner	87,570	Jane Blalock	.707	JoAnne Carner	72.87	JoAnne Carner	6

WOMEN'S AMATEUR CHAMPIONS

YEAR	U.S. AMATEUR	COLLEGIATE	USGA JUNIOR	USGA SENIOR	GOLF DIGEST #1 RANKING
1950	Beverly Hanson	Betty Rowland	Pat Lesser		
1951	Dorothy Kirby	Barbara Bruning	Arlene Brooks		
1952	Jackie Pung	Mary Ann Villegas	Mickey Wright		
1953	Mary Lena Faulk	Pat Lesser	Millie Meyerson		
1954	Barbara Romack	Nancy Reed	Margaret Smith		
1955	Pat Lesser	Jackie Yates	Carole Jo Kabler		Pat Lesser
1956	Marlene Stewart	Marlene Stewart	JoAnne Gunderson		Marlene Stewart
1957	JoAnne Gunderson	Meriam Bailey	Judy Eller		JoAnne Gunderson
1958	Anne Quast	Carole Pushing	Judy Eller		Anne Quast
1959	Barbara McIntire	Judy Eller	Judy Rand		Barbara McIntire
1960	JoAnne Gunderson	JoAnne Gunderson	Carol Sorenson		JoAnne Gunderson
1961	Anne Quast Decker	Judy Hoetmer	Mary Lowell	Maureen Orcutt	Anne Quast Decker
1962	JoAnne Gunderson	Carol Sorenson	Mary Lou Daniel	Allison Choate	JoAnne Gunderson
1963	Anne Quast Welts	Claudia Lindor	Janis Ferraris	Hulet Smith	Anne Quast Welts
1964	Barbara McIntire	Patti Shook	Peggy Conley	Hulet Smith	Barbara McIntire
1965	Jean Ashley	Roberta Albers	Gail Sykes	Maureen Orcutt	Nancy Roth Syms
1966	JoAnne Carner	Joyce Kazmierski	Claudia Mayhew	Marge Mason	JoAnne Carner
1967	Mary Lou Dill	Martha Wilkinson	Elizabeth Story	Carolyn Cudone	Mary Lou Dill
1968	JoAnne Carner	Gail Sykes	Peggy Harmon	Carolyn Cudone	JoAnne Carner
1969	Catherine Lacoste	Jane Bastanchury	Hollis Stacy	Carolyn Cudone	Catherine Lacoste
1970	Martha Wilkinson	Cathy Gaughan	Hollis Stacy	Carolyn Cudone	Martha Wilkinson
1971	Laura Baugh	Shelley Hamlin	Hollis Stacy	Carolyn Cudone	Laura Baugh
1972	Mary Budke	Ann Laughlin	Nancy Lopez	Carolyn Cudone	Jane Booth
1973	Carol Semple	Bonnie Lauer	Amy Alcott	Mrs. David Hibbs	Carol Semple
1974	Cynthia Hill	Mary Budke	Nancy Lopez	Mrs. J. Cushing	Debbie Massey

**Exclusive Golf Digest method calculated by dividing number of possible points (25 per tournament entered) into points earned (25 for first place, 24 for second . . .)

SPECIAL AWARDS

BYRON NELSON AWARD WINNERS
For most victories on PGA tour

Year	Player	Wins	Year	Player	Wins
1955	Cary Middlecoff	5	1965	Jack Nicklaus	5
1956	Ted Kroll	3	1966	Billy Casper	4
1957	Arnold Palmer	4	1967	Jack Nicklaus	5
1958	Ken Venturi	4	1968	Billy Casper	6
1959	Gene Littler	5	1969	Dave Hill	3
1960	Arnold Palmer	8	1970	Billy Casper	4
1961	Arnold Palmer	5	1971	Lee Trevino	5
1962	Arnold Palmer	7	1972	Jack Nicklaus	7
1963	Arnold Palmer	7	1973	Jack Nicklaus	7
1964	Jack Nicklaus	4	1974	Johnny Miller	8

MICKEY WRIGHT AWARD WINNERS
For most victories on LPGA tour

Year	Player	Wins	Year	Player	Wins
1955	Patty Berg	6	1965	Kathy Whitworth	8
1956	Marlene Hagge	8	1966	Kathy Whitworth	9
1957	Patty Berg	5	1967	Kathy Whitworth	10
1958	Mickey Wright	5	1968	Kathy Whitworth	10
1959	Betsy Rawls	10	1969	Carol Mann	8
1960	Mickey Wright	6	1970	Shirley Englehorn	4
1961	Mickey Wright	10	1971	Kathy Whitworth	4
1962	Mickey Wright	10	1972	Kathy Whitworth	5
1963	Mickey Wright	13	1973	Kathy Whitworth	7
1964	Mickey Wright	11	1974	JoAnne Carner	6

ROOKIE OF THE YEAR

	MEN				WOMEN		
Year	Player	Official Money	Rank	Year	Player	Official Money	Rank
1957	Ken Venturi	$ 18,761	10	1962	Mary Mills	$ 8,091	11
1958	Bob Goalby	11,062	31	1963	Clifford Ann Creed	13,843	5
1959	Joe Campbell	11,510	38	1964	Susie Maxwell	3,715	19
1960	Mason Rudolph	14,940	25	1965	Margee Masters	6,595	16
1961	Jacky Cupit	22,813	18	1966	Jan Ferraris	1,923	31
1962	Jack Nicklaus	61,868	3	1967	Sharron Moran	3,446	30
1963	Raymond Floyd	9,602	58	1968	Sandra Post	13,509	13
1964	R. H. Sikes	23,353	23	1969	Jane Blalock	3,825	37
1965	Homero Blancas	26,162	38	1970	JoAnne Carner	14,551	11
1966	John Schlee	21,442	48	1971	Sally Little	1,604	51
1967	Lee Trevino	26,472	45	1972	Jocelyne Bourassa	16,098	19
1968	Bob Murphy	105,595	10	1973	Laura Baugh	14,657	35
1969	Grier Jones	37,193	48	1974	Jan Stephenson	16,270	28
1970	Ted Hayes Jr.	28,500	77				
1971	Hubert Green	73,439	29				
1972	Lanny Wadkins	116,617	10				
1973	Tom Kite	54,270	56				
1974	Ben Crenshaw	71,065	31				

MOST IMPROVED PROFESSIONALS

	MEN				WOMEN		
1953	Doug Ford	1964	Ken Venturi	1954	Bev Hanson	1965	Carol Mann
1954	Bob Toski	1965	Randy Glover	1955	Fay Crocker	1966	Gloria Ehret
1955	Mike Souchak	1966	Gay Brewer	1956	Marlene Hagge	1967	Susie Maxwell
1956	D. Finsterwald	1967	Dave Stockton	1957	Mickey Wright	1968	Gerda Whalen
1957	Paul Harney	1968	Bob Lunn	1958	B. Randolph	1969	Donna Caponi
1958	Ernie Vossler	1969	Dave Hill	1959	M. MacKenzie	1970	Jane Blalock
1959	Don Whitt	1970	Dick Lotz	1960	K. Whitworth	1971	Jane Blalock
1960	Don January	1971	Jerry Heard	1961	Mary Faulk	1972	Betty Burfeindt
1961	Gary Player	1972	Jim Jamieson	1962	K. Whitworth	1973	Mary Mills
1962	Bobby Nichols	1973	Tom Weiskopf	1963	Marilynn Smith	1974	JoAnne Carner
1963	Tony Lema	1974	Tom Watson	1964	J. Torluemke		

MOST BEAUTIFUL GOLFER

1954	Dimmie Thompson, Greenville, S.C.	1965	Laura Anne MacIvor, Fort Walton Beach, Fla.
1955	Betty Jane Martinez, San Antonio, Paula Ann West, Sacramento (tie)	1966	Sharron Moran, Carlsbad, Calif.
1956	Barbara Williams, Richmond, Calif.	1967	Margo Fletcher Brinkley, Raleigh, N.C.
1957	Judy Easterbrook, Peoria, Ill.	1968	Carolyn Finley, Huntington Beach, Calif.
1958	Sally Bergman Robb, Cleveland, O.	1969	Priscilla Sauter Grosch, Switzerland
1959	Elaine Woodman, Wichita, Kan.	1970	Jane Fassinger, New Wilmington, Pa.
1960	Florence Zupnik, Washington, D.C.	1971	Laura Baugh, Long Beach, Calif.
1961	Sue Dobson, Macomb, Ill.	1972	Jonya Stapp, Miami, Okla.
1962	Carol Sorenson, Janesville, Wis.	1973	Debbie De Agostine, Walkill, N.Y.
1963	Nancy Albert, Trenton, N.J.	1974	Mary Cushing, San Antonio, Tex.
1964	Marlene Floyd, Fayetteville, N.C.		

224